The Empire Reformed

EARLY AMERICAN STUDIES

SERIES EDITORS
Daniel K. Richter, Kathleen M. Brown,
Max Cavitch, and David Waldstreicher

Exploring neglected aspects of our colonial, revolutionary, and early national history and culture, Early American Studies reinterprets familiar themes and events in fresh ways. Interdisciplinary in character, and with a special emphasis on the period from about 1600 to 1850, the series is published in partnership with the McNeil Center for Early American Studies.

A complete list of books in the series is available from the publisher.

The Empire Reformed

English America in the Age of the Glorious Revolution

Owen Stanwood

UNIVERSITY OF PENNSYLVANIA PRESS

PHILADELPHIA

Published by
University of Pennsylvania Press
Philadelphia, Pennsylvania 19104-4112
www.upenn.edu/pennpress

Printed in the United States of America on acid-free paper
10 9 8 7 6 5 4 3 2 1

Library of Congress Cataloging-in-Publication Data
ISBN 978-0-8122-4341-3

For Simon

Contents

Illustrations

Introduction: Popery and Politics in the British Atlantic World

ON 4 JUNE 1702, a crowd of worshippers gathered in Boston to pay homage to their departed monarch. William III had died the previous March, and as the Reverend Benjamin Wadsworth noted, seldom had there been a more heroic leader. William had been "A Good King," Wadsworth preached, because he "Imploy[ed] his Power and Authority for the good of his People." The king's greatest moment had been the manner in which he had come to the throne fourteen years earlier. At that time, England and its dominions were in "languishing circumstances," ruled by a Catholic monarch, James II, whose policies alienated many of his subjects. They were "quite depriv'd of *Liberty* and *Property*," Wadsworth remembered, "having their *Religion*, *Laws*, and *Lives* in utmost hazard; sinking under *Arbitrary Power* and *Tyranny*; almost overwhelm'd with *Popery* and *Slavery*." William, then the Prince of Orange, bravely "came over the sea to help them," engineering the coup that became known as the Glorious Revolution and establishing the Protestant faith and limited monarchy in Great Britain for good.[1]

In its time, Wadsworth's paean to William was an utterly uncontroversial statement—one probably recreated by dozens of ministers around the king's dominions. In this case, however, an ordinary event gave testimony to great political changes that had occurred on the far reaches of the empire. In the years before William's accession, colonial Americans had reputations as refractory subjects. None were worse than New Englanders, and in that region, Congregational ministers had particular reputations for disloyalty. The first royal governor in the region, Edward Cranfield of New Hampshire, believed there would be no peace in the colonies until the king "remove[d] all such their Preachers who oppose & indeavour to disturb the peace of this Government."

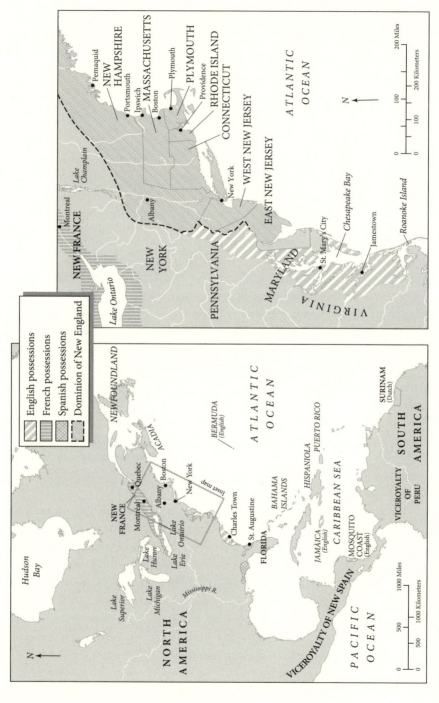

Figure 1. The British Atlantic world in the late seventeenth century.

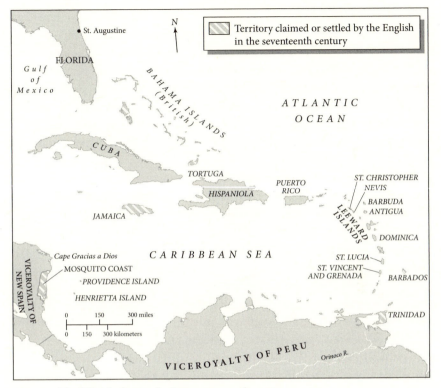

Figure 2. The West Indies in the late seventeenth century.

However bad the ministers were, they were only a step removed from colonial subjects as a collective group, who engaged in open rebellion with an
alarming frequency during the late 1600s. The problem was that rulers and
subjects often had different ideas about how politics and governance should
work, about how the empire should be constituted. These rifts combined self-
interest and ideology, with religion lying just below the surface. People like
Cranfield believed that the king had wide latitude to decide how he ruled his
foreign plantations, and that subjects had the responsibility to obey him—a
duty they cast in religious terms. Colonial subjects, on the other hand, had
become used to some degree of autonomy. Some of them, especially Reformed
Protestants like Wadsworth, believed that people had no duty to obey an ungodly or tyrannical ruler. The general disobedience of Americans led many
imperial administrators to believe that only a show of brute force could make
the empire work.[2]

After 1689, however, a new political culture developed in the American plantations. While they never lost their rebellious streak, colonial Americans came together, in the words of one New Yorker, as "true protestants subjects" of the English monarch. The reconstituted empire combined the centralization favored by royal agents like Cranfield with the militant Protestantism espoused by Wadsworth. This new kind of politics worked because ordinary people believed in it, and they did so, overwhelmingly, out of fear. From the 1670s through the beginning of the eighteenth century, colonial Americans lived in almost constant anxiety: of attacks by French and Indian enemies; of tyrannical exactions from their rulers; of subversion from within by dissident religious groups or by African slaves. In many cases, colonists described these threats using the language of conspiracies common in early modern Europe, especially the Protestant rhetoric of Catholic plots. Indeed, the language of antipopery provided a constant backdrop for political intrigue around the colonies. This fear had the potential to tear the empire apart, to cause rebellions against authority and subvert royal government. In some circumstances, however, fear could bring the empire together, as long as royal officials learned how to harness it. This book tells the story of how that happened, of how popular fear allowed the English, and after the Act of Union of 1707 the British, to build an empire.[3]

The story of the making of empire must necessarily be both intensely local and transatlantic in scope. Imperial leaders had to deal with dozens of local contexts: colonial societies that had developed, in some cases over decades, in relative isolation both from each other and from the metropole. What worked politically in a Puritan outpost like New Hampshire necessarily failed in a plantation society like Barbados. At the same time, colonial subjects of the crown, no matter where they lived, shared certain assumptions about politics. They can be boiled down into four basic rules. First, Anglo-Americans believed in the sovereignty of the king, that he enjoyed theoretical power in the plantations. Second, and somewhat contradictorily, they believed that local people, and the institutions of local governance, should have broad latitude in actually running things. Third, the vast majority felt that governments at whatever level should be Protestant, and defend subjects' "Protestant liberties." Finally, rulers had the obligation to keep people safe, to defeat whatever enemies threatened from within or without. These four rules, needless to say, contradicted each other in numerous respects. What was the line, for instance, between royal sovereignty and local autonomy? And what to do if a king, like the Catholic James II, seemed likely to subvert Protestantism? Finally, how much should people sacrifice the first three principles in the name of the fourth, a desire for security? English people struggled for most of the seventeenth century to answer these questions, and colonial subjects had their own answers.

The crisis that eventually produced this imperial consensus emerged from a particular moment in English and British politics. Inhabitants of the colonies, in many cases, came from England or Europe themselves; their political understanding depended on both the peculiar heritage of England and Britain, and a constant communication of ideas from one side of the Atlantic to the other. Of course, colonial subjects lived hundreds of miles from the center, and they never simply replicated English political culture. Nonetheless, the imperial transformation emerged from the complicated political and religious divisions of Restoration England and its British and European neighbors. During the late 1600s, England experienced a "crisis of popery and arbitrary government," an upsurge in fear that divided the nation into two rival parties, created new religious animosities, and eventually pushed England toward a new role in European power politics. Only by beginning in England can we understand how and why the empire changed.[4]

• • •

In 1678 rumors of a terrible plot surfaced in the city of London. According to a former Jesuit novice named Titus Oates, foreign and domestic papists were on the verge of carrying out a grand design to reduce the kingdom to "popery and tyranny." The undertaking would begin with the murder of King Charles II, which would pave the way for the burning of the city and the forcible conversion of the nation's Protestants, aided if necessary by French and Irish armies. The plot turned out to be a fiction, but it struck a nerve with English Protestants nervous that global Catholicism, led by the French king Louis XIV, was newly resurgent. The result was a political crisis that paralyzed the government, leading to a series of show trials and the hanging of nineteen Roman Catholics for alleged complicity in the plot. But even after the immediate crisis ended, the ramifications of the popish plot lived on. Not only in London but all around Protestant Europe, people remained fearful that Catholic enemies threatened them at every turn.[5]

Fear of Catholicism, of course, was not a new phenomenon in late seventeenth-century England. To one degree or another, every Protestant defined his or her faith against the Roman Catholic Church, and England had a particularly dramatic history of confrontation between Catholics and Protestants, from

"Bloody" Mary's persecutions of Protestants during the 1550s through Elizabeth I's feuds with Spain during the late 1500s and the infamous "gunpowder plot" of 1605 in which Catholic radicals attempted to blow up Parliament and assassinate England's political elite. But if antipopery was ubiquitous among early modern Protestants, it was historically contingent, dictated by local conditions and a changing global context. In addition, antipopery rarely functioned as a rallying cry for English Protestants, bringing them together against a common popish enemy. On the contrary, it often was a language of division: a rhetoric some Protestants used against others within the fold whom they viewed as insufficiently godly. The best example of this came during the 1630s and 1640s, when Puritans directed anti-Catholic rhetoric against King Charles I, claiming that his attempts to reintroduce ceremonies into the Church of England marked him as a closet papist. After parliamentarians executed Charles I in 1649, moreover, the king's defenders turned this anti-Catholicism right back at the Puritans, claiming that by killing a rightful Protestant monarch the Puritans imitated the "king-killing doctrine" of the Jesuits. Thus English anti-Catholicism was not a coherent ideology, but a rhetoric that could be applied to any number of political situations.[6]

Despite its diversity, though, English antipopery usually rested on a number of beliefs. It began with a view of history as a constant struggle between good, exemplified in the true church of Christ, and evil, represented by the church's enemies. These enemies, the forces of Antichrist, designed to replace Christ at the head of the church and thus monopolize wealth and power in their own hands. From the mid-1500s onward, most Protestant theologians confidently identified the pope as Antichrist, and they found plenty of evidence in scripture, from the Old Testament prophecies to the Revelation of St. John, that seemed to foreshadow the struggles between good and evil that were playing out in the sixteenth and seventeenth centuries. In these ministers' minds, "popery" was not a religion at all; it was an anti-religion, and in the typical words of one Cambridge theologian, papists were "Pseudochristians, or rather the Synagogue of Antichrist, who under pretence of professing Christ do most wickedly oppose him, by nulling his Laws, and barbarously murthering his true and faithfull Subjects." As a result, Protestants could identify the characteristics of true religion by examining popery—its binary opposition— and doing the exact opposite. Thus the impulse to view the difference between popery and Protestantism in terms of oppositions: light and darkness, liberty and slavery, reason and superstition.[7]

Aside from the identification of the pope as Antichrist, most English

Protestants agreed that the papists' program was political in nature. Unlike godly people, who focused their energies on the world to come, papists obsessed over worldly goals: the acquisition of money and power. Writing in particular about the Jesuits, one Englishman observed that "Riches, Dominion, Pomp and Glory, are the *Butts* they shoot at; and if ever they appear *Heavenly*, by tampering with Affairs of *State*, they mix *Heaven and Earth* together, to bring all into *Confusion*." Their most storied tactic was to subvert and undermine Protestant princes, either by infiltrating royal councils, by encouraging subjects to rebel, or in extreme cases by assassinating the monarch—as in the case of the French king Henri IV, murdered by a Catholic zealot in 1610 partly as punishment for issuing the Edict of Nantes, a law that guaranteed limited rights to French Protestants. With governments in their hands, papists would be free to beggar, harass, and persecute the people—and the result was almost always poverty and hardship, as was proven by the relative prosperity of Protestant countries in comparison to their Catholic neighbors.[8]

Finally, English antipopery rested on the belief that Catholics were unnaturally violent and cruel. The most famous English works of antipopish propaganda, beginning with John Foxe's sixteenth-century landmark *Acts and Monuments*, known to most readers as the *Book of Martyrs*, chronicled popish violence in the most graphic detail. The carnage took on two forms. First, there was the institutionalized cruelty of the Catholic Church, its tribunals like the Spanish and Roman Inquisitions, and popish monarchs like England's Mary I, who came to power in 1553 and attempted to turn back England's Reformation. The queen presided over the burning of dozens of Protestant martyrs at Smithfield, a time when "*England* was become such a Theatre of Fire and Faggot, as if *Rome* had design'd to have chang'd her imaginary, into a real Purgatory over all this Land." The second form of popish violence implicated ordinary people who, usually at the encouragement of scheming priests, set out to massacre Protestants, as in Paris on St. Bartholomew's Day in 1572, when "every Man seem'd a Fury; and as if they had bin transformed into Wolves and Tigres, out did the cruelty of Beasts." The most frightening of all these massacres and persecutions, however, was the Irish Rebellion of 1641, in which Irish Catholics—inspired, it was said, by priests who claimed it was not a sin to spill Protestant blood—rose up against their neighbors, depopulating much of the country and killing thousands. Protestant propagandists exaggerated both the numbers and the nature of casualties, turning the Rebellion into one of the signal acts in the annals of popish cruelty—and one acted by near neighbors against English and Scottish people.[9]

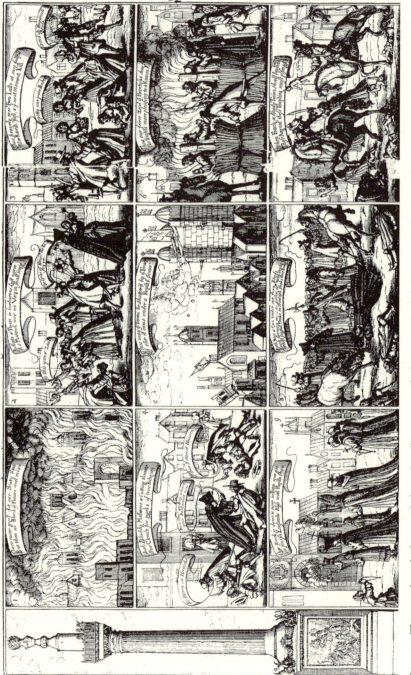

Figure 3. This 1681 broadside provided graphic illustrations of what some English Protestants feared would come to pass under a Catholic king, including the burning of London, destruction of churches, and cruel abuse and execution of Protestant men, women, and children. *A Scheme of Popish Cruelties* (London, 1681).

The anti-Catholic panic of 1678 drew from these traditions, but its key inspiration came from a tense geopolitical situation. The key factor was the rise of Catholic France as a major European and global power. In 1672 the Sun King's armies overran the Netherlands, long the center of international Protestantism, and threatened to expand his influence in Protestant Germany as well. In addition to his foreign adventures, Louis relentlessly persecuted his own nation's Protestant minority, giving an indication of how he would treat the inhabitants of conquered Protestant territories. "His Designs are so vast," wrote one English critic, "that in some short time all *Europe* will not be Elbow-room for his Ambition." The only way to bring him to heel, in the estimation of many English and Dutch Protestants, was a general alliance of all the Reformed people of Europe, who might be able to use their combined force to thwart his designs.[10]

While Louis XIV ran roughshod over the liberties of Europe, England's king Charles II proved reluctant to do his part for the Protestant cause. Indeed, the "merry monarch" seemed at times to be moving England closer to the French orbit, imitating Louis XIV's methods of governing and joining the French in a war against the Netherlands that was wildly unpopular in England. (In fact, Charles II signed a secret treaty with the French at Dover in 1670, so many of his subjects' fears were justified.) Even more ominously, the king's brother and heir to the throne, James, duke of York, revealed in 1674 that he had converted to Catholicism, meaning that—barring the birth of a male heir or a change in succession—the next king of England, Scotland, and Ireland would be a papist. All these circumstances lay behind the popish plot, when it appeared that the papists intended to bring their designs to fruition. And the people "who ought to stand by us in the day of Battel"—public servants—"have been the Persons in the World most likely to betray us, and lead us like Sheep to the Slaughter."[11]

The revelations of the plot, aided by the lapse of the licensing act that had allowed government ministers to police printing in the kingdom, resulted in an enormous outpouring of anti-Catholic propaganda. These tracts, books, and newspapers detailed the imminent popish threat to the English church and state, the Protestant religion in the world, and, indeed, the lives, liberties, and property of godly people everywhere. One of the most alarming publications, an anonymous tract entitled *An Appeal from the Country to the City*, detailed exactly what would happen if Catholics succeeded in their designs. First, the papists would set London on fire: "the whole Town in a flame, occasioned this second time, by the same Popish malice which set it on fire before."

Then, a military invasion: "Troops of Papists, ravishing your wives and your Daughters, dashing your little Childrens brains out against the walls, plundering your houses, and cutting your own throats, by the name of Heretick Dogs." For the survivors, then, torture and fire: "your Father, or your Mother, or some of your nearest and dearest Relations, tyed to a Stake in the midst of flames, when with hands and eyes lifted up to Heaven, they scream and cry out to God for whose Cause they die; which was a frequent spectacle the last time Popery reign'd amongst us." And if all this was not bad enough—your wives and daughters raped, your house in ruins, your parents burned at the stake, your own throat cut—business would also suffer: "Your Trading's bad, and in a manner lost already, but then the only commodity will be Fire and Sword; the only object women running with their hair about their ears, Men cover'd with blood, Children sprawling under Horses feet, and only the walls of Houses left standing."[12]

The only proper response to this danger, claimed the author and like-minded English people, was to change the line of succession to prevent the duke of York from becoming king. It was the interest, and indeed the duty of all good Protestants to ensure that a papist did not come to the throne; the *Appeal*'s author even suggested an alternative, Charles II's illegitimate son James, duke of Monmouth. "If the Papists make such plottings and designes to subvert our religion under a protestant prince," one advocate of exclusion noted, "how much more will they designe against us under a popish successour?" Contemporary circumstances in France seemed to provide the answer. In the early 1680s Louis was determined to sweep away the "Edicts and Arrests, Priviledges and Immunities, Liberties and Laws" that protected Protestant worship, and Huguenot refugees began an exodus to England where they advertised the Sun King's cruelty. As one leading radical Protestant wrote, "the severities exercised against those of the Reformed Religion in that Kingdom, are but a Copy of what we in these Nations are to look for, in case we should come under a Popish Prince."[13]

This so-called "exclusion crisis" marked the practical beginning of party politics in England. Advocates of the exclusion of the duke of York from the throne soon became known as the Whigs, and their program combined a fanatical and paranoid antipopery, a general tolerance for Protestant dissent, and a fierce advocacy of the independence of Parliament and local magistrates—the "country interest"—from the king and his royal court. As one Scottish Presbyterian noted around the same time, it was a goal of popish, arbitrary governments to bring about "a general or gradual unhinging of Legal

Constitutions, made for security of our Religion and Liberty." As a result, Whigs held fast to those "English liberties" that served as the greatest bulwarks to prevent a monarch or his "evil counselors" from pushing the kingdom toward "popery and slavery."[14]

While the Whig cause gained many adherents in the panic surrounding the popish plot, it was far from a unanimous movement among English men and women. Indeed, the exclusion campaign inspired the creation of a countermovement—which developed into the Tory party—that defended the king's prerogative in the face of rebellious subjects. The Tories were just as conspiratorial as their Whig counterparts, and also drew from the anti-Catholic tradition, but their emphases differed from those of the Whigs. Rather than look to France or Ireland, the Tories found their most potent example north of the border in Scotland, where radical Presbyterians, known as Covenanters, waged a sometimes violent struggle against the king's efforts to promote what they labeled "prelacy and tyranny"—the rule of the church by bishops and kings rather than Presbyterian synods. Some Covenanters were quite willing to kill and die to make sure the Scottish kirk remained sufficiently reformed. The most dramatic episode in the struggle occurred in 1679, when a gang of Covenanters murdered one of their leading opponents, Archbishop James Sharp of St. Andrews, and then faced off against the king's forces at Bothwell Bridge. The episode initiated what Presbyterians later labeled the "killing times," in which royal forces—led by the duke of York, who resided in Edinburgh during the early 1680s—rooted out the remnants of the Covenanting movement. Tory propaganda, whether targeting the Covenanters, English nonconformists, or the Dutch, drew from traditions of anti-Calvinism, forged during the years when Charles I had faced off against Puritans and stoked by memories of Britain's bloody civil wars.[15]

The Tories used the Covenanters to demonstrate the dangers of radical Protestantism and the need for royal authority. These radicals were the real plotters, Tories argued, and indeed their methods suggested affinities and probably even connections with the Jesuits. "Their Principles are incompatible with Government," asserted one Tory writer, "and the common Security that every man ou[gh]t to have in Human Societies." The chief goal of the Jesuits, after all, was to kill Protestant monarchs, and this is exactly what radical Protestants aimed to do; in 1683 royal officials uncovered the Rye House Conspiracy, a plot by leading English Whigs, aided by their counterparts in Scotland, to kill both Charles II and the duke of York, paving the way for the duke of Monmouth or, even worse, a "republic" in the fashion of the old

Puritan revolutionary Oliver Cromwell. Even those Whigs who did not advocate regicide encouraged the enemy by sowing divisions in both church and state. In the view of the Tories, therefore, the only way to defeat the papists and preserve England was to strengthen the royal prerogative and the Church of England, and to persecute dissent and eschew toleration of minority sects. Toleration would only "reduce Religion in *England,* and in other Heretical Kingdoms into so many Atoms, that nothing may unite them in a solid Body to oppose [Catholic] designs."[16]

In the early 1680s the king and his Tory allies conducted a vicious campaign against their Whig opponents and dissenters from the Church of England. In particular, they targeted dissenting preachers and the radical printers and booksellers who distributed Whig propaganda. One early example was the Baptist bookseller Benjamin Harris, who allegedly printed and sold *The Appeal from the Country to the City.* Authorities charged Harris with selling a libelous book. At his trial the notorious judge Sir William Scroggs called the *Appeal* "as base a piece as ever was contrived in hell, either by papists, or the blackest rebel that ever was." People like Harris, who "rail against the church and the government," revealed themselves to be "no Protestants." The jury found the bookseller guilty and Scroggs sentenced Harris to the pillory and fined him £500, an enormous sum that practically amounted to a prison sentence. Throughout the 1680s Whigs and dissenters faced threats to their lives and livelihoods. Mobs of ruffians ranged London, closing dissenting meetinghouses and imprisoning ministers, while the courts enforced the penal laws against dissent with exact precision. The campaign was largely successful: by 1685, when Charles II died, the exclusion campaign had failed, and most English subjects both supported the new king and believed that radical dissenters posed the greatest threat to the kingdom. The minority who continued to espouse the radical Whig cause found itself embattled and driven underground; many radicals chose exile, removing to the Netherlands or, like Harris himself, to the American colonies, where he later became a leading advocate for the Williamite Revolution.[17]

The years after the duke of York's accession to the throne as James II were dark ones for the Protestant interest in Britain and abroad. While most subjects supported the Catholic monarch, a minority decided on violent resistance. In the spring of 1685 James, duke of Monmouth, then living in Dutch exile, attempted an invasion of England's West Country, while the duke of Argyll mounted a similar expedition in the Scottish Highlands. The goal, as expressed by one of Argyll's supporters, was the "delivery of our native land from being again drowned in popish idolatry and slavery," and the rebels believed that "the standing or falling of the Protestant interest in Europe depended in a great measure upon the event of this undertaking in Britain." Both campaigns failed miserably, the two rebel leaders met their respective ends on scaffolds in London and Edinburgh, and royal officials executed or transported hundreds of rebels. Then a few months later matters became even worse when Louis XIV revoked the Edict of Nantes, that had guaranteed limited rights to France's Protestant minority, and forced his Protestant subjects to convert to Catholicism. By the dawn of 1686 the Reformed interest languished; about the only comfort came from the Huguenot theologian Pierre Jurieu, who argued that the wave of persecution suggested that Christ's return was imminent. If earthly leaders could not protect the godly, then the savior himself was the only hope.[18]

Thus in the mid-1680s James II's three kingdoms remained in ferment, with two groups of paranoid partisans facing off in what each saw as a critical struggle for the future of Britain and Protestantism. The battle was global in nature, stretching to the Netherlands and France, the free cities of Germany, the valleys of the Piedmont, and, indeed, the remote plantations of North America and the West Indies. The struggles between Whigs and Tories that convulsed England had the potential to have a great impact in the colonies, for a number of reasons. First, these overseas extensions of England had long provided refuge for those parts of the English nation most susceptible to Whig ideology. Second, the Stuart kings used the colonies as a kind of political laboratory during the Restoration, trying out political reforms that were not yet possible in England. Finally, the colonies were surrounded by French papists and their Native American converts and allies, thus making the danger of popery look less like an abstraction and more like a clear and present danger.

• • •

The colonies, like the three kingdoms, had a particular anti-Catholic heritage. The first English settlements functioned as challenges to Spanish pretensions in the continent, and each colony defined itself to one extent or another as a bastion of true religion amid popish and pagan darkness. The Puritan founders of Massachusetts Bay went the farthest in rhetorical terms, defining themselves not only against the Spanish but also as a corrective to "the *Baits of Popery* yet left in the Church [of England]," but they were not alone. The island of Jamaica, for instance, was a former Spanish colony captured during

Oliver Cromwell's Western Design during the 1650s—a vast, millennial plan to capture the remnants of the world's great Catholic empire. Even after the Restoration of Charles II, when the Stuart monarchs usually viewed the Netherlands as a more potent rival than Spain, South Carolina was intended in part as a haven for persecuted Protestants right under the nose of Spanish Florida. In addition, the colonies abounded with non-English Protestants who had their own anti-Catholic histories: most notably the Dutch in New York, but also a smattering of Germans and French Huguenots.[19]

The Protestant settlement of North America began with a shocking incident that reverberated for decades. During the sixteenth century Spain and Portugal had monopolized the Americas, and had combined this expansionist spirit with a militant Catholicism. As a result, European Protestants had particular reasons to challenge Iberian pretensions in America, and France's small but powerful Huguenot minority took the lead during the mid-sixteenth century. In the 1560s, after the failure of a colonial project in Brazil, the French founded a colony called La Caroline, located on the St. John's River in present-day Florida. Hearing about the colony, Spain's king sent an expedition under Pedro Menéndez de Aviles to deal with the interlopers. Landing on the feast day of Saint Augustine, Menéndez made quick work of the people he called "luteranos," claiming the country for both Spain and the Catholic Church. In doing so, the founder of Florida killed hundreds of Protestants, "because they were Lutherans and enemies of our Holy Catholic faith."[20]

The destruction of La Caroline proved a galvanizing event for Protestants of several different nationalities. Several witnesses of the carnage, including La Caroline's leader René Goulaine de Laudonnière, escaped to Europe where they published tracts that emphasized Spanish cruelty. During the rest of the sixteenth century both English and Dutch privateers worked to undermine the Spanish in the Caribbean and along the North American coast—a strategic area because the Spanish "treasure fleet" passed up the eastern seaboard in its annual voyage from Havana to Seville. Early English endeavors in the Americas were steeped in this global Protestant context. For instance, when Sir Francis Drake sacked St. Augustine in 1584, Drake's fleet learned they had captured the town when a French prisoner rowed out to the ship playing "the tune of the Prince of Orange his song" on a fife. Even thousands of miles across the ocean, the standard of Europe's Protestant hero, the Dutch prince whose challenge to Spanish rule in the Low Countries ended with his assassination that very year, bound coreligionists of different nationalities together against a common Catholic enemy.[21]

The first permanent English and Dutch settlements in the Americas, despite their obvious differences, all shared this common Protestant heritage. Advocates of the English colonial project during the Elizabethan era, like Richard Hakluyt and Humphrey Gilbert, promoted colonization as a way to "annoy the king of Spain." According to Hakluyt, the English could establish a different kind of colonial empire, one that instead of conquering and killing Indians, saved their souls and offered them the freedom of the gospel. The Spanish empire, Hakluyt claimed, pretended to be for the benefit of Christ, but that was just pretense; like the Roman Church, the Spanish aimed at "filthy lucre," and they used a combination of trickery and abject cruelty to keep the people of the Americas in "greate tyrannie." Following the Spanish Dominican friar Bartolomé de Las Casas, whose denunciations of the Spanish colonial project helped to create the "black legend" of Spanish cruelty, Hakluyt focused on cruelty toward the Indians. The Spaniards "teare them in peces," Hakluyt wrote, "kill them, martir them, afflicte them, tormente them and destroye them by straunge sortes of cruelties." The hypothetical Reformed empire, on the other hand, would possess the highest of motives. Its chief aim would be "the gayninge of the soules of millions of those wretched people, the reducinge of them from darkness to lighte, from falshoodde to truthe, from dombe Idolls to the lyvinge god, from the depe pitt of hell to the highest heavens." Moreover, Protestants could expect to be greeted as liberators by the grateful natives; after all, the two peoples were partners in suffering, as Spanish cruelties in America perfectly matched those used by Catholics during the Marian persecutions in England and the Dutch Revolt. The "western discoverie" would help to spread the "gospele of Christe." If it also served to enrich the Queen of England and her subjects, and provide employment for the poor, that was all the better.[22]

It was not until the seventeenth century that colonial founders actually made good on this inflated rhetoric. Sir Walter Raleigh's first attempts to found a colony in Virginia were famous failures, and only after years of struggle did Jamestown become a viable settlement. While most historians have stressed the worldly aspects of early Virginia, the colony's founders intended the colony in part as a challenge to Spanish, popish pretensions. While England and Spain were at peace during the reign of James I, official justifications of the early settlement of North America abounded in apocalyptic, anti-Catholic language, which was newly resurgent after the Gunpowder Plot by Catholics to kill the king and blow up Parliament in 1605. As one historian has noted, a "militant internationalist Protestant ideology" served to justify colonial expansion in Virginia as well as New England and the Caribbean. According to one minister preaching to a group of Virginia Company investors in 1610, for instance, the purpose of the colony was not "present profit," which was likely to be scant anyway, but "the destruction of the devils kingdom, and the propagation of the gospel."[23]

From this perspective, the militant Protestantism of the founders of New England was merely a continuation of earlier endeavors. True to form, the Puritans who settled the region justified their mission partly as a challenge to Spain. Some of their coreligionists aimed closer to the heart of the Spanish enterprise, establishing a plantation colony on Providence Island in the western Caribbean. While the Puritans continued the anti-Catholic colonization efforts of their Huguenot, Virginian, and Dutch forebears, however, the English state abandoned the mission, adopting a new style of Protestant worship under Archbishop William Laud that took a much softer line against the Roman church. As a result, from the 1630s through the execution of Charles I in 1649, the most militant anti-Catholics, in England as well as the colonies, were often dissidents, using the language of antipopery against a church and king that seemed insufficiently Protestant. Indeed, Charles I even granted one of his most prominent Catholic subjects, George Calvert, Lord Baltimore, the right to colonize the northern part of Chesapeake Bay, which became the colony of Maryland.[24]

While the English state shied away from directly confronting Catholics in the New World, the Dutch Republic began to assemble a colonial empire that also had strong religious connotations. From the beginning of their own struggle for independence from the Spanish Habsburgs, the Dutch had viewed the inhabitants of the Americas as fellow victims of Spanish tyranny. The eventual formation of the Dutch West India Company (WIC)—an American counterpart to the powerful Dutch East India Company or VOC—reflected a careful amalgamation of commercial and religious goals. Willem Usselincx, one of the company's early champions, hoped that it would function to liberate the Western Hemisphere from Spanish Catholic tyranny by promoting the Reformed religion, free trade, and the liberation of the natives. While the eventual Dutch colonies in the Caribbean and New Netherland did not live up to these high ideals, they did define themselves as Protestant havens. Some of the first settlers of New Netherland were French-speaking Protestant refugees from Wallonia, and throughout the seventeenth century many settlers in the colony called for a faith more pure and militant than that promoted by the States General and the WIC.[25]

The victory of the Parliamentary side in England's Civil Wars saw the temporary return of England to the vanguard of international Protestantism. One of Oliver Cromwell's boldest endeavors, the Western Design, aimed to conquer the Spanish empire. It represented the culmination of a hundred years of Protestant militancy in the Americas, beginning after the slaughter in Florida and continuing through the Elizabethan privateers, Dutch merchant companies, and Puritan colonization efforts in both New England and the Caribbean. As one New Englander later reported, Cromwell believed that the conquest of Spanish America "would be to dry up Euphrates"—a reference to apocalyptic prophecies—and that the Lord Protector would not stop "till He came to the Gates of Rome." Despite the successful conquest of Jamaica, the design ultimately failed. Even in New England Puritans showed little enthusiasm for leaving their homes and relocating to Jamaica. Cromwell's Western Design, much like his attempt to remake England into a Commonwealth, seemed to indicate the limits of radical Protestantism as a governing philosophy on either a national or an imperial level.[26]

By the time Charles II regained the throne in the Restoration of 1660, all the parts of his nascent empire shared a deep anti-Catholic heritage. Nonetheless, only in Maryland, where a Catholic proprietor ruled over an overwhelmingly Protestant colony, did antipopery routinely intersect with everyday politics. In the 1670s, however, this situation began to change. A number of factors, reflecting both a changing global dynamic and shifts in power relationships on the North American continent, combined to make antipopery a powerful political tool on the imperial peripheries.

On one hand, English subjects in the colonies simply reacted to the same fears that circulated in Great Britain and Europe. Within months of Titus Oates's revelations of popish plotting in 1678, ministers in New England knew about the conspiracy. The Reverend Increase Mather—probably the most connected member of Boston's clerical elite—first learned of the "deep & generall design amongst the papists to involve us in confusion & blood" from his brother Nathaniel, a dissenting minister in Dublin, in December 1678. Within months he received more details from English correspondents, along with numerous other reports of the languishing of the global Protestant interest. Mather and others like him efficiently passed the news on to their captive audiences on Sundays, and they received help from magistrates as well. During the late 1670s and early 1680s provincial and town officials around New England ordered frequent public fasts to pray for the "darke clouds . . . impending over the English nation" and the "deep consultations of the Antichristian party, who have been complotting the subversion of the true Christian Protestant Religion . . . in England, Scotland, & Ireland." In short, there could hardly be a person in the region unaware that something dramatic was occurring on the other side of the ocean.[27]

Beyond the news passed on in letters, colonial readers also consumed an array of books and printed matter from England. Once again, Increase Mather provides a vivid example of the circulation of books, since he noted his reading habits in his diary. In October 1682, for example, he read the trial records of Oliver Plunkett and Fitzharris, two of the popish plotters, along with the classic polemic *No Protestant Plot.* The following year he turned to "2d part of growth of popery," a reference to another leading Whig tract. Increase's son Cotton, meanwhile, provided some clues as to how such books traveled to the colonies. In a 1683 letter, the young minister requested that an English contact send him Henry Care's *Weekly Pacquet of Advice from Rome,* along with other Whig literature. Even in remote Henrico County, Virginia, the planter William Byrd knew enough of the volatile situation in Europe that he requested an associate to send him a copy of Pierre Jurieu's *Accomplishment of the Scripture Prophecies,* a book arguing that Europe's religious turmoil presaged an imminent Apocalypse. All these books served to underscore the same conclusion: that the Protestant world was facing a crisis unlike any other.[28]

Along with news and books came refugees—English dissenters, Scottish Covenanters, and French Huguenots forced out of Europe by persecuting kings and bishops. Some of these newcomers were simple fugitives from justice, like William Kelso, a Scottish surgeon who arrived in Boston on the *Anne and Hester* in the summer of 1680. Kelso had lent his services to the Covenanting army around the time of the Battle of Bothwell Bridge, and his flight took him around the British world—to Belfast, Dublin, London, and finally to New England, where he was received as a hero once magistrates there identified him as "a Scotch gentleman & Covenanter." They dutifully ignored a royal order to apprehend the fugitive. Many other similar migrants ended up in American ports during the 1680s—enough to populate new colonies like Pennsylvania, New Jersey, and South Carolina. Moreover, these newcomers brought harrowing stories of their ill treatment at the hands of their enemies in Europe, enemies that seemed to have designs on America as well.[29]

Of all the newcomers, perhaps the most important were the boatloads of French Protestants who settled in English colonies from St. Christopher to Massachusetts. The migration started early, in the 1670s, when significant numbers of Huguenots began seeking refuge in England, and a smaller number sought assistance from Parliament to move to places like South Carolina, which could serve as a "retreat for an infinity of people oppressed for their conscience in French colonies in the Antilles as well as Hispaniola and in Canada where they groan under the Cross." The proprietors of that young colony embraced this search for "forreigne Protestants" as something that would both bring revenue and security and solve a demographic problem in Europe, where refugees and undesirable radicals were filling up communities and taxing resources. Part of the plan involved settling a number of Covenanters in a village south of Charles Town, and the proprietors also proposed bringing in Protestants from the German Palatinate.[30]

The year 1686 marked the high point in this migration, as the combined suppression of Monmouth and Argyll's rebellions and the revocation of the Edict of Nantes increased the flow of dissenters of many nationalities. The Whig bookseller John Dunton, who came to New England to recover his debts that year, reported that Boston was the "common refuge" for "Monmouth's forlorn Fugitives." Farther south in the West Indies, meanwhile, nearly a thousand even more forlorn fugitives worked as indentured servants on plantations, sentenced to ten years of labor for their advocacy of Monmouth's cause. The effect of all these arrivals was to make almost everyone aware of the upsurge in persecution back home, and to assign the colonies a specific place in the Protestant world. If there was a place where godly people could continue to worship God, perhaps it was in these remote plantations, where the state did not possess as much coercive power.[31]

The rise in antipopery was therefore partly a result of the integration of the colonies into European confessional politics. But at the same time local circumstances in America served to reinforce these fears and make colonial subjects even more nervous. During the mid-1670s relations between Europeans and Native Americans took a particularly violent turn. First, in 1675, New England Wampanoags under the leadership of King Philip rose up against the English in Plymouth and Massachusetts, leading to a bloody war that threatened the annihilation of the New England colonies and eventually concluded in the removal of much of the region's native population. The following year, to the south in Virginia, conflicts between Indians and English settlers in the Potomac Valley led to an argument over Indian policy that culminated in civil war, as the planter Nathaniel Bacon led a movement that burned Jamestown to the ground and forced the governor to seek refuge on the Eastern Shore. Along with these two regional crises came a third in Barbados, which experienced its first major slave insurrection in 1675.[32]

As these events occurred few observers thought to relate them to each other, let alone to the alarms over "popery and arbitrary government" across the Atlantic. As time passed, however, and the rumors traveling through the Protestant world became more extreme, many people began to view these various disturbances as more than coincidences. When new arrivals warned of tyrannical designs in Europe, colonists started to fear that they too would fall to a global Catholic plot. This was the political and religious context of the unprecedented expansion of the empire under the later Stuarts, a design that succeeded in changing the way that crown and colonies related to one another—though not necessarily in the way that imperial officials envisioned.

• • •

The political circumstances in Britain itself combined with the crisis in the colonies to create the possibility of real political change in English America. However, this change was far from straightforward or inevitable. Stuart officials acted first, attempting to reform the empire by fiat in the late 1670s and 1680s, mainly through the revocation of various colonial charters. This program excited enormous opposition that eventually became subsumed in the empire-wide contest between Whigs and Tories after the popish plot. After some setbacks, however, James II managed to construct the Dominion of New England, a monument to enlightened, imperial absolutism that served as the cornerstone for a new empire.

This empire ultimately could not survive the crisis that forced James himself from the throne. The Glorious Revolution in England led to a period of profound fear and chaos in the colonies, and opened the door to a new form of imperialism, as anti-Catholic firebrands attempted to construct a decentralized union of colonies brought together by their common zeal for Protestantism. While these radicals gained control in several colonies, their dreams for remaking America collapsed in a sea of paranoia and fear—which allowed advocates of centralization to reemerge during the 1690s. In the midst of an actual war with France, imperial leaders used the promise of security, couched in the language of centralization and fear of popery, to build a popular movement for empire. By the eighteenth century, as Benjamin Wadsworth's sermon suggested, Anglo-Americans embraced their identity as subjects of a powerful English monarch.

While this study uses England's American empire as its canvas, I have not tried to give equal coverage to every part of it. In particular, a disproportionate amount of the action centers on the northeastern settlements from New York to Nova Scotia. I do not intend to argue that these colonies were more important than others, but at the same time the imperial transition did mean a bit more in this region for two reasons. First, imperial planners paid a lot of attention to these colonies, partly because of New England's reputation for independence, and partly because the duke of York centered his own ambitions on the region. Second, the colonies' proximity to New France made the fear of "popish plots" more intense and relevant than in some other parts of the empire. Nonetheless, while I pay a lot of attention to New York and New England, my purpose is to fit these peculiar places into a continental and global context. Despite their distinctive characteristics, all the various parts of the empire experienced these decades of change in broadly similar ways.

●　●　●

This book is based on extensive readings in official records, published tracts, and private correspondence. In the event that a single document has appeared in different forms, I have tried to cite the most easily accessible version. The one exception is for documents from the Colonial Office Papers housed at the National Archives in Kew. While many of these documents have appeared in the *Calendar of State Papers, Colonial Series*, my citations refer to the originals, since the versions in the *CSPC* are often incomplete. All dates are in the Old Style, with the year beginning on January 1. I have quoted the sources as they appear, but have modernized spelling and punctuation in some cases.

PART I

Empire Imagined

Chapter 1

Imperial Designs

BEGINNING IN THE 1670s administrators in Charles II's court sought to build a new empire. As an anonymous official noted, proper management of "forraigne Plantations" was of "great consequence . . . to the prosperity of [the] Nation." The king's empire was vast, but poorly regulated. Local officials in the various plantations worked in virtual isolation from authorities in Whitehall, and unlike other European states, England did not have a single office managing colonial affairs before the mid-1670s. The consequences of this oversight were profound; the king lost revenue and power, and colonial subjects languished on their own, as evidenced in the crisis of 1675–76, when New England nearly fell to a coalition of enemy Indians and Virginia experienced a massive civil war. If the empire was to work for the king and his subjects, it had to be brought into line.[1]

The later Stuart reorganization of the empire was a bold exercise in transAtlantic state building. It represented one strand of a campaign to augment the crown's power at the expense of the localities, reflected most notably in the reorganization of dozens of local corporations in England itself. Reformers hoped that England would soon have a much more streamlined state, one that reflected in some form the royal absolutist political philosophies pursued by Louis XIV in France at the same time. In order to do this, the king and his ministers had to reorganize the state on a grand scale, but in addition they had to change English political culture, which included a strong attachment to local customs, privileges, and liberties. If they were to succeed, crown officials had to convince people to view the king and the state in a new way.[2]

Thus royal officials had to translate this grand imperial vision in dozens of local contexts. In England the drama played out in counties and towns across the kingdom as local interest groups battled the crown for their privileges. Across the ocean, meanwhile, the theoretical issues were similar but the context very different. Zealous civil servants made the long trip to North America and the West Indies to accomplish what they hoped would be a simple task. The colonies were farther away and there was little money to help imperial officials build an empire, but few people lived in the plantations and they did not have entrenched interest groups like those in Britain and Ireland. Even the oldest colony, after all, was just over seventy years old. The crown began modestly: in 1678 it created a new royal colony in New Hampshire, a tiny outpost in northern New England, sending a minor courtier named Edward Cranfield to lead the colony into stability. Soon afterward, an English court revoked the charter of the Bermuda Company and took that island colony under its control. These minor conquests would pave the way for the royalization of New England, the most argumentative and independent of the colonies, and eventually all of the American plantations.[3]

This simple task proved very difficult for administrators to accomplish. In New Hampshire and Bermuda, the governors sent to oversee these changes met serious resistance—especially from the religious dissenters who formed majorities in both places. New Hampshire's Governor Cranfield quickly ran afoul of prominent landowners and assemblymen, surviving an attempted rebellion in 1683. In Bermuda, meanwhile, Governor Richard Coney managed to alienate virtually everyone, at one point confronting an armed mob right in front of his house, and declaring the colony to be in "actual rebellion." Beyond the physical perils of office, neither man was very successful at the tasks of governance, whether raising revenue or providing for defense. Put simply, colonial subjects refused to recognize their authority, meaning that both colonies were essentially without governments during much of the 1680s. The new empire did not come together as its planners envisioned; rather than uniting colonial subjects, imperial reform divided them into two hostile and irreconcilable camps.[4]

These reform efforts proved difficult because they ran into the conspiratorial political culture of popish and Puritan plots that poisoned Anglo-American politics in the Restoration era. Rather than bringing England and the plantations together in a more perfect union, the program of imperial centralization polarized colonists, creating two different factions or parties that took on slightly different forms from place to place but organized themselves around two conspiracy theories. One faction, which can be called the royal party, believed that a Puritan plot threatened the plantations; that Protestant dissenters, heirs to the regicidal impulses of their forebears, intended to undermine the Restoration monarchy and strip the king of his empire. The other side, which might be called the Protestant party, began to see imperial centralization as one plank in a popish plot, a design by Stuart officials, sometimes in collusion with French or Spanish allies, to reduce the plantations to popery and tyranny. With both sides dependent on such conspiratorial visions, the actual task of governance became much more difficult.[5]

•   •   •

In 1685 Nathaniel Crouch, a famous London bookseller known for his condensed histories and devotional tracts, issued a new title, *The English Empire in America*. The book was inexpensive and small enough to fit in one's pocket, and its 200 pages contained vivid, if somewhat remarkable stories about the history and present state of England's overseas plantations. The book would win no points for either originality or accuracy: as in his other histories, Crouch simply reprinted much of his material from other available printed sources, and selected anecdotes aimed at an audience more interested in curiosities than in the subtleties of colonial society or government. Nearly half of the book consisted of descriptions of native life culled from authors like Thomas Hariot and John Smith, while the chapters on the Caribbean Islands focused on sea monsters. But for all its eccentricities, Crouch's book teaches historians a very important lesson. Even among London's humbler classes, the American empire had begun to acquire a reputation. People knew about it, and wanted to know more. The colonies had entered the popular consciousness.[6]

It is hardly coincidental that Crouch's book appeared in 1685, the last year of Charles II's reign. Arguably no monarch in English history had presided over such a profound expansion of England's overseas empire. During the twenty-five years following the king's restoration in 1660 the plantations grew in both number and importance. Charles created five new colonies on the North American mainland by granting charters to royal favorites, while also expanding the scope of royal authority in existing colonies and handing more power to chartered trading monopolies like the East India Company or the new Royal African Company. At the time of the king's death his empire stretched from London to Newfoundland, Barbados, and India. Tens of thousands of his subjects lived overseas, along with many people of other nationalities who dwelled in his dominions, often against their will.[7]

But if Charles II's empire was mighty on paper, it was also diverse and diffuse. Not only in geography, but in economic livelihood, political form, and ethnic composition, each of the king's plantations was a world apart. Certainly it was a major goal of the king's ministers to impose some kind of order on the chaotic system he inherited from his father and grandfather, and he did preside over an unprecedented expansion of the imperial administration, but the farther one went from Whitehall the less this bureaucracy seemed to matter. Part of the king's irrelevance stemmed from his own inconsistency: just as he sought to eliminate the chartered corporations in New England and Bermuda that made the colonies so hard to govern, he also created new proprieties as late as 1681, when he granted Pennsylvania to the Quaker William Penn. This waffling has led many historians to downplay the significance of the Restoration empire and consider the eighteenth century as the true beginning of British imperialism.[8]

Despite its diversity, there was one thing that united the various parts of the Restoration empire, and that was fear. The expansionist push of the late 1600s did not stem, as one might think, from national self-confidence, but from the very opposite feeling, an anxiety that England was in danger of being subverted and undermined, or even destroyed, by its rivals. The identity of this eternal foe was a matter of some dispute, and English political writers engaged in a constant debate concerning which of the nation's chief rivals, France or the Netherlands, was more dangerous or cunning. But whoever the enemy was, most English people agreed that the proper response was an expansion of England's global influence. Thus, the empire that Crouch chronicled was in part a national attempt to save England and its interests from subversion.[9]

The champions of imperial consolidation came from a cadre of Stuart loyalists who shaped colonial policy on both sides of the Atlantic. The most ubiquitous was William Blathwayt, a political chameleon who never visited the colonies, but became England's most influential American expert, and a tireless advocate of a more centralized empire. While he rarely engaged in overt political sermonizing, Blathwayt left little doubt that he favored tighter controls over the colonies, and he also suggested why: without centralization, the king's rivals—especially France—would gain more power and resources in North America. In 1688 Blathwayt defended the proposed Dominion of New England by stating, "it will be terrible to the French and make them proceed with more caution than they have lately done." But if Blathwayt and other Stuart officials feared the French, they combined this anxiety with a great deal of admiration. Indeed, they proposed that the best way to defeat the French in America, as in Europe, was to emulate them.[10]

Two brief examples can serve to illustrate this anti-French imperialism. In the Leeward Islands of the West Indies, perhaps the most exposed of England's colonial possessions, the crypto-Catholic Tory Governor Sir William

Stapleton complained throughout the 1670s and 1680s of the attention the French king lavished on his island colonies, implying that if the Lords of Trade and Plantations did not imitate the Sun King and send a well-provisioned naval brigade, England's rivals could easily overrun the islands. In the meantime, another Irish Catholic, Thomas Dongan of New York, worked against French pretensions in the north by adopting French tactics. England's rivals had built a potent empire despite the perennial lack of migrants by cultivating Indian alliances that united the French, at least in theory, with natives stretching from Montreal to the Illinois Country. Dongan consciously imitated this alliance system by renewing the "covenant chain" alliance with the powerful Iroquois Confederacy dwelling north of the colony, which had been inaugurated by his predecessor Edmund Andros. At the same time, Dongan understood the role of Jesuit priests in expanding French trade and influence, and he proposed that the English expel the priests and replace them with English Jesuits—a tacit admission of the importance of missions in strengthening the imperial state. Indeed, the Jesuits had become leading vanguards of French expansionism, and Dongan understood their power.[11]

These Stuart planners perceived a hemispheric design by the French to dominate the continent both politically and economically. The Sun King and his minions would use every tool at their disposal—including military power and the more subtle efforts of the Jesuits—to win over the trade of the Americas for themselves, and with it land and power as well. The design was secular at its core, but had a strong religious component, since the French masked their true intentions under a religious veneer. Thus the Stuart vision of empire was based on a widespread fear of the French that was at least implicitly, and sometimes explicitly, anti-Catholic.

At the same time, they perceived another enemy that aided the French in their designs: radical dissenters. Along with the king's foreign rivals, these internal foes were the most dangerous enemies of the national interest. It was Puritans, after all, who had taken up arms against King Charles I and plunged the nation into civil war during the 1640s, and forty years later their heirs—usually labeled dissenters or nonconformists—appeared to be doing the same thing. By fomenting quarrels between English subjects and challenging royal authority, these subversives provided aid to the king's Catholic rivals. Stuart officials often made toleration a feature of their religious policy, but they accompanied this apparent moderation with a vitriolic condemnation of dissent, which often crossed the line from being a matter of conscience to a marker of treasonous inclinations. In addition, imperial planners used the *lack*

of religious toleration in New England, especially toward conforming Anglicans, as another reason to reform the colonies.[12]

The New England colonies provided the clearest indication of the dangers
of an empire run by dissenters. Edward Randolph, a royal officer sent to investigate the region in 1676, portrayed Massachusetts as an "arbitrary government" in the truest sense, as leaders claimed authority with no real mandate.
They flouted English economic regulations, passed laws that were "repugnant"
to the English constitution, and even harbored "regicides" who had signed
Charles I's death warrant in 1649. Reform was necessary, Randolph argued,
not just for economic reasons but for geopolitical ones as well. These perverse
"Independents" threatened to betray the colonies to a foreign power because
they fomented divisions among Protestants and rejected the king's authority,
and they occupied a vulnerable corner of the English dominions adjacent to
New France. "There are dangerous principles among them," Randolph complained, and if the crown did not exert some control, "the French will certainly
by degrees swallow up that great Countrey . . . & so at length become masters
of all his Maj[es]ties West Indian Plantations." Some Tories even went so far as
to suggest that an alliance existed between papists and dissenters, claiming that
Jesuits lurked in bastions of dissent like New England, where they encouraged
heresy against the Church of England in order to weaken their rivals.[13]

Luckily for the crown, Randolph thought that reforming this system
would be fairly easy. Most New Englanders, the agent claimed, did not hate
the monarch, and indeed would welcome greater imperial regulation, especially if it would provide safety against external enemies like the Indians who
had almost destroyed the colonies in King Philip's War. Randolph also noted
that New Englanders hated the French to an unusual degree, a factor that
could work in the crown's favor in the contest against its chief rival. It appeared to be obvious to all that a centralized empire, rather than a set of separate colonies that had trouble cooperating with each other, would best defend
America against the French. As bureaucrats like Randolph allied with military
men like Thomas Dongan to remake the colonies, therefore, they had high
hopes for success. These hopes proved short-lived, however, once they actually
attempted to implement their imperial policies.

•   •   •

The first experiment in Stuart imperialism was the remote colony of New
Hampshire. There were few places in the English Atlantic of less strategic

importance, but the province provided an opportunity for the crown to begin to restructure the political culture of the plantations. New Hampshire would not have attracted any attention in Whitehall but for the many petitions of Robert Mason, who claimed a title to New Hampshire based on a grant his grandfather had received from James I. Though he proved to be a poor politician in America, he played the game of court politics extremely well. His claim to New Hampshire was shaky, but he knew that if he agreed to share the spoils with the crown, he could succeed. So he presented his campaign for New Hampshire not as a design for personal profit, which it was, but as a means to buttress the king's authority, especially against Massachusetts Congregationalists, who had administered New Hampshire since the 1650s. "Mischiefe and miseries . . . have befallen those Colonies by reason of a divided and disjointed government," he wrote in one of his many petitions, and without "One General Governor," New England was "liable to become an easie prey to every Invader." In other words, both Mason and the crown viewed New Hampshire as a first step to the royalization of New England and, eventually, all America.[14]

The first royal government in New Hampshire, therefore, was a classic public-private partnership, combining aspects of the older model of chartered or proprietary colonies with a new, royal vision. Mason received title to all the province's land, meaning that he could legally charge quitrents from the inhabitants, provided that he could convince them to take out new patents acknowledging him as their landlord. The crown took on the right of government, which would be managed by a governor appointed by the king along with an appointed council and elected assembly. In an apparent act of magnanimity that may have been the price of doing business with the king, Mason agreed to give one-fifth of the proceeds from the land taxes to the provincial government to cover its costs. Thus the royal government appeared to be a winning proposition: it would help to establish royal authority in the region and support itself with the revenue from Mason's lands—which Mason assured Whitehall would be large.[15]

Of course, no one could deny that this design had certain pitfalls. The thorniest issue concerned the people who believed they already owned the land that Mason now claimed as his own. Not surprisingly, few if any landowners proved hospitable to Mason's claims, and to make matters worse, the initial commission that established royal government in 1679 gave political power to some of the men most likely to resist the proprietor's designs, like council members Richard Waldron and John Gilman, two of the colony's largest landowners. Faced with widespread disobedience, Mason waged a nasty battle with his political rivals, accusing Waldron and Gilman of being enemies of the king for several incriminating statements they had made. The council fought back by ordering Mason's arrest "to give Answer for his Usurpacon over His Ma[jes]t[ie]s Authority." In the main, the initial struggle between Mason and his enemies had little to do with royal government. Both sides accepted the king's authority, and claimed to be the true representatives of the royal interest. They differed on one very discrete issue: whether or not Mason had a right to the land.[16]

In 1682 the crown appointed a new governor, Edward Cranfield, to break the impasse. The reasons for his appointment are unclear: he was a military man, a minor officer in the queen's household, who had successfully negotiated with the Dutch in Surinam for the return of some English planters there in the 1670s. Some historians have argued that Robert Mason engineered Cranfield's appointment, knowing he would support the proprietor's interest, but there is no positive evidence for that assertion. In the main, historians have castigated Cranfield for his sins but done little to examine his policies, characterizing him as "rapacious," a tyrant interested only in self-aggrandizement. While Cranfield's tenure was an undoubted failure, such rhetoric is unfair. In fact, Cranfield was the most principled defender of the royal prerogative working in the colonies during the 1680s, and his detailed correspondence provides a wonderful narrative of how this early experiment in royal government capsized in a sea of religious paranoia and controversy.[17]

After his arrival in October 1682 Cranfield exhibited many of the same skills that had allowed him to negotiate successfully with the Dutch in Surinam. He set himself up, as his commission dictated, as an arbiter between the proprietor and his purported tenants. If anything—and in spite of historians' contentions that he was in league with Mason from the beginning—Cranfield sided with Mason's rivals. He reported that Mason had exaggerated both the wealth and the refractoriness of the king's subjects in the province. In truth, the colony possessed few resources; the people were generally loyal to the king but poor. Mason's proposals, meanwhile, had the potential to further impoverish the people. For instance, his attempt to seize common lands from the towns would have meant that ordinary settlers would no longer have any place to graze their livestock. As for Mason's opponents, Waldron and Martin, the governor found that "although there might have been some Heats of Spirit & undueness of Expression betweene Mr Mason and them while contending about property," it was "nothing to render them guilty of such disloyalty as they were charged with." One of Cranfield's first actions was to restore the two men to their seats on the council.[18]

Within two months of his arrival, however, everything changed. The conciliatory governor disappeared, replaced by a forceful and unbending advocate of centralization, by brute force if necessary. While some historians have blamed this change of heart on Cranfield's acquisitive nature—essentially contending that he abandoned the colonists when they refused to pay him enough—such a reading has little relation to the evidence. In fact, Cranfield was very clear about why he changed his mind: the situation in New Hampshire, he came to believe, was not a local dispute about property rights, but part of a transatlantic battle between the king and his enemies. A thorough royalist brought up in the age of civil wars and conspiratorial politics, Cranfield became convinced that a murderous Puritan plot, a "grand combination made up of Church members of Congregationall Assemblies throughout all the colonies in New England" intended to topple the king's government and, in effect if not in design, hand over America to Charles II's enemies.[19]

The governor's paranoia originated in a series of disputes with local interest groups that, at first glance, had little to do with each other. One rift involved a Scottish ship accused of trading in the colony contrary to the Navigation Acts. Under the recommendation of Edward Randolph, Cranfield prosecuted the ship's master, but found that since the master belonged to Portsmouth's Congregational church, the governor could not convince any jury to convict. At the same time, Cranfield ran into loggerheads with the colonial assembly, which refused to pass any of the governor's revenue bills. In an imitation of his master across the ocean, the governor dissolved the assembly, sparking the resentment of certain members. In a clear signal that he associated this resistance with the Congregationalists' longstanding antipathy toward monarchy, Cranfield scheduled a colony-wide fast for 30 January 1683, in order to commemorate the execution of Charles I by overly zealous Puritans 34 years before.[20]

This series of insults did not sit well with members of the assembly. By Cranfield's own admission, the people of New Hampshire had been fairly well disposed to royal government, only resisting Mason's designs on their land. Cranfield's actions convinced some that the new royal government, at least as it was currently composed, was illegitimate, and indicated another kind of plot, orchestrated by "papists," to erect an arbitrary government in New Hampshire.

The dispute manifested itself in the mysterious actions of one Edward

Gove, a member of the assembly and militia lieutenant from the town of Hampton. Gove had led resistance to Mason's land grab at the Hampton town meeting, but in January his anger toward the regime took on a different hue. Taking away land was just the first step in a general campaign against the country's "liberties," one that would culminate with the establishment of Catholicism. On 26 January 1683, Gove began riding around the province in attempt to raise a party to "stand against the governor." His exact intentions remain murky. Partisan accounts by Edward Randolph and Robert Mason claimed that Gove aimed to kill Cranfield and his allies while they paid homage to their martyred king on 30 January—a report sure to evoke a sympathetic response at Whitehall, but lacking corroboration. More likely, Gove wanted to raise up the militia as a show of force against Cranfield and Mason, a warning that the people of New Hampshire would not give up their land or liberties without a fight. While many people sympathized with Gove, however, he attracted few supporters. Only about a dozen teenage boys joined his cause, and they surrendered before the governor even arrived on the scene.[21]

Gove's "rebellion" marked an example of how paranoia could turn a simple property dispute into a cosmic drama in which some people were inclined to take up arms. The rebel's only written statement, penned in jail to the justices of the court that tried him, revealed a man convinced that New England stood on the precipice of doom. The rambling and barely coherent letter claimed, among other things, that his prison keepers fed him poison, but it ended with an alarmist biblical allegory. "If ever New-England had need of a Solomon, or David, or Moses, Caleb or Joshua, it is now," Gove wrote. "The tears are in my eyes. I can hardly see." Statements by his enemies, while biased, help to corroborate this vision of a man who believed New England's Protestant establishment to be in great danger. According to Randolph's account, Gove claimed that Cranfield's governorship was illegitimate because his commission was signed in Edinburgh by the Catholic duke of York, not in London by the king, and that Cranfield himself "was a papist and intended to bring in popery." In addition, Gove allegedly referred to a theological argument with Cranfield as one justification for the rebellion. The governor, citing the Gospel of Mark, argued for "the necessity of children's baptism," complaining that the Congregational system excluded the vast majority of New Hampshirites from the benefits of the sacrament, since only the children of church members could be baptized. Gove considered this "a great imposing upon the Ministry," and in the fevered atmosphere of January 1683 Gove combined this fear of ecclesiastical innovation with Mason's land designs, seeing both as elements in a global Catholic plot to extinguish the colony's civil and religious liberties. Gove may have declared that "his rising in arms was for liberty," but that "liberty" was very different from the modern definition.[22]

The aborted rebellion changed the nature of Cranfield's mission, and altered the way that people on both sides viewed the ongoing disputes over taxation and land tenure. Gove and Cranfield each saw the other's actions not as isolated events, reactions to local circumstance, but as parts of a global conspiracy. It was a battle of two universalisms: one rooted in radical Protestant thought, the other in royalist politics. With both sides so intransigent, there was little hope of compromise, and the situation in New Hampshire only deteriorated in the following months, as the colony's leading inhabitants divided into two hostile parties.

Cranfield's voluminous correspondence from this period allows for a close examination of his changing views of the imperial mission. If he originally considered himself as a neutral arbiter between Mason and the established colonists, such a role was altogether inappropriate in the face of a transatlantic design against the royal interest. The only way to make New England loyal was to refashion its political culture, to purge it of its seditious elements and train the people in loyalty—by force if necessary. Not surprisingly, his plan had a strong economic motive—he called for proper enforcement of the Navigation Acts—but his boldest policy proposals came not in the economic arena, but in the religious one. He believed, like many Tory royalists in the early 1680s, that radical preachers served as anchors of the Puritan Plot, poisoning the people from their true obedience, and he proposed that only by dealing with the ministers could the empire prosper.

The governor adopted these views during a lengthy residence in Boston, the regional center of sedition. He went there because he was frightened to remain in New Hampshire, believing his life to be in danger, but the time in Boston allowed Cranfield to "pry into the secrets of the faction." These investigations of the town's Congregational underworld led him to some dramatic policy proposals. First, he advocated the revocation of the Massachusetts charter, as the rulers of that government used their semi-independence to spread anti-monarchical sentiment around the region. They corresponded with and provided refuge to seditious elements from England, and they had their hands in everything unpleasant, from the Rye House Plot to Gove's aborted rebellion. Next, Cranfield requested a permanent military presence to enforce the king's will, a "frigate" that would defend the region not only from foreign enemies, but from domestic ones as well. But more than all these necessary measures, Cranfield demanded the authority to act against "the preachers." Congregational ministers, he claimed, did the most to excite the people against the king, because they had a captive audience in church each Sunday, and unusual powers of argument and persuasion. There could be no order in the region, Cranfield wrote, until he received a command to "remove all such their Preachers who oppose & indeavour to disturb the peace of this Government. Which method will be necessary to be observed in the Settlement of the Bostoners colony, & also in the Province of Main, from which I can only expect tricks & trouble, till annexed to this Government."[23]

Cranfield thus aimed not just at the structures of government in the region, but at New England's political culture: the beliefs and values that informed politics. In doing so, however, he did not make reference to a "New England Way" that distinguished the region from the rest of the empire. On the contrary, he saw the colonies as dumping grounds for the worst people and ideas of English (and Scottish) dissent, a place with a profound and deleterious connection to the wider world. At the same time, Boston served as a conduit, nurturing seditious ideas that could be repackaged and sent to other parts of English America, like New Hampshire or Bermuda. The key institution in this process was Harvard College, the local training ground for ministers. The college sent forth "Rebellious Trumpeters" who spread sedition around New England, meddling with local governments and encouraging everything from violation of the Navigation Acts to the harboring of regicides. Along the way, they excited the people against the established Church of England, as they "term the liturgy a precedent of superstition picked out of the Popish dunghill." In order to fix the problem, Cranfield demanded the power to turn out ministers and replace Harvard's faculty with orthodox preachers from England. Moreover, he proposed levying direct taxes in order to pay these Anglican ministers, bypassing the recalcitrant assemblies. Had it been implemented, Cranfield's all-out assault on Congregationalism would have transformed the region, establishing by fiat the kind of parish structure that existed in England.[24]

For the most part, Cranfield's English correspondents proved hesitant to move ahead on the governor's extreme proposals. The king's ministers did continue their legal campaign against the Massachusetts charter—a longtime goal of many Tories—but they would not send a frigate to New England or grant the governor power to turn out ministers. Indeed, they even took a softer line on the rebel Edward Gove than Cranfield believed was prudent. The rebel arrived in London in 1683 a condemned man, sentenced to be drawn and quartered for his act of rebellion. In a city teeming with rebels and traitors, however, this old New Englander was a very low priority. Consigned to the Tower of London, Gove repeatedly petitioned for release, while friends and family members testified that he had a history of mental illness. Soon Gove was given free rein to roam around the Tower grounds, and within a few years he received a full pardon and returned home to New Hampshire. Cranfield was long gone by that time, but he did complain bitterly when he heard of the prisoner's easy treatment, arguing that "if Gove escape[s] the sentence of the law there is an end of his Maj[es]t[ie]s business in New England."[25]

In the absence of meaningful assistance from his superiors, Cranfield was left floundering for any way to exert the king's will against those who conspired against him. He chose the worst possible battle, taking on Portsmouth's articulate Congregational minister in a struggle that made the governor look like a cruel and arbitrary tyrant, and undoubtedly caused many people to think Edward Gove had not been so crazy after all. Since his arrival in the colony, Cranfield had complained about the Reverend Joshua Moodey, who he believed was a covert enemy who encouraged the enemies of the king in New Hampshire, even Edward Gove. Since no evidence linked Moodey to such activity, the governor set a trap for his enemy, one that had the added benefit of furthering his design to establish the Church of England in the colony. He made clear that he expected the colony's ministers to administer the sacraments according to the custom of the Church of England, meaning that all children could be baptized, and all adults who did not lead "scandalous" lives could receive communion. In addition, he issued a direct challenge to Moodey, stating that he and several other prominent Anglicans would come to receive communion from the minister in December 1683.[26]

The governor's position had a logical consistency that was difficult to refute. Like many outside observers, Cranfield considered New England's ecclesiastical system hopelessly unfair and even un-Christian, since leaders of most churches limited the sacraments to those who provided direct evidence of being "visible saints." As a result, the vast majority of children in the colony were not baptized, even though everyone contributed to the minister's maintenance. In addition, Cranfield believed the Congregationalists were persecutors, particularly against those who advocated "Common Prayer Worship," and his action only took the logical measure of ensuring that those who worshiped in the national church were not objects of discrimination in a royal colony.

If Cranfield's motives made sense, his move nonetheless backfired. Moodey naturally refused to give communion to the governor. In retaliation,

Cranfield banned the minister from the pulpit and threw him in the common jail, also sending a letter to the colony's next most important minister, Seaborn Cotton, that Cranfield intended to seek communion from him as well. The results were predictable: by placing Moodey in prison, Cranfield turned the minister into a sufferer for the faith, the greatest reward for any Reformed cleric. Within days Moodey had advertised his state to friends around New England, not only complaining about the physical conditions, but also warning that such persecution would spread around the region. Soon other New England divines were using New Hampshire as an example of what would happen if the people surrendered to royal government: "The Cup is going round the world," warned Boston minister Cotton Mather, and would soon come to these remote provinces as well, recreating the familiar horrors of the Laudian persecution that had inspired the first Puritans to cross the ocean, or, even worse, the *dragonnades* currently rooting out French Protestants. In New Hampshire, meanwhile, all religious services ceased as the colony's other ministers fled to avoid Moodey's fate. "No public worship, no preaching of the word," railed one of the governor's enemies. "What ignorance, profaneness and misery must needs ensue!" In his attempts to allow freedom of worship for Anglicans, Cranfield had effectively shut down the colony's churches, blackening the reputation of royal government throughout the region.[27]

The Moodey debacle was a public relations disaster, and one that only made the more mundane tasks of governance more difficult. Cranfield found it virtually impossible to raise revenue, as the assembly refused to pass any money bills. In the meantime, Robert Mason had just as hard a time convincing New Hampshire's landowners to surrender their land and become his tenants, eliminating another source of revenue that was supposed to support the province and its executive. With no money coming from England either, Cranfield became desperate. He threatened to take landowners to court and force them to pay quitrents to Mason, charged exorbitant fees in the colony's courts, and eventually decided to enforce old revenue statutes from before his arrival in the colony, bypassing the legislature altogether. Like his campaign against Moodey, these moves made a fair amount of sense. Cranfield was personally broke. Never a rich man, he had sold his office to travel to New Hampshire. While his critics and historians characterize him as a greedy man intent on making a fortune, he may have never been paid a cent by anyone. Moreover, the government of New Hampshire had no funds to operate. Desperate times called for desperate measures, but these measures only cemented

Cranfield's reputation as a tyrant who aimed to subvert the colony's constitution.[28]

These efforts were all for naught, as the colony's inhabitants increasingly refused to follow any of their governor's orders. While there was no repetition of Gove's rebellion, no angry people taking to the streets and demanding their liberties, Cranfield's opponents did not completely reject violence. Revenue collectors routinely met resistance, including from women who threatened the men with "scalding water, & red hot spits," if they attempted to collect taxes. Far worse was the punishment afforded Thomas Thurton, Cranfield's provost marshal in the last days of December 1684. As he traveled around Exeter trying to serve arrest warrants, an angry mob followed and mocked him, on one occasion untying his horse while he visited a neighbor's house, and on another occasion stealing his sword. Thurton's deposition of these affronts reads like the complaint of a schoolboy facing off against bullies: at one point he refused to show his commission to the crowd, out of fear that they would take it and refuse to give it back. The mockery turned serious in early January. Thurton went to the house of Samuel Sherborn to collect a small fine, but found Sherborn in no mood to pay. Thurton and his deputy began to take the offender to jail, but on the way a group of Sherborn's friends freed him, and took Thurton into custody. Over the course of a harrowing two days, the provost marshal was tied up and imprisoned in a house in Exeter, dragged through the town with a noose around his neck, beaten with a cudgel, and eventually dumped over the border into Massachusetts, where he spent another 40 hours tied up in a stranger's house. Thurton knew most of his attackers, and he and several witnesses left detailed depositions of the affair, but the state of New Hampshire was such that it proved impossible to bring any of the attackers to court. Thurton, after all, was the face of royal authority, and the people had already demonstrated how much respect they had for him.[29]

By this time, in fact, Cranfield had essentially given up on New Hampshire. While agents from the colony worked to discredit him at Whitehall, the governor begged for a new assignment. He cited his deteriorating health, which he blamed on the cold weather, and requested a posting in a more "healthful" climate like Barbados or Jamaica. These later letters revealed a broken man, physically and mentally exhausted by his long political struggle with the New Hampshirites. When the Committee on Trade and Plantations finally appointed him to be customs officer in Barbados, he pronounced it "the greatest happyness that ever I had in my life . . . to remove from these unreasonable people." He served with distinction for over a decade in Barbados, where he successfully weathered the Glorious Revolution and the vagaries of politics in the famously tumultuous colony. Indeed, but for his two years in New Hampshire, Cranfield seems to have been a model public servant.[30]

The troubles in New Hampshire demonstrated both the possibilities and pitfalls of Whitehall's new imperial vision. There was no reason why Charles II's ministers could not build a centralized empire—in New Hampshire, after all, no one denied the king's theoretical power to rule his plantations. At the same time, however, the volatile political and religious situation across the Atlantic had the potential to complicate imperial plans, especially when people on both sides of the divide insisted on reading every local dispute as an element in a global design. In the midst of this controversy, one issue lurked just beneath the surface: defense against external enemies. On one occasion Cranfield tried, without success, to use fears of an Indian attack to shame the legislature into compliance with his demands. In the next experiment in royal control, on the island of Bermuda, the problem of defense jumped to the fore, causing a dispute perhaps even more dramatic than the one in New Hampshire.[31]

•   •   •

If New Hampshire was the most worthless corner of the king's dominions, Bermuda was not far behind. The island's 3,600 whites and 5,000 slaves produced low-quality tobacco and served as a way station for ships crossing the Atlantic, but the colony had yet to attain its later reputation as a shipping hub. In terms of politics and religion, Bermuda stood apart. Its rulers, the Somers Island Company (usually known as the Bermuda Company), held the oldest continuous patent in the New World, but their membership was severely depleted and they paid little direct attention to the colony. In terms of religion, most people were dissenters of one kind or another, but the colony maintained a parish structure that gave at least an appearance of conformity to the Church of England. Nonetheless, several of the island's ministers had ties to Boston.[32]

Like New Hampshire, Bermuda came to the attention of Restoration imperialists as a result of the efforts of several private interests. Throughout the 1670s parties in both London and Bermuda labored to break the Company's monopoly; by the early 1680s a Tory lawyer named Francis Burghill had become the leading advocate of royal government in the region. The Bermuda Company was a small, insignificant operation, but Burghill found plenty of sympathizers in Charles II's court who aimed to curb local corporations of any kind, especially those with historical ties to Puritanism or dissent. Burghill's grievances resembled those used against the Massachusetts Bay Company at the same time. The Bermuda Company, he claimed, was tyrannical—it oppressed the king's subjects and took their property without due process of law. Company leaders were also guilty of economic mismanagement, especially in their stubborn refusal to allow Bermudians to export tobacco except in one annual company "magazine ship." Finally, Company leaders were traitors, adherents to the old Puritan cause who would betray the colony to the king's enemies in a heartbeat. Burghill contended that an old Company governor allowed the Dutch to scout out the island's harbors and fortifications during the Third Anglo-Dutch war, and that the Company also harbored a number of known rebels. The foremost example was William Milborne, a Baptist radical who had lived on the island for many years and had once publicly compared King Charles II to a dog. The colony's governing council suspended Milborne for his seditious speech, but according to Burghill, the very fact that such a man was allowed to maintain a position of influence painted the Company as hopelessly disloyal.[33]

If the case against the Bermuda Company appeared to be a classic example of Tory empire building, a closer look reveals a more complicated picture. Indeed, most of Burghill's allies on the island were not Tories or royalists, but radical dissenters—including the island's ministers and even William Milborne himself. These radicals, most of whom had lived in Bermuda for decades and were a bit out of touch with English politics, had both economic and political grievances against Company rule, which they compared to the "Grand Signiurs"—meaning that that paragon of arbitrariness, the Ottoman sultan. But they seem to have given little thought to the realities of royal government. As the last Company governor, Richard Coney, noted, the people of Bermuda believed that the coming of royal government would lead to less, rather than more regulation. "They aim at the sole Government themselves," Coney complained, "many of them saying His Ma[jes]ty will not concern himself with them, a small Island of Rocks, and such poor people as they are God bless him hee hath enough to doe at home, they can look after themselves."[34]

This odd partnership succeeded in breaking the Company and turning Bermuda into a royal colony, but not without some tension. Burghill's letters to his Bermudian allies reeked of condescension and frustration. He berated them for failing to send enough money or sufficient evidence to prosecute the case against the Company, and he also chided them for their dedication to

Whig political principles at a time when these ideas had little purchase in the Stuart court. On one occasion, the Bermudians requested that the king give them complete control of the island's judiciary, a request Burghill considered to be a major affront to the king's authority. "Is it reasonable," Burghill asked, "to thinke the Kinge willbe Setting up Comon welthes in any of his Dominions at this tyme of Day?" Such rhetoric was bound to strengthen the hand of the Company, who could easily paint Bermudians as disloyal subjects. On the island, meanwhile, Company advocates also attempted to use Whig, anti-Catholic rhetoric to urge people to resist royal government, claiming that the end of Company rule would lead to "Loss of their Landes, Poperey & voyalence."[35]

The breaking of the Company led to a period of profound chaos in Bermuda. It is easy to read these events, like those in New England, as disputes between local interest groups and overbearing outsiders, but in fact such an interpretation would be too simple. Bermudians had successfully worked with metropolitan agents—including some with very different political principles—in their efforts to break the Company, and the issues of dispute were even clearer than in New Hampshire. A sympathetic royal governor could have easily brought the island to an accommodation with the new imperial system, merely by opening up the island's trade and giving leading inhabitants a modest voice in local affairs. After all, most people had earnestly desired royal governance, even if they had little sense of what it entailed. As it happened, though, Bermudian politics fell victim to the same process that struck New Hampshire—people began to view local events in global terms, as manifestations of a larger battle between cosmic forces intent on world domination. And as in New England, the Bermudian political nation polarized into two hostile factions.

The Bermudian crisis was driven by two sets of international events. The first centered on the Caribbean islands and especially the Bahamas, a true periphery of the empire that had longstanding connections to Bermuda. Throughout the early 1680s, English and Spanish mariners menaced each other in spite of official peace between the two kingdoms, usually justifying their conduct by claiming that the other side violated international law by engaging in piracy. The struggle culminated in two Spanish strikes, the first devastating New Providence Island in 1684, the second destroying the Scottish Covenanter community at Stuart's Town, South Carolina, in 1686. In both cases, the Spanish claimed to be retaliating against piratical assaults on St. Augustine and surrounding Indian missions, and English officials forbade their own subjects from fighting back. Nonetheless, word of these incidents spread alarm across the English Atlantic, as refugees dispersed as far away as New England. In a conspiratorial time, such attacks could only feed into fears of a generalized popish conspiracy against Protestantism, especially when so many of the victims were dissenters. Bermuda welcomed many survivors from these assaults, and the close proximity of the incidents combined with Protestant zeal only increased the fear of an imminent Spanish invasion.[36]

The second outside influence came from the uncertain state of English politics around the time of the fall of the Bermuda Company. In February 1685 Charles II died, leaving the throne to his Catholic brother James. Most subjects accepted the succession with little apparent alarm, but a minority of radical Protestants in both England and Scotland refused to countenance the accession of a popish monarch. During the summer of 1685 two prominent nobles—the duke of Monmouth in England and the duke of Argyll in Scotland—led expeditions aiming to overthrow the new king. Both rebellions failed miserably, and the two ringleaders died as traitors within months. In the American colonies, however, where European news was often out of date and unreliable, the rebellions caused a minor crisis, as many people came to believe—by a combination of wishful thinking and inaccurate news—that Monmouth and Argyll had succeeded and that the King James set to take the throne was the Protestant Monmouth rather than the Catholic York.[37]

Monmouth's level of support in the colonies is difficult to ascertain. No one openly admitted favoring the duke's cause, and the writers who claimed widespread support for Monmouth in America were all imperial officials attempting to blacken the colonists' reputations and underscore their own loyalty. Nonetheless, there is no doubt that the rebellions caused a great deal of confusion and excitement. In Boston, according to one report, Congregationalists welcomed the news of the victory of the "Protestant Prince," calling it "an answer of their prayers." In Virginia—not usually considered a center of radical Whig thought—the news of the invasion "so farr Imboldened" the people "that their Tongues runn at Large and Demonstrated the wickedness of their harts." The governor responded by issuing a proclamation against the spreading of rumors. In Bermuda, speculation about Monmouth combined with fear of the Spanish and local political uncertainty to inspire a true rebellion, a temporary chaos that again revealed the limits of imperial policies.[38]

The crisis in Bermuda owed much to the policies and personality of the island's governor, Richard Coney. While his initial commission came from the Bermuda Company, Coney owed his appointment to the king, who essentially forced the Company to appoint him, and his political predilections reflected the high Tory ideals of the royal court rather than the moderate Whiggism of his original superiors. Indeed, Coney's wife and children were Catholic—a fact never publicly mentioned by Bermudians, but one that could not have escaped their notice. Coney secured a royal commission after the Company's fall, overcoming Francis Burghill's attempts at the office. The fact that the last Company governor stayed on as the first royal governor only exacerbated the crisis, as some Bermudians questioned the validity of Coney's commission. More than that, Coney seemed to inspire great passions in people. Even before the royal commission arrived, he faced an armed mob in front of his house, narrowly escaping death, or so he claimed, by the heroic appearance of one of his slaves.[39]

As Bermudians simultaneously learned of unrest at home and the dissolution of the Bermuda Company, they challenged the governor over the issue of defense. As for many English plantations, Bermuda's defenses consisted of a few aging fortifications and a small cache of arms and ammunition, and when word of the Company's demise reached the island the governor and his enemies began to argue about who controlled these resources. Local militia officers claimed they did, and proved willing to support their claims with force, occupying the forts and demanding that Coney give up any pretensions to control the colony's stores of arms. In the meantime, Coney set out to strengthen the fortifications on his own, actions that he assumed to be prudent, but that worried his opponents, who believed Coney to be an illegitimate governor with Spanish sympathies. One Bermudian suggested that it was "treason" to build fortifications without the king's direct order. Over the course of 1685, further rumors of Coney's treasonous nature circulated, mostly reports that the governor intended to "betraye the Island" to Spain.[40]

The tension led to a confrontation between the governor and militia leaders in October 1685. Seven leading officials appeared before the governor demanding powder from the governor's store, noting "The nakedness, distres, & necessity of that Country, for want of arms & ammunition." He refused, leading to a sustained argument, as the militia leaders complained that Coney had turned out qualified militia officers and claimed supplies that rightfully belonged to "the Country." In the heat of argument, two of the officers said, "clapping their hands uppon their brests, That they believ'd in their conscious, That the Govor intended to betray the Island." They added that if Coney did not name them to his council, they would refuse to recognize his authority— leading to a constitutional crisis on the island not unlike the one that Cranfield faced in New Hampshire.[41]

In Coney's view, the rebellion he faced in 1685 was just like the one at home—a treasonous combination of preachers and other radicals intent on subverting the king's authority and ultimately handing Bermuda to England's enemies. The governor and his few allies—almost exclusively ship captains passing through Bermuda—made great note of the timing of the Bermudians' actions, just as news of Monmouth's rising reached the island, and of the Whig, anti-Catholic rhetoric they used to justify their actions. Coney noted that one opponent claimed he had "noe power to Governe but by the Duke of Yorke who is a Papist," and questioned whether "a papist" should "comand this country"—a dangerous statement, since Monmouth justified his rebellion in much the same terms. Indeed, in another letter Coney claimed to hear one of the rebels proclaim that "The Right of the Crown was in the Duke of Monmouth; and that hee was noe Papist; that the Protestant Religion now profest in England was Popery; and that the Pope was the Whore of Babilon and drunk with the bloud of the Saints." At times, Coney even suggested that his enemies had secret knowledge of the risings at home, especially the minister Sampson Bond, the island's most prominent divine and a man with longtime links to the dissenting interest in England.[42]

Beyond their specific links to Monmouth, Coney and his allies noted the Whig rhetoric the colonists used to justify their conduct. Indeed, they seemed to be intent, as the visitor from New England William Phips observed, "to sett up for a free Comon wealth & to follow piracy." The people were devoid of any natural loyalty to their sovereign, but served only their own interest, which meant they would freely give up the island to the highest bidder. They justified their actions, naturally, by the disloyal rhetoric in English opposition literature. Captain George St. Lo, a visiting naval officer (see below) who sided with Coney against the Bermudians, noted that one opponent of the governor showed him "a Booke entituled the Liberty of the Subjects of England, by which he would make it appear, that they had the power to send the Governor home prisoner, but not the Governor them." St. Lo eventually came to the conclusion that they were "a mutinous turbulent, hypocriticall people, wholly averse to Kingly Government."[43]

The governor's response to the plot against him surpassed even Cranfield's actions in sheer foolishness. Since he had virtually no allies on the island, and no support from the crown, Coney deputized the captains and crews of passing ships to serve as councilors and provide assistance against the rebellion. His foremost ally was Bartholomew Sharpe, who sailed into St. George Harbor to purchase provisions for a return voyage to the Leeward Islands. A zealous defender of the king's prerogative, Sharpe was only too happy to devote his ship and crew to the cause of defending the new royal colony against the rebels. Sharpe was less than an ideal lawman, however, since he was also one of the most notorious pirates in the Caribbean. In fact, he came to Bermuda after a lengthy romp around the West Indies, in which he had threatened the provost marshal of Jamaica, plundered a New England merchant ship, and sacked a Spanish settlement at Campeche, capturing thirty Indian slaves he intended to sell at Bermuda. Despite his Toryism, in other words, Sharpe was an unlikely agent of empire.[44]

Over the next few months the colony verged on civil war. On Coney's orders, Sharpe imprisoned Richard Stafford, an elderly leader of the local opposition. Stafford quickly played the role of Joshua Moodey in New Hampshire, becoming the symbol of Coney's oppression, locked in irons in the hold of Sharpe's ship and not allowed to venture outside. Meanwhile, Sharpe's men— many of them escaped servants from the West Indies—ranged around the island intimidating the governor's opponents. One petition to Coney gave a sense of how the people viewed Sharpe, begging "That there bee no more rude men sent arm'd into the Country swearing & threatening to kill the Kings Subjects putting them in fear & takeing w[ha]t they please wch by the law is no less than robbery under the pretence of Authority." In response, many Bermudians turned their homes into garrisons, hunkering down in anticipation of an impending strike from the tyrannical governor, his pirate sidekick, or even their possible Spanish allies. In an incendiary letter to local justices of the peace, William Peniston virtually called for armed resistance against Coney and Sharpe, protesting that the people's "lives & estates" had been "vilely prostituted to the rage & fury of pirate Roags" who ran roughshod over the country. He urged the justices to act unilaterally against Sharpe, whom he defined as an enemy of the king, and noted how the pirate had imprisoned Richard Stafford "wth Irons on both leggs."[45]

Undoubtedly Sharpe's actions did more than anything else to dampen enthusiasm for royal government in Bermuda. He combined a thirst for power and authority with an almost fanatical opposition to dissent. In a brief letter to the Lords of Trade—his sole statement of his role in Bermuda's political crisis—Sharpe wrote that "the Islands here are all in Rebellion agt his Majtie, and will nowaies believe that there is any other King than Monmouth Living." All their complaints about Coney's tyranny were mere pretenses; they really hated him because he represented the king, "for they are so contentious that they will alwaies be kettling against Monarchy." For Sharpe, zeal for monarchy and distrust of dissenters went together; one witness said Sharpe "Swore

Severall times that he . . . would bee . . . a plague to the New England men and the Burmudians." And a plague he was: aside from imprisoning Stafford and confiscating arms from unruly subjects, he also hounded merchants, confiscating the sails of one ship that refused to lower them in recognition of the king's standard, which Sharpe confidently displayed on his own ship. Such actions did allow Coney a measure of control, but at the cost of his legitimacy. As word circulated around the country that Sharpe was suspected of piracy, the governor's reputation among his people dipped even lower. One opponent called him "the pitifullest Domineeringst rascall in the world"—a description that most of the island seemed to endorse.[46]

The end of Sharpe's term as royal enforcer came in the spring of 1686. The royal frigate *Dartmouth* arrived in Bermuda, commanded by an actual naval officer, George St. Lo, who carried a warrant for Sharpe's arrest. St. Lo shared Sharpe's politics but not his tactics. The officer surveyed the situation and spoke to partisans on both sides before concluding that Coney was right and the Bermudians had no legitimate grievances against the governor. When he departed during the summer of 1686 he carried off both Sharpe—to face trial for piracy in Nevis—and five leading opponents of the regime, sent like Edward Gove to face trial and punishment in England.

At this point a measure of calm returned to Bermuda, but for Coney the damage was done. His efforts to royalize Bermuda had been even less successful than those of Cranfield. Moreover, officials in Whitehall proved reluctant to take a hard line against the rebels. Almost as soon as they arrived in London, the five opponents of Coney petitioned for their freedom, and within six months they returned to Bermuda and presented a petition to receive reimbursement for their forced confinement and transportation. The new governor, Sir Robert Robinson, viewed local politics in a much less paranoid manner than his predecessor, and as a result his rule was remarkably free of drama. Indeed, as former Bermudian William Milborne joined his fellow Bostonians in overthrowing their governor during the revolutionary turmoil of 1689, Robinson and his people sat tight, confused but not particularly alarmed by the tumultuous politics in England.[47]

• • •

The ordeals of royal administrators in New Hampshire and Bermuda demonstrate some important truths about the Restoration empire. In both places, reformers had grand ambitions and expectations for success, not least because so many local inhabitants expressed theoretical support for royal governance. As they set out to govern, however, the governors and their primary opponents fell prey to the conspiratorial outlook that pervaded English politics during the 1680s. Moreover, while officials in Whitehall theoretically supported their officers in the field, they proved reluctant to provide any actual support, leaving the new royal governments as mere ciphers with great theoretical powers but no means to turn their ideals into reality. The result was chaos and rebellion, the first examples of colonial subjects rising up against imperial centralization. At the same time, however, the news was not all bad for bureaucrats in Whitehall. After all, no one in either Bermuda or New Hampshire questioned the king's right to remake the plantations; people simply disputed whether their governors were legitimate royal representatives. If the king found wiser men to rule the colonies, and supported them with even a few royal soldiers, future royal projects might prove more successful than the false starts in New Hampshire and Bermuda. In addition, the Bermuda debacle especially underscored the importance of security in colonial politics. In that case, it was fear of Spanish enemies, and the widespread belief that the governor was in league with them, that doomed the government. If this issue had been neutralized, it seemed, the people would have been more compliant.

In many ways, the campaign to remake Massachusetts reflected the lessons learned in the other old Puritan colonies. Unlike New Hampshire or Bermuda, Boston *was* important—not an economic powerhouse, perhaps, but a center of commerce with a large and growing population. Moreover, it had a longstanding reputation as a haven for radical dissenters, exacerbated by the virtual independence that the Bay Colony enjoyed under its 1629 charter. In many ways, the royal campaigns in both New Hampshire and Bermuda were practice runs for the much more critical design against the Massachusetts charter, and in turn, the events in each of those colonies only underscored how Boston served as a center for antimonarchical sentiment in America. Cranfield had blamed Harvard College for trumpeting sedition, and rebels from both New Hampshire and Bermuda fled to Boston to avoid punishment. As Edward Randolph told the Archbishop of Canterbury, "they give encouragement to Phannaticks of all sorts & receive them from all places." The town and region were filled with refractory subjects from all over the empire, and a firm action against the charter would send a message to all enemies of the king that they now had nowhere to hide.[48]

The battle over the Massachusetts charter—beginning with Edward Randolph's arrival in 1676 and ending with a ruling against the colony in the

Chancery court in 1684—appears in many historical accounts as a contest between core and periphery, Puritanism and empire, America and England. When compared with New Hampshire and Bermuda, however, the long process of royalization appeared both moderate and more or less consensual. Randolph hurled vitriol at his enemies and they hated him in return, but he always believed that a majority of New Englanders would welcome royal government once they understood that it would guarantee their rights against an overbearing Congregational "oligarchy" and protect them from outside enemies. He was at least partly right: while Cranfield and Coney inspired a large majority of subjects in their colonies to resist royalization, people in Massachusetts divided into two more or less evenly matched parties. On one side stood not just new arrivals like Randolph, but the colony's few Anglicans and even many self-styled "moderates" such as Governor Simon Bradstreet, one of the original Puritan settlers, and Joseph Dudley, whose father had been one of the first governors. The opposition party, led by a cadre of church members and eventually championed by the Rev. Increase Mather, attempted to use conspiratorial politics to inspire a popular movement against imperial regulation. At least at first, however, the attempt to build a consensus in favor of defending the charter did not succeed. New Englanders were divided on how to deal with the empire, mainly because royal officials acted with more moderation than Cranfield or Coney had done. Most historians have labeled Mather's group the "popular party," thus implying a high level of opposition to imperial plans; in fact, neither side could claim a popular mandate at the outset of the controversy.[49]

While some royal officials aimed at the Massachusetts charter as early as the 1640s, the campaign resumed during the Restoration and reached a crescendo in the mid-1670s. King Philip's War devastated New England, reminding imperial administrators of the dangers of allowing a large and strategically placed region essentially to rule itself. These issues appeared clearly in an anonymous report filed in 1675. The author objected to the religious life and antimonarchical bent of New England's leaders, but his main objections concerned defense. New Englanders argued constantly among themselves and "they cannot I doubt at present make a sufficient defence of his Majts Territorys & Subjects in those parts, if a more powerfull Enemy should invade." The author recommended sending "some Gentlemen, residing there, by his Majte authorized to make appeales unto to end their Differences, and keep unity amongst them"—an appointed royal council to serve as the face of authority. This particular plan proved too cumbersome or expensive to realize; instead, the king's ministers went after the Massachusetts charter in the courts, much as they opposed the charter of London during the same period.[50]

The circumstances of the delivery of the *quo warranto* against the charter demonstrated the diversity of New Englanders' responses to the royal campaign. A common legal tactic in Charles II's time, the order demanded "by what warrant" the Massachusetts Bay Company exercised power over the colony, charging that the company had violated the terms of the charter and therefore possessed no rightful authority. When Edward Randolph delivered the *quo warranto*, he pleaded with the rulers of Massachusetts to relinquish the charter without a legal challenge, ensuring that the king would deal with them tenderly as he designed the new royal government. In order to help the process along, Randolph brought two supporting documents: the first a guarantee of liberty of conscience, to dissuade the people from the belief that the king had any designs on their churches; and the second a declaration of how the corporation of London had surrendered its charter without a fight.[51]

Evidence from within Massachusetts indicates that the colony's inhabitants were divided over how to respond to the loss of the charter. No angry crowds met Randolph when he delivered the writ to Massachusetts officials, and even among the magistrates there was an air more of resignation than of resistance. After all, Charles held out an olive branch to the colonists, offering them the chance to submit input regarding a new charter that would better acknowledge the king's sovereignty. Governor Bradstreet and many of the more prominent magistrates favored submission, and so did many of the colony's clergy—though not without consternation. The diary of Peter Thacher, the minister at Milton, provides some indication of how people away from the colony's center viewed the events over the course of 1683. Thacher spent much of the 1680s, like his neighbors, praying for the Protestant cause and "for the Continuation of our libertys sivil & sacred," and he was horrified when he received news of the court action against the charter. On 31 October 1683 he met with other ministers to decide what to do—the matter was so sensitive that Thacher recorded his observations in cipher. Several days later, after the General Court met to consider the matter, Thacher revealed the predominant opinion of the gathered ministers: "tht if the patent was forfeited by law, thn it was best to resigne it up to his majesty for such regulation as might make it most fit for his Majesty's service, tht so the Essentialls of the patent might be continued." In other words, even the ministers, those trumpets of sedition, thought twice before offering offense to the king, preferring a pragmatic course over confrontation.[52]

Despite the moderation of many New Englanders, however, there were others who resisted any compromise regarding the country's "liberties." Alongside the longtime firebrand, Deputy Governor Thomas Danforth, Increase Mather emerged as the most eloquent spokesman against surrendering the charter; he did so by linking the design against the country's liberties to the ongoing popish plot. Such an interpretation was not altogether fanciful. Many New Englanders knew that the campaign against corporations in England was primarily a means to remove dissenters and their allies from positions of authority, and pamphleteers noted that the same thing had happened in France before Louis XIV escalated his campaign against the Huguenots. An exasperated Edward Cranfield accused radical ministers of "infusing the people, that it is God's cause and that they may lawfully draw their Swords in the defence of the Charter." This was surely an exaggeration—no one openly favored armed resistance—but opponents to royal government were beginning to endorse aspects of Calvinist resistance theory, arguing at least implicitly that people, or at least inferior magistrates, did not have to obey their rulers if they turned against God.[53]

The confrontation over submission climaxed in Boston's town meeting in January 1684. In a ritual repeated all over the colony, the city's inhabitants met to consider the design against the charter. The same divisions existed in Boston as in the colony as a whole, but in this case the radicals ruled the day by a combination of parliamentary tactics and soaring rhetoric. First, leading radical Samuel Nowell dismissed all nonfreemen from the meeting, ensuring that only church members would be present for the discussion and vote on the charter. Then Increase Mather rose and addressed the crowd, using examples from the Old Testament and the recent past—including contemporary events in New Hampshire—to urge resistance. In response, the freemen of Boston pledged that they would not voluntarily relinquish their charter, and essentially dared the king to take it.[54]

Despite the drama, however, Mather's speech did not usher in a new age of resistance in New England. Throughout 1684 and 1685, as anarchy reigned in New Hampshire and Bermuda, inhabitants of Massachusetts continued their lives much as before. The most notable event was the electoral defeat of several prominent moderate magistrates, but at the same time Governor Bradstreet won reelection. In 1685 colonists learned that the king had chosen Percy Kirke as their governor, an unwelcome choice for radical Protestants. Kirke had been commander of the royal regiment at Tangier—afterward known as the Queen's Regiment—a division known for its popish leanings. Moreover, after presiding over the abandonment of Tangier—also cause for suspicion among many Whigs—Kirke gained a particular reputation for cruelty in his response to Monmouth's Rebellion, where he allegedly "Invited 30 Gentlemen to dine with him, and after dinner hanged them up in his hall to satisfie his popish and blood thirsty Cruelty." Such stories traveled around New England, but in the end the king passed over Kirke—a narrow escape according to Increase Mather, who claimed that "Bloody Kirk would in a few weekes have made horrible slaughters."[55]

In the end, however, the coming of royal government to Massachusetts did not bring about bloodshed of any kind. Instead, the change in administration occurred slowly and a bit haphazardly. It also showed the influence of the most hated man in New England, Edward Randolph, who had a very different approach to colonial governance from that of his ideological allies Cranfield and Coney. For all his hatred of New England's Puritan past, Randolph retained the belief that most New Englanders were naturally loyal, and he recommended giving a great deal of power to reliable local people. He also eschewed extreme tactics like imprisoning opponents or interfering with the region's religious establishment, which would only play into the hands of his radical enemies. Indeed, Randolph's moderation eventually set him at odds with Cranfield in particular, who he complained was "of the most arbitrary nature I have heard of." It seems probable that Randolph used his connections at Whitehall to secure freedom for both Edward Gove and the prisoners from Bermuda, understanding that the creation of martyrs would only hurt his cause. "They are very numerous," Randolph wrote of the colonists, "and it is far easier to affright them into rebellion than to obedience."[56]

The first royal administration in Massachusetts bore the marks of Randolph's moderation. Rather than Percy Kirke, the king commissioned the most reliable moderate in the colony, Joseph Dudley, to be council president, meaning that control passed to the son of a Bay Colony founder rather than an outsider like Kirke. Dudley's commission brought howls of protest from his political rivals; outgoing secretary Edward Rawson, for instance, lodged a protest that the new commission violated the colonists' "rights as Englishmen" because it did not provide for an assembly. The protest never left the council chamber, however, and it seems that historians have noticed the lack of representation much more than ordinary New Englanders did at the time.[57]

Dudley's presidency was short-lived, however, replaced at the end of 1686 by the new Dominion of New England. The main difference between the two commissions was that the Dominion extended much farther, incorporating all the New England colonies under one government, and eventually annexing New York and both New Jersey colonies as well. In addition, an outsider, former New York governor Sir Edmund Andros, served as the Dominion's governor, and he arrived with several regiments of redcoats and some allies from his days in New York. In some ways the Dominion was an experiment in absolutism, planned in James II's court with little input from people with actual experience in the colonies. More than that, however, it was created to defend the king's interest against the French. One internal memorandum, written sometime in 1688, made clear that the king had joined the colonies together so that "the Frontiers of his Ma[jes]ty's Dominions in those Parts, with the Beaver Trade, [would be] more easily secured." The same report devoted more pages to French pretensions in Hudson's Bay than to any other single colony, demonstrating the degree to which geopolitics shaped colonial policy in James II's court.[58]

The Dominion of New England, in the long run, represented a more focused exercise in royal power than previous regimes in New Hampshire and Bermuda. Andros was a competent administrator not liable to the conspiratorial outlooks of many contemporaries, and he also had the support of royal troops and resources. While he did attempt, and in many ways accomplish, a thorough remaking of the region's political culture, his correspondence is surprisingly free of the unrest that often accompanied such changes. At the dawn of 1688, advocates of royal government could look with some pride on a system that actually seemed to work. It was only when the new regime failed to deliver on its main promise—defense against external enemies—that conspiratorial fears and partisan divisions once again came to the fore.

Chapter 2

Catholics, Indians, and the Politics of Conspiracy

IN THE SUMMER of 1688 the governor of the Dominion of New England, Sir Edmund Andros, faced a political crisis. A group of hostile Indians had attacked the colony's northern and western borders, killing and capturing a number of English settlers and causing frightened townspeople to take refuge in garrison houses. Even more alarming than the violence, however, were the colonists' reactions. In Maine, local officials foolishly imprisoned several Abenaki chiefs, while the people of Marlborough, Massachusetts, assembled in arms without any instruction from the governor. To calm these fears, Andros sent his lieutenant, Francis Nicholson, on a good will tour of the New England backcountry. He assured the people, both English and Indian, that they were safe "under the protection of a great King, who protects all his Subjects both in their lives and fortunes." In the eyes of Andros and Nicholson, New Englanders' hysterics made little sense. The Dominion of New England—a potent union of all the colonies from Maine to New Jersey under the command of an experienced officer—provided the best defense against external enemies that the region had ever possessed. The king and his redcoats, not a motley local militia, would keep the plantations safe.[1]

The crisis in the Dominion represented the first major setback in what had been a fairly successful example of imperial state building. The key to the Dominion was protection, represented perfectly in the new union's official seal. The design featured James II, "Robed in His Royall Vestments and Crowned, with a Scepter in the Left hand, the Right hand being extended towards an English Man and an Indian both kneeling, the one presenting the Fruits of the Country and other a Scrole." Above them a flying angel held a banner with the Dominion's motto, "Nunquam libertas gratior extat," "never

Figure 4. Seal of the Dominion of New England, 1686. William Cullen Bryant and Sydney Howard Gay, *A Popular History of the United States* (New York, 1879), 3: 9.

does liberty appear in a more gracious form [than under a pious king]." The monarch received allegiance and tribute and provided protection, which was the key to political stability. Andros and his allies knew that the Dominion's programs would excite opposition from New Englanders who defined both "liberty" and "piety" in very different ways from James II's allies. However, they believed that they could keep control as long as they upheld their promise to provide protection—and they were mostly right. Despite some opposition, the Dominion did not fall until subjects began to believe that their leaders were not protecting them at all, and in fact aimed to subvert and destroy the country. The opposition to the Dominion grew as a result of its failed Indian policy; as native enemies attacked the borders, New Englanders turned against their leaders.[2]

The wave of fear that threatened the Dominion combined several different varieties of popular anxiety. Aside from the popish plot alarms that periodically struck both England and its colonies, settlers in North America also obsessively feared Indian attacks. Europeans and natives had experienced tensions since the newcomers arrived on the continent, but the violence increased during the 1670s. First, in 1675, a coalition of Indians under the Wampanoag sachem Metacom (King Philip) attacked English settlements in New England in response to land disputes and religious tensions, dramatically revealing the region's vulnerability. The following year Indian attacks on the frontier of Virginia inspired a massive popular revolt against Governor William Berkeley by subjects, led by the upstart Nathaniel Bacon, who believed the governor was not protecting the colony from Indian enemies. While peace had returned to both places by 1677, the legacy of this unrest remained. As a result, the fears of popish plots that crossed the Atlantic after 1678 arrived in places already primed to expect the worst.[3]

Popular panics of the 1680s proved particularly powerful because they combined the tropes of antipopery with homegrown racial fears. Increasingly, people became apprehensive of a massive plot that combined papists and Indians into a gigantic, diabolical coalition that aimed to push English Protestants off the continent. This belief did not come naturally; indeed, during the first period of colonization many English settlers had expected that Indians would be natural allies against a common Catholic enemy that, according to the "Black Legend" of Spanish cruelty, had victimized both groups. In time, however, Protestants began to redefine natives as violent enemies who were particularly susceptible to the temptations of priestcraft. In making these arguments, colonists drew on another form of anti-Catholic rhetoric perfected in Ireland, where the "wild Irish" had proven impervious to Protestantism, and outsiders explained this religious intransigence by pointing to a lack of civility among Irish Catholics.[4]

By the time Andros faced his troubles in 1688, the identification of Indians and Catholics had become widespread. This development marked the Americanization of antipopery, the adaptation of a set of European fears to explain conditions on the colonial frontier. The results were dramatic and long lasting. On one hand, the wave of fear endangered the program for imperial reforms, giving a new opening to those Protestant radicals who believed that centralization was merely another branch in a popish plot. But at the same time, the common fears of a Catholic-Indian design gave colonists across the colonies a common political language, one that combined their desire for security, their Protestant heritage, and their nascent sense of racial privilege. Fear could tear the empire apart, but it could also put it back together again. The results of the crisis depended a great deal on how Andros and other imperial officials responded to popular fear.

· · ·

The first reference to a Catholic-Indian conspiracy appeared, ironically enough, in the private correspondence of colonial America's most prominent Catholic. Cecil Calvert, the second Lord Baltimore, founded the colony of Maryland in 1634: a bold experiment intended to demonstrate, among other things, that Roman Catholics could be loyal English subjects and work for the king's interest. His plans for religious neutrality inspired opposition, however, and not just from Protestants. Members of the Society of Jesus, who had provided spiritual support for the first colonists and endeavored to convert local Indians, resent Baltimore's refusal to grant them preferred status in what they considered a Catholic colony, even threatening at one point to have the proprietor excommunicated. This dispute led Calvert to suspect the Jesuits of more sinister designs, confiding in a letter to his resident governor that the priests intended to employ local Indians to destroy anyone who stood in the society's way, including the Catholic proprietor. In Baltimore's mind, the Jesuits used religion as a pretense to further their political goals—and they were not afraid to encourage violence if it brought them to power.[5]

It is a testament to the power of anti-Catholicism in seventeenth-century English thought that even a prominent Roman Catholic used antipopery to criticize his rivals. Indeed, it demonstrates the extent to which "popery" as a construction was detached from actual relations between Catholics and Protestants, or even among groups of Catholics and Protestants. Perhaps unconsciously, Baltimore drew on two strands of anti-Catholic thought, each of which became important in the colonies over the next half-century. First, he painted the Jesuits—hated agents of the counter-Reformation—as devious papal agents who would stop at nothing to accomplish their worldly ends. Second, he argued that the priests would employ impressionable, weakminded foreigners—in this case Indians—to accomplish their goals. This aspect of antipopery also had a history in Europe, but it soon became even more important in the colonies, where foreigners were particularly strange and the Jesuits made great efforts to convert them.

In Protestant propaganda, Jesuits were the very worst of the papists.

Founded by Ignatius Loyola in the 1520s, the order had gained a reputation as the strictest defender of Catholic orthodoxy during the counter-Reformation. Polemical Protestant diatribes against the society abounded in northern Europe during the 1600s, stressing several different sides of the Jesuit character. First and foremost, the Jesuits were defenders of papal authority and the foes of Protestant princes, and they would do anything to serve their master's cause, even if they had to murder recalcitrant monarchs—as they did French king Henri IV in 1610. Beyond their ill intentions, the Jesuits were also master tricksters. They blended into their surroundings by dressing in disguises, speaking numerous languages, and using personal charms to insinuate themselves into Protestant society in order to undermine it. Both of these fears appeared in an English newspaper report from 1679, just after the revelations of the popish plot. The paper reported that a man in a London coffeehouse revealed himself to be a Jesuit in disguise, and when asked whether he endorsed "the Doctrine of Killing of Kings," responded "*That their Doctrine was to Kill every one that stood in their way.*"[6]

Beyond being violent tricksters, Jesuits were also known for their skill in converting people to Catholicism. The priests themselves encouraged this reputation by publishing reports of their missionary successes in the Far East and America, and while these *Relations* served primarily to encourage support for the Jesuits in the Catholic world, they had the additional effect of confirming Protestant fears. Enemies of the order explained its success in much the same way modern historians do, by arguing that the Jesuits encouraged pagans to become Catholics by drawing on similarities between Christianity and paganism. In a fictional dialogue among three Jesuits published in 1689, for instance, a missionary to Siam bragged that he stressed the common points between Catholicism and the local religion, especially "Worship of Images" and "a blind tame submission to the Doctrines, Worship and Ceremonies of their false Religion, [which] makes them resemble our People absolutely." If this tactic did not work, the missionary advocated changing the principles of Catholicism to suit local circumstances; for instance, he believed that by deifying the saints he could convince adherents of polytheistic eastern religions to embrace the faith. To Protestants, these reports—fabricated though they were—reinforced the Jesuits' reputations as dissemblers and casuists who would lie without shame to advance their cause, and who had particular success with impressionable pagans. It also proved that their true goals were not religious, but worldly: they wanted power above all else, and would not let principles stand in their way.[7]

The picture of Jesuits in propaganda was exaggerated and in some respects entirely false, but it did bear at least a superficial resemblance to reality. Many Jesuits did pride themselves on their ability to win back "heretics" to the true faith, and especially in the English dominions the priests considered the re-establishment of Catholicism as a primary goal. The behavior of Maryland Jesuits helps to demonstrate why Protestants were afraid. Even without the establishment they desired, Maryland provided the priests a degree of freedom unknown in England or other colonies: they no longer needed to travel in disguise, and they could openly conduct worship services. As one prospective priest put it in a letter asking to be assigned to the new colony, "Where I live, I am abriged of liberty in doing the good I could wish, wch maks me more earnest to be els where imployed." Besides ministering to Maryland's small but influential Catholic population, the priests set out to create as many new Catholics as they could. This goal appeared clearly in a catechism from the mid-1670s that survives in the archives of the Maryland Province of the Society of Jesus. Probably intended as a guide to young priests in proper doctrine, it attempted to combat the most fundamental Protestant teachings. It stated that the Church received its imprimatur from Christ himself, and therefore "we cannot call in question the truth of any one thing the Catholick Church teaches without making Christ a Lyar." It also argued that scripture only contained part of the truth, and "we cannot tell wch is the true scripture from the false" without help from the church. In short, Maryland Jesuits traveled the countryside extolling with great zeal a message that directly refuted the most basic tenets of Protestantism. It is not surprising that many people took offense.[8]

Another story from the Jesuits' own writings helps to illustrate the threat the order posed to Protestantism. From its earliest days, and especially after the 1640s, Maryland welcomed a large number of Reformed Protestants, many of whom migrated from the less tolerant Anglican colony of Virginia and settled near the Severn River in a community called, in typical Puritan fashion, Providence. These settlers saw the Jesuits as devious rivals who would do anything to convert heretics, as one episode made clear. In the late 1630s, according to a Jesuit report, a Protestant man fell ill from a snakebite. A local Jesuit endeavored to see the sick man, partly to treat him, but mainly to win his soul for the Church before he died. These deathbed conversions were particularly offensive to Protestants, who believed that Catholics took advantage of the mental and physical weakness preceding death to poach souls. In this case, a friend of the sick man stood guard to make sure the Jesuit could not gain access to the patient. "Nevertheless," the report stated, "the priest kept on the watch for every opportunity of approach; and going at the dead of night, when he supposed the guard would be especially overcome by sleep, he contrived, without disturbing him, to pass in to the sick man; and, at his own desire, received him into the Church." Despite appearing in a Jesuit letter, this story could have served as a potent piece of anti-Catholic propaganda, as it reinforced the belief that Jesuits used trickery and artifice to advance their cause.[9]

The Jesuits' penchant for trickery made it critical for Protestants to resist the order in any way they could. Some colonies banned the presence of Jesuits, and even in places like Maryland where the priests could legally reside Protestants prided themselves on the ability to resist their advances. But even if all Protestants stayed true to the faith, the Jesuits posed a problem. As one tract explained, resistance to their designs only made the Jesuits more devious: "where they cannot convince," it explained, "they labour to destroy." They could succeed because of a network of foreign allies whose main ambition was to "massacre the whole Protestant Party" and clear the way "to build a corrupt Church." In England opponents of the Jesuits believed that the order intended to invite the French or Spanish to invade the kingdom, but another tactic was to target inhabitants of foreign nations who did not have the training or intellect to resist Jesuit advances. This had particular relevance in America, where a large population of natives lived among the colonists, and where Jesuits had already begun to establish missions.[10]

In the 1640s, particularly in Maryland, English colonists began to worry about what would happen if the Jesuits insinuated themselves into Indian communities. They had a useful precedent from Ireland, another part of the empire where Jesuits and other popish priests had labored, with astonishing success, to infiltrate a population of common people most English considered impressionable and uncivilized. The lessons from Ireland could not have been encouraging. Despite the expectations of reformers in the sixteenth century, the "wild Irish" clung tenaciously to the Catholic faith, and Protestant observers tended to blame two factors: the depraved state of the populace and the underhanded methods of the clerics. Moreover, the priests' successes had dire consequences for Ireland's Protestant minority, as the Irish peasantry became willing shock troops for the Catholic cause.[11]

The Irish Rebellion of 1641 was an epochal event in the history of British anti-Catholicism. Before this time, antipopery had been a less potent force in Ireland than elsewhere, mainly because the vast numbers and diversity of the Catholic population forced Protestants to accept that the true face of

Catholicism was more complex than their conspiratorial logic suggested. The events of October 1641, when Irish Catholics rose up in a bloody rebellion against English Protestant rule, immediately prompted Irish Protestants to place their own struggles within a global context. More important, the reports of "popish" atrocities in the rebellion quickly spread to England and beyond, becoming an important source of propaganda as the nation moved toward civil war.[12]

This propaganda—as popular in the 1680s as in the 1640s—provided a salient example of how uncivilized people could aid the popish cause. Protestant writers targeted the usual shibboleths of antipopery: Jesuit priests; infiltrators from foreign countries, especially Spain and France; and unscrupulous "evil counselors" who pretended to be Protestants but really promoted popery. None of these masterminds could have succeeded without "the blind, ignorant, and superstitious people," who "rise up and execute whatever they command." In addition, the wild Irish served as the agents of popish cruelty: according to one propagandist, "they acted with that brutish fury, as if the wild Beasts of the Deserts, Wolves, Bears and Tigres, nay Fiends and Furies had been let loose from Hell upon the Land." Not even unborn children were safe, as "their Hellish Rage and Fury extended also to the Babes unborn, ripping them out of their Mothers Womb, and destroying those Innocent Creatures, to glut their Savage Inhumanity." In this reading of the rebellion, the Jesuits were the masterminds, but the wild Irish provided the savage violence that brought the rebellion to its terrible conclusion. It would not be difficult to imagine a similar scenario in America, and in time colonial witnesses would describe native attacks using almost identical language.[13]

Nonetheless, there was no reason to assume that Indians would naturally fall into the role of the Irish. Early colonization tracts usually expressed optimism that the Indians would gravitate toward alliance with the English, especially when they recognized the contrast between good Protestants and cruel, rapacious Spaniards. In the logic of antipopery, moreover, pagans usually occupied a step above papists. The English poet and politician Andrew Marvell wrote that "The Pagans are excusable by their natural darkness, without revelation," while "the Pope avowing Christianity by profession, doth in doctrine and practice renonce it." From the 1640s, therefore, a few colonists had good evidence to suspect that Indians could be auxiliaries in a Catholic cause, but such beliefs were not widespread.[14]

Not surprisingly, Maryland's political situation provided the most fertile ground for fear that Indians could fall to the temptations of popery. Founded by Catholics, the colony nonetheless welcomed a large number of Protestant dissenters, drawn to the colony by Lord Baltimore's generous policy of religious toleration. Proprietary authorities understood that they ruled over a powder keg, where religious passions could explode into violence at any time; they attempted to avoid such a scenario by restricting religious speech. Accordingly, the 1649 "Act concerning toleration" including a long list of outlawed religious slurs: calling your neighbor a "Jesuited Papist" or a "schismatick" could result in a ten-shilling fine.[15]

On the whole, these attempts to promote religious understanding failed. During the turbulent Civil War years of the 1640s and 1650s, when rumors of Catholic plotting reached fever pitch in Britain, Protestants in Maryland rejected Lord Baltimore's authority in large numbers, mounting two successful rebellions. Only through impressive maneuvering in London—and an improbable alliance with Oliver Cromwell—did Baltimore manage to hold onto his colony.[16]

In the meantime, the proprietor's opponents barraged him with a number of charges. One tract claimed that Baltimore's intention was to create a "receptacle for Papists, and Priests, and Jesuits," and that he even intended to bring 2000 Irish to the colony who "would not leave a Bible in Maryland"— surely an alarming prospect only a decade after the 1641 rebellion. Colonial agent Leonard Strong was even more blunt when he described the series of events that led a cadre of Protestants to throw off the lord's authority, claiming that Baltimore required subjects in Maryland to "countenance and uphold Antichrist," meaning the Catholic church, and he was willing to use tyrannical force to ensure submission. This force extended even to employing Indians. When proprietary forces faced off against Protestant dissidents in the "Battle of the Severn" in 1655, according to Strong, "the Indians were resolved in themselves, or set on by the popish faction, or rather both together to fall upon us: as indeed after the fight they did, besetting houses, killing one man, and taking another prisoner." Baltimore's enemies had no direct proof, but they could only assume that the natives were under his authority, especially since his government maintained such close alliances with local tribes, and even employed Jesuits to work among the Indians.[17]

The decade after 1660 represented a period of relative calm in the colony, but by 1676 discord returned. In the wake of Bacon's Rebellion in neighboring Virginia, opponents of the new Lord Baltimore, Charles Calvert, sent an appeal to England that expressed many of the fears that would become commonplace around the colonies in the next decade. The "Complaint from

Heaven" represented Baltimore as a partner in a global Catholic design: "the platt form is, Pope Jesuit determined to over terne Engl[an]d with feyer, sword and distractions within themselves, and by the Maryland Papists, to drive us Protestants to Purgatory . . . with the help of French spirits from Canada." The petition used the Catholic plot to explain recent attacks by Susquehanna Indians, as well as the unwillingness of Baltimore and Virginia governor Sir William Berkeley to meet the Indian threat. The "Huy and crye" also described a plan by Jesuits to infiltrate the colonies by sending priests in disguise. "These blake spirits disperse themselves all over the Country in America," the writers claimed, and held secret correspondence with French Jesuits, plotting destruction for American Protestants. The petitioners used this argument to plead for an end to Baltimore's government and, in direct contrast to those in New England, for an increase in royal authority. In order to defend against French Catholics and their Indian allies, the writers suggested that the king send "a Vice Roye or Governor Generallissimo" to preserve the colonies from external enemies.[18]

In 1681 these fears of Catholics and Indians combined to create a crisis that foreshadowed later troubles in New England. The problems began in the summer, when some "heathen Rogues" attacked the borders of the colony, killing several settlers on the upper reaches of the Patuxent and Potomac Rivers. These Indian attacks, probably Iroquois or Susquehanna strikes against people they believed were harboring their enemies, caused massive panic in both Maryland and Virginia, where inhabitants became "greatly dissatisfied" that their governors could not protect them from the enemy. In this climate of fear, some eventually concluded "that it is the Senaco Indians" who had committed the depredations "by the Instigacon of the Jesuits in Canada and the Procuremt of the Lord Baltemore to cut of most off the Protestants of Maryland." This identification reflected the tendency among colonists in the Chesapeake to describe all northern Indians as "Senecas," in reference to the westernmost nation of the Iroquois Confederacy, and constituted the most elaborate theory to date of how Baltimore, French Catholics, and Indians had banded together. The proprietor blamed "some evile ill disposed spirits" for spreading these rumors, and he pointed to two men in particular: Josias Fendall and John Coode.[19]

The two ringleaders of the opposition in 1681 were among the most interesting and enigmatic figures in early Maryland history. Fendall had been a governor under Cecil Calvert, but the proprietor removed him from office for his role in fomenting a previous rebellion in 1660; since that time he

had stayed out of politics but remained an irritant to the proprietary interest. Coode was a younger man and a more recent arrival to the colony. An
ordained Anglican minister, he served in the colony's lower house as a representative of Calvert County, and had not yet acquired the reputation as a
"perennial rebel." While the two men's motivations are not entirely clear, they
tapped into a deep undercurrent of fear and resentment that had the potential
to topple the government.[20]

Coode allegedly began his plotting in May 1681 at the house of Nehemiah
Blackiston, when he said in the company of many people that within four
months no Catholic would own "a foote of land" in the province, and that
Coode could "make it high water" whenever he pleased: meaning that he had
the power to cause a popular insurrection. (Coode objected to that assertion,
claiming he was only "alludeing to a bowle of Punch wch they were then
drinking wch he could make ebb or flow at pleasure.") He apparently put his
plan into operation in July after the murder of one Thomas Potter and some
other English people near Point Lookout. When a neighbor observed that
Indians killed the colonists, Coode responded that they "were not murdered
by Indians, but were Murdered by Christians," a clear implication of Catholic
authorities.[21]

Fendall harbored the same suspicions. One of his employees reported that
around the time of the murders Fendall "did severall times say that he beleived
in his Conscience the Papists and Indians joined together, and that . . . my
Lord [Baltimore] did uphold them in what they did, and he beleived my Lord
and they together had a mind to destroy all the Protestants." The rumor may
have originated with Daniel Mathena, a neighbor in Charles County who
had received an Indian visitor en route to deliver a packet of letters to the
"Senecas" several years earlier, containing, Mathena claimed, orders from Lord
Baltimore "to come and cutt off the Protestants." His evidence was not compelling, and showed the intellectual leaps that English people made when they
feared a conspiracy was afoot. The Indian visitor mentioned that he carried
letters from Baltimore to the Senecas, and when Mathena's wife asked how
the Indians could read the letters, "the Indian answered that the French were
hard by and that they could read them." After the murders, this rather obtuse
report of French presence in the backcountry became solid evidence of a massive popish plot.[22]

Fendall and Coode decided to take action. They visited Nicholas Spencer,
the secretary of Virginia, notifying him "that the Papists and Indians were
joined together." Spencer, for his part, discounted the rumors and advised

them to "be quiett at home," advice that prompted Coode to swear "God Damn all the Catholick Papist Doggs" and resolve to "be revenged of them, and spend the best blood in his body." The two men's motivations cannot be known for certain. Fendall in particular seems to have been attempting a return to political power, and understood that the Indian troubles provided an opportunity to undermine his old rival; one man reported that Fendall "hath been soliciting the people to choose him Delegate in the Assembly and hath told them that were he Commandr of the County Troope he would Destroy all the Indians." Additionally, witnesses implied that both men hoped to increase their property holdings by confiscating land from Catholics. At the same time, Coode's actions remain somewhat more difficult to interpret. He already possessed both a seat in the lower house and a militia commission. While most historians have branded him a self-interested demagogue, his anti-Catholicism appears to have been heartfelt, if not always internally consistent.[23]

Baltimore responded to these threats by throwing Fendall and Coode in prison. Motivated by memories of Bacon's Rebellion in Virginia and the numerous insurrections his father had faced, the proprietor believed that only decisive action would demonstrate the consequences of rebellion. His approach backfired, however, because he underestimated the degree of popular support for the two men's actions. For one thing, the lower house refused to remove Coode from its ranks or even discipline him. More ominously, a Charles County justice of the peace named George Godfrey hatched a plot to break Fendall out of prison, receiving commitments from forty men at church one Sunday. The design failed, and Godfrey joined the two other malcontents in jail. In November colonial authorities put the men on trial and convicted Fendall, who was banished from the colony, and Godfrey, whose death sentence was commuted to life imprisonment. The jury acquitted Coode, leaving him free to get his revenge another day.[24]

The denouement of the episode represented only a partial victory for Baltimore. He remained in control of the colony, but did little to regain the trust of his people. According to authorities in Virginia, Maryland remained dangerously unstable throughout the 1680s. A letter from the end of 1681 suggested that the proprietor only retained control by "keeping forces in Armes" and imprisoning anyone who questioned his authority, leaving "the Common people in great dread and feare." A report by Virginia governor Thomas Culpeper about the same time noted that "Maryland is now in Ferment, and not onely troubled with our disease, pouverty, but in very great danger of falling into peeces whether it be that the Old Lord Baltimores politick Maximes are not pursued and followed by the Sonne or that they will not doe in this Age." In recognition of the precarious nature of imperial politics, Culpeper implored the Lords of Trade to take steps to stabilize Maryland, lest the disease spread to its neighbors.[25]

The governor's warning proved to be prescient. While Baltimore's political difficulties appeared to be peculiar to his own situation as a Catholic ruler in a Protestant colony, the same political language could apply throughout the English colonies. In essence, ordinary Marylanders were attempting to explain the inexplicable: why a distant, mysterious Indian nation had decided to attack them, seemingly without provocation. With reports of popish plots traveling around the English world at this time, many colonists easily molded the familiar language of antipopery to this unfamiliar situation, implicating both the French and local Catholic leaders whose loyalty seemed to be suspect. In a sense, however, Baltimore's Catholicism was not the main issue. As future events would show, the same tactics could be used against Protestants as well.

• • •

If rumors of a Catholic-Indian conspiracy proved particularly potent in Maryland, by the 1670s they had begun to appear all over the colonies. The ubiquity of these fears came out clearly in the travel journal of two members of an obscure Dutch Calvinist sect, the Labadists, who ranged from Maryland to Boston in 1679 and 1680 looking for land for their communitarian settlement. The two men, Jasper Danckaerts and Peter Sluyter, heard talk of popish plots almost everywhere they went. In Maryland they learned that Jesuit priests "hold correspondence" with all the Indians between the English and French colonies, and related that "some people in Virginia and Maryland as well as in New Netherland, have been apprehensive lest there might be an outbreak, hearing what has happened in Europe, as well as among their neighbors at Boston." Once they reached New England, meanwhile, popular anxiety began to have a deleterious effect on the men's travels. As strangely dressed foreigners Danckaerts and Sluyter stood out, and many Bostoners feared they were papists in disguise. "Some declared we were French emissaries going through the land to spy it out," Danckaerts noted, "others, that we were Jesuits travelling over the country for the same purpose; some that we were Recollets, designating the places where we had held mass and confession." Only with some difficulty—and a lot of explanation—were the two men able to find lodging in the town.[26]

These fears came out of several recent incidents. The most distant was in 1673, when a similar European stranger appeared in Boston during a more innocent time. The man proved to be an astute scholar, and he charmed New England's clerical elite with his wit and learning. In time he began to raise suspicions, however, because "although he was disguised," New Englanders believed the man might be a Jesuit. In fact, he was a priest named Jean Pierron, a member of the Society of Jesus stationed in Acadia who had spent the winter exploring the English colonies. In particular, he had sought to create ties between French and Maryland Jesuits, perhaps inspiring the fears of coordination expressed by Marylanders in the 1676 "hue and crye." Only after his departure from Boston did the townspeople realize that an inveterate enemy had been among them; Pierron boasted on his return he had converted several "heretics" to the Catholic faith.[27]

Several years after this unwelcome visit a major Indian war convulsed the region. The paramount Wampanoag sachem in the region, known to the English as King Philip, led a coalition of Algonquians who threatened the colony's very existence in 1675 and 1676. The region's leaders agonized over the causes of the war, and most came to blame sin and backsliding. God was angry, the ministers said, and they demanded a return to the zealousness of the colony's founding years. For some people, however, there was another explanation: it was priests like Pierron who inspired the bloodshed. Just after his arrival in Boston the royal agent Edward Randolph heard that "vagrant and Jesuitical priests" had worked for years "to exasperate the Indians against the English, and to bring them into a confederacy, and that they were promised supplies from France, and other parts, to extirpate the English Nation out of the Continent of America." This alternate explanation for the war seemed more persuasive after the General Court voiced its suspicions that the French had supplied arms to the enemy, several of whom had taken refuge in New France. Indeed, charges of French collusion became common both during and after the war, in spite of the lack of any real evidence.[28]

The next evidence of a plot against America came in 1679, when a fire raged through Boston, destroying much of the town's North End. Such conflagrations were not uncommon in early modern towns and cities, but New Englanders naturally suspected that papists had a hand in the disaster, since they were known to favor such tactics: many people continued to believe that the London fire of 1666 was a Catholic affair. Suspicion came to rest on a

Frenchman named Peter Lorphelin, and though investigators could find no sufficient evidence to tie him to the crime, word of the fire traveled through Protestant networks as far as Ireland and the Netherlands. It appeared to many that the papists were beginning to pay attention to America, and some people at least were inclined to think of Indians as partners in the design.[29]

In 1680, nonetheless, most American colonists continued to view Catholics and Indians as two distinct threats. When Indians captured a young New Englander named Quentin Stockwell in 1677 and carried him to Canada, for instance, he never made any connection between the two groups, and praised the French for providing food and care for him during a sickness. He even related an argument between the French and Indians regarding his treatment, after which the natives charged that the French "loved the English better than the Indians." For Stockwell, the civility and Christianity of the French was enough to place them above the Indians, whom he perceived as cruel pagans. But if he could separate the two groups in 1677, other New Englanders began to view them as partners in the same cause. Two broad changes began to occur: first, the English saw Indians as turning French, especially in their increasing adherence to the Catholic faith; and second, the French began to look more like Indians, due to their tolerance for miscegenation and ability to adapt to backcountry life.[30]

During the 1680s periodic violence continued to plague the New England frontier. But more damaging than actual attacks were the rumors, usually bringing reports of a new Indian conspiracy. In 1682 at the Cape Porpoise River Falls Mill in Maine, for instance, reports circulated that nearby Abenaki Indians "doe Intend to Rise again this Summer," gathering at the head of the Merrimack River "so to destroy so far as thay Can." Around the same time New Hampshire's Governor Edward Cranfield claimed that the "Indiens . . . are well Armed by the French which makes them verry Insolent." Two years later an Indian boasted to an Englishman in Pemaquid "that he would Burne the English houses and make the English Slaves to them as they ware Before," and others added "that they would go to Canada and fetch some strength to fall on the English and some of the Chefe of them is gon to Canada all Ready to fetch guns and amanition and they said they would make the greatest armie that ever was yet among them."[31]

English witnesses saw several connections between the latest alarms and the French. First, many refugees from King Philip's War had taken refuge both in Abenaki country in northern New England, and in New France, where they gathered in the mission towns of Sillery and later Odanak, located on the

St. Lawrence River between the towns of Québec and Trois-Rivières. Jesuits founded the latter mission specifically for the refugees, and according to an early report they were enthusiastic converts. Many of the neophytes already knew much of the catechism when they arrived at the mission, and they exhibited a devotion to the faith, one missionary claimed, that surpassed all other Indians in North America. They also bore some animosity toward their former enemies, the Iroquois Confederation in particular, and by extension their allies the English colonists. One priest even suggested that he might accompany the Indians in battle if they chose to venture out against their enemies.[32]

The second "French connection" involved an eccentric trader named Jean-Vincent d'Abbadie, baron de Saint-Castin, a French noble who lived in the borderlands between Maine and Acadia. The baron was a classic middleman trader, with trading partners in Boston and Port Royal, and impressive connections to local Abenaki villages through his marriage to a sachem's daughter. His main desire, according to all evidence, was to stay outside the purview of any one colonial government, so he carefully cultivated his ties to Massachusetts authorities, even pleading, in one letter to the governor in Boston, that he be considered neutral in case of "war between the two crowns." Despite his official neutrality, however, Saint-Castin was rapidly acquiring a different reputation among the English, as a French partisan who used his natural affinity with the Abenaki to cement an alliance between the two groups. John Nelson, a friend and trading partner of Saint-Castin, reportedly told one Englishman that the baron would never give allegiance to the English, but was "Comisinated from the King of France, and Likewise from the Gover[no]r of Canadey to Kepp the Rite and posesion of those prts." When the man protested that there were not enough French people to keep the territory, Nelson replied "that these and all the Indeans were Ingaged to him in these prts" and if the English paid Saint-Castin any insult they "would sone be Cut of, and the plases Left in Ashes." This report led local officials in Maine to urge Massachusetts authorities to be very careful to avoid any "misunderstanding" with the baron that could "proove a great Mischiefe to all the English Intirest in those parts."[33]

By 1684 nearly everyone thought that an Indian insurrection was in the works, and that Saint-Castin was the mastermind behind it. New Hampshire's Governor Cranfield confided to his counterpart in Plymouth that "there is a strong suspicion of a sudden rising of the Indians to attack the English at the eastward, being thereto instigated by one Castine, a Frenchman," and he urged the colonies to band together and provide for the common defense. Cranfield also wrote to New York's governor, Thomas Dongan, to seek the aid of the Mohawks and Senecas against the insurrection, believing that other Indians were "best acquainted with the manner of these Indians' skulking fight."[34]

New Hampshire's embattled governor understood that such rumors could impact politics in the region. Panicked people, in his estimation, were very difficult to govern. But while the Indian assault did not occur, neither did the rumors go away. The following year the patriarch of the Connecticut Valley, Springfield's John Pynchon, reported a rumor "that the French have In-tended [to establish] Settlements on Conecticot River about fifty miles above Squakeake"—near the present site of Brattleboro, Vermont—and suggested that the General Court find "some meete way of Possessing & settleing them before others." Combined with the continuing fears of Indian attack, the re-port suggested a combined French-native design that threatened the region's security and demanded a strong response.[35]

Sir Edmund Andros sailed into this cauldron in December 1686. Few men seemed better positioned to deal with an Indian crisis than the man the king had chosen to rule the newly formed Dominion of New England. As governor of New York during the 1670s, Andros had not only cemented the "Covenant Chain" alliance with the Iroquois; he had also mobilized them to intervene in King Philip's War, perhaps saving New England from greater destruction. Recent historians, like many contemporaries, have praised the governor's handling of Indian affairs, even while criticizing other aspects of his rule. Nonetheless, the series of events that occurred after his arrival proved beyond even Andros's considerable abilities. While most of his actions made perfect sense in terms of Indian policy, he did not appreciate the role of fear in colonial politics. It was his miscalculation of the mood of the people he governed, more than any other factor, that doomed Andros and his imperial designs.[36]

In January 1687—less than a month after the new governor's arrival—familiar rumors of an Indian design circulated around the Province of Maine. This time they centered on one of the most influential Abenaki sachems, named Hope Hood. Visiting the home of Ruth York, Hope Hood complained that the English had killed or kidnapped his brother. In the company of York's husband, the sachem made what the Englishman considered a violent address to a group of Indians. The evidence was far from overwhelming, but enough to convince the Yorks that a design was afoot.[37]

In the meantime, Andros took steps of his own to place Indian relations on a firmer basis. His main goal, in keeping with his mission, was to solidify the king's authority over the Eastern Country, a region claimed by both England and France. Andros believed, in typical Stuart fashion, that stability would come if he established both political and economic order, along with guarantees of allegiance from the principal inhabitants of the area, whether English, French, or Indian. He intended to create the ideal world represented in the Dominion's seal, with the Indian and colonist united in their devotion to a benevolent monarch. His first project was the baron of Saint-Castin. Andros understood, as his secretary Edward Randolph wrote, that Saint-Castin was somewhat of a free agent who "does not well like to be under the French government, [but] desires to live indifferent," and thought that by winning him over with a mixture of coercion and inducement the English could gain all the eastern Indians as allies. Andros especially hoped to gain the affinity of Saint-Castin's powerful father-in-law, the Kennebeck sachem Madockawondo.[38]

The baron's main problem, in Andros's eyes, was not his Frenchness or his Catholicism, but his ignorance of commercial regulations. As a result, the governor aimed to warn Saint-Castin that he had to give the king's customs officers their cut, while also promising that the king would protect his interests if he pledged his allegiance to England. In May 1688 Andros learned "That Severeall Goods wares & Merchandizes have lately been Imported into the River of Penobscott . . . Contrary to Law," and he resolved to teach the baron a lesson. The governor sent the royal frigate *Rose* to Saint-Castin's trading post at Pentagouet, but found the post deserted. The governor and his men entered the baron's house "and found a small altar in the common roome, which altar, and some pictures and ordinary ornaments, they did not meddle with any thing belonging thereto, but took away all his armes, powder, shott, iron kettles and some trucking cloath and his chaires, all of which were putt aboard the Rose and laid up in order to a condemnation of tradeing." Andros's assault was judicious: he made clear that his quarrel with Saint-Castin was economic rather than religious, and he also left word with a nearby Indian that if the baron would "come under obedience to the King" he could reclaim his goods.[39]

In fact, Andros's assault probably pushed Saint-Castin into the arms of French officials he did not entirely trust. By September he had pledged to help the governor of Acadia to establish French authority west of the St. Croix River; the governor bragged that the baron was leading "a more regulated life" and "promised to work to make an establishment in this country." A large component of this labor involved keeping the local Abenaki Indians in the French camp: not difficult, the governor believed, since "they are rather affectionate to the French and hate the English." In coming years many New

Englanders referred to the conflict with the Indians that started in 1687 as Castine's War. While they may have exaggerated the baron's role in the conflict, there was no doubt that in the eyes of both French and English authorities Saint-Castin controlled the balance of power in the eastern borderlands. In this as in so many cases, Europeans had trouble understanding that natives could have reasons of their own to resist the expansion of settlements, preferring to view them as pawns in an imperial chess game.[40]

After looting Pentagouet, Andros turned to the other volatile borderland in his Dominion: the region between Albany and Montreal. He renewed the Covenant Chain alliance that he had been so instrumental in creating a decade before, urging representatives of the five Iroquois nations both to stop deserting to the French, and also to refrain from attacking them without express permission from Andros. The governor was optimistic about Indian relations in the region, but during his stay in New York Andros received alarming reports from the Eastward. The peace he desired was not to be.[41]

Residents of Maine noticed a sea change in Indian relations after Andros's assault on Saint-Castin. Several inhabitants of the town of New Dartmouth noted that "after the Report of . . . Andros Robbing one Casteen a french man at Eastward, we never did see any Indian Come to our Plantation . . . but in an hostill manner, although before tht time they used to come and trade at sd Towne frequently." In August 1688 a number of thefts occurred, but the offending Indians disappeared—"Bound to Canneda," one official believed. The conflict escalated when the Abenaki took several English captives, and English officials retaliated by imprisoning twenty Abenaki chiefs who probably had little to do with the original kidnappings. Along with this violence came increasingly bellicose rhetoric on both sides, as the Abenaki claimed that the new war would be different, since the Mohawks had promised to stay neutral.[42]

English officials in Maine believed that both French priests and Saint-Castin stood behind the violence. A leading inhabitant of the region, Edward Tyng, claimed that the Indians "Intend a Warr with us, & we Question not but there is a Strong Combination with them and the french against us, and are afraid that the Captives are Carryed to the french & Indians at Penobscott"— meaning Saint-Castin's outpost at Pentagouet Harbor. Once captives began returning home, they told stories of French machinations. One captive reported that a French priest visited the Indians as they traveled, "& in that time was frequent with them in Consultation." Several days later they acquired new stores of powder, lead, and guns from the Jesuit, "who they said was gone to Canada & would send them more Armes and Amunition as soone as the frost came & an Army of men from Canada." The Indians also received guns from Saint-Castin, who had a large store he had bought from Boston traders, and was determined, according to the Indians, "to be revenged" for the insult Andros had given him.[43]

While trouble brewed in the east, another crisis struck western Massachusetts. In August two separate attacks claimed the lives of ten English settlers and allied Indians near the towns of Deerfield and Springfield. While the attackers slipped off before the English could apprehend them, a group of Schaghticoke Indians encountered the party and reported on their motives. The strange Indians told the locals that "we live in Canada" and "are going to fight by ordre off the Governr off Canida who told us, the maquaas [Mohawks] have done great mischief in Canida" The French governor allegedly instructed the warriors to avenge themselves on Indians or Christians. In addition, other evidence seemed to suggest French involvement. Before the attack, the Indians had traded with their victims, and sold "some small Papers [with] French pictures, as also bags, One mark't Roy"—the French word for "king."[44]

By the end of summer 1688, there was more evidence than ever before of a general design against the colonies, including many different Indian nations, and inspired by French malice. In the minds of most of the king's subjects in the colonies, this conspiracy demanded a strong response, a show of force to demonstrate that the English would not surrender to the combination that threatened them. As a military man with extensive experience in backcountry politics, Andros did not flinch in accepting the challenge. From the beginning, however, his response to the crisis differed from that of most colonists, and he played right into the hands of his political rivals—radical Protestants who viewed the enemy in a very different light from the Tory governor.

When Andros heard about the crisis his first action was to chastise his subordinates in the Eastern Country for their rash actions in imprisoning the Abenaki chiefs. He wrote that "by your seizing and disturbing the Indians you have Alarmed all your Parts and putt them in a posture of Warr." The governor quickly left New York for Boston "to prevent a second Indian warr." Returning to Boston, he freed the prisoners, demonstrating the kind of acumen in Indian affairs that scholars have repeatedly praised. Andros believed that the Abenaki could be valuable allies, and while he took a hard line against anyone who denied the king's authority, the governor wanted to underscore that the king's officers would rule fairly—showing that the Indians would enjoy the legal privileges of all subjects. Once again, the governor's policy gestured to the theoretical equality of settlers and Indians as subjects of a benevolent king. As sensible as the policy was, however, it looked very strange to colonists who believed that the Indians were partners in a Catholic conspiracy. For the first time, the governor himself appeared as if his own commitment to defending the colonies from Catholic and Indian enemies could be compromised.[45]

The release of these prisoners was not the only action that raised suspicions among New Englanders. Almost as soon as the attacks occurred Andros decided to raise an army to seek out the Indians who were really responsible— an action that should have raised his stock among the people of New England. The way he conducted the campaign, however, only fed into the conspiratorial thinking. On 10 September he impressed 32 men from Boston "to goe to the Eastward, by reason of the fears and dispersions people there are under." Within months he had sent around 700 men out of Massachusetts towns to Maine. The governor believed this policy to be sound. Impressment was a standard procedure during wartime, but New Englanders had little experience with the practice, and it appeared to them that Andros was draining the towns of their best bulwark in the case of an attack—the young men who made up the bulk of local militias. Indeed, Andros showed a marked hostility toward allowing townspeople to defend themselves. When he and Edward Randolph found the people of Marlborough in arms on their way from New York to Boston, they warned the people that their actions verged on treason or rebellion, and that they could not act to defend themselves without orders from authority. The dispute reflected different military cultures, but to the townspeople it appeared that the governor cared little for their safety.[46]

Once the newly impressed soldiers reached the Eastern Country, their suspicions only increased. The officers showed little tenderness toward the new recruits, and both their words and actions fed into popular fears that they were in on the conspiracy. Two soldiers from Haverhill reported that when they arrived the officer, James Weems, said "Hell is like to be youre winter quarters, & the divel yor Landlord." The officers swore and beat soldiers; one beat a young man to death because he was too weak to stand. None went farther than John Jourdan, who also happened to be Catholic. He once tied a soldier he accused of stealing biscuits up at a stake for hours to coerce a confession, and when "this punishmt failing of his desired End he Wickedly, Divellishly & after the Popish Cruelty studdyd & Invented new Torm[en]ts." Other New Englanders claimed that Jourdan treated them "not as Englishmen nor Christians but rather as Indians."[47]

While they treated their charges with "popish cruelty," the officers were somewhat more lenient toward their purported enemies. One soldier complained that while the men nearly starved, Andros ordered the merchant John Alden to distribute provisions to Saint-Castin, even though the baron was "looked at to be an enemy to the Interest of the Kings subjects & an aider & abetter of our enemies the Indians." On another occasion some soldiers witnessed their superiors giving ammunition to the wives of two prominent sachems, including Saint-Castin's father-in-law Madockawondo. Again, these actions probably represented a sensible policy on the part of Andros, who hoped to win over leading Abenakis to the English side. But, combined with the forms of military discipline New Englanders had never experienced before, this mild treatment toward the Indians only served to confirm suspicions that Andros and his men cared more for the Indians than for their own people. Even worse, the officers showed a general animosity toward New Englanders. When one soldier commented to John Jourdan that he would like to find some Indians to fight, Jourdan replied "that he had rather there were a thousand or Two Indians on Roxbury neck to [fight] against the Boston Bores."[48]

By the fall 1688 a new climate of fear had descended on the Dominion of New England. In an adaptation of a form of political discourse common in Maryland for decades, New Englanders had begun to suspect that their own leaders might be complicit in a conspiracy among the French and Indians to destroy English America. These kinds of rumors would have been damaging in any time and place, but they proved especially potent in New England because they played to a powerful minority who had been preaching for years that royal officials like Andros were partners in an evil popish plot—until this point with little success. In 1688, thanks to the addition of Indians to the plot, fear of Catholics moved out of the Congregational churches and became a mass movement capable of changing the face of imperial government.

Long before the Indian troubles started, some members of New England's clerical elite already believed that the region's new leaders had suspicious leanings. They represented a Catholic king, James II, who many radical Protestants feared would set up a popish "arbitrary government" in both England and its colonies, and their actions in revoking the old charter, abolishing the legislature and town meetings, and assessing new taxes, seemed to confirm their absolutist predilections. Nearly from the moment Andros arrived, his enemies tried to discredit him, and one of the main ways they tried to do so was from the pulpits.

Imperial officials understood that ministers possessed great political power in New England, and they often charged the preachers with spreading sedition.

A perusal of some of the surviving sermons from the Dominion period partly confirms these fears. While few ministers were brazen enough to call openly for rebellion against authority, many of them laced their sermons with coded messages implying that the Andros administration intended to persecute the Godly, and that accordingly true Christians were under no obligation to obey their commands. These messages drew on the long traditions of Calvinist resistance theory, and were driven by the belief by many leading radicals that the recent rise of persecution represented the last strikes of a dying beast, as the reign of Antichrist ended and Christ returned to Earth.[49]

Political messages abounded in sermons during the mid-1680s—and they were not limited to either printed sermons or those delivered by New England's more radical preachers. For example, Salem's John Higginson—a minister known as a common-sense moderate who often had good relations with royal authorities—preached a sermon on the "two witnesses" of the book of Revelation that directly addressed the popish conspiracy that he perceived to be targeting the region. Unlike some of his more radical counterparts, Higginson denied that ordinary people had the right to resist their rulers, but he also made clear that it was all people's duty to witness for Christ against "the Idolatries, Heresies, and Superstitions of the Popish Religion," and that it was impossible to stay neutral. Anyone who did not stay true to Christ would "by degrees fall to and fall in with the Antichristian party." He claimed that for years the "Popish Party" had wanted to destroy the "City set upon a hill," and that now New Englanders could expect a "fiery Tryal" as forces of good and evil collided. That final phrase, taken from the third chapter of the Book of Daniel, appeared in another incendiary sermon delivered several years earlier by a purported moderate, Samuel Willard, who counseled his charges to expect that the fires of popish persecution common in so much of the world would soon come to New England as well.[50]

These sermons appeared in print just before Andros's arrival, after which the new authorities ensured that no seditious messages came off the presses. As a result, ministers had to limit their politicking to ordinary weekly sermons. This was little impediment, however: as historians of Restoration England have asserted, spoken sermons could be as effective as printed ones in spreading political messages. One minister who took up the challenge in Boston was Joshua Moodey, the scourge of royal governors in New Hampshire who had fled Portsmouth to take a post at Boston's First Church. A notebook kept by an unknown auditor recorded the subject matter and fundamentals of Moodey's sermons during the Dominion years, revealing a nearly constant stream of coded political messages. In October 1687 the minister began a series of sermons on Psalm 1:1, declaring that "The only blessed man is a nonconformist to the Ungodly," a thinly veiled call for resistance to authority. In July 1688 he moved on to 2 Cor. 7:1: "let us cleanse ourselves from every defilement of body and spirit, and make holiness perfect in the fear of God." While the message sounds innocuous enough, Moodey took it from the section of Paul's letter to the Corinthians that contained one of the favorite verses of anti-Catholic radicals: "What accord has Christ with Belial? Or what has a believer in common with an unbeliever?" Certainly all Moodey's auditors knew the verse, and it took on a new meaning in the summer of 1688 when ungodly authorities seemed intent on compromising with the enemy. While we cannot know how his flock interpreted the sermon, his intentions could not be clearer: the minister exhorted the people to resist the imposition of royal authority.[51]

While they preached against the Dominion, the ministers also pointed out the strange innovations that the new rulers had brought to New England. In 1687, for instance, some inhabitants of Charlestown erected a maypole—the kind of lewd, pagan amusement Puritans had crossed the ocean to avoid. The maypole's very existence demonstrates that New England was not as uniformly devout as some historians have assumed, but the government's allowance of such blasphemy could only confirm that the region was sliding toward perdition. On a similar note, Governor Andros and his friends had introduced the Church of England to the colony, first at Boston's town house, and later in the Third Church, which they requisitioned for their own use in a move that was highly incendiary and probably illegal. The establishment of "common prayer worship" prompted Increase Mather to cross the river to Cambridge and break into the now defunct college press, publishing a clandestine tract warning that "the English Liturgy is taken out of the Popes Mass Booke," and adding "as to worship and discipline they are Extremely Popish." He claimed that "should I once go to hear Common Prayer, I seriously profess I should not know how I should bee able to look my Father in the Face in the other world."[52]

These ministers effectively built an opposition to Andros's reforms, but they did not immediately inspire a mass movement. Some New Englanders danced around the maypole and attended Anglican services, exhibiting an understandable curiosity about the new kind of worship. Even Andros's political innovations—abolishing the legislature and restricting town meetings, questioning the land tenure system, and imposing new taxes—prompted only one noteworthy act of resistance before changes in England altered the political calculus. A group of leading citizens of Ipswich, led by minister John Wise, refused to appoint a tax collector, claiming that the governor's warrant was illegal and to "Comply with the same were to lose the liberty of freeborne English men." Wise used the rhetoric of English liberties that would become so popular in eighteenth-century America, and his objections appeared to be remarkably secular, but he was also driven by a conspiratorial Protestant worldview. Wise believed that by taking control of people's estates by levying arbitrary taxes Andros could more easily force religious changes. In essence, Wise took the old storyline of a conspiracy against true religion, and cloaked it in constitutional rhetoric—just as many English Whigs were doing on the other side of the ocean.[53]

Yet while historians have focused on Wise's objections as a precursor to both the rebellion of 1689 and the more substantial revolution a century later, there is no indication that his cause was a popular one in the colony as a whole. Andros easily dealt with the "uprising" by imprisoning his opponents and depriving Wise of the right to preach. Aside from this one example, Andros reported few problems collecting taxes or convincing New Englanders to accept his authority. They grumbled about his impositions on land in particular, as Andros forced subjects to take out new patents from the king, but no one lodged an official challenge to the governor until he ended up in prison in 1689. People might not have liked the Dominion, but unlike earlier experiments in royal rule in New Hampshire and Bermuda, it actually worked. Given the difficulties of building a mass movement, opponents of the Dominion combated the regime in the most classic manner, sending Increase Mather to England to complain about the government's excesses to King James himself. The Catholic king, Mather and his allies hoped, would stop the "popish" innovations that Andros inflicted on New England.[54]

When the Indian troubles commenced, however, these old intrigues took on new meaning, and in retrospect the ministers who warned of a Catholic conspiracy appeared to be prescient. While many ordinary New Englanders showed little concern over a maypole or even a new structure of taxation, they did feel strongly that their leaders needed to protect them from external enemies. Indeed, the Dominion's framers justified its existence by claiming that it could provide greater security than a number of "petty" colonial governments. In 1688, however, the people of New England were no longer safe, and the discontented populace became more willing to believe the alarmist rhetoric coming out of the pulpits.

While the opposition to imperial centralization was especially strong in

Boston, the rumors of Andros's duplicity moved beyond the usual opposition circles. Even in New York, those with personal grudges against the governor spread rumors that questioned his commitment to the Protestant cause. The most extreme report came from a Huguenot merchant named Pierre Reverdy, who had asked for a patent to make salt in America, which Andros's council rejected as "impracticable and also detrimentall to the fishery & Navigation of this place." In retaliation Reverdy circulated what could only have been an outright fabrication. He claimed that Andros corresponded with the governor of Canada and heard "of severall protestant people" who had left Canada and sought work as laborers in New York. The governor then advertised for a gardener, and when several French Protestant refugees came to work Andros "sent them to the Westward Islands," presumably as forced laborers. The story was false, but it played into popular fears that Andros could not protect his people—and may in fact have been contributing to their demise.[55]

By late summer of 1688, therefore, popular impressions of the Dominion government had shifted from positive or neutral to negative, and the change was almost entirely due to worsening relations with Indians. Many people believed that Andros not only failed to stop Indian attacks, but even encouraged them. As a later report stated, there were "great jealousies and Suspicions of Sinister designs in the Gov[erno]r as to our Troubles by the Indians," especially as Andros's robbery of Saint-Castin's trading post had started the conflict. An official in Plymouth named Samuel Eldred spoke to an Indian in September 1688 who claimed that 500 armed Indians waited on Martha's Vineyard, but that "our Governour did not dare to Disarme them for that the Governor had more love for them the sd Indians then for his Majestyes Subjects the English."[56]

Correspondents were understandably circumspect about the rumors that circulated in late 1688. Writing to Increase Mather in London, Joshua Moodey mentioned "strange Conjectures wch I dare not write," but another anonymous letter—copied for the Committee on Trade and Plantations by Mather—provided more details. The correspondent wrote that "the alarum of war & Garments rolled in blood is now among us," as the Indians had attacked and many suspected that the Indians and French "are armed & Gathered together at a place called Pennycook where they have erected a Fort . . . & were there holding a consult about a war with the English." What's more, the writer suspected that some English people were in on the design: "I do heartily wish that some of our owne Gent[leme]n have not had too much of a hand in this evil designe, For I have been informed by Credible psons that some in power have said that it is not for the King's Interest that this People should injoy it, & if another People had it it would be more for the King's Interest." In this letter we can see the various conspiracy theories and rumors woven together: an Indian conspiracy, engineered by the French, and supported by foreign rulers who hated New England and wanted to destroy its liberties.[57]

The person who advanced the most coherent anti-Catholic interpretation of the Indian war, strangely enough, was himself a target of suspicion: Dominion secretary Edward Randolph. He had long believed that the French used the pretense of religion to win the beaver trade, and in 1688 he endorsed former New York governor Thomas Dongan's proposal to send English Jesuits to establish missions, even writing to a leading Catholic noble about the plan. At the same time, Randolph began to express anti-Catholic sentiments much more in line with his enemies in Massachusetts than he probably knew. In a letter to William Blathwayt he charged "the priests" and unscrupulous merchants with being "the onely fomenters of the warr," and he told the story of a French cleric who traveled with enemy Indians and supplied them with arms and ammunition. By January 1689 he drifted into the classic tropes of antipopery, blaming a Jesuit emissary from New France who visited, and allegedly tricked Thomas Dongan into letting down his guard before the hostilities started. He also claimed the French seduced the Indians from their allegiance "by their Jesuites [who] strangely allure them with their beads crucifixes and little painted images, gaining many new converts." The fact that even a royal official, who had every reason to look kindly on Catholicism, resorted to such classic anti-Catholic explanations of the conflict, shows how much power such imagery possessed. And it also shows the precarious position that Andros occupied as he dealt with a crisis that had spiraled out of his control.[58]

In the midst of these rumors another set of reports came from across the Atlantic. James II's reign had taken some dramatic turns. The king's key political goal was the establishment of religious toleration for Catholics and, by necessity, other religious minorities. While he preferred to work through Parliament, James did not hesitate to use questionable tactics to push through his measures. In April 1687 he issued a Declaration of Indulgence that essentially nullified penal laws against dissent, and the following year he instructed every Anglican minister to read the Declaration from his pulpit. When seven bishops refused to administer the order, he briefly imprisoned them, leading to an uproar, as many English people believed the king meant to undermine or destroy the established church. In fact, James's regime foundered because, like some of his American associates, he played directly into his subjects' conspiratorial fears. While his program for toleration attracted quite a bit of support from radical dissenters—including Increase Mather and other New Englanders—it appeared to most mainstream English Protestants that the two great menaces, Catholics and radical Protestants, had joined forces and threatened to bring down the realm in blood and fire. The situation worsened in June 1688, when James II's wife, Mary of Modena, gave birth to a son, an heir who guaranteed that a Catholic could inherit the throne. Soon after this, a cadre of leading nobles issued a secret message to William of Orange, whose wife Mary was James's eldest daughter and thus second in line to the throne. The nobles basically invited the Dutch stadholder to invade England and take over the government, saving England from popery and slavery. By the fall James himself knew that he faced a dire threat from his daughter and son-in-law, and he readied his army for attack. When the invasion came, however, James's shaky coalition quickly crumbled and the king himself fled London in disgrace, leaving England, Scotland, and Ireland in political chaos, without a proper monarch.[59]

People in the colonies learned slowly of the problems at home. When the Prince of Wales was born, for instance, officials throughout the king's dominions celebrated the event with the appropriate jubilation—an official celebration in Boston; a day of thanksgiving in Maryland, presided over by the colony's Catholic council president and resident Jesuit priests. As events developed, however, both colonial officials and ordinary people began to realize that the revolution in England was an imperial revolution as well, a rupture that created new dangers and possibilities for those who hoped to rule the various colonies.[60]

PART II

Empire Lost

Chapter 3

Rumors and Rebellions

IN THE LAST months of 1688 a new wave of fear swept England's American colonies. On the island of Barbados, white planters believed themselves to be targets of a vast design by popish recusants, French Jesuits, and Irish servants, a plot to reduce the island to "popery and slavery" and perhaps deliver it to France. By January 1689 almost identical rumors appeared in New England, where Indians joined the list of enemies, and two months later settlers on the frontier of Maryland and Virginia began whispering of the same plot. At the same time, rumors of a different sort arrived from Europe, telling of William of Orange's invasion, James II's abdication to France, and a possible change of government. This combination of fears and great expectations pushed matters to a crisis: by April colonists in Boston took to the streets demanding a change in government, and before the summer's end political strife had spread to many, if not all, of the colonies. By that time one former governor languished in prison, two more had been forced to resign, and another had surreptitiously abandoned his post, sailing for England. All told, the rebellions of 1689 marked the most dramatic political disturbance in the colonies before the next revolution a century later.[1]

To casual observers, the turmoil of 1689 spelled the end of the Stuart design to reform the empire. The effort at imperial centralization had moved farthest in Boston and New York, the constituent parts of the ambitious Dominion of New England, but several days of popular turmoil succeeded in erasing over a decade's worth of work by imperial leaders. By the summer of 1689, when England's new monarchs William and Mary attempted to take firm control of their dominions, many American colonies were in administrative chaos, without functional governments of any sort. Even Edward Randolph, the man who had worked so hard to build a new empire, and had expressed repeated confidence that it could be done, took on a less optimistic tone. Writing from the "common jail in New Algiers"—as he termed Boston—Randolph wondered if the colonies were just ungovernable, stating that "force is the Onely Argument to convince & oblige them" to submit to authority. Maybe Edward Cranfield had been right, and only a strong military presence, and the firm establishment of Anglican conformity, could bring the colonies into line.[2]

If one looked beyond Boston and New York to other parts of the colonies, however, the lessons of 1689 were not so negative. In fact, in the ashes of Stuart imperial reforms lay clues as to how to build the empire again. The crisis had revealed something very important: despite their differences, English colonists in America spoke the same political language. From the summer of 1688 throughout the crisis nearly identical rumors circulated around the empire. However, not every rumor led to political chaos. In some places, like Barbados and Virginia, they actually strengthened the hand of authority and ushered in a new era of political stability. The variable, of course, was how local officials responded to the rumors. Those who took them seriously, who made a stand against the real or imagined Catholic enemies that threatened their polities, weathered the crisis and came out unscathed. Those who downplayed or discounted popular fears, on the other hand, paid for it with their jobs and reputations.[3]

The rumors and rebellions of 1688–89, therefore, represented an important turning point in the history of imperial politics. They demonstrated that Stuart absolutist plans for the empire were untenable, but they also pointed the way toward closer coordination between colonies and metropole, enabled by a common fear of Catholic rivals. If imperial officials could promote themselves as guardians against a popish enemy, perhaps they could build the level of public support necessary to create a permanent imperial establishment in America.

• • •

The story of the rebellions of 1689 began not in Boston or New York, but in the West Indies. In August 1688 the people of Barbados witnessed one of the most extravagant displays of loyalty to ever appear in the English colonies. Lieutenant Governor Edwyn Stede had recently received word of the birth of a male heir to James II, and he was not content for a simple day of thanksgiving or firing of the fort's cannon. In addition to those ordinary measures, he organized a vast procession of all the island's prominent people dressed in their finery, followed by hundreds of horse and foot soldiers, and punctuated by the "most magnificent Entertainment, such as the present state of the West-Indies never Saw & the future age will admire," a feast for more than two thousand people with enough wine to drink the health of the entire royal family. The whole display demonstrated "that the Comands of his Prince shall never be Obstructed by unwillingness nor retarded by Negligence." The people of Barbados, Stede declared, were the king's most loyal subjects. Thus the surprise that the first stirrings of trouble in the colonies in 1688 came not from a den of sedition and Puritanism like New England or Bermuda, but from this cradle of monarchism.[4]

Despite their longstanding loyalty, however, people in Barbados and the king's neighboring island colonies had good reasons to be afraid in 1688. Beyond the constant fear of slave conspiracies, the islanders also lived in close proximity to two groups of strangers that they did not entirely trust. The first were their indentured servants, many of whom were of Irish Catholic origin, a fact that proved particularly vexing in the years after the Irish Rebellion of 1641. The exact number of Irish servants in the islands is difficult to measure—and their religious composition even more so—but they probably made up a majority on the island of Montserrat throughout the seventeenth century and a substantial minority on the other English islands.[5]

The second threat in the 1680s came from another variety of papist, the French. The two nations had coexisted in the region, not always peacefully, for decades, even sharing the small island of St. Christopher, but after Louis XIV's rise to power the French menace became a preoccupation of both English governors in the region and ordinary people. By 1688 Stede had taken on the role of the foremost challenger of the French in the islands. His main focus was on the islands of St. Lucia, St. Vincent, and Dominica—thinly inhabited, mountainous bastions that lay within the official bounds of Stede's commission but contained only a few French and Carib Indian inhabitants. Stede forcibly ejected the islands' French residents on several occasions, sending a clear message that he would not tolerate interlopers. In his estimation, the French were bad neighbors, enemies to the king's interest, despite the official peace in Europe.[6]

The history of the Leeward Islands, those more marginal English colonies to the north and west of Barbados, showed the dangers of both French and Irish enemies. In 1666, the last time the two kingdoms had fought, the French had overrun the English half of St. Christopher along with Antigua and Montserrat, plundering English plantations and making off with hundreds of African slaves. While the English eventually regained most of their land, they were still campaigning for reparations twenty years later. Ominously, the French had been aided by some of the Irish servants on the islands—an indication that these faithless people could prove to be a fifth column that would bring down the colonies from within. The events of 1666 cast a long shadow, even in a place like Barbados that was geographically remote from the French.[7]

It was during this period of fear and uncertainty that a number of questionable visitors arrived on Barbados. One was Sir Thomas Montgomery, the king's choice for attorney general. Like other officials on the island, he was fanatically loyal—but with a difference, as he was also Irish and allegedly a Catholic convert. This meant that Montgomery favored royal policies, like religious toleration for Catholics and Protestant dissenters, that many of the king's Tory supporters could not completely endorse, and as the king's legal representative he felt compelled to promote them. In addition, he appealed to a new constituency: the Catholic servants who, despite their checkered pasts, appeared to Montgomery as dependable subjects to an increasingly embattled Catholic king. Early in his tenure Montgomery complained to the Lords of Trade that Barbadian servants were "used with more barbarous Cruelty then if in Algiers . . . as if Hell Commenced here and but continued in the world to come." Such sentiments could only serve to alienate the planter elite, who quickly came to see the attorney general as a particular enemy.[8]

The second unwelcome visitor caused much more alarm: sometime during the summer of 1688 a French Jesuit priest arrived in Barbados from Martinique. The Jesuit, named Father Michel, seemed to have come with the support or at least connivance of English authorities. Lieutenant Governor Stede promised the president of the Committee on Trade and Plantations that he would not allow anyone to "molest, affront, abuse or scoff at him," though he noted that the presence of a French man on the island at that time of tension "made the People here to Conclude him Rather a Spye than a Priest." Montgomery, meanwhile, took a much more active approach, offering the priest lodging in his house, though he later claimed he did so out of obligation rather than pure charity. It was at this time, according to his enemies, that Montgomery actually converted to Catholicism.[9]

The priest's activities during his six months in Barbados remain shrouded in innuendo, but he seems to have spent most of his time ministering to the colony's substantial Irish Catholic population. He held mass both at Montgomery's house and at the dwelling of another prominent planter named Willoughby Chamberlain. Later investigations revealed the names of at least 44 people who attended the services, but rumor had it that some services attracted more than 200 Barbadians, "[in] generall Irish men, and them of the poorer sort, and many of them Servants." Chamberlain and Montgomery supposedly scoured the countryside to inform the colony's Catholics of the rare opportunity to receive genuine religious instruction, and even offered "treats" to entice them to attend. The depositions of Irish servants who attended the services hint at a brief golden age for the island's Catholics, a time when the combination of a Catholic monarch and relaxation of the penal laws provided new opportunities for public expression of faith. Many Catholics evidently embraced the new freedom, as political and religious arguments moved out of the council chamber and coffeehouse into the island's fields and curing houses.[10]

To the island's respectable Protestants, it appeared that Montgomery and the Jesuit had emboldened Barbados's unruly Irish population. For instance, in September 1688 a laborer named William Kelly charged the minister of St. Lucy's Parish, John Wilson, with "Uttering or Speakeing of Treasonable words." The incident occurred early in the morning on 2 September, when Wilson awoke to the sounds of Kelly beating one of the minister's servants. When Wilson confronted the intruder, Kelly accused him of threatening to chase all Roman Catholics out of his parish, after which the minister allegedly made some unkind comments about the Catholic king—charges he vehemently denied. Kelly could find no one to back up his story, and he did not help his case when he claimed to be the disinherited son of Irish nobility, but the fact that the court heard his testimony at all demonstrates the strange state of colonial politics in 1688. One fellow servant testified that Kelly had told him "you will see an alteracon of affaires in a short time and that he himselfe should be a great man," and that "two Preists" had confirmed that dramatic changes were imminent.[11]

Such evidence begged for a conspiratorial interpretation. All the pieces were there: the scheming, foreign Jesuit; the turncoat recusant; and the Irish shock troops that would provide the manpower to bring the plot to its conclusion. But in November 1688 it was still dangerous to speak out loud about a popish plot, so most prominent Barbadians expressed themselves with great care. Edwyn Stede, for example, denounced Montgomery to authorities in Whitehall, but he couched his criticism in language calculated not to offend his royal master. Stede had no problem with Catholicism, he pledged, nor did anyone else in Barbados, but Montgomery had raised up the people against him due to his immoderate zeal in promoting his new faith. The attorney general "makes it his buisness to quarrill with every body about it," Stede wrote,

"& Not Onely threaten them with Law & his Ma[jes]ties Displeasure, but upon Suprise falls upon them . . . which breeds much heart burning with the People." The problem lay with Montgomery and not the people of Barbados, who remained loyal subjects of their Catholic king. But one could sense the uneasiness in Stede's writing: he knew that it might become difficult to remain loyal to the king and also maintain order among nervous colonists.[12]

As if the king's representatives in the West Indies did not have enough problems, they soon began to hear rumors of a different sort. There was trouble at home, though the exact dimensions of the crisis remained unclear. By 20 November word of an impending Dutch invasion of England had reached the Leeward Islands—just two weeks after William of Orange's landing at Torbay. The news, vague as it was, caused a great deal of consternation. Already in late November an inhabitant of the Leewards named Colonel Beach spread rumors—which no one dared repeat in print—that King James might have lost the throne. When the Assembly of Nevis declined to affix their names to a late declaration expressing joy over the birth of the Prince of Wales, Leeward Islands governor Nathaniel Johnson accused them of giving too much credence to the rumors.[13]

As fall turned to winter Barbadians received more news—but none of it official or particularly reliable. Various reports arrived of William of Orange's landing, his triumphant march toward London, and James II's flight to France, but it was impossible to know for sure whether William had really defeated James, and if so, whether he could hold onto power. In some ways, the reliable communication links between the islands and England were harmful rather than helpful: by February most people knew at least something of the revolutions at home, but their leaders did not have enough information to take any definite action. Official correspondence from this time contained more than a little desperation—Thomas Montgomery and Nathaniel Johnson even took the step of writing to the French governor in Martinique seeking more reliable news. The results must have only added to the confusion, since the comte de Blenac assured Montgomery in early January that William of Orange's invasion force had returned to the Netherlands in disgrace.[14]

The frequency of communication meant that Stede had to act in order to maintain stability, but he faced a terrible choice. Choosing the wrong side would mean his political downfall in the best of circumstances, and could lead to charges of treason. But if he stayed neutral others with more strident beliefs, like Montgomery, would undoubtedly fill the vacuum, perhaps pulling the island toward civil war. Faced with this dilemma, Stede decided to cast his lot with William of Orange—sort of. At the end of February he called the council together to consider the island's security during these times of troubles, and they produced a document that was at once an act of incredible daring and a study in vagueness and equivocation. It saved Stede's career, ended Montgomery's, and could have stood as a model for how colonial governors should deal with such crises.

The stated reason for the council's emergency session was the danger of a French invasion. Several reports of a French fleet in Martinique had circulated around the island, and Stede argued that the colony must put itself in a better posture of defense against the enemy. Nonetheless, in February the council did little to prepare for an invasion. Instead, it turned against the island's Catholics. Stede and his councilors must have had access to official justifications of William of Orange's invasion, as they consciously adopted much of the anti-Catholic language that had become fashionable in England. They blamed all the king's problems on "the subtile, wicked, horrid and abominable contrivances of Popish Recusants, and more particularly those called Jesuits, who goeing about with their head & father the devill . . . have for many years been undermindeing and Endeavouring to destroy, overturne, and utterly abolish the truely antient, Catholicke and apostolicke Protestant faith." The wording of the declaration was curious in that it adopted an anti-Catholic interpretation of the Glorious Revolution but studiously avoided any acknowledgment of the revolution itself—just vaguely thanking God for preserving the laws, liberties, and religion of England in the face of the Catholic menace. The text even implied that England's Catholic king was himself a victim of popish plotting—merely tricked by the machinations of recusants and Jesuits.[15]

Stede and the council did more than just yoke Barbados's fortune to the Protestant revolution at home. They illustrated how the problems plaguing Europe, caused by recusants and crafty Jesuits, had come to the plantations as well. There was indeed a popish plot against Barbados and all of the English empire, Stede asserted, a design to replace the perfect English system with "popery and slavery" and subvert the Protestant faith. Its champion was the convert Thomas Montgomery, aided by another convert, the planter Willoughby Chamberlain. Stede urged the council to act quickly against the threat, not only by disenfranchising Catholics, which they did, but also by imprisoning the two ringleaders (the Jesuit had wisely left Barbados in January). The council concurred, charging that Montgomery and Chamberlain had "suffered themselves to be perverted, & reconsoled to the Popish Religion," helped a Jesuit priest proselytize contrary to the law, and attempted to "subvert the Government, and change the true, and Established Protestant Religion" to popery.[16]

The actions of the lieutenant governor and council were both dramatic and politically astute. They had received no official word of any change in government at home, but they acted anyway, essentially undoing James II's decree of religious toleration and, indeed, throwing his appointed legal representative in jail. Some would have interpreted it as an act of rebellion against authority, albeit one championed by the executive. But it was also a necessary rebellion if Barbados's leaders hoped to hold on to power. Stede and the councilors surely knew that their past loyalty to James II would not serve them well with their subjects or the people who were likely to wield power in the new government. They needed to shield themselves from both popular rage and recrimination from their new masters, and they did so by presenting themselves, rather incredibly, as the saviors of Protestantism. They also created a scapegoat, Montgomery, whom they could paint as the real Jacobite in their midst.

In order to do this Governor Stede gathered nearly a hundred pages of evidence against Montgomery and his accomplice Chamberlain that related "their popish tricks and Evill Corrispondencies." The collected material, which included incriminating letters to the attorney general as well as numerous depositions about him and other Barbadian Catholics, constitutes one of the most stunning examples of how Protestants could imagine popish plots even without the benefit of much solid evidence, especially as Stede provided extensive commentary on many of the documents telling his readers in Whitehall exactly how to interpret them.[17]

The primary charge against Montgomery and Chamberlain was that they harbored the Jesuit priest, who had come to the island with the goal of undermining the true Protestant church and establishing popery in its place. One of Montgomery's servants provided the corroborating details, confirming that Father Michel made "his Generall abode" at Montgomery's house "and read and said Mass Publiquely." The attorney general, meanwhile, not only countenanced such activities but "officiated at the service thereof," even though he required lessons in Roman Catholic liturgical practice from his own servants. This was one of the central pieces of evidence for the assertion, which Montgomery always denied, that he had abandoned the Church of England and turned to popery. Stede gathered similar evidence against Chamberlain, taking depositions from numerous servants and neighbors who either witnessed the frequent masses held at his house or heard about them from others. Many of these same witnesses also testified that Chamberlain frequently declared his

Catholic faith: even the minister of St. Philip's Parish declared that the planter had pledged to "spill the last dropp of his Blood" for the Roman Catholic Church.[18]

Stede presented this evidence as proof that Montgomery and Chamberlain had violated English laws against recusancy and the harboring of popish priests. To do so required the governor and council to make a fairly novel argument about the strength and limits of English law in the colonies. On the one hand, they contended that English laws—specifically the penal laws that criminalized Catholicism—had as much force in Barbados as in England, even if they had never been officially endorsed by the local legislature. At the same time, they declared invalid James II's toleration decrees, depending as they did on the dispensation or suspension of parliamentary laws. Montgomery responded that some degree of religious toleration had always applied in the colonies, "whose fundamentalls are upon much different grounds than those of England," and that at any rate he was obligated as a servant of the king to obey his master's directives. Few unbiased readers could have failed to see the hypocrisy in Stede's arguments, since the lieutenant governor had pledged himself to enforce liberty of conscience and protect the visiting priest only five months earlier. Stede had been smart enough to sense the change in rhetoric in England, however, and knew that he would be better off choosing parliamentary supremacy over the royal prerogative.[19]

Beyond harboring the Jesuit—a charge that neither man could completely deny—came more ominous allegations. In particular, Stede argued that after their plan to promote the Catholic faith failed, they resolved to betray Barbados to the French, paving the way for an invasion that would accomplish by force what the Jesuit could not by persuasion. The main evidence for this charge came from several letters from French correspondents that Stede's men found after Montgomery's arrest. It was the very existence of these letters, rather than their contents, that most impressed Stede. The comte de Blenac, French governor of Martinique, simply passed on some false reports from Europe in a January letter, probably responding to queries from Montgomery before he had reliable news of what had happened in England, but this was enough evidence for Stede that Montgomery was "frenchified" as well as Catholic. Along with Blenac's letter were three from ecclesiastical officials: Latin letters from the Jesuit superior on Martinique and from the lady superior of the island's Ursuline nuns. Stede appeared not to have read the Latin letters, but he speculated that they were part of a design to have more Jesuits sent to Barbados "by which our p[ro]testant religion would be weakened, &

the French intrest strengthened." At any rate, the fact that priests and nuns considered him a friend seemed further to establish Montgomery as an internal enemy.[20]

The next plank in the plot involved the "rude debauched, drunken swearing hactoring Irish papists" that Montgomery and Chamberlain had entertained at their houses. These were the shock troops that would allow the French to conquer the island, rising up as one when their master Montgomery directed them. Most of the evidence of the Irish uprising had little or no relation to the case against the attorney general, but Stede included it in the same packet—unfortunately with very little commentary—in order to underscore the connection between Montgomery's intrigues and the Irish threat. For example, he included several depositions concerning an Irish servant named James Jordan who "had spoken very Irreverently and prophanely of the holy Bible and other bad Expressions of Englishmen," as well as a man named Dominick Rice who assaulted a neighbor for refusing to drink the pope's health. Both incidents appeared to be the result of mixing drink and politics during a tense time, but their accumulated effect was to ratchet up the level of fear in the colony.[21]

Despite their marginal relevance, these documents spoke very clearly to the level of panic in Barbados in the early months of 1689. If Stede was taking advantage of an opportunity to destroy a political rival, he was also responding to real alarm on the part of subjects, who were conditioned by both upbringing and experience to fear the Irish. For instance, a servant named John Thompson provided an eyewitness account of an attack by James Jordan, in which the Irishman assaulted Thompson for reading a Bible and "said he hoped to see all the Bibles Burnt & all the protestants hanged or killd." The news of the outburst quickly spread by word of mouth. A week later one John Bowen heard about the incident from another witness and spread it around the neighborhood, but changed the details a bit, claiming that Jordan said he hoped to soon have "an hundered such English Doggs to bee his Slaves." The rhetoric was alarming in any case, but the second report turned a vague threat into a virtual conspiracy to conquer and enslave Protestants. As rumors traveled, in other words, each auditor added or changed details to increase the sense of alarm.[22]

This process appeared even more clearly in the case of Cork Farley. In November 1688 this former servant was at the house of Tom and Martha Custley, where a third "young man" was reading a popular Protestant devotional tract, and commented to the Catholic Farley that "he Must not Worship Images"; Farley replied "angerly that Bibles where Bookes that Caused a great Deall of differences, & that the Roman Religion was the first Religion that was Upon the earth & that it would be the Last." This was how the incident appeared to an eyewitness, but by the time Tom Custley told a neighbor the story had a new wrinkle, that Farley had also pressured the young Protestant to turn Catholic "& told him if he did not turn to that Religion he [would] repent it for that he hoped to see the blood of the Protestants swim on the ground." As they heard reports of these everyday arguments about politics and religion, people added gory details that happened to adopt the language of Irish atrocities popularized by Sir John Temple in his famous book about the Irish Rebellion of 1641.[23]

If fear of the Irish depended very much on Old World prejudices, another element of the plot was distinctly American. At a dinner of the leading gentlemen of Christchurch Parish on 25 February, after the quarter sessions, conversation turned to fears of a French invasion. One planter observed that if the French did invade they would have a difficult time as "there was severall good trusty negroes" that would gladly fight and "venter their lives" to defend the island. At this Sir Thomas Montgomery was incredulous: he speculated that as soon as the French arrived on the island they "would give all the Negroes their freedomes" and the slaves would desert en masse to the enemy, joining the island's servants who "would fall upon us first." Apparently the planters had never considered that their slaves might join an invading army: they upbraided Montgomery for even voicing such a thought, especially since several black slaves were in the room at the time, and they suspected him of trying to inflate the strength of the French and dissuade his neighbors from resisting them. With this comment—which strikes the modern reader as quite logical—Montgomery connected the longtime fears of French and Irish Catholics with homegrown anxieties over slave insurrections. Within a week he was in prison.[24]

The final set of charges against Montgomery involved his designs on the governorship. Along with plotting a bloody invasion, the attorney general also attempted to bring about regime change in a more traditional way, by complaining to superiors in England about Stede's conduct and urging Whitehall to appoint a new governor—perhaps Montgomery himself. Of all the charges, this was the least serious and also the least supported by evidence. There was hardly a royal appointee in the colony who did not angle for a promotion, but Stede's only evidence was the fact that Montgomery had corresponded with several members of James II's privy council, including his hated Jesuit confessor Fr. Edward Petre, in what could only have been another round of popish intrigue. In fact, Stede turned Montgomery's possible attempt to secure a promotion into an act of treason by connecting it with the larger popish plot. Montgomery opposed Stede, the lieutenant governor argued, because the governor was an "obstinat heritick" who "opposed them and their popish Superstitions and Idolatrus religion" and resisted their campaign for "Setting up popery in this Island."[25]

Taken as a whole, Stede's campaign against Montgomery aimed to discredit his rival and save himself and the council from the taint of their past loyalty to James II. In both goals he succeeded admirably, defining himself simultaneously as a loyal subject of the new king and a zealous Protestant who would protect the island from popery. Events over the course of the summer only strengthened his position, when the French attacked and conquered St. Christopher, with the help of the island's Irish servants. Stede was the first colonial official to use fear of Catholics to buttress state authority, and as a result Barbados managed to avoid any major political strife. In other parts of the king's dominions rulers were not so astute.[26]

● ● ●

If Barbadians had a reputation for loyalty, their counterparts in New England appeared almost the opposite. In the minds of most royal officials, they were the most refractory of subjects: they harbored several regicides after the Restoration, ignored economic regulations, and repeatedly asserted their independence from royal authority. The customs agent William Dyre described this independent spirit in colorful terms: New Englanders were "raging furious fanatick Whiggs . . . Rebellious & unnatural hators & warr[i]ors Ag[ain]st the true mother church." The proclamation of James II as king, Dyre added, was "Cold & heartlessly performed, Coursly, and Carelesly Slubber'd over in that place . . . which is a shame to Relate." Dyre had a particular grudge—his mother had been one of the Quaker missionaries executed by Massachusetts authorities in 1660—but he was not alone in his sentiments. It was this reputation for disloyalty and irregularity, along with the region's strategic position alongside New France, that prompted royal officials first to revoke the Massachusetts charter, and then to create the Dominion of New England. Such a potent union, officials believed, would force New Englanders to behave, while also defending the colonies from foreign designs.[27]

Given the region's history, therefore, one would almost expect that the region would experience troubles as word of unrest at home crossed the ocean.

And indeed, the news of revolution did convulse the region, eventually leading to an uprising nearly as dramatic as the one at home. It is tempting to
blame this crisis, as royalist officials did, on the region's peculiar principles, but
this would be incorrect. In fact, the rumors that inspired colonists to rise up
against the Dominion of New England were almost identical to the ones circulating in the West Indies—and may have even been inspired by correspondence from the islands. The main difference was the reaction by royal officials,
who uniformly rejected popular fears of a popish design. This was the central
lesson of the rebellion of 1689 in New England: not that New Englanders were
impossible to govern, but that they had to be governed in a particular way.

During the first months of 1689 New Englanders suspected that dramatic
events were occurring in England, but had no reliable information about
them. While the Gulf Stream and the moderate weather allowed information to travel quickly from England to the West Indies, the voyage across the
North Atlantic was nearly impossible during the winter months, and as a result New Englanders received much of their news from the Caribbean rather
than Europe. What they received in 1689, therefore, was recycled news—
probably variations on the rumors spread by Colonel Beach in the islands in
November—along with the occasional newsletter or reprint of a pamphlet or
newspaper. Only in January did New England officials learn of the impending
Dutch invasion, and it was not until 11 February that New Yorkers received "a
flying reporte from Virginia; that the Prince of Orange was landed in Tarrbay,"
three months after the fact. About the same time a ship from Nevis brought
similar news to Boston, along with the Prince of Orange's Declaration, one of
the key pieces of Williamite propaganda. Within a few months more ships had
spread news of William's victory, but the details remained unclear. Even as late
as April a Boston merchant complained to a business partner in Rotterdam
that while "we have heard by way of Virginia of strange & great Revolutiones
In England . . . .we doe all Long for a Shipe directly from England," and could
not be sure of exactly what had transpired.[28]

Just as in the islands, these rumors landed in a place already primed to
fear the worst. In the summer of 1688 a series of Indian attacks claimed a few
lives and caused great consternation around New England, especially when
colonists learned that French authorities in Canada may have authorized the
attacks. Moreover, when the governor, Sir Edmund Andros, impressed hundreds of men from Massachusetts towns to raise an army to fight the natives, this only increased suspicions, as it seemed that the governor was leaving
the towns defenseless just at the time they needed their young men most. As

summer turned to fall, many ordinary New Englanders came to believe the alarmist rhetoric of Andros's enemies, who claimed that the governor and his cronies were crypto-Catholics whose sympathies lay not with the Protestant colonists, but with the French enemy.

As soon as news of a possible revolution at home reached New England, colonists began to integrate their own troubles into the larger story. The first rumors probably came from discontented soldiers in Maine, who overheard and dutifully reported a number of odd comments and behaviors on the part of their officers. When two men suggested to the governor that he should hire the Mohawks—New England's fiercest Indian allies—to fight the Abenakis, Andros cryptically objected, saying "they may be [of use] to me another time." To the two men, this comment indicated that Andros intended to hire the Mohawks for a later assault on New England—a rumor soon confirmed by reports of two local Indians who had spoken with a Mohawk messenger. Soldiers who returned from the frontier brought these reports home to Massachusetts. William Sargeant told his Amesbury neighbors that "the great man," meaning the governor, "had hired the Indians to come downe on the English, to destroy them, & had given some Coats & some money."[29]

These reports soon became fodder for the governor's enemies. According to one official, "some Ill Spiritts" in New England persisted in "Scattering & publishing Seditious & Rebellious Libells." While the official did not relate the contents of these libels, he may have referred to the "paper" found by the side of the highway in Newbury by Joseph Bayley. While walking down the road in January 1689, Bayley discovered a handwritten tract in verse that warned New England to "rise and be armed" and "let not Papist you charme." The anonymous author claimed that the war against the Abenakis was merely a ruse to drain New England towns of their young men, leaving them vulnerable to an attack by "Indians french and papist[s]." Unfortunately no copy of the paper itself has survived, and its provenance and authorship remain unclear, but it points to an inclination among some New Englanders to interpret their troubles in light of a global Catholic conspiracy just like the one that had recently struck Barbados, as well as a communication network that sought to spread the alarm around the countryside by an interesting combination of print and word of mouth.[30]

Evidence from local Indians provided more specific revelations about the plot. In the town of Sudbury, for example, a Christian Indian named Solomon Thomas told some English neighbors that Governor Andros visited the praying Indians of Natick and told them of a plan for a Catholic and Indian force to overtake New England. If the English army proved victorious against the enemy Indians, the governor claimed, "in the spring french and Irish would Com to Boston" with a large number of Indians. After destroying the capital the popish army would continue to "the Countery townes." To remove any doubt of his motives, Andros gave the Indian "a booke that was better than the bible" that contained pictures of the Virgin Mary and the twelve apostles, and claimed that "all that would not turn to the governor['s] reledgon and owne that booke should be destroyed." According to this Indian informer, the governor was a confirmed Catholic, and his impending plan to invade New England reflected his religious goals. Another Indian in Sudbury claimed that Andros distributed gifts to Abenaki leaders as "commissions" to fight the colonists.[31]

Rumors of the governor's misconduct circulated beyond Massachusetts. In New York, which James II added to the Dominion of New England in 1688, Dutch and English inhabitants of Westchester County heard of a plan by Andros to invade Manhattan at the same time as the alleged expedition against Boston. A local sachem told a Dutch colonist named Barent Witt that the governor "did promise him a brib of twelf pounds to be ready with a Company of Indians so many as he could get at Manhatans Island in the month of April." In addition, Witt also spoke to some Frenchmen who passed though the region, who confirmed that "some ships were arrived" in Canada that would soon set out to conquer New York—again, a rumor almost identical to the one circulating in Barbados. When Witt brought his concerns to the leading landowner in the region, a prominent merchant and member of the Dominion's council named Frederick Philipse, the councilor laughed and said "it was foolish to be afraid," which led Witt and his neighbors to suspect Philipse as well. They also connected their anxieties with the sanguine imagery common to Protestant propaganda. Barent Witt's wife believed that "she would be the first which should be burnt in case the French should take the place," probably because she was a French Protestant. New York had a large Huguenot population, and these recent refugees from Louis XIV's regime feared that the Sun King would deal with them cruelly if he gained control of the colony. New Yorkers had shown little organized resistance to imperial reforms in the years immediately before 1689, but revelations of a popish plot caused some of them to develop new suspicions about their leaders.[32]

The rumors that circulated around the Northeast in early 1689 looked quite similar to those in the West Indies. In both cases, vague reports of political turmoil at home combined with specific fears of local officials and suspicious outsiders to cause popular panic. What was different, however, was the official reaction. First of all, Governor Andros and his deputies did all they could to suppress any rumors of the revolution in England. When Andraes Greveraet and George Brewerton arrived in New York with the "flying reporte" of William's landing at Torbay, Lieutenant Governor Francis Nicholson expressed dismay, "saying, hath he [William] not had an example of Monmouth," referring to the duke of Monmouth's unsuccessful invasion in 1685. He ordered the men to keep quiet and sent the report on to his superior in Boston. In the meantime, Governor Andros imprisoned a man who distributed Orangist publications and spread news of the prince's victory around Boston. Dominion authorities were merely being cautious; they had no official word that the crown had changed hands, and they remembered that premature reports of Monmouth's victory had flooded the colonies in 1685.[33]

In addition to suppressing news from Europe, Dominion leaders also dealt harshly with those who circulated rumors within the colony. When Newbury magistrate Caleb Moody told two justices of the peace about Joseph Bayley's "paper," they charged him with "publishing a Scandelous & Seditious Lybell" and threw him in jail. The justices immediately branded Caleb as a malcontent, probably because he was a brother to one of the Dominion's most bitter enemies, the Boston (and former Portsmouth) minister Joshua Moodey. They did the same to the Sudbury residents who told local officials about the Indian testimony against the governor. Watertown Justice William Bond asked the men "what mony wee gave the indian to tell us such nuse," while Boston judge Benjamin Bullivant complained that "a parsell of felows had devissed a parsell of lys and had fathered them on a pore Indean." New England authorities made a fatal mistake: they viewed the rumors as so patently ridiculous that they did not even answer them. They did not realize that idle talk of a Catholic conspiracy could motivate previously neutral colonists to join forces with local leaders who had long resented the increase of royal authority.[34]

By April Boston teetered on the brink of political chaos. According to one observer, the streets buzzed with "many foolish and nonsensicall storys, and pretended wonderfull discoveries of horrid Plotts against the Country." Many of the rumors concerned the Mohawk Indians, fierce allies who, according to some, "were to be brought down" to kill the inhabitants. In addition, some Bostonians whispered that "there were several Fire-works prepared in the Fort and Vaults dug under ground to blow up the Town," that the soldiers in Maine had been "poisoned with Rum," and that thirty French frigates lurked off the coast. These tales circulated widely around the populace, since "when any came to Town, some secretly told them the same things and others shook their heads and made ugly faces, whereby they concluded all to bee true, which was reported amongst them: So that it was but a sounding of a Trumpett or beating a Drum, and the Majority of the People was ready to rise against the Governour, who, as they were made to believe, was the great Enemy of the Country." The trumpet sounded on 18 April, when thousands of people descended on Boston, imprisoning the governor and other imperial officials and placing power in the hands of a coalition of local gentlemen. This bold act by the people of Massachusetts quickly unraveled over a decade's work by imperial officials who had hoped to remake New England.[35]

Officers of the Dominion of New England believed themselves to be victims of a well-planned coup. They charged that longtime opponents of royal government, made up of "the Preachers and their Adherents," had labored for months to spread lies about the governor and his party and inspire the "mobile" to rise up against him. The ringleader of the rebellion, according to Dominion Secretary Edward Randolph, was New England's agent in London, Increase Mather, who sent letters home to his county folk "in which he encouraged them to go cheerefully" into revolution. The ultimate goal, Randolph claimed, was to turn back imperial reforms and resume the old Massachusetts charter that had been vacated by English courts. Interested parties carefully disseminated stories of Catholic and Indian plots to influence ignorant commoners, since, as an English Tory writer noted, "the People are ductile, and easily drawn to any design, when they think Heaven is in the Plot, and God is one Party thereof."[36] Most historians have adopted this contemporary interpretation, fashioning Boston's rebellion as a "Protestant putsch" by self-interested elites. There is an element of truth to this, but it ignores the role of both ordinary New Englanders and inept officials in causing the crisis. The key cause of the rebellion was popular fear of an imminent Catholic plot, and local elites only capitalized on this fear by providing protection from the popish design that Andros and his underlings refused to acknowledge.[37]

The first signs of trouble had appeared on the northern coast of Maine several weeks before 18 April. In the middle of March Governor Andros, who had spent most of the winter searching for Indian enemies with his troops, heard urgent reports of political strife in Boston. He sailed back to the capital on 15 March, and in his absence morale among the troops reached new depths. Sometime before 12 April "Severall of the Souldiers" in John Floyd's Saco garrison "in a Mutinous manner Left & deserted their post & Station" and began "Marching towards Boston without the Officers Commands." Andros learned

of the desertion and ordered Floyd and other commanders to force the mutineers back into service. At the same time, the governor heard that Lieutenant John Puddington, the commander at Kennebunk, had "Quitted &
Discharged the Garrison & Souldiers" contrary to orders. A week before the
insurrection, Andros knew that at least a hundred angry mutineers had begun
to march toward the capital.[38]

The governor's leading opponents also received word of the troops heading for Boston. According to Samuel Mather, a son of Increase and brother
of Cotton, the "gentlemen" of Boston feared that deserting troops from the
"Eastern War" would "make a great Stir and produce a bloody Revolution,"
perhaps even killing the governor. The town's leading citizens met to consider such a possibility, and while they opposed revolt, they resolved that if
"the country people to the northward" descended on the city, "some of the
Gentlemen present would appear in the Head of what Action should be done;
and a Declaration was prepared accordingly." Thomas Danforth corroborated
Mather's account, claiming that the "ancient magistrates and elders" were
"compelled to assist with their presence and councells for the prevention of
bloodshed, which had most certainly been the issue if prudent counsells had
not been given to both parties." The elite rebellion, in other words, was one of
necessity rather than choice.[39]

Matters came to a head several days before 18 April. The carpenter of the
king's frigate in Boston Harbor, the *Rose*, deserted his post and joined the "rebels" in town, claiming that Captain John George and other officers had made
disparaging comments about William of Orange's victory in England. Some
of the crew prayed for King James, and one man even expressed hope "that it
would Raine hell, fire, & Brimstone upon the Prince of Orange, London, &
ovore all England for seven days." Captain George, meanwhile, pledged that
since "the King [James] was fled into france," the captain would "carry his
ship" there as well, supporting himself by raiding merchant vessels heading
for Boston. Additionally, according to Small, George and Andros conspired
to escape from Boston in a blaze of glory. The governor "intended to fire the
Towne at one end," while the *Rose* fired on the other, after which the officers
would "goe away in the smoake, designeing for France."[40]

The insurrection started early in the morning of 18 April. In the town's
North End, Samuel Prince "saw boys run along the streets with clubs in their
hands, encouraging one another to fight." Within minutes a crowd of more
than 1,000 people had gathered at the two ends of the town. They formed
themselves into militia companies and beat drums to call people to action.

Around ten o'clock the crowd seized Captain John George. When he asked by what authority they took him, the men "shewed their Swords, saying that was their Authority." The newly formed companies then confronted the few redcoats stationed at Boston's fort and castle, who despite orders refused to fire on the colonists. By two in the afternoon townspeople from around the province surrounded the fort. Witnesses estimated their numbers at twenty companies or over 5,000 men in arms. The throngs of angry colonists outnumbered the governor's troops many times over.[41]

The "strange and sudden appearance" of so many subjects in arms surprised Governor Andros. Around noon several men approached the fort and desired an audience with the governor. They handed him a printed declaration explaining why the people had risen against him and demanded that Andros surrender both himself and the keys to the town's fort, located in the South End, and the castle in Boston Harbor "in order to appease the People." The governor initially refused, but when he ventured to the town house to negotiate with members of the newly self-appointed "Council" they took him prisoner. Within a day the rebels obtained the surrender of both of Boston's fortifications, as their commanders recognized themselves to be hopelessly outnumbered. Miraculously, the revolution occurred without any reported casualties.[42]

The "seed of Sedition" quickly traveled from Boston to outlying parts of the far-flung Dominion of New England. Reports of Boston's revolution alarmed residents of Suffolk County on Long Island—an English Congregational stronghold that had always looked to Boston rather than New York as its exemplar. The "freeholders" of the county declared their readiness to defend their liberty and property "from the Intented invasion of a foraign French design" and reflected on "more than Turkish crueltyes" already acted by the French on English people in other parts of the world. In Westchester and Queens Counties as well as Suffolk, colonists turned out magistrates and officers who had served under the old Dominion government, believing that these officers were unable or unwilling to defend their communities from attack.[43]

Rebellious Long Islanders declared the colony's security to be their first concern. In the town of Jamaica in Queens County, for example, residents worried that the fort in New York City was not strong enough to endure a French invasion. On 15 May the town's militia marched toward the city, "exceedingly concerned and zealous for the safety of the Citty and fortt against any attack or invasion off the French." Nicholson believed that enemies of the government incited the crowd in order "to stirr up the Inhabitants of this City to sedition and Rebellion." Still, he recognized that he had to take action to quiet his subjects, and worked to strengthen New York's fortifications. While not willing to go as far as Stede in endorsing the uncertain revolution in England, New York's embattled leader had begun to understand the delicacy of his position.[44]

Nicholson and his associates had to act carefully. As officers in Edmund Andros's government, they deplored the illegal acts committed by "the rabble" in Boston. As time went by, however, no one dared make any public pronouncements against New England's revolution. In late May, for example, Nicholson requested that two local magistrates travel to Boston and demand the governor's release from custody. The two men respectfully declined. One New Jersey official worried that his absence "might throw the people in mutiny or rebellion," while a Long Islander claimed that his subjects "already shoocke off this governm[en]t" and if they considered him "a papist or a frind of them . . . the people in his towne would rise and plunder his house, if not offer violence to his family." Not only was it a risky political move to criticize Boston's rebellion; local magistrates feared for their lives.[45]

In the meantime, various rumors circulated around the province that fed popular fears. Some of the reports questioned Lieutenant Governor Nicholson's Protestantism. One colonist claimed to have seen Nicholson attend a Catholic mass in England, while another complained that he neglected to destroy the popish "Images" erected in the fort by his predecessor, Catholic governor Thomas Dongan. Other rumors indicated that French or Indian war parties approached the colony, and that "several Souldiers, of which there was a number of Papists," had escaped New England and now resided in New York's fort. The most potent rumor, according to an anti-revolutionary pamphlet, told of a "horrible design" to murder the city's inhabitants on the first Sunday in June "as they were worshipping of God in the Dutch Church within the Fort." While authorities tried to suppress these reports, New York Mayor Stephanus van Cortlandt claimed that the people were "so possest with jealousyes and feares of being sold, betrayed, and I know not what, that it was almost impossible to do anything that would please them." On 18 May "severall of the Inhabitants" of New York City presented a paper to the city council "containing severall jealousies and demonstrations of their disturbed minds." The council granted all but one of their unspecified requests, refusing only to force ex-governor Dongan to remove from his Long Island estate to a more visible residence in the city.[46]

Fear flowered into open rebellion on the last day of May. On that day a Dutch militia captain named Hendrick Cuyler approached Francis Nicholson and asked to place a sentinel at Sally Point. The contents of their conversation are murky, as Cuyler claimed not to speak English, but apparently Nicholson became angry at the request. He had been deluged with demands from subordinates and wanted to make his authority clear. According to witnesses, the lieutenant governor berated Cuyler and threatened to "Pistoll" another officer who accompanied him. In his anger, Nicholson made an unfortunate comment; he shouted that if the militia did not become more obedient, he would turn the fort's guns on New York and "set the town a fire." The comment played right into the hands of his nervous opponents, since many Protestants believed that Catholics had a penchant for arson.[47]

Nicholson's outburst traveled around the town. For the nervous militia men who already suspected foul play on the part of their leaders, this latest development proved that Nicholson was a "pretended protestant" who would not defend the town from the papists who threatened it. As a result, the local militia took action. According to van Cortlandt, the fort filled with burghers, "armed and inraged," who declared that they were "sold, betrayed and to be murdered, [and] it was time to look for themselves." Most of the militia commanders—including a German-born merchant and devout Calvinist named Jacob Leisler, who eventually became the movement's de facto leader—placed themselves at the head of the trained bands and demanded the keys of the fort from Nicholson. The council met and decided that they had no choice but to surrender "to prevent bloodshed." New York's only substantial military body had turned against its government.[48]

In New York, as in Massachusetts and Barbados, power devolved to those who acted most decisively against the popish threat. An incident on Staten Island revealed how fear helped to shape politics. Around the time of the rebellion, authorities heard reports that "the Papist" on Staten Island "did threaten to cut the inhabitants throats & that the People had left their Plantations & were running in the woods." The reports also claimed that the Catholic in question—a Mr. de la Prairie—stockpiled weapons at his house and that Thomas Dongan's brigantine sat off the coast "fitted out with a considerable quantity of Guns & amonitions." The papists awaited reinforcements from Boston to begin their design, which included burning the city of New York. The militia commander and Nicholson partisan Nicholas Bayard visited the island to investigate these reports, and found that the islanders "were afraid to Lay in their beds for fear of the Papists." Bayard belittled their fears, claiming that the island's Catholics were too few in number to threaten Protestants. After the rebellion, however, representatives of New York's new "Committee of Safety" returned to Staten Island. They took depositions recording Bayard's misconduct, and confiscated arms from one "known papist" on the island. These actions gave legitimacy to the new government by showing that they would provide protection against enemies of the community.[49]

By June the Dominion of New England, the great experiment in direct royal rule, had ceased to exist. All its ringleaders were either in jail or fled to England, chased out by a combination of elite opposition and popular rage. With the benefit of hindsight, it is easy to declare that the Dominion failed because it offended the colonists' republican sensibilities, yet on examination the crisis in New England and New York appeared remarkably similar to the one in Barbados. There too, a Stuart appointee ruled in an arbitrary fashion, making many enemies among the planter elite. There too, rumors of a popish plot caused panic in the countryside. But Edwyn Stede survived, while Edmund Andros ended up in prison. The difference between the two men was less in political ideology or methods than in rhetoric: Stede cast himself as a defender of Protestantism, while Andros would not. The easiest option would have been for Andros and Nicholson to turn against the region's Catholics. The former New York governor Thomas Dongan was an obvious choice, and there were several Catholics in inferior civil and military offices in the Dominion who could have played the role that Montgomery did in Barbados, taking the fall so that the rest of the government could keep functioning. Instead, by downplaying anti-Catholic fears, Andros and Nicholson lost control—a lesson future imperial governors would not forget.

•   •   •

A third major region in English America—the tobacco settlements on Chesapeake Bay—also experienced turmoil in 1689. If the West Indies represented one extreme and New England another, then the Chesapeake fell firmly in the middle. One of the region's administrations, in the royal colony of Virginia, managed to avoid trouble by responding to the panic much as Stede did in Barbados. The other one, in the proprietary colony of Maryland, refused to give credence to popular fears, and ended up falling to a rebellion very similar to those in Boston and New York. In some ways, the Maryland rebellion stands alone, as colonists there dismantled a proprietary regime rather than a royal colony, and Roman Catholics controlled the government. Nonetheless, the rumors that brought about the crisis looked quite similar to those in other colonies, as did the behavior of local officials.[50]

When word of a revolution at home began to circulate, Maryland's governors acted more suspiciously than their counterparts in neighboring colonies. Unlike Andros, Maryland Council President William Joseph actually was Catholic, like the absent proprietor, Lord Baltimore, and many other prominent men in the majority-Protestant colony. These Catholic officials suppressed news of William's victory in the colony and made several comments that indicated their support for James II. Jesuit priests publicly prayed for the success of the king's armies and spread rumors of James's victories over "the rebells as they tearmed the protestants." Besides suspecting that their Catholic overlords prayed for James's victory, Maryland Protestants leveled specific charges against their leaders, charging that Catholic officials contracted with Indians and the French to invade the colony and kill Protestants.[51]

The first step in this plot was to confiscate the colonists' arms. On 19 January 1689 Maryland officials ordered all subjects to deliver their weapons to the county sheriffs. The sheriffs then sent the arms to smiths to be "amended fixed and made ready and fitt for service" before being returned to colonists. Colonial leaders claimed that they only aimed to put the colony in a better posture of defense in case of a Dutch invasion, but many colonists believed their leaders had other motives. By depriving people of their arms, Maryland's leaders prepared the country for an Indian assault that would preserve the colony for King James.[52]

In March 1689 word spread around Charles County of a large force of Indians gathered at the head of the Patuxent River. This army, which some claimed to be larger than ten thousand men, allegedly consisted of Seneca Indians and local Nanticokes, aided by the French. For decades Marylanders had hated and feared the "Senecas," a label they assigned to any northern Indian, not just the westernmost tribe of the Iroquois Confederacy. Even though Virginia's governor had recently traveled to Albany and signed a treaty with the Iroquois, many colonists still believed the Indians had bad intentions. To make matters worse, they also began to suspect that their own leaders, especially the Catholic Lord Baltimore, commanded the Indian army that lurked on the colony's frontier. Rumors implicated three Maryland officials in the plot. According to a colonist named Matthew Tennison, proprietary official Henry Darnall—like Sir Thomas Montgomery, a recent convert to Catholicism—and two of his cohorts had approached some local Indians and hired them "to fight for My Lord [Baltimore] against the Protestants." Baltimore's administration had always maintained good relations with local natives, making it easy, his opponents believed, to enlist them in the popish army.[53]

These reports probably originated across the Potomac River in Stafford County, Virginia. In the middle of March residents of that county began to hear "some discourse that was talked by the Indians." The county court ordered Burr Harrison to examine the Indians in question, who related that Henry Darnall had contracted with Seneca Indians to "kill the protestants." They had to act quickly, Darnall claimed, so that their bloody work would be complete before word of William's victory arrived from England, at which time "the protestants would kill all the papists and then all the Indians." Harrison and his partner—a local clergyman named John Waugh—spread this Indian report around the region, not only to neighboring Rappahannock County but to Maryland as well. As colonists learned of the popish plot against them, they scrambled to arms and declared their support for William and Mary, opposing any magistrates who did not act to ensure public safety.[54]

Ordinary people placed authority in the hands of local leaders who would provide for local defense. In Charles and Calvert counties colonists "Assembled in Armes" under a militia officer named Henry Jowles, who informed officials in St. Mary's of the widespread rumor "That the Catholicks and Indians have plotted together to disturb [and] cutt off all the protestants in the province." The people felt that their leaders had the duty to protect them from enemies, and they believed that the confiscation of their arms by the central government undermined their ability to defend themselves. Jowles demanded that the governor "returne the Armes with powder and bulletts sufficient for the defence of the Countrey," and warned that "until you doe that," the people "will hold themselves betrayed by your hon[o]r to the Comon Enemy." Moreover, Marylanders proved all too willing to look across colonial boundaries for assistance. When Darnall arrived in Charles County, he found that "the people" were "sending for the Virginians to come to their assistance." Relations between Maryland and Virginia had never been tranquil, but the "common enemy" inspired residents of both places to fashion an alliance.[55]

Officials in both colonies reacted to the panic in a very different way from their counterparts in the Dominion of New England. Instead of believing the rumors to be attacks from political rivals, they saw class motives at work. According to William Joseph and his deputies, certain "ill minded persons" of "the meanest quality" spread the rumors "to affright then confuse and then to pillage and plunder the people Especially such as had anything to loose." Virginia secretary Nicholas Spencer, the caretaker of a government whose executive had recently sailed for England, agreed, claiming that the rebels targeted their economic betters, "good men who had any estate." These attacks had little to do with politics, Spencer claimed, since "to have an Estate [was] a Crime sufficient to have laid a man open to popular Rage, w[hi]ch would not be assuaged but by satiating their appetites with plunder." While these statements reflected the class biases held by leading planters in the Chesapeake and elsewhere, they indicated that leaders in Maryland and Virginia understood the power of rumor in a way that northern officials never did. They recognized that the opposition to their administration was a popular front, rather than a small interest group.[56]

Maryland officials attempted to provide public assurances that the rumors were not true. After learning of the panic, Joseph sent two of his deputies, William Digges and Henry Darnall, to investigate the alarms. In the company of Henry Jowles and another militia officer, Ninian Beale, they ranged the woods of Charles County and confirmed that no army of Senecas threatened the colony. They also collected depositions establishing the innocence of the proprietary officials accused of being parties in the plot. Darnall convinced Jowles and others to sign a declaration that the conspiracy was "groundless and imaginary" and had been "fomented by the Artifice of some ill minded persons." In the most critical concession to popular opinion, Joseph ordered that confiscated weapons be returned to the counties. These actions seemed to calm people's fears.[57]

Virginia officials reacted in a similar fashion. They worked to discredit the plot, finding the Indian who disseminated the rumors and convincing him to recant his story. They also ordered the three men who spread the reports to appear before the General Court, which prohibited John Waugh from preaching "Publickly or Privately," since he "Stirs up the People in Stafford to Sedition by his Sermons." Besides punishing these malcontents, officials also investigated the reports. They searched the home of Stafford County's most prominent Catholic, George Brent, whom they confined at the house of a local magistrate. This public investigation showed the people that Brent had not hoarded weapons on his plantations and probably saved him from being plundered by a local mob, "For the Stafford men were wholly intent to kill robb and burne what Capt Brent had." According to Nicholas Spencer, by the end of March "the fears and Jealousies of the people" in Stafford County had "much abated."[58]

Virginia authorities took a final step to assuage popular fears. On 27 April, the colony became the first to declare publicly that William and Mary were the rightful monarchs of the English empire. As Secretary Spencer explained to royal officials, "the difficulties of maintaining order would have remained insuperable" without proclaiming the new monarchs, since many people be-lieved "that there being no King in England, there was no Government here." Maryland authorities refused to follow suit, even though the colony's inhab-itants were "rageingly earnest for proclaimeing their present Majesties." In Spencer's view, the reluctance of his neighbors to proclaim William and Mary risked a popular revolt that could "unhinge the whole Constitution of that Government And dissolve the whole forme of it." The secretary's prediction proved to be prescient. Of the four mainland colonies that experienced panics in the spring of 1689, only Virginia weathered the crisis.[59]

From March to July proprietary officials in Maryland maintained a pre-carious hold on their troubled province, allaying the fears of its frightened inhabitants by employing "a company of men[,] all Protestants, to range in the woods to make all discoveries they would be capable of." Nonetheless, Maryland's Protestants were unhappy that their leaders still refused to pro-claim William and Mary. In mid-July reports surfaced of another Catholic plot against the colony, and popular fervor finally became more than propri-etary officials could handle. The new alarms resembled previous ones that had struck the colony. A group of armed men gathered in Charles County on the Potomac River, motivated by reports "that the Papists had invited the North-ern Indians to come down and cutt off the Protestants and that their descent was to be about the latter end of August." The leaders of the armed men were longtime opponents of Lord Baltimore, including Nehemiah Blackiston, the Calvert County militia captain Henry Jowles, and his lieutenant Ninian Beale. The central figure in the brewing insurrection, meanwhile, was also a familiar name in Maryland politics: the longtime malcontent John Coode.[60]

Coode bore a striking resemblance to revolutionary leaders in other parts of North America. Like Jacob Leisler, for example, he combined religious zeal with military acumen. Ordained as a minister in the Church of England, Coode lacked the orthodox Calvinist beliefs that defined his counterparts to the north, but he displayed a paranoid hatred of popery that rivaled anyone on the continent. Also like Leisler, he was a militia commander, and became politically active in order to save the colony from impending attack. Oppo-nents of the rebel leaders in Maryland and New York described the two men in nearly identical terms. One of Baltimore's allies referred to Coode as "our Masinella"—referring to Tomaso Aniello, or Masaniello, the fishmonger who led a popular insurrection in Naples in 1649 and epitomized the dangerous consequences of allowing common people to rise to positions of leadership.[61]

In late July Coode's "mob" set out from Charles County toward the

provincial capital at St. Mary's. The force intended to seize the colony's records—probably to search for evidence of popish plotting—and place local
government in the hands of the militia. Baltimore's men showed no inclination to surrender to such a motley rabble. Henry Darnall and Nicholas Sewall
tried to raise a party of men to meet the rebels, but while many militia officers
joined their ranks, "their men were possessed with the belief that Cood rose
only to preserve the Country from the Indians and Papists and to proclaim the
King and Queen." Since they thought the rebels would "do them noe harm,"
most men refused to march against them. The underlings of one militia officer, Richard Smith, told him that "they were willing to march with him upon
any other occasion, but not to fight for the papists against themselves." When
the rebels reached the state house, most of the men who defended it were
"not willing to fight." The lieutenant governor and his partisans retreated to
Lord Baltimore's estate at Mattapany while the rebels occupied the capital. By
convincing their neighbors that the ensuing political conflict was a religious
matter, Coode and his allies neutralized their opposition.[62]

Baltimore's men hoped they could wait out the storm in the security of
their lord's country estate. But once again, they underestimated the amount
of rage that ordinary people possessed against a colonial government they believed to be conspiring against them. Coode's troops surrounded Mattapany
House, and grew in size as reinforcements arrived from throughout the colony.
According to Henry Darnall, the rebels circulated more rumors in order to set
the people against the proprietor. While the militia camped out at Mattapany,
for example, the ringleaders allegedly "caused a man to come riding Post with
a Letter wherein was contained that our neighbour Indians had cut up their
Corn and were gone from their Towns, and that there was an Englishman
found with his belly ript open." Within days, Darnall and his men realized
they had "no hope left of quieting or repelling the People thus enraged," and
they surrendered to Coode and the rebels on 1 August. The terms allowed all
armed men in the garrison to return home, but pledged that "noe papist in
this Province" occupy "any Office Military or Civil." In a matter of days, the
people of Maryland turned from power many of the men who had determined
colonial policy since its founding.[63]

The circumstances in the Chesapeake could not be directly compared to
the other regions of English America, since the rebellion dismantled a proprietary colony run by actual Roman Catholics. It would have been difficult if not
impossible for Catholic officials to stay in power in 1689 without renouncing
their faith, and they did not have the option of diverting popular rage toward

inferior officers. At the same time, however, the parallels are striking. The similarities in the composition of the rumors points both to a common world view shared by Protestants around the empire and a subterranean communication network that must have spread details of the plots by word of mouth from Barbados to New England to the Virginia frontier.

One final piece of evidence gives a sense of the depth of these intercolonial communication networks. Among the items sent to Whitehall as evidence against Sir Thomas Montgomery, Stede included a letter to the Barbadian official from a Capuchin monk in Virginia named Alexander Plunkett. The short letter, written in February 1689, claimed that Montgomery's "endeavours for the propagation of the Holy Catholick Religion has spread itself farr & neare & extended itself to those parts of Virginia where now I am." The comment is tantalizing in that it gives a glimpse of a vast network of rumor and correspondence that is all but invisible to historians. Perhaps Plunkett heard from other Catholics, traveling through Virginia in disguise, that an official in far off Barbados was doing good service for the church. Or maybe he overheard some of his Protestant neighbors speaking about a diabolical plot against the empire, one that implicated a minor officer in a colony hundreds of miles away. Either way, it demonstrates that the colonial peripheries were not aloof from the political and religious intrigues that convulsed Europe in the last years of the seventeenth century. [64]

Chapter 4

The Empire Turned Upside Down

IN THE WAKE of the rebellions of 1689, people from London to Boston debated the structure and meaning of the English empire in America. Not surprisingly, the colonists who had overthrown the Dominion of New England represented their action, like the larger Revolution in England, as a moderate, conservative, and consensual event. The people who took to the streets in Boston, New York, and Maryland were not firebrands but good English patriots, preserving the plantations for their rightful monarchs William and Mary against the tyrannical agents of the deposed James II. The former agents of the Stuart empire quite naturally saw matters differently. In the words of some of Jacob Leisler's opponents in New York, the revolutionaries sought "to Turn all upside Downe," to utterly subvert the old empire and build something new in its place. Whatever James II's sins had been—and no one sought to defend him in the political atmosphere of 1689—his imperial reforms had been necessary and beneficial, and proved even more so with the renewed threat of a war with the French and Indians. The rebels of 1689, in the view of their enemies, were opportunistic fanatics who took advantage of the chaos at home to throw off all authority and regulation, and aimed to set up "a Republick Government." The result would be the utter ruin of the empire and the English interest in America.[1]

In a sense the critics of the Revolution were right. The pretense of moderation aside, the rebels of 1689 did turn the empire upside down. They deposed many of the people who had been running the colonies for years—in New York, for example, the anglicizing Dutch merchants who had controlled the scene since the English conquest found themselves suddenly and dramatically out of favor, while Maryland's Catholic leaders were legally barred from government. But more than that, the revolutionaries consciously set out to construct polities very different from the Restoration colonies that Stuart officials had laboriously built over the past decade. The political thought that justified the revolts drew, in pragmatic fashion, from a number of traditions—from the Whiggish rhetoric of "English liberties" then in vogue with the country party; from the traditions of Calvinist resistance theory, honed in the Protestant struggles against papists in Germany, France, and the Netherlands, which valorized the role of inferior magistrates in resisting tyrannical monarchs and preserving the true church; and, especially in New York, from the Orangist rhetoric of municipal autonomy combined with strong military leadership. More than philosophy, however, the revolutionaries claimed that their brand of empire was a practical necessity, the only way to turn back the popish plot and save Protestant America. By giving power to local administrative bodies—committees of safety, in the parlance of the time—the new English monarchs could be sure that these territories would, like the semi-independent provinces of the Dutch Republic or the Protestant cantons of Switzerland, do their part for the common cause. The people of New England and New York, and to a lesser extent Maryland as well, sought very consciously to build a Reformed Protestant empire.[2]

While the critics of the revolution were correct about the movement's radicalism, they did not recognize the cosmopolitan, global nature of the Protestant vision of empire. In an effort to discredit their rivals and paint them as opponents of the English interest, the Stuart apologists presented their enemies, especially in New England, as isolationist reactionaries who wished to return to a pristine past before the imperial reforms of the 1680s. In fact, nothing could be further from the truth. The radical Protestants who took control of the old Dominion of New England were, if anything, better connected to the wider world than their opponents. They understood America as a partner in a global Protestant movement, now led by the new monarchs William and Mary, that sought first to hold off French advances on the continent, and second to advance true religion, whether by rooting out those with popish leanings within the colonies, or expanding the reach of the empire itself. At the same time, they rejected centralization—a popish idea, after all—and promoted local control within a loose confederation as the best way to further the cause. In this debate, the revolutionaries frequently made use of a word that had appeared often in the political debates of Restoration England, and would become even more ubiquitous in American political discourse: liberty. While they did not use the exact phrase, the architects of this prospective colonial system sought an "empire of liberty"—a confederation of likeminded people joined together for the greater good, but retaining their liberties, property, and especially the right to maintain the true Protestant religion in the face of its enemies.[3]

The Protestant empire, as we will see, was a dismal failure. But at the same time, much of the language and ideology of the Protestant revolution of 1689 became dominant even after the particular programs of the revolutionaries went down in flames—even influencing those on the opposite side of the political spectrum. When Thomas Jefferson proposed building an "empire of liberty" in the early nineteenth century, he advocated a similar vision of expansion and empire, though shorn of its obvious theological content. The Protestant vision of empire, therefore, continued to motivate colonial Americans even as the urgency of the struggle against popery diminished in the eighteenth century.[4]

• • •

Soon after the Dominion of New England went down to defeat, the region's new leaders set about rewriting history. The complicated events of the past half-decade needed to be placed in a simply storyline, one that vindicated the colonists' rebellions and defended against the charges of disloyalty and rebellion that Andros and Edward Randolph were sure to bring against them. Accordingly, colonists painted the defunct Dominion of New England—a government that had aroused relatively little opposition during most of its short life—as the worst of popish, arbitrary governments, and as a plank in the global plot by papists and their abettors to extinguish true religion and replace it with "popery and slavery." This propaganda campaign was so successful that it has continued to influence opinions of the Dominion up to the present: still, most accounts of the period from 1686 to 1689 depend on the retrospective accounts penned by people defending themselves against legitimate charges of treason and rebellion.

At the same time, the accounts of the Dominion produced after the revolution served a different, somewhat more lofty purpose. Like English accounts of Louis XIV's government, or chronicles of the "oriental tyranny" of the Great Turk, these visions of the popish, arbitrary dominion functioned as a mirror of sorts, a vision of the exact opposite of what an imperial government should look like. Thus it is useful to spend some time drawing this picture of the evil empire, since it allows us to begin to construct its binary: the good, Protestant empire that colonists hoped to build in its place.[5]

New England propagandists began their task by placing the Dominion

THE
Declaration,

Of the *Gentlemen, Merchants,* and *Inhabitants* of *BOSTON,* and the Countrey Adjacent.   *April 18th.* 1 6 8 9.

§ I. WEE have seen more than a decad of years rolled away, since the *English* World had the Discovery of an horrid *Popish Plot*; wherein the bloody *Devotoes* of *Rome* had in their Design and Prospect no less than the extinction of the *Protestant Religion*: which mighty Work they called *the utter subduing of a Pestilent Heresie*: wherein (they said) there never were such hopes of Success since the Death of Queen *Mary* as now in our dayes. And we were of all Men the most inexcusable, if we should apprehend a Countrey so remarkable for the true Profession and pure Exercise of the Protestant Religion as *New England* is, wholly unconcerned in the Infandous Plot; to crush and break a Countrey so intirely and signally made up of *Reform'd Churches*, and at length to involve it in the miseries of an utter Extirpation: must needs carry even a Super erogation of merit with it, among such as were into it cated with a Bigotry inspired into them by the great *Scarlet Whore*.

§ II. To get us within the reach of the desolation desired for us, it was no improper thing that we should first have our *Charter* Vacated and the hedge which kept us from the wild Beasts of the field effectually broken down. The accomplishment of this was hastned by the unwearied solicitations and slanderous accusations of a man for his *Malice* and *Falshood* well known unto us all.

Our *Charter* was with a most injurious pretence (& scarce that) of Law, Condemned before it was possible for us to appear at *Westminster* in the legal defence of it; and without a fair leave to answer for our selves concerning the crimes falsly laid to our charge, we were put under a *President* and *Councill*, without any liberty for an Assembly which the other *American Plantations* have, by a Commission from his *Majesty*.

§ III. The Commission was as *Illegal* for the forme of it, as the way of obtaining it was *Malicious* and *unreasonable*: yet we made no resistance thereunto as wee could easily have done; but chose to give all *Man-kind* a demonstration of our being a people sufficiently dutifull and loyall to our King: and this with yet more Satisfaction because wee took pains to make our selves believe as much as ever we could of the Whedle then offer'd unto us; That his *Majestys* desire was no other then the happy encrease & advance of these *Provinces* by their more immediate dependance on the *Crown of England*. And we were convinced of it by the courses immediately taken to damp and spoyl our *trade*; whereof decayes and complaints presently filled all the Countrey; while in the mean time neither the Honour nor the Treasure of the King was at all advanced by this new Model of our Affairs, but a considerable Charge added unto the Crown.

§ IV. In little more than half a Year we saw this Commission superseded by another, yet more Absolute and Arbitrary, with which Sr. *Edmond Andross* arrived as our Governour; who besides his Power, with the Advice and Consent of his Council, to make Laws and raise Taxes as he pleased; had also Authority by himself to Muster and Imploy all Persons residing in the Territory as occasion shall serve; and to transfer such Forces to any English Plantation in *America*, as occasion shall require. And several Companies of *Red Coats* were now brought from *Europe*, to support what was to be Imposed upon us, not without repeated Menaces that some hundreds more were intended for us.

§ V. The Government was no sooner in these Hands, but care was taken to load Preferments principally upon such Men as were strangers to, and haters of the People: and every ones Observation hath noted, what Qualifications recommended a Man to publick Offices and Employments, only here and there a *good man* was used, where others could not easily be had.

Figure 5. The Massachusetts declaration of 18 April 1689 provided official justifications for the overthrow of Sir Edmund Andros and the Dominion of New England. *The Declaration of the Gentlemen, Merchants, and Inhabitants of Boston, and the Country Adjacent* (Boston, 1689).

of New England in historical context. The beginnings of the struggle that climaxed on 18 April 1689 lay about a decade earlier, when "the *English* World had the Discovery of an horrid *Popish Plot*; wherein the bloody *Devotoes* of *Rome* had in their Design and Prospect no less than the Extinction of the *Protestant Religion*." The reference, of course, was to the fictional "Popish Plot" revealed by Titus Oates in 1678, the panic that had inspired the campaign to exclude James Stuart from the throne and ultimately led to the official reaction against dissent that resulted, among other things, in the coming of royal government to New England. It was natural that the papists would seek to extend their plot to New England, the declaration asserted, because the region was "so remarkable for the true Profession and pure Exercise of the Protestant Religion." The authors thus integrated America into the global battle against popery even as they celebrated New England's piety. The controversy there was not a simple struggle between imperial overlords and local elites, but a version of the same battle occurring in Protestant places from Ireland to Bohemia.[6]

In many of these places, the popish plot went along with a campaign to establish an "arbitrary government." Whig poet and politician Andrew Marvell made one of the most famous connections between these two concepts in a 1677 book, which claimed the existence of a design "to change the lawfull Government of England into an absolute Tyranny, and to convert the established Protestant Religion into downright Popery." In the eyes of Marvell and other writers, popery and arbitrary government were a natural fit. First of all, the pope ran his church in an arbitrary way, making it logical that papists would attempt the same in civil government. The pope "can change the very nature of things, making what is Just to be Unjust, and what is Vice to be Virtue"—an apt description of the arbitrary monarch who ran roughshod over the laws and liberties of his kingdom. Propagandist Henry Care illustrated the link: "that Principle which Introduces *Implicite Faith and blind Obedience in Religion*," he wrote, "will also Introduce *Implicite Faith and blind Obedience in Government*, so that it shall be no more the *Law* in the one than in the other, but the will and power of the Superior that shall be the *Rule and Bond* of our Subjection." Care's observation underscored the instrumental relationship between popery and tyranny. Monarchs who aspired to absolute government recognized that popery was a good tool toward ensuring the blind loyalty of their subjects, since the random decrees and impositions of the church made people poor and servile. Simultaneously, arbitrary government allowed the further expansion of popery, as monarchs could change the faith of their kingdom by fiat. The "ancient Landmarks" of the English constitution, after all, existed primarily for "the preservation of our religion." With these laws and institutions destroyed by an overreaching monarch, the door would be open for that same king, usually under the spell of Jesuit councils, to simply decree the reestablishment of popery. The people, poisoned by the errors of popery and beggared by taxes and impositions, would be powerless to resist.[7]

The surest way to set up an arbitrary government was to shackle local authorities, especially the corporations that controlled so much of day-to-day governance in England. Virtually every arbitrary ruler began by curbing these local "liberties," and America was no exception. Just as Charles II, inspired by "evil counselors" under the "French Interest," had revoked dozens of borough charters in England during the 1680s, so too did he threaten colonists' liberties by vacating their charters. The Massachusetts patent, declared the rebels on 18 April, had been "the hedge which had kept us from the wild Beasts of the field." Once it was gone, the door was open to other innovations, the end of which was "to destroy the Fundamentals of the English and to Erect a French Government." In this reading the charter—and all similar documents that defined relations between king and people—stood as a counterpart to Magna Carta, described by Benjamin Harris as "the *Corner-Stone* of all our *English* Freedoms." With the charter gone, the king and his representatives had nothing to prevent them from taking subjects' property and even their lives. In New England, they set about doing this by eliminating the colonial assembly, meaning that the governor and council had the power to seize people's goods without their consent.[8]

After dispensing with the charter, the next step in the quest to erect an arbitrary government was to infiltrate the courts. In Henry Care's estimation, the right to judgment by a jury of one's peers was, next to the right of representation in Parliament, the bedrock of English liberty. It ensured that the king or his favorites could not arbitrarily dispose of subjects' liberties and properties. During the 1680s Whigs perceived a concerted design by their opponents to hijack the legal system. The villains of this design were royal favorites, under the influence of foreign, popish powers, who bought off judges, packed juries, or used technicalities to gain convictions even in the face of little evidence. New Englanders found plenty of signs that Sir Edmund Andros and his creatures had acted similarly in their jurisdiction. The trial of Charlestown minister Charles Morton was a case in point. In 1686 Morton, headmaster of a famous dissenting academy at Newington Green, near London, came to New England, partly because the new charter of the Dominion of New England guaranteed a degree of liberty of conscience that was impossible in England after Monmouth's Rebellion made dissent a byword for treason. When Morton preached that "persecution . . . was come amongst us and settled amongst us," and called for the restoration of the "rulers of Jerusalem," he found himself under arrest for preaching sedition. In an action reminiscent of the measures used against many of Morton's friends and allies in England, Andros moved the trial from Middlesex County, where the alleged crime occurred, to Suffolk County, where he could pick a reliable jury made up of his underlings and allies—many of them "meer Strangers in the Country, and no Freeholders." Protestants interpreted this rejection of the rule of law was as a central characteristic of both popery and arbitrary government, which depended on the will of an infallible master rather than due process.[9]

Beyond the manipulation of the legal system, Protestant propagandists argued, popery and arbitrary government depended on brute force. A hardy, freedom-loving people like the English would never surrender their liberties and property on their own, so papists and their adherents did not shy away from using violence to advance their designs. This was the rationale behind establishing a standing army—a professional class of soldiers in the king's constant employment—and disbanding or shackling the citizen militias that theoretically kept England safe from its enemies. While Charles II and James II's standing armies inspired howls of protest, the worst example of military excess was across the channel in France, where Louis XIV used his *dragonnades* to enforce the Revocation of the Edict of Nantes. Stories of the military's excesses—some true, many embellished—traveled around the Protestant world, even to New England, so that when Andros arrived in Boston with 100 redcoats, Increase Mather claimed the king had sent "some French Dragoons amongst them to *Teach them Succoths Lesson* by the *Briars and Thornes of the Wilderness.*" In truth the soldiers and their officers—even the few Roman Catholic officers among them—did little to inspire much complaint, short of their harsh treatment of impressed soldiers in the eastern campaign, but they were definitely outliers in the Congregational town: "A crew that began to teach New-England to Drab, Drink, Blaspheme, Curse, and Damm." Moreover, they were a sign of things to come; especially after word of James II's flight to France reached the colonies, many feared that more troops—this time actual French dragoons and vicious Irish Catholics—were on their way, ready to carry out the same bloodshed as had occurred in Ireland and France in previous decades.[10]

Finally, all these political and military innovations would allow the papists to accomplish what had always been their goal: reestablishing the Roman Church. By the time of the Revolution, many New Englanders and New Yorkers confidently argued that this was Andros's goal, even though he purported to be a Protestant. Indeed, it was often High Church Anglicans rather than actual Catholics who did the most to promote popery, a fact noted by the Presbyterian Roger Morrice in his many diatribes against "hierarchist" enemies. Henry Care warned against "those that *play the Protestants in Design, and are indeed disguised Papists*, ready to pull off their mask on the first opportunity, whenever times serves." These imposters could be identified by their advocacy of the popish successor and their ill treatment of Protestant dissenters. In this light, Andros's promotion of the Church of England, and especially his seizure of Boston's Third Congregational Church for Anglican services, looked like tyrannical measures leading toward popery. In one pamphlet, Increase Mather even claimed that Andros defended his conduct by pointing to the example of contemporary France, urging New Englanders to "*Consider what Effects the Stifness of the Protestants in France had,* who would not *Yield in what they might have done* (note that well) *and now there is not the name of a Protestant in France.*" The episode was almost certainly contrived, but its propaganda value was clear: Andros had brought the arbitrary government of Louis XIV to America, complete with *dragonnades* and the seizure of places of worship.[11]

The common theme in this portrait of the evil empire was that of centralization, the expansion of a tyrannical authority that swept away all dissenters and imposed uniformity in both state and church. This authority was coordinated in the hands of "*Priest,* and *Prince,*" who "may, like *Castor* and *Pollux,* be worshipt together as Divine in the same temple by Us poor Lay-subjects." In this genealogy of evil, however, the priest easily outdid the prince—even James II's most determined foes preferred to blame evil counselors, especially Jesuits, for his worst excesses; and pamphlet literature about Louis XIV did the same, often portraying the king as a good man led astray by bad counsel. The centralization of the state, whether in England or America, was thus a plan foisted by agents of the church on unknowing kings. This interpretation allowed Whig theorists to seem slightly less treasonous, but it also emphasized the extent to which the good empire, like the good state, would be not a republic but a limited monarchy, in which the guarantees of "English liberties" ensured that the king got advice from the right people.[12]

As this brief exposition has demonstrated, many post facto depictions of the Dominion of New England adopted the Whig political rhetoric opponents of the Stuart kings used to challenge their pretensions. This is not surprising, considering both the close connections between Puritanism and country thought, and the integration of the colonies into international Protestant networks. When it came to proposing remedies, however, the Protestant imperial vision differed in important respects from the Whig attempts to remake the English state after 1689. Colonists claimed that they enjoyed the rights of Englishmen, but they did not view their own relationship to the king to be the same as, for example, that of an English province. Instead, they used the language of composite monarchy to describe their ideal relationship with the center, understanding that New England, like Scotland or Ireland, had particular qualities the monarch had to respect. Moreover, they described the empire fundamentally as a defensive coalition attached not just to England, but more broadly to the global Protestant interest. Just as King William promoted himself as a Protestant hero, his new subjects reimagined his empire as a global force to defend true religion against popery.[13]

The Protestant empire drew on precedents that stretched back to the dawn of the Reformation. As early as the 1520s, Protestants in Switzerland attempted to form a "Christian Civic Union," led by local magistrates, to defend and spread the faith among Catholic neighbors. The Lutheran Schmalkaldic League, while led by princes rather than magistrates, echoed this plan in Germany during the 1540s. While late seventeenth-century thinkers knew of these earlier precedents, they were more influenced by two more recent unions: the United Provinces of the Netherlands, which had successfully vanquished the Spanish Habsburgs and become the vanguard of the Protestant interest; and the "Solemn League and Covenant" that bound Scots and English together in a common cause to defend true religion in the 1640s. In each case, local magistrates decided that they could no longer obey the commands of a monarch who had shirked his pledge to defend local rights and, more important, who acted against God by supporting the Catholic Church and persecuting Protestants. As one Scottish minister noted of James II, "the King is expressly limited and qualified thus, *In the preservation and defence of the True Religion, Liberties, and Laws of the Kingdom.*" Any king who acted against his own people was no longer properly king, and it was the duty of lesser magistrates to resist him.[14]

There was no time that called for Protestant unity more than the late 1680s, when the forces of popery appeared ascendant from the British Isles to France to Hungary and Bohemia. "Disunion and Division hath proved our ruine," wrote the influential Huguenot theologian Pierre Jurieu, "it is a re-union and conjunction alone that can save us." Boston's Cotton Mather, filling his absent father's role as political broker, adapted these theories to the colonies in a thanksgiving sermon he preached in December 1689. After a lengthy description of the providential events of 1688–89, Mather placed New England in global context, contrasting its recent salvation to the hardships still faced by Protestants in other parts of the world. America had escaped the popish plot for now, but just barely, and its people needed to do their part for the larger cause. This meant that Protestants had to stop their internecine quarreling; the minister hoped for "*War* with none but *Hell* and *Rome.*" In addition, each component part of the new Protestant coalition had to act offensively against neighboring papists—in New England's case the French and their Indian allies—and open their doors to Protestant refugees. Mather urged his auditors to act with a "public spirit," so that "a *New England man*, may be a Term of Honour in the world."[15]

The new polity that Mather outlined depended on the active involvement of ordinary citizens—especially magistrates and militia officers. The only way to defeat the plot, in this vision, was to remain vigilant about any attempts by superiors to impose an arbitrary government, and to keep the community safe from outside attack. Two examples from the Dominion era illustrated the virtues of active citizenship. First, there was the Rev. John Wise and his fellow selectmen in Ipswich, punished by Andros for refusing to appoint a tax collector in 1686. This relatively minor dispute became a cause célèbre after the revolution; one official's unfortunate outburst that "you have no more priviledges left you, than not to be sold for Slaves" confirmed the Dominion's absolutist proclivities. At the same time, Wise's active citizenship stood as a model; only if ministers and magistrates stood up for their "liberties" could they defeat their enemies' tyrannical designs.[16]

The second example was more obscure, but no less important. In the summer of 1688, alarmed by Indian attacks and rumors of French involvement, many Massachusetts towns fortified themselves. Edmund Andros and Edward Randolph passed through one such town, Marlborough, on the way from New York back to Boston. While there, Randolph had a telling argument with one of the town's militia officers. Annoyed that the town had come to arms without orders from the governor, Randolph asked what would happen if the sentries shot and killed a suspicious Indian. "We would be in our way," the officer said, implying that local people, in the form of the militia, had the authority and indeed the responsibility to defend the community from hostile outsiders. "You would be in the way to be hanged," Randolph countered, worried that the foolish actions of paranoid officers could embroil the whole region in an unnecessary Indian war. The role of militias was one of the central disputes driving the revolution in the colonies—in each colony that rebelled, militia leaders played critical roles in both the planning of the rebellions and the conception of the new empire. The issue was defense— New Englanders like John Wise and the Marlborough officers defended local autonomy not on philosophical but on practical grounds. With the central government infiltrated by enemies, local people had to act to save themselves and defend the Protestant interest.[17]

The Protestant imperial vision also depended on the defense of property rights. In this, colonial writers closely approximated the Whig position, famously articulated by John Locke, that those who cultivated and improved

the land had a natural right to it. In a colonial context, this debate had somewhat different implications, both because the availability of land led to more
landowners, and because the king claimed a more direct right of possession
than in the Old World. The best statement of the colonial position came from
the Reverend John Higginson of Salem, who testified to an argument he had
with Andros in 1687. The governor asked Higginson "*Whether all the Lands in*
New-England *were not the Kings?*" Higginson replied that the land belonged
to the inhabitants, both because they had "subdued and replenished" it, and
because they had purchased it from "the Indians, who were Native Inhabitants." The minister added a religious gloss to the argument, denouncing Andros's position as a "Popish Principle, that Christians have a right to the Lands
of Heathen," which was "disowned by all Protestants." While this defense of
property rights was not novel, it cast ordinary property-holders as the vanguard of empire. It was these people, after all, whose labor and "*Vast Charges*"
had "*conquered a Wilderness*" and expanded the king's influence. To restrict
these rights to property was not only unjust but foolish, as "what Englishman
in their right Wits will venture their Lives over the Seas to enlarge the Kings
Dominions, and to enrich and greaten the English Nation, if all the reward
they shall have for their cost and adventures shall be their being deprived of
English Liberties, and in the same condition with the *Slaves* in *France* or in
Turky!" And as everyone knew, most kings proved quite unwilling to spend
their own treasure conquering foreign lands.[18]

Colonial writers articulated a new political vision for the continent, one
that privileged local magistrates, militia officers, and individual landowners.
It was explicitly not, however, a rejection of empire as such. Indeed, the writers of the most detailed justification of the revolution underscored that New
England was indeed part of the king's empire, rather than part of the king's
"dominions," as one of Andros's allies claimed. The semantic difference was
critical: the king possessed sovereignty in his empire, and its people owed him
their allegiance, but the very word implied diversity. Scotland was also part of
the king's empire—subjects in that kingdom honored the king just as much
as the English, but their exact relationship to him was modified by contract
and local custom. The king's dominions constituted his real property—lands
in which he could decree whatever he desired. Wales and perhaps Ireland, as
conquered territories, were closest to this ideal. New England's agent in London, Increase Mather, reinforced this definition when he promised that King
William "might easily be Emperour of America" as long as he granted a new,
liberal charter to the region. The people would be so grateful to the king that

they would freely devote their lives and resources to expanding the monarch's power and influence.[19]

If this vision limited the king's authority, it was not antimonarchical in any meaningful sense. Even during the reigns of Charles II and James II most colonials refrained from criticizing the kings themselves, preferring to blame their counselors, but after William and Mary's accession the colonies erupted in a spasm of love for the new monarchs. Rebels in all three colonies defined themselves as staunch Williamites—and not only out of practical necessity. For over a decade the Dutch stadholder had promoted himself as the chief defender of the Protestant interest against Louis XIV and popery, and his combination of qualities made him attractive to many segments of the colonial population. Committed Calvinists, whether English, Dutch, or French, perceived William as a coreligionist who would defend their cause. A correspondent of the Plymouth minister John Cotton described the new king as "a real godly man (a rare thing upon that throne)" who had been "a seeker of God since he was 8 years old," and therefore a natural enemy to "the Devil & pope & Jacobites." Dutch settlers in New York, familiar with the historic role of the House of Orange in battling popery, were even more enthusiastic. Officials of New York's Dutch church noted that love of the new monarch was "natural to the Dutch nation," since "his forefathers had liberated our ancestors from the Spanish yoke and his royal highness had now come again to deliver the Kingdom of England from Popery and Tyranny." Colonists came together behind the monarch, but it was a curious kind of monarchism, based on the king's status as a Protestant hero who, unlike his predecessor, pledged to keep his subjects safe from papists.[20]

In its broad contours, the political thought of the American revolutionaries of 1689 fit comfortably into a Whiggish narrative stretching back at least to the 1620s and forward to 1776. Reacting against the centralizing tendencies of the Stuart kings, these American Whigs adapted a version of English "country ideology" to their own purposes. At the same time, the Protestant revolutionaries differed from their eighteenth-century descendents in a number of ways. First, most revolutionaries viewed this philosophy as a means to an end; they favored a decentralized government not out of a natural love of liberty, but because they believed it would best defend the country against the timeless and diabolical popish plot. Second, there was another strand to the revolutionaries' thought that rarely appeared in their printed tracts, but lurked just beneath the surface: apocalypticism. Many of the leaders of the rebellions—divines like Cotton and Increase Mather and secular leaders such as Jacob

Leisler—believed that the tumultuous events of the late 1600s predicted the return of Christ to earth. The coming apocalypse had political implications that helped to define the Protestant empire.[21]

Most radical Protestants believed that the reconstruction of the invisible church was impossible in a sinful world. Thus the Reverend Samuel Lee, a leading English Congregationalist who preached in Plymouth Colony during the late 1680s, ridiculed the Roman Church for its claims to universality, and cautioned Protestants against attempting to imitate Christ's church on earth. "The true Church hath an admirable union," Lee preached, "one Lord, one faith, one baptism, *Jerusalem* is a Citty compact together, and at unity within herself." This true church would not be attainable, however, until Christ returned, when the enemies of Christ would fall and his followers come together in perfect unity.[22]

In the heady days of the late 1600s, some Protestants began to apply this ecclesiastical theory to the world of secular politics. One of the first was John Eliot, minister in Roxbury and "apostle to the Indians," who laid out his millennial political vision in a 1663 letter to Presbyterian leader Richard Baxter. Eliot proposed "to advance the Kingdom of Jesus Christ, which shall be extended over all the Kingdoms and Nations of the Earth . . . Not by the personal Presence of Christ, but by putting Power and Rule into the Hands of the Godly, [and] Learned in all Nations." Eliot was too infirm to take part in the excitement surrounding the revolution, but Cotton Mather echoed and expanded upon these sentiments. Mather wondered in 1689 "Whether the Day is not at Hand, when the *Kingdoms of the World, shall be the Kingdoms of our Lord, and of his Christ*," and speculated that the godly monarch now on the "British Throne" might lead the charge to defeat Antichrist, in the form of "the Tyrannous and Treacherous *Grand Seigniour of France*," and bring about a new age of peace and unity.[23]

Mather's friend Samuel Sewall went even farther in illustrating the millennial empire. In a series of letters and in a 1697 book, Sewall made a case for America's critical role in the last days. Noting that Christianity was nearly extinct in Africa and Asia and "choaked with Thorns of worldly Hypocritical Interests" in Europe, Sewall wondered if "possibly this place that was lately none at all; and is still last of all, may in time, be made the first." Sewall based his speculation on a number of scriptural passages that predicted the discovery of America and its integration into the Christian world, most notably the tenth chapter of Revelation, in which an angel—identified as Christ by Sewall—set his "right foot upon the sea," signifying the New World, "and his left foot on the earth," signifying the Old. This proved, in Sewall's opinion, that Christ's empire on earth would be a transatlantic one, and he advocated a number of policies to ensure that this came about. In addition to promoting mission work among the Indians, Sewall also cast his eye toward Latin America and especially Mexico, where the Spanish had "planted Antichristianisme in the room of Heathenisme." He understood New England as a godly beachhead in a land once controlled by Satan, and hoped "that Christ will be so far from quitting what He hath already got in *New England*; that He will sooner enlarge His Dominion, by bringing on a glorious Reformation in *New Spain*; and so making the New World deserve the significant Name of *Columbina*." To bring this about, Sewall supported such ventures as New Englanders planting new towns in South Carolina, nearer to the Spanish, as well as the Scottish efforts to set up a colony in Central America (Darien) in 1700. With Christ's help, Sewall hoped that the Protestant empire would soon stretch from Canada to Mexico and beyond.[24]

The Protestant vision of empire, therefore, was a combination of the practical and the prophetic. Its strength rested on the assertion that a decentralized empire, anchored by local magistrates and militias under the sovereignty of a distant monarch, could best subvert the plot and keep the colonies safe. At the same time, many of its leaders had loftier plans for the new union, viewing it as a tool to construct Christ's empire on earth, a glorious coalition that would defeat Antichrist in America as well as Europe. As might be expected, this tension led to problems as colonists tried to build new polities in the wake of the revolution. The Protestant cause depended on unity in the face of the popish threat, but the conspiratorial outlook of many radical Protestants made this unity elusive. At the same time, millennial expectations added urgency to the cause that did not necessarily result in clear thinking.

• • •

In the last half of 1689 the new leaders of New England, New York, and Maryland attempted to reimagine imperial politics in their respective regions. They did so in different ways and with little coordination, and as a result the polities took on different forms. Magistrates in Massachusetts and Connecticut resumed old arguments about the nature of sovereignty in their provinces; Marylanders excluded Catholics and prepared for a royal government; and New Yorkers under Jacob Leisler attempted North America's most radical experiment in Calvinist state-building. Despite their differences, however, these three regions all adhered to larger patterns. Each of them built consciously on English, Dutch, and Huguenot revolutionary thought as they defined their relationship to the center; each one considered defense against Catholics as the state's primary mission; and finally, leaders across the continent realized that they needed to band together to be effective. This meant both closer ties with England and, perhaps most important, closer ties with each other.

The task of building a new empire began shortly after the fall of the Dominion of New England on 18 April 1689. The group of elite New Englanders who had placed themselves at the head of the popular rebellion needed to form a government, and fast, to keep the country from slipping into chaos or falling prey to invaders. They did so by creating a "Committee of Safety" made up of dissident members of Andros's council, former magistrates under the charter government, and prominent merchants. The last charter governor, eighty-seven-year-old Simon Bradstreet, presided over the committee; Wait Winthrop commanded the militia. The balancing of factions on the committee allowed defenders to argue that the people had been "unanimous" in their opposition to Andros, but the committee's name also beckoned back to a more radical heritage. The original Committee of Safety, after all, had been formed by Parliament in 1641 to coordinate military efforts against Charles I, and the concept remained controversial for many English. A few years earlier, Bermuda governor Richard Coney had charged rebellious subjects with forming such a committee of safety—an act he clearly did not approve of.[25]

The main task of the committee, as its name implied, was to keep the country safe. Its existence implied a state of war, in which normal rules of state did not apply, and as a result the militia took on a prominent role. While the revolutionaries cloaked their message in the rhetoric of moderation, they had essentially engineered a military coup: the former rulers, they claimed, were "Enimyes to the protestant religion, & to the Libertyes of the English Nation," and removing them was the only way to ensure safety. But even with Andros and his minions behind bars, the plot lived on, and to assuage the armed companies that occupied Boston, the country's new leaders had to do something about it.[26]

Tensions in the ruling coalition appeared from the very beginning. The first major conflict between the people and their leaders concerned the governor's imprisonment. While they distrusted Andros and probably believed many of the stories circulating about him, members of the committee treated the governor "with all the Respect that could be due unto his Character." After his imprisonment, they confined him in the house of one of his political allies, merchant John Usher. For the country people who had streamed into Boston over the past day, this action proved insufficient. According to one witness, armed men from surrounding towns came "in such rage and heat, that it made us all tremble to think what would follow." They demanded that Andros "be bound in chains and cords, and put in a more secure place, and that they would see [it] done ere they went away, or else they would tear down the house where he was to the ground." In the first of several concessions to the mob, the committee obeyed, sending Andros to the fort, where he endured conditions that few seventeenth-century gentlemen experienced.[27]

A similar controversy surrounded the treatment of Joseph Dudley, the foremost local defender of royal authority. When the rebellion occurred Dudley was out on his judicial circuit in Rhode Island, but agents of the revolutionary government quickly apprehended him. Unlike the other prisoners, however, Dudley was a native, and though "the object of the peoples displeasure," the past and future governor had great influence in both old and New England. This clout won Dudley an early release from custody, but when he returned home to Roxbury in mid-July he found an angry mob surrounding his house. He escaped to a friend's home, but the mob followed him there, breaking the house's windows and demanding Dudley's surrender. As one of his neighbors reported, "the Rabble arose and Brought him like a dog to Gaole againe, In spite of the Governor and Council." Bradstreet wrote Dudley a regretful letter asking him to remain in jail until "the fury of the people be more allayed." In the view of Edward Randolph, the incident demonstrated "the inability of the Government to defend their own act and the power [that] the Rabble do upon all such suddaine Emergencyes exercise."[28]

In the months after the rebellion, the Committee of Safety spent more time investigating the contours of the plot than actually governing. They collected numerous depositions detailing the sins of Andros and his allies, and confiscated the papers of the "evil counsellor" Edward Randolph. Officials also took down the sails of the royal frigate *Rose*, to prevent it from deserting to the French. In the midst of all this panic and innuendo, both rulers and ordinary people had to deal with the question of governance. Everyone knew that the Committee of Safety was temporary, and New Englanders divided over the next proper step.[29]

Perhaps the most dramatic confrontation occurred in Connecticut, where traditional hierarchies collapsed under the strain of popular fear and uncertainty. When Connecticut's leaders received copies of Boston's declaration, they first acted to prepare the militia to meet any possible invasion. Like their counterparts elsewhere, colonial authorities did not take measures to change the structure of government, waiting for orders from England. For members of the "popular party"—the faction that had defended the Connecticut charter against the expansion of the Dominion—this inaction was not acceptable. The popular leader James Fitch called for a new election on 9 May, soon after he heard "the late news from Boston," hoping that in the excitement following the revolt voters would decide to resume government under the old charter. Several prominent gentlemen worried about the people's resolution, fearing that frightened colonists would elect "narrow Spirrited men" who would use their new authority to persecute anyone who was not of "the Congregational way." The colony avoided such a scenario because Fitch's proposal for a new election of representatives never materialized, but the freemen did vote to "re-establish the Government as it was before and at the time when Sr Edmond Androsse tooke the Government."[30]

Competing parties in Massachusetts also feuded over the settlement of a new government. Like their counterparts in Connecticut, many people desired to return to their old patent, but the colony's new leaders resisted following this path. After all, the king's court had vacated the charter, and probably would look askance on a colony claiming authority to overturn court decisions in England. Additionally, some members of the coalition that took power on 18 April—especially Anglican merchants like John Nelson—never liked the old charter, since the old system gave voting rights only to members of Congregational churches. The new council trod carefully as it considered a course of action. Afraid to contradict the will of the freemen of 66 towns who requested a resumption of charter government, the council declared that all officers serving in 1686—the last year of the old charter—would be reinstated. They carefully added that they "do not intend an Assumption of Charter Government," but only endeavored to settle affairs until further orders arrived from England. This decision resulted in an immediate withdrawal of merchants from the ruling coalition, but it did little to assuage the people. While colonists had been nearly unanimous inclination in their dislike of Andros, they disagreed about what to do in his absence.[31]

The fall of the Dominion led to a similar political reckoning in the colony of New York. The rebellion there had begun, like the one in Massachusetts, as an uprising by the local militia, who seized control of the fort but initially did not interfere with the civil government. When Lieutenant Governor Francis Nicholson left, the colony militia officers formed their own Committee of Safety. The political circumstances in New York were very different from those in Massachusetts. For one thing, the colony had no lost charter rights to regain, and the majority Dutch population brought very different political assumptions to the table. Nonetheless, the debate in New York came down to many of the same issues as the one in New England, centering on local privileges and ways of maintaining security in a time of war.[32]

The central figure in New York's revolution, and perhaps the most committed Protestant leader in America, was merchant and militia captain Jacob Leisler. The son of Frankfurt's French Reformed minister, Leisler was a member of the religious faction known in the Netherlands as Voetians—extreme Calvinists who called for orthodoxy and resisted any "popish" innovations in Reformed churches. Leisler had acted as an advocate for Calvinist orthodoxy in New York in the past, but he became even more radical after Louis XIV revoked the Edict of Nantes, that had guaranteed toleration for France's Protestants. Leisler used his clout as a merchant to buy land for Huguenot refugees at New Rochelle, and while he remained a member of New York's city council, he became a fierce opponent of Catholic officeholders in the colony. A few days before the rebellion he refused to pay customs duties on a shipment of wine because the collector, Matthew Plowman, was Catholic. While not an original ringleader of the rebellion, Leisler quickly emerged as its principal spokesperson, primarily due to his vociferous anti-Catholic rhetoric.[33]

Leisler believed that "Combinations of the Forces of hell itselfe" threatened New York's Protestants. On 3 June, while Leisler occupied the rotating captaincy of the city's trained bands, an alarm circulated that a French fleet was approaching the city. In response, Leisler mobilized the militia and started a campaign against papists and members of their party. Leisler dismissed the customs commissioner Plowman, since he was "a Papist and the people [were] much incensed against him." He also turned his attention to former governor Thomas Dongan, placing him under house arrest, seizing his old commission from James II, and eventually chasing him out of the colony, since the people suspected Dongan of gathering arms at his estate. Meanwhile, signs of the plot continued to be manifest in New York. In late June Leisler reported a "miraculous deliverance" from a fire that threatened to consume the Dutch church at the fort and perhaps the rest of the city as well. The deed was "suspected to be done by one Papist who had been there before;" only the fortuitous presence of a black slave prevented him from carrying out his "hellish designe."[34]

In response to these plots Leisler essentially declared martial law. According to one critic, the Committee of Safety searched every vessel that arrived in the port and confiscated news and mail, "some whereof were open'd, and publickly read amongst the People." By performing such searches of suspected parties, Leisler rendered the plot transparent, and satisfied the angry crowds who demanded that their rulers protect the community from Catholics. This campaign against local papists quickly moved beyond the colony's small Catholic population. The captain charged that anyone who questioned New York's revolution was "Popishly affected." Leisler considered ex-Dominion officials John Palmer and John West papists because they briefly sent their sons to a Jesuit school in the city. Captain George Mackenzie, meanwhile, had once called the local Jesuit, Father Smith, a "very good man." Anglican minister Alexander Innes commented that Jesuit priests in Canada "ware good people" and "the Catholicks Romish Religion was the best and true Religion." Dutch ministers Henry Selyns, Rudolph Varick, and Godfrey Dellius were "popish trumpets" because they "Preach[ed] up the damn'd Doctrins of Passive Obedience and Non Resistance." Local magistrates like van Cortlandt and Bayard showed their popish leanings by refusing to declare the new monarchs William and Mary. In Leisler's binary vision of the world, any person who held a commission under the Catholic King James could not be a good Protestant. He filled the colony's prisons with many of the people, English and Dutch, who had stood at the center of colonial government for the previous two decades.[35]

Leisler's enemies denounced his regime as an "arbitrary government" that ran roughshod over the liberties of his enemies. In truth, however, Leisler was not a simple tyrant. As several historians have noted, he operated within a Dutch Orangist political tradition that stressed rigid Calvinist orthodoxy, the autonomy of local corporations, and the central role of the militia under a single commander—the Dutch stadholder. Like English Whig ideology, Dutch Orangist thought originated in Calvinist resistance theory and the sixteenth-century struggles against Spanish papists. Moreover, the exile of leading English, Scottish, and French thinkers in the Netherlands during the 1680s allowed for ample cross-fertilization between these various intellectual traditions. In the port city of Rotterdam—a place with close connections to both Boston and New York—such diverse thinkers as Pierre Bayle, Pierre Jurieu, and John Locke rubbed shoulders in the months before the revolution, and the town's printing presses turned out a large number of Orangist and Williamite tracts, many of which ended up in America.[36]

This Whig-Orangist political philosophy found its purest expression in Leisler's contest against the convention of Albany. When news of revolution arrived in the fur trading village, its merchant leaders acted cautiously. Mayor

Peter Schuyler proved reluctant to distribute Boston's declaration of 18 April, fearing that the town's inhabitants would "run mad" when they heard the news. At the urging of a visiting officer from Connecticut, Schuyler eventually shared the report with other leading gentlemen in the town, who acted quickly to disarm the town's Catholics, but controversy remained. As Leisler and his party consolidated power, Albany's rulers—led by Schuyler and Scottish merchant Robert Livingston—refused to submit, leading to a political contest that very nearly turned violent.[37]

The key confrontation occurred in November 1689. Leisler sent one of his deputies, Jacob Milborne, to Albany to force the convention to acknowledge his authority. An English merchant from a family of radical Protestants, Milborne had spent the past several years in Rotterdam, where he had advocated on behalf of the Orangist cause. His father-in-law had been one of the key incendiaries in New York's rebellion, while his brother William—the same one who had caused trouble in Bermuda a few years earlier—played a major though somewhat shadowy role in Boston's uprising. Milborne had known Leisler for years, and on returning to New York in the summer of 1689 quickly became one of his leading confidantes. In October Albany's leaders heard rumors that Leisler intended "to send up armed men to overthrow the government of this Citty," and "turn the government of this Citty upside doune." The rumors turned out to be true; on 9 November Milborne and his retinue marched into Albany in the name of William of Orange, "to Redeem them from Arbitrary Power, and to free them from the Yoke of Popery."[38]

Milborne and his foes conducted a delicate political debate that combined tropes from Dutch and English political culture. On one hand, the leaders of Albany claimed that their local corporation had privileges that could not be abridged by outsiders—a position that resonated in the Netherlands, where municipalities held extensive powers, and also drew on the recent resistance to Stuart centralization in both Britain and America. Milborne effectively turned this rhetoric against Albany's leaders by presenting himself not as an outside agitator, but as a liberator. The town's current leaders were illegitimate, Milborne claimed, because they held power under a commission granted by the popish and tyrannical James II. Since James was gone, the charter no longer stood, and "now the Power was in the People to choose both new Civill and Military officers as they pleased." While Albany's leaders defended themselves with the rhetoric of local liberties, Milborne went a step farther, claiming that his rivals were illegitimate rulers and "the People," vaguely defined, held the real power. He went so far as to invite leading Leislerians from the neighboring villages of Kinderhook and Schenectady—places excluded from the fur trade by Albany's officially sanctioned monopoly—to come to Albany "to Receive Priviledges and Libertyes." As in New England, the debate centered on the legitimacy of officers appointed by the deposed king and the right of the people to hold elections without instruction from Whitehall. Leisler and his allies went beyond their neighbors to the north, however, in both the tone of their rhetoric and their tendency to use force against rivals. In this particular drama, Milborne came up short. Mohawk warriors, watching from outside the town gates, threatened to fire on the New Yorkers if they did not leave. Not willing to alienate the colony's most steadfast native allies, Milborne did as instructed, and the tension between Albany and New York City continued to rise.[39]

The situation in Maryland—the last colony to forcibly remove its governor, in 1689—appeared at first glance to be much more moderate than that in the former Dominion of New England. Rebel leaders there requested a royal government and the establishment of the Church of England, and the "Associators' Convention" that took charge in the wake of the rebellion included moderate Anglicans as well as a smattering of radicals. Even with a significant Roman Catholic minority, the colony's new leaders managed to rule without violence, and they never filled the prisons to the extent that Leisler did. Nonetheless, there was a latent radicalism in Maryland's revolution, and it drew from many of the same political traditions. Even the name of the colony's caretaker government—the Protestant Association—drew from radical Whig thought. The first Association had been founded in Elizabethan times as a pact between leading gentlemen who pledged to take over the government should papists kill the queen. Whigs resurrected the idea in the 1680s, leading to charges of sedition from royalist opponents, and in the wake of William's invasion his English supporters founded an "Orange Association" to promote the prince's cause.[40]

Like the Committees of Safety in Massachusetts and New York, the Association represented a tactical alliance of local power brokers who had long resented Lord Baltimore's government and ordinary colonists who believed the proprietor had sold them out to the French and Indians. Their published declaration showcased both views. On the one hand, it detailed decades of misconduct on the part of the proprietor, who had usurped the role of the monarch by exercising "absolute authority" over his subjects, levying unreasonable taxes, and limiting the rights of the colonial assembly. Beyond these constitutional complaints, however, the rebels objected to the religious objectives of Baltimore and his allies, who were "Papists . . . Guided by the Counsels and Instigations of the Jesuits." Baltimore's men had reserved the best offices and best land for Roman Catholics, placed Protestant orphans in Catholic families, and protected a notorious Catholic murderer. Like the people of New England, Marylanders tried to endure hardship, but had to take action when they learned of "the Practices and Machinations that are on foot to betray us to the French, Northern, and other Indians, of which some have been dealt withal, and others Invited to Assist in our Destruction." Only the threat of invasion pushed colonists to act for their own self-preservation.[41]

Maryland's new leaders attempted to take the revolution into the localities. They called for each county to elect representatives for a new assembly, a move that proved as controversial as similar measures in Connecticut and Massachusetts. One county, Anne Arundel, refused to hold elections, preferring to await clearer orders from England. Critics alleged that almost none of the people who called for elections were "men of Estates or men of note," but rather "the most contemptible and the most factious." As in New York and New England, opponents of the revolution dared not speak in public. In a letter to Baltimore, Peter Sayer complained that no one had courage to challenge the "damn'd falsities" contained in the revolutionary declaration; one official warned "that if any body should contradict anything, in that humour the people were in, they should have all their brains knockt out."[42]

Once in power the Associators took steps to ensure that local papists could no longer threaten the colony's safety. The new assembly appointed a "committee of secrecy" which predictably concluded "that the late popish Governors have contrived, conspired and designed by villanous practises and machinations to betraye their Majestie's Protestants Subjects of this Province to the French, Northern, and other Indians" and that the people of Maryland remained in "eminent danger of our lives libertyes and estates." According to Peter Sayer, the committee's report led to a full-blown campaign of persecution. The Associators "fixed upon the State house Doore a prohibition that no Papist should come into the citty dureing the Assembly," and they continued to investigate rumors that certain Catholics held unlawful meetings with Indians. Within months Catholic lawyers could no longer practice in Maryland courts, and the province's Jesuit priests kept low profiles as they attempted "to render what consolation they can to the distressed Catholics." The disfranchisement of Catholics satisfied both elite Protestants and common people in Maryland by opening up offices to Protestants and removing the popish councilors who had allegedly conspired against their own people.[43]

Aside from seeing to internal affairs, Maryland's caretaker government took the lead in building an intercolonial coalition against the popish plot. In a letter to Jacob Leisler, John Coode declared that the deposed governors of the three colonies had formed "a Caball & held a great correspondency ag[ain]st the Protestant Interest" in America. Moreover, even in the wake of the revolution the "great design" lived on. Coode complained that Maryland papists took refuge in Virginia, where uncooperative magistrates refused to arrest them, while Leisler countered that "papist grandees" resided in Philadelphia, and that the Quaker inhabitants of that city pledged to send their powder to the French if a war broke out. This conspiracy called for a coordinated response, and Coode and Leisler each pledged to keep the other informed of popish intrigues.[44]

Leisler also turned his attention beyond the North American mainland. In particular, he maintained an active correspondence with Edwyn Stede, the Barbados lieutenant governor who led his own, simultaneous campaign against papists and the French in the islands. Unfortunately none of Stede's letters to Leisler survive, but Leisler seems to have been well informed of events in the Caribbean, including the French sack of St. Christopher. Leisler in turn told Stede about the mainland rebellions, and also sought to forge an alliance against the popish threat. In particular, Leisler reported on two Irishmen in New York who had come from Martinique where they allegedly passed intelligence to the French. Leisler sent them back to Barbados, but the men escaped and fled south, where John Coode questioned them "upon suspicon, being Strangers, Irishmen, and papists," before they absconded again, one as far as North Carolina. With such malcontents freely ranging around the colonies, coordination among the region's leaders appeared all the more critical.[45]

• • •

Advocates of a centralized empire in North America viewed the revolution as a major setback for the imperial cause. One disgruntled merchant declared in the wake of the rebellions, "Now Each Tub stands upon his owne Bottome," meaning that "each Colony or Governm[en]t" looked out for its own affairs without considering the welfare of the mother country or its empire. Another colonist complained that "Every man [is] a Governour," while a Rhode Islander asserted that "wee are heare in Great confution & without any Goverm[en]t." In some cases, these opponents of the Protestant rebellions advanced their own constitutional vision, one in which the king's power in the plantations was nearly absolute. In the opinion of John Palmer, a former

Dominion official who wrote the most strident denunciation of Boston's revolution, colonies were conquered territories, and colonists did not enjoy the same privileges and liberties as subjects in England or Scotland.[46]

Opposition was not limited to outsiders and royal officials. The most strident critic was Connecticut physician, former minister, and member of an old New England family Gershom Bulkeley, who believed the revolution had opened up Pandora's box. The people of New England had no authority to rise up against their rulers and demand the resumption of old charters, Bulkeley claimed, because they based their actions on incomplete information received from England, and "Rumours are but a sandy foundation to ground such assertions, or to change & build Government upon." Additionally, Bulkeley saw dangerous principles behind the rebellion; he argued that certain ringleaders intended "to promote an Oliverian republic" and demonstrated "A levelling, independent, democratical principle and spirit, with a tang of the fifth-monarchy, which is a very churlish drug." While he did not defend Andros's regime, Bulkeley claimed the aftermath of the rebellion was far worse, because the new regime had no sanction from the king; "now all is arbitrary," he wrote, "and we have nothing but Will and Doom."[47]

Bulkeley and likeminded colonial and imperial leaders also decried the popular use of antipopery to justify the revolution. He complained that all people who questioned the conduct of the revolution were "most opprobriously defamed" as "papists, wicked incendiaries, disturbers of the peace" just for advocating the preservation of order. Radical Protestants used charges of popery to defame their opponents not because they believed them, but because they worked; as the Virginian William Fitzhugh observed, being branded "a Papist . . . is enough to set the Rabble to do a mischief to the Person so Taxt." Anglicans in New England also claimed persecution; Boston's Church of England minister alleged that "Our Church is perpetually abused," the windows broken and smeared with excrement, due to "the Rage and Fury of the People." Edward Randolph blamed Congregational ministers, whose sermons against Common Prayer worship caused the people to "account us popish & treat us accordingly." Bulkeley tried to turn this anti-Catholic ideology back against the revolutionaries, raising the possibility that "some Jesuit . . . foisted in this Project [the revolution] . . . as the most probable way to ruin us at this time; for it is the trade of that Diabolical sort of men by their plausible crafty Counsells, to make protestants destroy themselves, by stirring up, and fomenting divisions among them."[48]

Bulkeley's attention to the dangers of division revealed a key position of those who opposed the revolution. While revolutionary leaders claimed that a decentralized, Protestant union could best defeat the papists, Bulkeley and Palmer thought otherwise. Indeed, the fall of the Dominion of New England made the colonies far more vulnerable to attack, they claimed, because it replaced a streamlined, effective royal government with a chaotic coalition of zealots who were overly influenced by the "giddy multitude." The Dominion had been founded, after all, as a bulwark against the French, and now that it was gone, there was nothing preventing the enemy from accomplishing its design. According to Edward Randolph, Massachusetts leaders had no interest in helping their more exposed neighbors, and self-interested Boston merchants even sold arms to Indian enemies. Meanwhile New York mayor Stephanus van Cortlandt expressed fear that "if an Ennemy should come wee are in a bad condition having no head to command us, every one being Captain."[49]

Leaders in the hamlet of Albany—the English town with the closest ties to New France—added a new twist to the argument. This division and confusion within the English ranks, they claimed, would cause the crown's Iroquois Indian allies to desert to the French, leading to an inevitable French victory. Albany's leaders understood that the Covenant Chain alliance, which provided more protection against French attack than anything else, could be jeopardized if the natives came to believe that the English were much weaker than the French, and nothing displayed weakness and indecision like an altercation between two distinct factions on the steps of the town hall. In addition, the Albany Convention—as the town's leaders called themselves—crafted a self-serving argument that in order to maintain the alliance, they needed to stay in power. The Iroquois knew and trusted Mayor Peter Schuyler and his deputy Robert Livingston, while Leisler and Milborne were unknown to them.[50]

Revolutionary leaders in New England, New York, and Maryland understood their precarious position. To consolidate their political gains they needed to do what Andros and his cohort could not: keep the region safe from Indian and French enemies. And while colonial leaders suffered from a frustrating dearth of European news during the summer of 1689, they assumed that the revolution in England would likely lead to a new war with France. As a result, the region's leaders worked to shore up defenses, by both reinforcing fortifications and negotiating with local Indians. In fact, the Indian policy of the Massachusetts Committee of Safety did not differ in its fundamentals from that of the hated Edmund Andros. The committee sent an envoy to negotiate with the Abenaki—the same Indians who had caused such panic among New Englanders the previous summer—and even proposed reimbursing the baron of Saint-Castin for the goods Andros had seized from him in 1688. Officials in New York acted similarly, rushing out to negotiate with the very Indians that they believed to be plotting against them. In general, these negotiations failed: by August the Abenaki had already attacked several towns in New Hampshire and Maine, even seizing the English fort at Pemaquid, and panicked inhabitants of Albany threatened to desert the town.[51]

The escalation of conflict in the east led New Englanders to forge closer ties to the Iroquois. One of the most potent rumors in the spring of 1689 concerned a "Mohawk plot"—the belief that the most powerful and war-like Indian nation, the westernmost of the five Iroquois nations, had turned against the English and was preparing to descend on the Protestant colonies. Rumors of a different sort circulated through Indian country, that the English intended to kill all the Indians, who had better band together and save themselves by striking first. The English blamed these rumors on crafty Jesuits, and in the summer of 1689 several prominent New Englanders traveled to Albany to make sure that the Mohawks remained faithful to their old allies.[52]

The envoys' speeches to the Indians laid out their political vision more directly than any other document. First, the delegation—led by Springfield patriarch John Pynchon—explained how "the late King James, being a Papist and a great friend of the French," had been replaced by "professed enemies to the French interest." With "the Quarrell now Depending Between Protestants and Papists," King William had "united the English and Dutch to be as one" and "resolved to ruin the French King." Since the Iroquois were longtime enemies of the French, the English urged them to join William and Mary's potent coalition and ignore the stratagems of the Jesuits. "So long as the French king and the Jesuits have the command at Canada," Pynchon claimed, "you can never live at peace." The English expected at any moment to receive official word of a war between England and France, at which time they "shall not be wanting to doe our uttmost for the Rooteing out and Extirpation of your and our Enemies at Canada."[53]

These speeches painted a clear picture of global politics in the wake of the revolutions in Europe and America. William and Mary now stood at the head of a glorious Protestant cause, a grand coalition that targeted the popish, tyrannical designs of Louis XIV. American Protestants defined themselves as partners in the cause, and realized that they had a specific mission: to save America for England and Protestantism by vanquishing the French in Canada. Neighbors like the Iroquois—while not technically Protestants—had common interests and therefore had to be integrated into the struggle, just as

William himself brought the Austrians, Spanish, and other Catholics into the League of Augsburg. Colonial leaders hoped to build a new kind of Protestant American empire, one that allowed each province to rule itself, but bound them together in a common cause. In order to make it work, however, they had to make good on their boastings, and actually confront the French.

PART III

Empire Regained

Chapter 5

The Protestant Assault on French America

In July 1693 a large flotilla of English naval vessels, led by Sir Francis Wheler, limped into the port of Boston. Months earlier, Wheler had sailed from England to Barbados with 3,000 men and a mandate to destroy French America. His assault on the French Antilles had foundered, however, and along the way the fleet met a more formidable adversary than the French: disease. Hundreds of men died in a plague so virulent that Wheler worried whether anyone would be left to man the ships. When they arrived in Boston, the next stop on the tour, he predicted that the locals "will fly into the Country from us, as if wee were Turks" when they saw how sick the sailors were. In fact, his prediction was not far off. New Englanders were unhappy to house a crew of sick, disorderly seamen, but their complaints were a bit different from those lodged against the last Redcoats in Boston who had accompanied Sir Edmund Andros. People were not upset that the troops were there; they were angry that they had fought so badly. Probably no one was more disappointed than Massachusetts governor Sir William Phips, who had made the conquest of French Canada a main ambition. The governor knew, however, when the sickly sailors arrived in Boston far too late in the season to plan an effective assault on Canada, that their design would fail, and he recommended that they head home to England instead. The conquest would have to wait.[1]

Wheler's disastrous expedition marked the end of a four-year English campaign to eliminate the French presence in America. Just after the revolution and rebellions of 1689, the French and their allies—Indians, Irish servants, and on some occasions African slaves—began to attack colonial communities in both the West Indies and the mainland. While the attacks often reflected local histories of conflict, combatants on both sides connected them with global events. English leaders understood that they fought for King William and the Protestant cause, as well as for the expansion of the English empire, while the

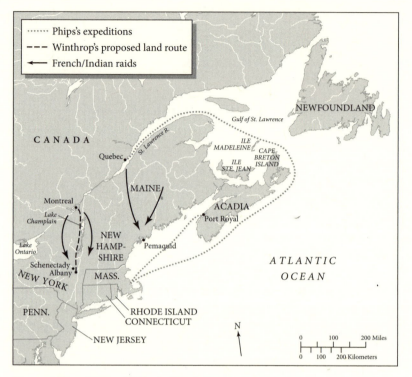

Figure 6. King William's War in North America.

French contended for the Catholic Church, Louis XIV, and the deposed James II against usurpers of the English throne. Thus, King William's War—as it was later known—had the potential to bring the colonies far more comfortably into an imperial orbit. The war allowed inhabitants of various parts of the colonies, from the northern borderlands of New England to the plantations of Barbados, to connect their local circumstances with the larger Protestant imperial cause. So in New England and New York tensions with Indians became something more than a local concern, while ethnic and racial divisions in the Caribbean hardened. In addition, colonists in each region had to rethink their relations with imperial power, and figure out how much of their autonomy they should surrender in the interests of security.[2]

The first major effect of King William's War was the drawing of new lines of inclusion and exclusion across the continent. Of course, long before the declaration of war inhabitants of the colonies had spent a great deal of time identifying possible conspirators, but the task took on new urgency after the

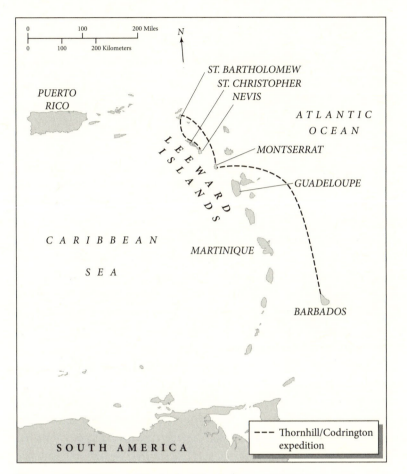

Figure 7. King William's War in the West Indies.

start of open warfare. Nearly everyone defined the enemy, above all, as French and Catholic, a force determined to extinguish Protestant liberty in America and replace it with popish slavery. Beyond this universal definition, however, colonists added other groups to the enemy ranks depending on their local predilections. In the mainland colonies, this meant above all Indians—both those natives who really had joined the French cause, and also many who had not. In the islands, however, Irish servants played the role of the fifth column, while both West Indian and, to a lesser extent, mainland planters suspected black slaves as well. In limited circumstances, local officials or subjects could target other groups, including Quakers, French Protestants, or even, in the town of Salem and neighboring Essex County, alleged witches. The purpose of all this finger pointing was to police the lines of belonging, to determine who had a place in the empire and who did not. As the turmoil of the decade showed, however, few people agreed on how these lines should be drawn.

In order to meet the threat, the leaders of various colonies led their own efforts to thwart the enemy. In particular, the war provided opportunities to various interest groups to prove their effectiveness as leaders and partisans of the imperial cause. In Barbados, the opportunistic Lieutenant Governor Edwyn Stede used the war to burnish his questionable reputation, while others who had run afoul of James II for their Whig sympathies tried to regain power. In the north, meanwhile, rebel leaders like Jacob Leisler and Sir William Phips attempted to take charge and thus show that their particular version of empire—a loose coalition of Protestant colonies under the protection of a distant monarch—could keep the continent safe. These various efforts had some early triumphs, including the recapture of St. Christopher and the conquest of Acadia, but met bitter failure in a coordinated assault on Quebec City in 1690 that bankrupted the northern colonies and spelled doom for the Protestant coalition that had ruled the region since 1689.[3]

In the wake of the failure at Quebec a new age of empire began. Even ordinary people in the colonies began to realize that they needed help from the imperial center if they hoped to vanquish the enemy. This revelation led to a gradual political shift away from the Protestant firebrands who had championed a decentralized empire, and toward some of the very people who had faced disgrace and imprisonment in 1689. The new context led to new imperial possibilities. At the same time, however, colonial subjects would only embrace the empire if imperial leaders did their jobs, and as Wheler's debacle showed, defending America required both skill and money. Thus Francis Wheler's failure introduced the tension of empire in the eighteenth century: the French enemy united the various colonies in a firm union, but the difficulties of war created new divisions.

• • •

King William's War began with a series of frightening attacks on English colonial communities. The first troubles occurred in the Leeward Islands, where the English and French lived in close proximity to one another, even sharing the island of St. Christopher. On the very day that New Englanders imprisoned Sir Edmund Andros, 18 April 1689, a West Indian planter remarked that "the Irish on Montserrat are very insolent and threaten the English, And they on St. Christophers are much in fear of the french who promise the Irish to Assist them likewise on Montserrat." By July these fears were realized, as the French overwhelmed the English half of St. Christopher, finding many Irish inhabitants all too willing to desert and join the invaders. The Irish majority on Montserrat appeared likely to do the same, thus robbing the English of two valuable sugar colonies. The situation was clear: in the eyes of English planters, the French had found it easy to trick weak-minded people into joining their cause, not only "the bloody, popish, Irish rebells," but also "Molattos, Musteses and Negroes that are Inbodyed with the Irish."[4]

The war soon erupted in the northern colonies as well, though the first combatants were Indians rather than French or Irish. During the summer and fall of 1689, Indians struck English settlements in New Hampshire and Maine, and they offered clues that they had been, as one colonist later put it, "Frenchified both in spirit & apparell." They claimed alliance with the French, and even left small Catholic devotional items behind when they retreated after their attacks. By the end of the summer dispatches from Whitehall confirmed the speculation: England and France were at war, and the troubles in America were just elements in a global struggle between William and Mary and the French king, a contest that could have dire implications for Protestants everywhere. The official declaration of war complained, among other things, that Louis had "invaded our Caribbean Islands" and "that they would take over, by force, our lands in the province of New-York and Hudson's Bay."[5]

The connections between local violence and the global cause appeared clearly in the hamlet of Schenectady on 8 February 1690. A French and Indian war party descended on the town at 11 o'clock on a snowy night, finding the gates to the Dutch village wide open. The invaders devastated the town, killing 60 people and carrying off about 30 prisoners. A survivor escaped and trudged through the snow to Albany, where he reported that "the french and Indians had murthered the people of Skinnechtady." Within days word of the attack spread around the colonies, and it acted as a galvanizing event, demonstrating that the savage Catholic violence that periodically struck Europe had made an appearance in America.[6]

Rhetoric about the Schenectady attack adopted wholesale the language of anti-Catholic propaganda. The Connecticut militia captain Jonathan Bull first reported on the slaughter, and it was horrifying: the minister, Petrus Tesschenmaker, "kild & burnt in his house;" "the wife of Adam Vroman shot & burnt her childe the brains dashed out against the wall." The carnage corresponded to most Protestant conceptions of popish violence: the attackers burned the town, as papists were wont to do, and they performed acts of gratuitous violence, focusing on the town's Protestant minister and innocent women and children. But as stories spread, they became even more explicit. On 4 March Jacob Leisler wrote to authorities in Maryland about the "sad and deplorable massacre," claiming that "women with child [were] ript up, children alive thrown into the flames, some their heads dashed ag[ains]t the doors & windows." Leisler's description of the violence at Schenectady lifted details from Bull's report but added particular images common to anti-Catholic propaganda, in particular Charles Blount's *Appeal from the Country to the City*, which had warned of what would pass if the Popish Plot had come to fruition. The depiction of papists ripping unborn babies from pregnant women's bellies was one with a long genealogy, beginning with John Foxe's martyrologies and making appearances in propaganda about the 1641 Irish revolt as well as persecution of French Huguenots in the 1680s. By evoking such imagery Leisler meant to place American frontier violence in context, as the latest strike of the Antichristian beast that had terrorized Protestants for over a century.[7]

Imagery from the Schenectady attack reappeared across England's colonies. Even far from actual French colonies, colonists saw popish influence behind every act of bloodshed. In 1696, for instance, unknown Indians attacked a plantation in Henrico County, Virginia, on the falls of the James River. The carnage was terrible: witnesses saw the bodies of their neighbors cut into pieces and hung from trees. On seeing the bloodshed, one observer noted "this was like the Papists way," and another "believed there were either Papists with them or they were hired by Papists." The power of propaganda was so widespread that even on the far edges of empire, English people interpreted violent acts as elements in a global popish plot.[8]

The French Catholic plot against English America combined political and religious objectives. Perhaps the best illustration of the design came from Silvanus Davis, a militia officer and magistrate in Maine who became a prisoner to the French and traveled to Quebec in 1690. Davis asked New France's governor Louis de Buade, comte de Frontenac, why he targeted settlers in Maine, when it seemed that his real grievances lay with the Mohawks and their abettors in New York. "I Towld him that New yorke & Boston was tow distincte Govourments," Davis reported, but Frontenac disagreed, countering that "wee ware one nation," and that people in New England shared responsibility for the conduct of their brethren elsewhere on the continent. Moreover, the French quarrel with the English was not just due to Mohawk and Seneca attacks; it was prompted by political quarrels at home. New Englanders were "Rebells against our King," Frontenac told them, and "if the Government had not bin Chainged & that Sr Edmund Androus had Contenued go[verno]r whee should have had noe wars betwixt us: but wee shoold have bin all as one people."[9]

Davis's report portrays how one man suddenly became a believer in the popish plot against America. Before his arrival in Quebec he had been genuinely confused about the Indian attacks that struck the Eastern Country. Intercultural violence was nothing new in the borderlands, but it usually represented local grievances, and the years before 1688 had been comparatively tranquil. When he heard Frontenac's arguments, however, Davis realized that the remote province of Maine had become embroiled in a contest that stretched far beyond its borders. The French governor's argument was essentially political: that subjects of the two kings, however far they traveled, still bore responsibility for their monarchs' actions. North America was not, as some would have it, "beyond the line." Davis and others on the English side naturally added a religious angle to Frontenac's speech, which prompted Davis to "beleve there was a papist designe against the prodestant Intrest in New England as in other parts of the world."[10]

This global plot required a strong response. Almost as soon as war began, leaders began to plan elaborate and ambitious designs to extinguish the French presence in America. These assaults looked somewhat different in the Caribbean and the mainland, but had several common features. Most especially, they required the creation of coalitions that incorporated diverse members of colonial societies, even at a time when the conspiratorial logic of American politics made it very difficult for people to trust one another.

The first version of this political dilemma occurred in the Caribbean. In July 1689 leaders in Barbados received distressing reports from St. Christopher. Irish servants on the island had "Declar[ed] themselves for the late King James," and set out to "kill, burne, and destroy all that belongs to the Protestant Intrest in that Island," forcing Protestant planters and their slaves to take refuge in the island's fort. One English planter described the Irish as "worse Enemies" than the French, since many of them had received preferment under James II and "remain in Comand among us & exercise their Religion openly." This situation could not have been aided by Sir Nathaniel Johnson, Tory governor of the Leeward Islands, who decided to resign his commission rather than serve the new monarchs. The governor decamped for South Carolina after rivals charged him with conspiring to betray the island to the French—a charge that closely paralleled those against Andros and Nicholson in the Dominion of New England. Soon the embattled English people abandoned the island entirely, surrendering after a lengthy siege, and word from Montserrat—where the Irish made up a distinct majority of the white population—suggested that the same thing could happen there as well. Irish inhabitants of the islands openly favored James II over William and Mary, and when forced to choose sides almost universally stayed neutral or deserted to the French. As English planters understood it, the French on St. Christopher and Martinique were using religion as a pretext to encourage a rebellion and conquest of the English islands. Since war had not officially been declared, the French claimed to harbor the Irish "for protection in point of Religion, as heretofore the English Received the French fugitive protestants on the like occasion." Nonetheless, it was clear to both sides what was happening: war was imminent, and the side that acted first would be able to make great conquests.[11]

One of the initial proponents of war in the islands was the self-serving Lieutenant Governor Edwyn Stede of Barbados. After he used focused anti-Catholic rhetoric to secure his own position in the wake of the Glorious Revolution, Stede turned his attention to the French threat. Like the rebel leaders in the mainland colonies, Stede understood that the fearful populace would only support someone who defended the islands against papists, so he began planning an expedition to regain St. Christopher and stabilize Montserrat. In fact, Stede had a history of taking on the French; during James II's reign he had attempted to enforce English claims to the islands of St. Vincent and Dominica until royal officials ordered him to stop. As he argued in 1687, the French were "the great, if Not the Onely Cause of makeing Enmity betweene the English and the Indians in these parts of America," referring to the Carib Indians who continued to raid English islands from their base on St. Vincent. He was happy to restart his campaign under the command of a more sympathetic monarch, but ended up collaborating with some strange characters, most notably Sir Timothy Thornhill, a disgraced councilor who had been one of Stede's foremost rivals.[12]

Thornhill had been almost the perfect archetype of the wealthy, dissolute West Indian planter. During the 1680s he had been a hard drinking member of the island's governing council, a member of a prominent family. Stede described him as "A man of such vitious Inclinacons, and soe full of all manner of Lewdness, Debauchery that most of our youth are Corrupted by him." In the 1680s, when any sign of Whig political leanings spelled trouble for colonial politicians, Stede and his faction decided to use Thornhill's penchant for speaking too freely to end his political career. In a conversation at a tavern, Thornhill allegedly spoke ill of the planters who, decades earlier, had violently resisted the coming of Parliamentary rule to the island after Charles I's execution in 1649. While he denied making such seditious statements, a jury found otherwise, fining Thornhill and turning him out of his office.[13]

In 1689, as Stede and the council set out to deal with the crisis in the Leeward Islands, Thornhill set out "to Recover his Lost Creditt." He volunteered, as Stede reported, to "serve their Maties in this Expedition, and to bear what Command I though fitt to trust him with." The council sent off 300 men under Thornhill's command to relieve St. Christopher, where Thornhill became a deputy under the new governor of the Leewards, the planter Christopher Codrington. They arrived too late to help, but they did manage to keep the Irish of Montserrat from rebelling, in part by transporting many of them to Jamaica. In an account that may have been a bit overblown, Stede presented the war as something that brought together everyone in the islands against the Irish and French enemy. "Never Men went more freely to the Warrs then these Men that are now gone to Releive the Leeward Islands," Stede wrote, "Haveing noe other designe but pure duty & service to their Maties not haveing so much as pay or the Prospect of Plunder." The council dared not levy new taxes to pay for the expedition, demonstrating the fragile state of Barbadian politics after the revolution, so they started a subscription campaign, "In which indeed the People proved more Gennerous and free than I Expected, for they gave very frankly to the Occasion."[14]

Over the next year Thornhill stayed in the Leeward Islands and assembled a motley collection of militia members and seamen with the goal of conquering St. Christopher and, with luck, all the French islands. A virulent outbreak of disease on Nevis made recruitment difficult, but soon after arriving Thornhill took the small French island of St. Bartholomew, where after the French surrender he obtained an additional victory by getting a Franciscan friar so drunk that he "spoke Latin so fluently on *Transubstantiation*, that he confounded himself on his own argument." After winning that island, Thornhill moved on to St. Christopher, putting together nearly 3000 men, a force that included such familiar figures as the old pirate and royal enforcer in Bermuda Bartholomew Sharpe, now commissioned as a captain, and future pirate William Kidd, who would go on to surpass Sharpe's reputation as a villain by the end of the decade. The invaders faced not only the French but also the Irish,

Carib Indians, and their own former slaves, who fired many of the island's houses as the English came through. After a significant fight the English forces succeeded in taking the whole island.[15]

Official and unofficial dispatches presented the conquest of St. Christopher as a great victory for the English interest in the islands. Thomas Spencer, the secretary of Thornhill's forces, credited both "the forwardness of the soldiery" and "divine blessing" for the triumph, which he hoped would soon "root the French interests out of that part of the world." Another account focused on the amount of plunder, claiming that the invaders brought back over £100,000 worth of "Victory and Spoil." Nonetheless, cracks appeared in the coalition in 1691. Thornhill established himself as a champion of the common soldier, and soon started a feud with Christopher Codrington, claiming with typical slander that the governor placed his love of French ladies over his allegiance to the English interest. Meanwhile, a commander on St. Christopher complained that the islands "are but in a very weak condition to receive an Enemy, should a Fleet come from France and Command the Sea, our Condition would be more misserable than now it is, for want of Provisions, of which we have a great scarcity occasioned by the Warr in Ireland and New England, which were our constant supplies." In other words, West Indian planters could only put aside factionalism for so long; they needed assistance from London if they hoped to defend territory and expand their conquests.[16]

As islanders fought the French, a parallel situation developed on the mainland, especially on the frontiers of New England and New York. There, however, circumstances proved far more complicated because of the precarious politics in the region after the Glorious Revolution and the role of Indian nations in the conflict. To win the war colonial leaders needed to put aside their petty differences and come together against a common enemy, but this was a difficult task for people who tended to view every rival as a possible conspirator with the forces of evil.

As in the islands, the war in the Northeast created odd alliances. Two of the most unlikely partners in this campaign were Cotton Mather and Robert Livingston: the former one of Boston's most influential Congregational ministers, the latter a wealthy Scottish merchant in Albany who had held numerous offices in the duke of York's government. After the attack on Schenectady, the Albany Convention sent Livingston on a tour of New England to plead Albany's cause and seek assistance for the unfortunate town. While he undoubtedly wanted to save the place his family and business were located, he also had practical reasons to leave. Jacob Leisler was in the midst of a campaign to neutralize his political opponents—many of them already confined in prison—and had made Livingston, who refused to acknowledge Leisler's authority, his number one target. Indeed, soon after Livingston left town Leisler's men came to Albany to search his house. They found that Livingston had taken most of his financial papers with him, but there were some suspicious materials, for example, a chest full of papers and items that had belonged to a French Jesuit named Pierre Vaillant who had visited the town a few years earlier during Thomas Dongan's administration. Leisler's men also took depositions from several locals who remembered Livingston making untoward statements about the Prince of Orange during the months before William's victory was certain, comments that riled some of his Dutch neighbors. Leisler was attempting to build a case against Livingston as he had done against several other rivals, painting him as a closet papist and Jacobite who would betray the country to France at the first opportunity.[17]

By the time Leisler's men ransacked his house, Livingston was in Connecticut, where he presented Albany's case to the governor, council, and assembly. He aimed in part to discredit "Leislars his violent and monstrous proceedings" and preserve support for the current leaders of Albany, but he also urged that people "lay aside all animosities and private differences and contests and joyne heart and hand with all might and force against the Common enemy." He claimed it was "every true Englishmans interest" to help Albany, which was the bulwark of all the colonies. If Albany fell, Livingston pleaded, the rest of the colonies would soon follow. The message seemed to go over well. The influential merchant had many friends in Connecticut, where the moderate sensibilities of most magistrates contrasted with Leisler's bombastic approach. They refused even to consider Leisler's demand that they confine Livingston and extradite him back to New York.[18]

By 17 March Livingston was in Boston, where he delivered an ingenious appeal that presented the most articulate case to that point for an offensive strike against the French. Livingston claimed that only an invasion of Canada would protect the colonies in the future; once the French were gone all the Indians would naturally surrender to the English, who would own the continent. He was also the first to spell out exactly how the attack could succeed: as a joint mission by land and sea, with New Yorkers and their Iroquois allies attacking Montreal while a naval force traveled from New England to Quebec. Lest any pious New Englanders miss the subtle antipopery of his appeal, Livingston made it explicit as he developed the argument, defining the assault

on Canada as a religious mission: "all true protestants subjects" should partici-
pate in the conquest of New France, Livingston argued, and as the most zealous Protestants of all, New Englanders were the only ones "capable in these
parts of performing soe glorious a design." Livingston included two details
that established his Reformed Protestant credentials. First, he mentioned the
importance of missionary work among the Indians as an adjunct to military
invasion, boasting of the efforts of Albany's Reformed minister Godfrey Dellius, but also urging Massachusetts to send its "young divines" west where they
could do good service for the Protestant cause. Second, he ended his statement with an apocalyptic message, "there are diverse good omens that God
Almighty has determined the downfall of Anti-Christ, in our days," Livingston told his sympathetic audience, "this is the only meanes in all probability
to effect itt in America."[19]

One man in Boston who would have been particularly interested in Livingston's statement was Cotton Mather. The young but precocious minister of
Boston's North Church, Mather had been a central player in Boston's revolutionary politics, though he often obscured his role out of a sense of political
pragmatism and necessity, since ministers were supposed to be advisors rather
than leaders in New England's government. After the beginning of the war
Mather preached several sermons underlining the cosmic importance of the
impending struggle. The fullest exposition came in a sermon to an artillery
company in the fall of 1689, after the first Indian attacks on Maine and New
Hampshire but before the deadly Schenectady raid. Along with the usual valo-
rization of military service that always appeared in artillery sermons, Mather
compared New England's current "Just War" to the prophetic struggle between good and evil that would precede Christ's return to earth. The minister
described Indians as "a wretched party of Mankind" who had been shielded
from the light of the gospel by "the *Divels*," and in more recent times by "the
Papists" who "say *Mass* with them" and attempted to turn them against the
true Christians who had settled in New England. Good Protestants did not
need to fear, however, because according to Mather's interpretation of the
book of Revelation, the "whole *Papal Empire* . . . is very near its *End*, when
none shall help it; and that the *twelve Hundred and sixty Yeares*, during which
the people of God, were to be harrassed by it, are not far from their Expira-
tion." The minister urged his charges to take the fight to the enemy not only
to defend their communities, but also to aid the global Protestant cause and
help to usher in the apocalypse.[20]

The Mather-Livingston interpretation became the leading ideological justification for an invasion of Canada. By mixing the apocalyptic specula-tion of the radical Protestant fringe with a kind of Reformed ecumenism and a secular emphasis on imperial unity, the two men offered a rationale for war that could appeal to almost everyone, from the hottest Protestants to more practical-minded men like Anglican merchant John Nelson, who took the lead in planning the early stages of the campaign. And the message seemed to spread, as is evidenced by the diary and correspondence of that most ubiqui-tous late Puritan, Samuel Sewall. In the early months of 1690 the influential merchant and judge not only came to be a key promoter of the war effort, but also a particular friend of Albany, declaring in a letter to officials in Con-necticut that "Albany is the Dam" that kept the French from overpowering New England.[21]

Even as Americans came together against the popish threat, there were indications that such unity might be more difficult than it seemed. Indeed, Livingston himself was a refugee, not from popish persecution but from a radical Protestant, Jacob Leisler, who believed him to be a covert papist rather than a fellow Protestant. As this example demonstrates, the ecumenical anti-Catholicism of Mather and Livingston remained fairly novel; more powerful, at least in some circles, was the Manichean impulse to view anyone who devi-ated in the least from Reformed Protestant orthodoxy as a popish agent who could not be trusted.

On 1 May 1690 representatives of several colonies met in New York City to coordinate the war effort. The representatives left few records of their pro-ceedings—even Samuel Sewall, one of the delegates from Massachusetts, failed to provide any substantive commentary—but many of the participants under-stood the novelty of their actions. Massachusetts governor Simon Bradstreet best expressed the stakes of the meeting. "The advantage of the enemy is so great that our united strength will be found little enough," the governor wrote, unless the delegates achieved "a good understanding between their Majesties' Governments . . . in this public concern against a common enemy."[22]

The meeting did not quite live up to these high expectations. The host, Jacob Leisler, had sent invitations as far as Maryland and Virginia, but in the end only the New England colonies sent representatives. Nonetheless, they managed to settle on an invasion plan with little acrimony, mainly by adopting wholesale the plan espoused by Robert Livingston. Despite Leisler's hatred of Livingston, he must have realized that his rival's plan provided the best chance to defeat the enemy. The colonists would mount two invasions, one by land, led by New Yorkers and assisted by the Connecticut militia and

Iroquois, the other by sea, managed by Massachusetts and Plymouth. As they decided on the proper distribution of troops and supplies, the delegates not only worked to save themselves from a formidable enemy; they also labored to prove that a decentralized Protestant union could effectively defend the king and queen's interests in America. This was to prove a difficult task.[23]

By the time of the New York meeting, New Englanders had already begun to take the offensive against the French. Their first project was Acadia, the sparsely settled French province to their east and north. New England merchants often traded in the region, and the best connected of these traders, John Nelson, led the campaign to reduce Acadia before targeting Quebec, not only providing a rationale for the assault but also coordinating a private fundraising campaign among Boston's merchants. But just as Leisler stole the limelight from his rival Livingston, Nelson also found himself eclipsed by the less competent but more dramatic Sir William Phips. Nelson lost his position as commander of the expedition against French Acadia because "he was a Merchant & not to be trusted," replaced by one of the shadiest characters in New England, who appeared to have no religion at all before being quickly admitted to Mather's North Church in 1690. Perhaps it was less Nelson's occupation that compromised him than his Anglican faith and previous friendly relations with the French, another casualty of the Protestant impulse to view the world in binary terms.[24]

Phips possessed one of the more compelling biographies of any seventeenth-century American. According to legend he was one of 22 children from a small town in Maine, an unlikely hero who married the daughter of a wealthy Bostonian and gained wealth and a knighthood by discovering a Spanish wreck off the coast of Hispaniola. His early years revealed little religious zeal, and in several instances he appeared almost royalist in politics. He defended Bermuda's embattled governor Richard Coney, and even helped deliver the *quo warranto* that challenged the Massachusetts charter. Only one incident presaged his future career as an anti-Catholic firebrand. In Jamaica in 1684 Phips shot a volley at a Spanish ship he believed did not pay proper respect to the king's standard, an incident that ended with Phips demanding compensation for the shot from the Spanish commander "wth a Crowd of Rabble at his heeles." According to the governor, Phips had become embroiled in the controversy over special privileges given to Spanish traders in the colony. While a relatively minor incident, it indicated two things: Phips did not look kindly on Catholic rivals; and he was popular with the common people. By 1690 he had retained his favor with the "rabble," but added important ties with influential patrons like the Mathers, though his detractors continued to characterize him as an illiterate mariner.[25]

Despite Phips's popular appeal and political connections, the Acadia expedition met several obstacles. First, New England's leaders found that few New Englanders wanted to leave home to serve against the French. The commander managed to attract volunteers by promising them a share of the plunder—a valuable incentive at a time of economic instability—but he still had no real way to prevent men who had already committed themselves to the expedition from deserting if they became tired of the service. By the end of March, moreover, colonial authorities realized that the number of volunteers was insufficient. On 15 April the council ordered the constables of Boston to impress 30–40 men, and later the government resolved to finance the mission publicly by raising taxes, since contributions from leading merchants failed to provide sufficient funding. In the meantime, some argued that the expedition was not the best strategic move at such an early stage in the war. Robert Livingston believed that Port Royal was an insignificant target, and would only divert energy from the more important drive against French Canada. But as casualties mounted in the Eastern Country, New England's leaders needed to take some action, and in late April Phips left Boston with five ships and nearly 800 men. The declaration of war explained that the English were merely defending themselves in attacking Acadia, since French subjects there had assisted "the Heathen-Enemies in their Bloody Invasions."[26]

The conquest of Port Royal proved to be easier than any of New England's leaders imagined. Despite being the capital of Acadia, the town was barely more than a hamlet by New England standards, and the meager fortifications and garrison could offer no challenge to such a large invasion force. As they approached the harbor Phips received word from a friendly Acadian of the garrison's weakness; when the fleet entered the harbor a priest named Louis Petit came on board as a representative of Governor Louis des Friches de Meneval under a flag of truce "to acquaint our General that he was willing to surrender upon our Terms and comply with the Proposals." In a subsequent meeting with Meneval, Phips worked out the details of Port Royal's surrender. The English promised the governor that his garrison could retain their arms and would be sent to Quebec. Phips also promised to respect the property of the town's French inhabitants and allow them liberty of conscience to practice their Catholic faith.[27]

Once the fort was safely in English hands, however, Phips violated the terms of surrender. First, he imprisoned Meneval and other officers, as well as the two Jesuit missionaries Petit and one Father Trouvé. Then the English invaders descended on the town itself, "pillaging the houses of the great part of the inhabitants, from which they stole the goods and the livestock, without pretext." The invaders reserved their most brazen conduct for the village church. The author of the published proceedings claimed that "We cut down the Cross, rifled the Church [and] Pu'lld down the High-Altar, breaking their Images." French reports described the same incidents with outrage, noting that, "The church according to their good custom was dishonored by many mockeries and infamous actions," and that the iconoclasts stole the church's "ornaments." While these actions broke the terms of the surrender, they pleased both the invading party and their brethren back in New England. Since many people believed the conflict to be a religious war, they would have been scandalized if the raiding party had spared the church. Accordingly, Phips not only allowed his men to pillage the place of worship, but also made sure that descriptions of the desecration appeared in the published description of the attack—in marked contrast to Edmund Andros's previous strikes against the French.[28]

Phips violated the surrender terms to make sure the conquest produced the expected economic rewards. Massachusetts authorities had only attracted men to the expedition by promising them a share of the plunder, not unusual for military expeditions during that era. When the enemy surrendered without a fight, however, it was difficult to justify pillaging a town that did not even resist the invaders. Phips allowed his men to plunder Port Royal, however, probably because he knew that they would be angry—perhaps uncontrollable—if they did not profit from the assault. The merchants who helped bankroll the expedition also expected their share, as did the nearly bankrupt Massachusetts government. Phips pleased all these parties: he returned to Boston with so much booty that the General Court had to appoint a committee to dispose of it all. It included several "great guns" and other military implements that the government retained for the war effort, significant quantities of claret and brandy, furs and skins, saws, kettles, fish hooks, blankets, and a variety of Catholic baubles, including surplices, communion wafers, and priestly vestments. The returning party also brought a number of French soldiers as captives. Governor Meneval and the two Jesuits remained in close custody while authorities granted the soldiers liberty "to dispose themselves into such familyes as shall be willing to entertain them." Some colonists, therefore, even gained extra laboring hands from the successful expedition.[29]

The assault on Port Royal seemed an auspicious start to the offensive war. Colonists not only struck back at the Catholic enemy; they also reclaimed territories that had once been part of the king's dominions. Cotton Mather told a friend that "we have newly made an expedition against Nova Scotia, and old Scotland will not complain of it that we have brought that country under the English government." Governor Bradstreet bragged to Jacob Leisler that Phips returned to Boston "with the Governor of Port Royall two Priests, & about Sixty Souldiers with their great gunns & Stores of Warr & other Plunder." Knowing Leisler's penchant for iconoclasm, Bradstreet made sure to mention that "The Fort [was] demolished & their Crosses & Images broken downe." Another writer claimed that "the greatt conquest made at Port Royall" had inspired "greatt talk of Sending for Canada, the people generall Supposeing to have thatt upon as easy termes as the former." But even as colonists celebrated their victory, the enemy proved to be resurgent, as Indian war parties desolated English communities on Casco Bay in Maine, causing Massachusetts to call back the soldiers they had committed to the land expedition against Montreal. They may have attained victory in Acadia, but the people of New England would not be safe until they vanquished Canada, labeled by Mather as "the seminary of our troubles from the Indians."[30]

Planning for the land expedition met troubles early on as well. The first dispute concerned who would lead the assault on Montreal. Leisler commissioned his political ally Jacob Milborne for the task, but Milborne proved unpalatable both to the Albany Convention and to New England allies. Robert Livingston complained that Milborne was unqualified for such an office by virtue of his humble background, being "formerly a servant to a man at Hartford," and promoted his friend Fitz John Winthrop of Connecticut for the job. Winthrop was both the heir of New England's most distinguished family and a veteran of military service in England, and he gladly accepted the post, noting that "The Gen[era]ll Calamity that hanges over our heades, & points us out for Sorrow, calls for every ones help; and being myself Sollicitous for the Safety & prosperity of the people, am ready to be in Armes for their defence." Leisler initially resisted the appointment, but relented after Simon Bradstreet endorsed Winthrop as well. Nonetheless, relations between the commander and New York's lieutenant governor remained chilly. Winthrop had political and economic ties to Leisler's enemies in New York, and expressed wonder that people in the colony "should be soe blind & deluded with such a one, wch is a great dishonour, and besides a mischeif to the managemt of affaires at this juncture." Leisler undoubtedly knew that Winthrop was a friend of Robert Livingston, and perhaps not as zealously anti-Catholic as befitted the leader of such an expedition.[31]

Aside from personality disputes, planners of the expedition also had trouble filling their ranks. First, Massachusetts reversed its previous troop commitment, since new attacks in Maine required it to devote more soldiers to defending the eastern frontier. And Maryland, which had promised 100 troops, never sent the men, prompting Leisler to remind John Coode that he could not maintain Maryland's alliance with the Iroquois unless he received help against the "threatening dangers of the french." Near the end of June, Leisler complained that only 70 of 525 promised soldiers had arrived at Albany. He still hoped for at least 1,800 Iroquois warriors, but feared that the expedition would be difficult with so few men. Even official dispatches to London hinted at the colonists' desperation. One letter claimed that the people were "extraordinarily spirited and importunate" to attack Canada, but requested supplies from England to help with the task. Even at this early juncture, colonial leaders realized that their promise to conquer Canada without English assistance had been somewhat foolish.[32]

In the months before the expedition the colonies remained in a "distressed Condicon." The Massachusetts and New York governments used extreme methods to raise the money and men necessary to mount their coordinated assault. Benjamin Bullivant noted that "The Bostoners now print Their Laws, raise Taxes, force open Warehouses, press all sorts of Goods, have set up the Excise"—all actions that, in Bullivant's view, usurped the king's rightful authority over the region. Leisler reportedly threatened to collect taxes by force if people did not voluntarily support the war effort. Despite these measures, however, most New Englanders were unwilling to answer the call. Cotton Mather blamed a lack of public spirit, but a letter from Gloucester's minister suggests that local communities had other, less selfish reasons to oppose the expedition. The minister complained that the impressment of 47 men from Gloucester threatened the town's future, since it was left with no one either keep watch for the enemy or harvest crops. If the men were not released from service, he warned that "wee must all be forced to leave the towne" or else "be made a prey to the enemy." Two militia commanders made a similar protestation to the General Court, claiming that "if so many be press'd for Canada" as the government intended, "the fronteers shall draw in" as inhabitants of outlying towns fled to the coast.[33]

On 21 July Winthrop arrived in Albany, where he was alarmed at the state of the preparations. As he reported to his Connecticut superiors, "the designe against Canada [was] poorely contrived & litle prosecuted." The commander had less than 400 "Christian" troops at his command, and the Iroquois alliance had not even been finalized. Even New York had not met its quota. Many of the troops suffered from smallpox, and the men had very few provisions. Most critically, they lacked canoes to take them up Lake Champlain and into Canadian territory, which they had expected Indian allies to provide. They also lacked ammunition. Winthrop confidently cast blame for the lack of supplies on Jacob Leisler and his adherents, denouncing them as "unreasonable men wholy tyed up to their owne intrest." Former New York mayor Stephanus van Cortlandt, also in Albany at the time, agreed with Winthrop, citing the "division and Contrision" occasioned by Leisler's "illegall and Arbitrary Actions." Jacob Milborne, for his part, urged Winthrop to go on despite the disadvantages, since "all things on the French's side [were] looking to their disadvantage, praying that the heavens may be propitious to your undertakings."[34]

On 8 August Winthrop convened a council of war to decide how to proceed. The results of the meeting with Iroquois allies provided further discouragement. The Indians were offended that the English blamed them for the lack of canoes, claiming that they had never promised to provide them, and complained that Winthrop did not bring the belts of wampum customary for such meetings. When the commander asked if the Indians would accompany him against Montreal, they answered ambiguously, saying "it was not for them to ly ther, for ther was no provision to be had," and suggesting that the party strike at a lesser target, as the French had done at Schenectady. In the end, the Indians only supplied 300 of the 1,400 warriors they promised, claiming "sicknes, or some trifles." Winthrop believed that the Indians' cold response to his arrival "did not sufficiently engage them in the design against Canada." Without adequate provisions, with disease ravaging both Indian and Christian troops, and with no hope of future provisions, the council of war reluctantly agreed to abandon the assault. Johannes Schuyler and Sander Glen took a small party north by canoe "to do [the French] all hurt and mischief," but the party only succeeded in taking a few prisoners. The ambitious plan against Montreal had been a miserable failure.[35]

News of the disappointment quickly reached New England. By 23 August Connecticut authorities learned "to our great griefe" that the invasion had been "retarded by the faylure of the Indians to accompany them and furnish them with Cannoes." The colony's leaders ordered all their forces in Albany to return home, "for the sicknesse being so rife there it seemes not advisable to let them lye there." By the 28th word of the retreat reached Boston, where authorities ordered a "Publick Fast." The expedition's failure caused great consternation in both New York and New England, as it suggested that the conquest of Canada would not be as easy as some had predicted. In the meantime, the various parties in the intercolonial coalition began blaming one another for the misfortune.[36]

Jacob Leisler had staked his political future on the success of the expedition. His claim to power rested on his pledge to subvert the Catholic plot— the "Combination of the forces of hell" that threatened the colonies. With the resistance to the French in shambles and civil strife rampant in the colony, Leisler's hold on power was weaker than ever. When he learned of Winthrop's shameful retreat, he reacted predictably by pointing once again to the popish conspiracy. He ordered that the commander be placed in prison, accusing him of "unaccountable and unchristian behaviour" that resulted in the expedition's failure. Winthrop was flabbergasted by the indignity; he believed that retreat had been the only sensible option given the lack of men and provisions, and that a person of his stature should not suffer the shame of being thrown in jail by a purported ally.[37]

Leisler created an elaborate defense of his decision to imprison Winthrop. He argued that the general had joined a popish conspiracy led by Robert Livingston, "the Chief Instrum[en]t to create all our Evills." Leisler originally gave Winthrop the benefit of the doubt, but became suspicious when he learned that he "lived in open adultries in despight of your lawes, and other crimes which are the ruines of civill government, without the least mark or signe of repentance, to the shame of all Christians." More disturbingly, Winthrop soon became "a toole fit for the wicked purposes" that Connecticut secretary John Allyn and Robert Livingston "had contrived." Livingston and Allyn were political allies who had both—like Fitz John Winthrop—held commissions under the Dominion of New England, and Leisler believed that no one with ties to the old regime could be trusted. Livingston had returned to Albany with Winthrop, who used his house as a headquarters, and Leisler believed Livingston influenced Winthrop to abandon the assault, despite its likelihood of success. Leisler also charged that Livingston and his adherents "sent a bribe to the Indians to stop their March."[38]

New York's leader went beyond blaming Winthrop and Livingston for the failure. In a series of incendiary letters, Leisler blamed all of New England for its "perfidy." While they once had been "a people professing Christianity so eminently beyond others," New Englanders had become nothing more than hypocrites, aiding the papists in their design against Protestantism. Their conduct, he continued, "astonishes all the protestant world," since in the face of God's deliverance the people of New England "trust to your wicked crafts and inventions." In the end, however, when Christ returned, New England would be held to account. Leisler ended one diatribe with a scriptural flourish, warning that "when you are searched with candles, it will be known who are guilty of this accursed thing, & your nakedness will be uncovered, wherefore yow who have not struck hands with the authors hereof, it behoves you arise & shew yourselves men for cause of God & Zion, that you partake not of their abominations." Because they had "struck hands" with suspected popish agents like Livingston, Leisler considered New England Congregationalists—perhaps the world's most reliable Protestants—of being covert papists. In accusing his neighbors of such a sin, Leisler committed political suicide, alienating his only allies in the name of religious purity.[39]

Connecticut's leaders reacted to Leisler's actions with indignation. John Allyn wrote an angry letter protesting that "a prison is not a catholicon for al State Maladyes, though so much used by you," and added that New York's actions "infringe our liberty" and damaged future attempts at cooperation. The colony's legislature perused Winthrop's report and concluded that he acted "with good fidelity to their Ma[jes]ties interest, and that his confinement at Albany on the acco[un]t thereof deserves a timely vindication, as being very injurious and dishonorable to himselfe and the Colonyes of New England, at whose instance he undertook that difficult service." With enemies gaining power in his own colony, friends deserting him, and ordinary subjects up in arms, Leisler's days in power were numbered. He released Winthrop from prison not to assuage New England, but because local Mohawk Indians threatened violence against Leisler if the general remained in jail. New Englanders could not admit that the scion of their leading family was a popish agent, and many of them began to view Leisler not as an ally in the Protestant cause, but as an unbalanced lunatic whose rash actions compromised the war effort.[40]

New Englanders still held out hope that the naval assault on Quebec could succeed despite the land expedition's failure. During the summer colonists had been bullish about their planned invasion of Quebec, which, like the earlier strike against Port Royal, was to be commanded by Sir William Phips. Governor Bradstreet hoped the strike would put an end "to this troublesome war," and reports of Canada's weakness buoyed New England's spirit. "Canady is poor and discouraged," one correspondent reported, while Fitz Winthrop noted that "every thing Seemes to favour [the fleet's] designe," as "the Merchants" had raised over £6000. The expedition spoke to both the patriotism and religious duty of New England Protestants. The Reverend John Hale of Beverly, for example, determined to "goe to Cannady" as a chaplain over the objections of his wife and congregation, saying "God calls, th[i]s Country cals, Authority cals and Christs Interest cals." One member of the expedition who later wrote an anonymous account succinctly expressed the importance of the design: the fleet intended "to Endeavour the Extirpation or Subjugation of the French & Indians, who by the bloudy Instigation of fiery Jesuits, were designing no Lesse ag[ains]t us & Consequently all the English America."[41]

The fleet departed amid much fanfare on Saturday, 9 August 1690. Phips had delayed his departure several weeks waiting for supplies from England, but while the Committee on Trade and Plantations had ordered assistance to the colonists in June, the shipment would not arrive until 1691. Phips also worried about the land assault, since rumors circulating around the town in July had already indicated that Winthrop's troops were ill prepared. Despite these qualms, the general set off for Canada with a substantial fleet, numbering 34 vessels and about 2300 men. The expedition included a number of learned divines—not only John Hale, who dined with Phips and Samuel Sewall the night of August 8, but also John Wise of Ipswich, who had resisted Edmund Andros several years before, and Nehemiah Walter of Roxbury, who spoke fluent French.[42]

The passage to Quebec proved more arduous than Phips had imagined. The general could not find a good navigator, and contrary winds prevented the fleet from making a timely ascent of the St. Lawrence River. By the time Phips approached Quebec it was already October, nearly two months after his departure, and his men suffered from disease and low morale. While the fleet slowly approached the target, an Abenaki messenger traveled overland to share the news that "a very considerable fleet" had left Boston "with the design to come and attack and take Quebec." Local officials sent a dispatch to Governor Frontenac, who was residing in Montreal at the time, who summoned "all the troops and *habitants* of his government" to march day and night to save Quebec. The English expected to face little resistance in Quebec, since they had heard several rumors that the town was weak and the people eager to surrender. Instead, they encountered over 2,000 spirited men in arms. As one

French official said, "it seemed that everyone wanted to take part in an action that each person hoped to be glorious for Canada."[43]

The next act of the drama underscored the political consequences of the battle for both sides. After assembling his fleet before the town, Phips sent his lieutenant Thomas Savage to deliver a letter to Frontenac. The letter explained why the English had to take the city. Phips mentioned the global conflict between their two kings, but focused on "the *Destruction made by the* French and Indians, *under your Command & Encouragement.*" These "Cruelties and Barbarities" demanded a severe response, but the general offered to allow Frontenac to surrender the town and return all English captives.[44] The governor was in no mood to capitulate. He charged the English with being "unfaithful to king James, their legitimate prince," and since he did not recognize William's authority, he treated the fleet not as agents of another state, but as pirates. According to the baron of Lahontan—a French writer sometimes accused of exaggeration—Frontenac erected a gibbet and intended to hang Savage until the bishop and intendant dissuaded him. When the frightened lieutenant asked the governor to provide an answer to his commanding officer, Frontenac issued a call to arms, daring the English to try and take the town. The governor general would give no response, he said, "but from the mouths of our cannons and shots from our muskets." Both sides related their struggle to larger political currents: Frontenac determined to chastise the "vieux parlamentaires" of Boston in the name of King Louis and King James, while the English attackers chanted "Vive le roi Guillaume" as they came toward the city.[45]

While both commanders presented the conflict in political terms, it also had strong religious overtones. Ecclesiastical officials in Quebec called their charges to action by pointing out that the attackers were "enemies not only of the French, but of our faith and of our holy religion," but the French also understood what was likely to happen if the Protestants won. Nuns at one convent hid "the church's silver and all the sacred vases" in the garden "to prevent their desecration." A priest spent the first night of the attack consuming consecrated hosts for the same purpose. Several French prisoners who had recently returned from Boston circulated stories that the English were particularly eager to lay their hands on the six chandeliers at the Jesuit church. The invaders had designs for the colony's religious as well, hoping "to drive from Canada the Ecclesiastics and the Nuns, to take the latter to Baston, and to send the former back to France; but, as for the Jesuits, they were to cut off the ears of all these, to make chaplets for the bandoleers of the soldiers,

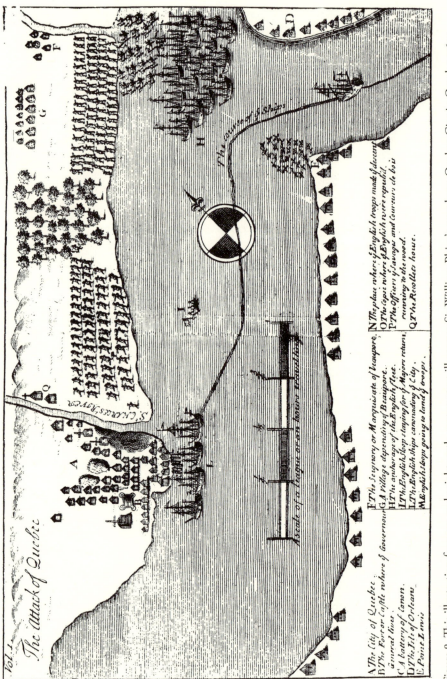

Figure 8. This illustration from an early eighteenth-century text illustrates Sir William Phips's assault on Quebec City in October 1690. Louis-Armand de Lom d'Arce, baron de Lahontan, *New Voyages in America* (Chicago, 1905), 316.

and then break their heads." The French responded to the threat by resorting to prayer and worship; divine services continued as usual, which caused the English "to infer that we had no fear of them, which made the greater part very dismayed." [46]

The assault began in earnest the day after the encounter between Savage and Frontenac. Phips endeavored to bombard the town from the water, while Lieutenant John Walley of Plymouth went ashore with the land forces, which approached the city from the north. The army proved to be poorly disciplined and ill prepared to fight an enemy that knew the terrain and could endure the unseasonably cold weather. As the campaign wore on the troops became disillusioned, and Walley could not convince them to follow orders or continue their assault. While they outnumbered the French and their Indian allies many times over, the English became terrified when the enemy began to fight "in the manner of the savages," hiding in the "swamps" and picking off the English as they approached. According to a French nun, the English "persuaded themselves that all the neighboring mountains were populated by indians who came to take them from behind." The troops then fell into "confusion and disorder, . . . [and] betook themselves to flight, crying out, *Indians, Indians.*" As the English stumbled toward their ships, they abandoned several of their "great guns"—leaving them as an unintended gift to their enemies. The panicked retreat illustrated just how terrifying the "common enemy" appeared to most colonists, and how the French and Indians utilized psychological techniques to defeat far more numerous adversaries. The Reverend John Wise blasted the men for their "cowardize," claiming that "there is no less than Death deserved" for such conduct. He continued, "when we desert our Dutie and buisness we were sent about by God and Countrey." "God follows Us with Crosses and Confusion." [47]

The shameful actions of Walley's men brought a practical end to the siege. Over the next few days Phips and his senior officers waited for another opportunity to attack, but the weather worsened, many soldiers suffered from smallpox, and ammunition supplies ran low. At a difficult council of war Phips decided to conduct a prisoner exchange with the French and retreat. The trip back to Boston proved even more arduous than the voyage to Canada. Contrary winds pushed the fleet apart, and disease killed far more men than French bullets had. Several of the ships were lost, and one was blown all the way to Barbados. Stephanus van Cortlandt reported with some satisfaction, "Baston hath Loste [in the expedition] many Vessels, above a thousand men, their Reputation, Incouraged the french, and brought their gouvernm[en]t above 40000 pounds Indebted." The expedition had accomplished almost the opposite of what its planners intended, plunging the region into a depression and proving to many outside observers that colonial leaders could never work together without English assistance and coordination.[48]

•   •   •

In the wake of the failed Canada expedition the Protestant assault on French America appeared to be in dire straits. In the Caribbean infighting between commanders and lack of resources threatened to undo early English victories, while lack of strategy and paranoia had doomed the design against Canada and thrown the northern colonies into chaos. Over the next few years English colonists turned on one another with far more commitment than they had shown against the enemy, leading to a virtual civil war in New York, a witch-craft outbreak in Massachusetts, and a slave conspiracy scare in Barbados. In this chaos, however, lay the possibility of imperial regeneration. As colonists observed the way lack of unity had delivered victories to their enemies, more people began to see wisdom in the kinds of imperial reforms people like Edmund Andros had tried to implement.

No one had banked more on the Canada expedition than Jacob Leisler. Not surprisingly, he fell first and hardest after it failed. As early as December 1690, subjects on Long Island began to "mutiny" in response to the high taxes Leisler demanded to subsidize the war effort. The lieutenant governor decried the protesters as "Rebells & Trait[or]s to their Majties," and sent Jacob Milborne and a party of soldiers to chastise them. While Leisler's men forced the rebels to retreat and plundered the house of their ringleader, they could do little to assuage his subjects' discontent toward a regime that many of them now viewed as arbitrary. One of Leisler's allies in Boston wrote a letter expressing regret that "things are Com to open arms, espessialy when Settlements from the King is deemed to be so neer." The writer urged his friend to act carefully toward his enemies, noting that "gustis with moderation and mersy is becoming all persons." This moderation was especially necessary since a new governor, Henry Sloughter, had already left England to take up his post, accompanied by several hundred redcoats under the command of Richard Ingoldesby, and both men had ties to Leisler's influential enemies.[49]

Despite the advice of his friends, Leisler's extreme anti-Catholic world-view made it difficult for him to show moderation toward people he deemed to be agents of Antichrist. When Richard Ingoldesby arrived on January 30,

Leisler refused to recognize his authority. His stated reason was the lieutenant's lack of a proper commission, but the real cause was Ingoldesby's alliance with disaffected subjects on Long Island and other enemies of Leisler's regime—people Leisler considered popish agents. Former New York mayor and anti-Leislerian stalwart Stephanus van Cortlandt met Ingoldesby's ship as it arrived in New York Harbor, and from that moment the commander became a dedicated ally of Leisler's enemies. Ingoldesby demanded that Leisler surrender the fort, but Leisler refused to give the keys to anyone except William and Mary's commissioned governor, who remained stranded in Bermuda. In the meantime, Leisler accused Ingoldesby of encouraging "great numbers of disaffected persons to the King's interest, Papist[s] & others who are fled from justice" to come into the city "and Comit insolencies agreable to their disposition." In essence, Leisler began to view the king's soldiers as agents of the popish plot, and, in a remarkable twist of logic, as enemies of the king.[50]

Over the next two months New York teetered on the brink of civil war. Leisler's men retained control over the fort, but Ingoldesby's soldiers installed themselves at City Hall and occupied the blockhouse. Leisler and his allies continued to insist that the city was under siege by enemies. One witness alleged that Ingoldesby had become the dupe of enemies of the regime, "some of which were papists and many french." Another claimed that the anti-Leislerian faction also gave arms to black slaves. Leisler's enemies directed similar charges at their rival, insisting that he was not a true partisan of William and pointing to his German heritage to suggest that he "preserveth this Province for some foreign Prince or State." Ingoldesby claimed that by denying his authority Leisler had declared himself opposed to William and Mary as well. By March both sides had become bold. Ingoldesby's men turned their guns on the fort in an act of provocation, while crowds of ordinary people thronged the streets of New York registering their political opinions. Eventually the mayhem led to bloodshed. In one exchange Leisler's soldiers shot and killed several of their opponents, including a prominent Scottish officer named James Macgregory. In the eyes of his opponents, this incident made Leisler not only a rebel but a murderer as well.[51]

When governor Henry Sloughter finally arrived in New York, he predictably sided with his political ally Ingoldesby. He arrested Leisler and other rebels and commissioned an "impartial" jury that consisted almost exclusively of men who had grievances against the lieutenant governor, led by the New Englander Joseph Dudley, then resident in the city. Sloughter put Leisler and his chief lieutenant Jacob Milborne on trial for levying war against the king and queen and committing murder, and on 16 May 1691 the two men were hanged for the crimes. To his death, Leisler insisted that he acted only "to maintaine against popery or any Schism or heresy whatever the interest of our Sovereign Lord & Lady that now is & the reformed protestant Churches in thos parts." After his death, many of Leisler's followers viewed him as a Protestant martyr, describing the men who killed their hero in apocalyptic terms as "the dragon, the whore, & the Croaking Froggs of the Pitt." By 1691, however, this rhetoric could no longer build a popular political movement in the colony. Leisler's failure to vanquish the real papists—the common enemy that lurked beyond the borders—damaged his reputation to the point that many New Yorkers welcomed any change in leadership.[52]

New England experienced similar political troubles that stemmed directly from the failed military expedition—but they manifested themselves very differently. Instead of turning against their leaders, New Englanders turned on each other, and the near-political vacuum turned a minor local disturbance into a province-wide crisis. In early 1692 several teenage girls in Salem Village had begun charging neighbors with witchcraft. The Salem Village minister Samuel Parris related these charges to the larger battle against popery, noting that "Devils, & Idolators will make war with the Lamb, & his followers," and that "in our dayes . . . the Bloody French Monarch" was the foremost enemy of Christ. Along with King Louis, the devil also instigated "Multitudes of Witches & Wizards . . . to attempt the overthrow of Religion." The minister adopted the same Manichean world view that doomed Jacob Leisler to the gallows as he reflected on the crisis, noting that "Here are but 2 parties in the World, the Lamb & his Followers, & the Dragon & his Followers: & these are contrary one to the other. Well now they that are against the Lamb, against the Peace & Prosperity of Zion, the interest of Christ: They are for the Devil. Here are no Newters. Every one is on one side or the other."[53]

The conspiratorial fears that abounded in New England after the failure of the Canada expeditions helped to inspire the Salem witchcraft crisis. As recent scholars have noted, many of the accusers and accused had ties to the war in the Eastern Country, and some of the depictions of violence inflicted by the accused witches resembled French and Indian tactics in war. But more than the personal connections, the crisis grew out of the peculiar political culture of the time. New Englanders faced a terrifying enemy that lurked everywhere, and the logic of antipopery asserted that even the most unlikely candidates could have ties to the enemy. After the region's leaders proved inept in defeating the French and Indians, ordinary New Englanders began to accuse the only people they could find—locals whose unorthodox lifestyles or strange behaviors suggested they could be part of the diabolical coalition against the colonies. Magistrates responded to these charges because they needed to regain power after the embarrassing failure against New France. By executing nineteen witches, the leaders of Massachusetts hoped to show their subjects that they could act boldly against the colony's enemies at home, even if they could not abroad. In the end, of course, the Salem witchcraft debacle only proved—to contemporaries and future generations—how desperate and powerless the region's leaders had become.[54]

The final kind of domestic panic to hit the colonies during wartime involved slaves and servants. The plots and panics of the late 1600s occurred at a time when the numbers of African slaves were rising in many parts of British America, and it is unsurprising that some people began to view impressionable slaves as possible Catholic agents. In Essex County, Massachusetts, just before the witch obsession began, authorities apprehended a native of the island of Jersey named Isaac Morrill, accused of "consspercy with the common enmye" by bringing various disgruntled servants together to aid a French invasion. The plan, as shared by one Robert Negro, was for Morrill to lead "all the negros" to Canada where they would join an invasion force, returning to New England where they would "distroy all the English and save none but only the Negro and Indian Servants." Very similar fears appeared in Barbados about the same time: a place where the large black majority made the fear of slave conspiracies much more powerful In 1692 word spread of a slave plot, in which an army of African slaves intended to take advantage of the chaos of war to stage a rebellion and set up their own republic, one that would depend on the assistance of Irish servants as well as the French. While relatively isolated, these conspiratorial fears presaged the much more widespread alarms of the eighteenth century, when whites in New York, South Carolina, and the Caribbean routinely believed that Catholics labored to encourage slave insurrections.[55]

The widespread panic of the early 1690s provided a perfect opportunity for advocates of a centralized empire to make a political comeback. Some of the loudest voices for imperial rule came from New England. After the Canada expedition's failure, a disgruntled Charlestown magistrate named Lawrence Hammond charged that the expedition's planners had disingenuously played to the people's fears of popery to drum up support for the design. Hammond claimed that the government manipulated people into volunteering for service, "so that partly thro' fear of Violence us'd with them, and partly great Expectations of success and much plunder, which was trumpeted about in the Country by some busy Agents (and some Clergymen in *Boston* and some other places Crying Victory, Victory over Antichrist in their Pulpits &c.) the Poor people were enticed and drawn in to their own and the Countries (almost) utter ruin." Any people who opposed the government "were call'd King *James*'s men, Friends to the *French* and Papists, Enemies to the Country &c. for so doing." Hammond considered all the talk about "our zeal against Antichrist" to be mere pretense, and charged that the planners really intended only to aggrandize themselves. Connecticut physician Gershom Bulkeley believed Massachusetts never intended to succeed in Canada, but just used it as an excuse "to entangle, harass and beggar the people."[56]

Connecticut magistrate Samuel Willys provided the most thorough critique of the decentralized vision of empire. While no Jacobite, Willys came to believe that the events of 1689 had been ill conceived, that a "head strong multitude" had seized power, to the detriment of all order, and that Edmund Andros had been no traitor, but just a zealous defender of kingly government—not a bad idea when compared to the near anarchy that followed. The Canada expedition, meanwhile, was a foolish ploy by a weak government to try and gain some credibility, but doomed to failure, and probably illegal to boot: "kings do seldome take pleasure," Willys noted, "to see their subjects grow so big as to undertake the conquest of countries." The best option would have been to wait for approbation from Whitehall, along with supplies and reinforcements, so that the design would have possessed a proper legal footing and a better chance of success.[57]

Many of these critics were longtime advocates of imperial rule in New England, but soon even charter advocates joined the chorus. Samuel Sewall, for instance, realized that Massachusetts could not survive without extensive help. The region's colonies needed to come together, "But now they are at their Liberty, whether they will doe any thing or no towards defraying the necessary charge we are at in defending the Common Interests of the Crown." His recommendation was that "these lesser Governments [should] be firmly compacted together in one." Of course, Sewall imagined that his own colony, Massachusetts, would retain an important leadership role over its smaller neighbors.[58]

In this time of uncertainty colonists in New England and the rest of North America longed for someone who could save them from destruction. For the people of Boston such a savior appeared in 1692 in the familiar personage of Sir William Phips, who returned from a sojourn in England with a commission to be the first royal governor of Massachusetts. The arrival of the new charter

marked an important turning point in colonial politics. While the charter preserved the colony's legislature and other local governmental bodies, it called
for the governor to be appointed by the crown and altered the franchise in the
colony, ending the Congregational churches' lock on power by decreeing that
a property requirement, rather than church membership, determined eligibil-
ity to vote. Many elements in New England society had fought for years to
fend off royal control of the province, but Phips did not meet angry crowds
as he landed in Boston. Instead, he found a desperate people willing to accept
political change if their new leaders could defend them against the common
enemy. The Protestant assault on New France had strengthened and reinforced
the anti-Catholic views of most Americans, but also led to a fundamental shift
in popular opinion. The exigencies of war caused many colonists to give up
their fear of political centralization, and led them closer to the empire.[59]

New England's "adjustment to empire" looked more dramatic than the
transitions in other colonies, but represented an empire-wide pattern. Every
part of the colonial world experienced difficulties defeating the enemy without outside assistance, and colonists expressed willingness to formalize bonds
to England in exchange for more reliable military aid. The process proceeded
most rapidly in the vulnerable Caribbean colonies. Edwyn Stede of Barbados
was one of the first officials to ask for help, back at the war's outset. Stede
wrote to superiors in London, "had I a few men of war here and the help of
a Thousand or fifteen hundred men to be added to those I could spare here,
I make no doubt but that I would give their Ma[jes]t[ie]s the possession of
all the French Islands." These additional supplies would "enable us not only
to defend this their important Island but to Enlarge their Empire in America
which will be greatly to their Mats Glory and Honour and Improvement to
their Revenues & Treasure."[60]

Stede's successor as the primary royal enforcer in the islands, Christopher Codrington, put matters somewhat more bluntly. Like many before and
after him, he found some of his fellow islanders "turbulent and disagreeable."
In particular, the Assembly of Nevis took on a "high and mighty" style, setting themselves up as a mini-Parliament against Codrington's personification
of royal authority. Codrington called for a show of force to save the colonies from the French and from themselves, since "some here have almost the
vanity . . . to fancy these Colonys Independent States," which would lead to
factions and divisions and "enervate all government." His answer was somewhat novel: Codrington proposed eliminating local assemblies entirely and
"annexing of these islands directly to the Kingdomes of England, allowing us

representatives in an English Parliament." The proposal aimed to centralize authority in a way that avoided the common charges of "popish tyranny" that had followed previous attempts at centralization, and it showed that advocates of centralization had altered their methods but not their fundamental goals in the wake of the Glorious Revolution.[61]

Codrington's proposal proved too utopian for the times, but the crown did follow through on the requests for military assistance. In 1692 officials in Whitehall began to plan a new, ambitious assault on all of French America, led by Sir Francis Wheler, that had the potential to shape the new empire. Imperial planners intended that Wheler's expedition would accomplish with the power of the Royal Navy what Phips, Codrington, and Leisler could not: the complete defeat of the French in both the Caribbean and North America. Wheler would begin by taking Martinique, with the aid of Codrington's local forces, before heading north and conquering Quebec as fall turned to winter. Wheler himself was a fitting instrument for the conquest, a well-connected naval officer whose father, Sir Charles Wheler, had been a previous governor of the Leeward Islands during the reign of Charles II. Wheler's force included twelve ships and nearly 3000 men, a sure demonstration of naval power that would overwhelm the French and set the terms for a new imperial union.[62]

In the end, however, Wheler's mission just demonstrated that building the empire and defeating the enemy were no easier for the English than for colonials. The mission began auspiciously, as Codrington and Wheler coordinated an attack on Martinique, but the raids accomplished little, and disease spread through Wheler's forces, killing hundreds. In addition, the English fell victim to the same paranoia that struck local officials. Many of the naval forces, both sailors and locals, were "Irish Papists Persons in whose fidelity, wee cannot confide, many having already deserted to the Enemy, the rest only wanting an Opportunity to doe the same." When a Council of War met to determine whether or not to continue their assault, they pointed to this possible fifth column as a reason to give up. The Irish claimed to be loyal, the Council claimed, but "they take all occasions in their Cups to Drink a health to King James, whose intrest they still seem (tho privately) yet Stifly to Espose."[63]

Wheler's fleet gave up on Martinique, to the anger of Barbadians, and set off for New England. While the New France phase of the expedition had been something of an afterthought, it represented a great opportunity to realize longstanding goals of building up the empire in New England by forging a popular alliance between the crown and local politicians. In particular, the new royal governor, Sir William Phips, had made the conquest of Canada one of his primary goals. He needed to do so to restore his reputation: though he had defenders, some New Englanders were upset at having surrendered the charter. Hatred for the French remained high, and Phips could "doubt not but that they will readly and Cheerfully assist to the utmost of their power in Subdueing Cannada, and bringing it under their Majties obedience." In February, as Wheler was in the West Indies, William Blathwayt told Phips of the plan to take Canada. Wheler would lead the fleet, but Blathwayt instructed Phips to raise New England volunteers, much as he had three years earlier. The expedition aimed at "a Conquest of Nova Scotia and Canada, the only means to make New England happy and secure hereafter." It would also allow "the People to shew their Zeal for their Religion and Love to their King and Country."[64]

In July Wheler came into Boston to carry out the design. There was one problem: due to the vagaries of transatlantic communication during wartime, Phips received Blathwayt's dispatch only days before Wheler's beleaguered fleet arrived. Wheler wrote to the governor and council asking whether it would be practical for him to go toward Quebec "in their Present Condition," or better simply to attempt to make a strike at Newfoundland on the way home. The commander noted that the coordination required for the expedition would take months, and they had "not half of crew left alive." On 12 July Phips responded that there was no way the fleet could succeed, since the season was so late and the governor could not raise troops without the assembly, which had recently adjourned. "I cannot express my greife for the loss of this opportunity of Subdueing Cannada," Phips lamented to Blathwayt. "I fear there will scarce bee for the future such an opportunity." Nonetheless, the conquest would have to wait. Wheler's men left Boston, to the relief of the inhabitants, eventually meeting more misfortune in a hurricane off the coast of Spain that killed the commander and virtually everyone on his ship.[65]

Wheler's failed expedition showed both the possibilities and the pitfalls of imperial coordination. On one hand, imperial designs had a fair amount of public support during the 1690s—far more than during the reign of James II. Yet at the same time, imperial leaders would not succeed until they learned to do two things. First, they needed to figure out how to balance local and central power, to solve the problem confronted by such people as Edward Randolph and Christopher Codrington. How to build a union that navigated between these different interest groups, and more important, how to sell it to colonial subjects who generally distrusted centralized power? Second, imperial leaders had to actually make the empire work. Phips noted that English America's key problem was the French Catholic menace. "While that remaines a French Province," he wrote of New France, "New England is subject to frequent allarmes and must allwayes be on guard." In order to gain legitimacy after the Glorious Revolution, imperial leaders had to meet the threat.[66]

Chapter 6

Ambivalent Bonds

THE BLOODY CONFLICT of the 1690s created a great dilemma for many colonial Americans. Nowhere was this dilemma more visible than on the Isles of Shoals, a set of rocky outcroppings off the coast of New Hampshire. The islands were famous for their independence: though they were nominally part of New Hampshire, no authority possessed any real control there, and the Isles were known as way stations for smugglers and pirates. With England and France at war, however, the islanders suddenly developed a grudging respect for authority. Fearing an enemy attack, they wrote to the provisional government in Boston in 1691, requesting forty soldiers. In February 1692 the troops arrived, but the inhabitants proved reluctant to provide them lodging or provisions. As the commander of the force noted, the islanders were "like Bullocks unaccustomed to the yoke." They had "com from the maine to avoyd all publique Service," and even when faced with their own destruction, did not want to cede control to outsiders.[1]

These tiny islands represented a microcosm of the colonial peripheries in general during the years following the Glorious Revolution. Especially after the failure of the Canada expeditions, colonial subjects realized that they needed the protection of the imperial state to survive in a more dangerous world. This change in attitude presented an opportunity for imperial administrators—many of whom were holdovers from the Stuart era—who still wanted to streamline colonial administration. At the same time, however, colonists showed little enthusiasm for the empire—they wanted protection, but did not want to pay for it. The challenge for royal governors, therefore, was to build some sort of emotional tie between rulers and subjects, in order to convince people that closer regulation was not just a necessary evil, but a positive good. The rebellions of 1689 had proved that such bonds could not be created by coercion. At the same time, however, the lessons of that year

Figure 9. Portrait of Richard Coote, earl of Bellomont, governor of New York, Massachusetts, and New Hampshire, 1697–1701. Frederick De Peyster, *The Life and Administration of Richard, Earl of Bellomont* (New York, 1879), v.

suggested a formula for imperial success. If representatives of the English state could successfully promote themselves as defenders of the region's Protestant liberties, then perhaps they could further the imperial mission with the people's tacit support.

The most interesting theater for this struggle was the former Dominion of New England. Now divided again into several colonies, the region witnessed the most intensive efforts at imperial state building, especially during the rule of a particularly ambitious governor around the turn of the century. An Irish peer and staunch Williamite, Richard Coote, earl of Bellomont received a commission in 1697 to become governor of New York, Massachusetts, and New Hampshire. In some ways, Bellomont's commission marked a cautious return to the ideals of the Dominion of New England. Like Sir Edmund Andros, Bellomont labored to bring the colonies under a closer dependence on the crown, especially in the economic sphere, through enforcement of the newly strengthened Navigation Acts. Unlike Andros, however, Bellomont understood how the rhetoric of antipopery could aid the imperial mission. This became most clear in the winter of 1700, when rumors of a new Indian conspiracy rocked New England. Instead of discounting popular fear, Bellomont embraced it, using the rumors as a call to arms against enemy Indians and Jesuit missionaries who labored to destroy English America. As a result, there was no political crisis in 1700, no repeat of the turmoil of 1689. In this case, fears of Catholicism worked to bring English subjects together rather than divide them—at the expense, of course, of their Catholic and Indian neighbors.[2]

Bellomont's death in 1701 left many of his plans unfulfilled. But his legacy lived on, as more and more imperial leaders realized that anti-Catholic fear could be the ideological glue that held the Anglo-American empire together. When England declared war on France and Spain in 1702, beginning the War of the Spanish Succession, colonial governors of all political persuasions promoted themselves as guardians of the people's Protestant liberties. As a result, the refractory inhabitants of the colonial peripheries gradually acquired a new reputation, as loyal subjects. "Whatever Hardships our *American* Colonies . . . have met with at home," declared one writer, "nothing has ever been able to shake their Loyalty to the Crown of *England* . . . . They have ever been zealous for the Service of the Prince, and as hearty for that of the Publick." While it blatantly ignored the colonies' recent history, this statement faithfully represented American sentiments at the beginning of Great Britain's imperial century.[3]

• • •

From the perspective of bureaucrats in Whitehall the problem of colonial governance remained the same at the end of the century as it had been in the 1680s. After the Glorious Revolution destroyed the Dominion of New England, the colonies went back to their former "independency," and while the mid-1690s witnessed the beginning of royal government in Massachusetts, Maryland, and Pennsylvania, local power brokers ruled most American territories with minimal supervision from London. As one New Yorker commented to the colonial administrator William Blathwayt, the colonies maintained "devided interests" because each one possessed a distinct government and considered itself a "comonwelth or principality in it self." The correspondent predicted that "should an enimy invade any one govern[men]t here, the rest would sitt still and see it ruin'd." If the colonies were to successfully resist French inroads in North America and serve the king's interests, they needed to be placed under a single administration, or at least combined into fewer units—as James II had envisioned before his fall from power.[4]

Over the course of the decade many people in the colonies began to agree with their purported superiors about the need for greater imperial regulation in America. Local authorities in the larger colonies became the first to invite greater imperial oversight, though often for selfish reasons. Representatives of both Massachusetts and New York sent appeals to the king calling for more assistance in the war effort, calling for "royal aid" in securing the reduction of Canada, an act that would strengthen the king's interest while providing both security and material rewards to colonists. Both colonies requested that the king send troops and supplies, and Massachusetts added their hope "that yo[u]r Ma[jes]tys several Governments within these Territorys"—and here they referred specifically to small neighbors like Connecticut—"be jointly concerned in the prosecution of the War, and Supporting the Charge thereof." Leaders of both Massachusetts and New York wanted the crown to take on a new role, essentially forcing each colony to contribute to the war effort. They still had no desire to surrender autonomy, but recognized that divisions between the colonies hampered their military capabilities.[5]

North Americans outside government proved even more insistent in their demands for greater royal oversight in the region. Simply put, many colonists blamed their local leaders for failing to protect them from enemies, and they advocated the consolidation of the "many little petty Governments" into a larger union. As one petition from a group of New England merchants stated, the region was "much Depopulated, wasted, & brought into a deplorable miserable & weak Condition, by the Warr." The merchants noted that political divisions in the region provided a stumbling block, and recommended that "some good form of Government may be established for the uniting of so many Interests as is occasioned from the divers Separated Governments." Stephen Sewall—the brother of Samuel and no defender of the royal prerogative—believed that the king should send a "viceroy . . . that may Comand all in this difficult time of Warr," and recommended the new ruler be a "Great & Noble man that is a soldier." Some correspondents realized that they were requesting the same government they overthrew in 1689, but the merchants' petition claimed no opposition to "the union of the Colonies" in principle, but only to the "Exorbitant and illegall Commissions" granted to officials in the Dominion of New England. Americans saw no reason why they could not retain their local rights and customs within a closer imperial union.[6]

A number of interested parties on both sides of the Atlantic offered specific suggestions on how to bring about this closer imperial union. One of the most vociferous was the Boston merchant John Nelson—a ringleader of the 1689 insurrection who quickly ran afoul of the revolutionary government and spent the rest of the decade demonstrating against it. Nelson was the primary author of the merchants' petition calling for unification of the northeastern colonies, and he also left behind several other detailed appeals to the crown proposing a new colonial policy.[7]

The merchant spoke from experience. Not only was he a veteran trader in New England, Acadia, and New France, but he also spent most of King William's War in Canadian and French captivity, where he added to his already formidable knowledge of French colonial policy. His advice, put simply, was to imitate the enemy. Despite having a much smaller population, the French were winning the contest for North America, and the English had to learn from their example if they wanted to claim their rightful place as rulers of the continent. Some changes had been suggested by other contemporary observers: the colonies needed to be placed under closer supervision of the crown; and England had to support the colonies—as the French did—by sending adequate troops and provisions. But, significantly, the most specific changes Nelson suggested related to Indian relations. In his view, New France's intricate system of native alliances kept the colony strong beyond its meager population, and Nelson suggested that the English copy the French in giving "seasonable presents" to the Indians and inviting them to London to "dazell them with the greatness and Splendor" of the imperial capital. These measures would help to ensure that the English became sovereign over the American interior, since "those who are masters of the Indians, will consequently prevaile in all places."[8]

Other observers echoed Nelson's plan for union but added touches of their own. The Pennsylvania proprietor William Penn, for instance, drafted "A Briefe and Plaine Scheam" for a union of the colonies, designed to make them "more usefull to the Crowne, and one anothers Peace and safety." His plan significantly preserved the rights of individual proprietors like himself but proposed a yearly meeting of representatives to discuss common concerns, and recommended that the governor of New York serve as the king's representative to make sure each colony contributed to the imperial mission. In times of war, the same official would become the military commander for all the mainland colonies. If Penn's scheme paid little attention to the enforcement of its provisions, another proposal from a more obscure source recommended a much more invasive royal presence. John Miller served for several years as the Anglican chaplain at Albany's fort, and on his return he concocted a detailed plan not only for conquering Canada, but also for ensuring the "settlement & improvement of Religion & Unity both among the English subjects that are already Christians & the Indians supposed to be made so." Like Penn, Miller called for the governor of New York to be the military chief of the colonies, but he added a new twist: the commander should be an Anglican bishop, with control over political, religious, and military affairs in the colonies.[9]

These plans stood little chance of success. Every design for colonial reorganization had to navigate the thicket of court politics, in which various factions tried to scuttle any proposals that did not advance their particular political agendas. More important, however, the shadow of 1689 hung over any plans for centralization. As every imperial administrator knew, colonial subjects had previously dismantled an imperial system primarily because they considered it to be popish and arbitrary, and in intervening years they had often vocalized against maintaining Indian alliances. Few proposals could have appealed less to militant Protestants than an attempt to establish a state church and curry favor with Indians.

While they never admitted the legitimacy of public opinion, some authorities in Whitehall had learned from the events of 1689. One student of New England politics, an Englishman named Richard Daniel, recommended that royal officials move firmly but cautiously toward greater regulation, taking special care to guarantee liberty of conscience, property rights, and the preservation of local assemblies. Daniel even suggested that the crown supply the salaries of Congregational ministers, in order to convince them "to submitt to the Government"—showing how little he understood the fundamentals of Congregationalism. While these guarantees would keep the people obedient, a "loyal, wise, & generous govern[o]r" would restore order to the region with the aid of a small regiment of redcoats, turning New England from an unsettled place to "one of the best flowers in the English garden."[10]

The policies of the new Board of Trade, founded in 1696, reflected some of the numerous petitions and reports it received. Most prominent imperial strategists agreed that a new, streamlined colonial system would help win the war, but they realized the political dangers inherent in any plan for centralization. Accordingly, in September 1696, when philosopher and board member John Locke drafted a proposal for uniting the colonies, he suggested that the king send a "captain general" to America who would act as a commander-in-chief and control the war effort but allow the individual colonies to maintain their separate political establishments. The board's proposal incorporated many of John Nelson's suggestions. In particular, the captain general would rule "by having constant intelligence from the neighbour Indians . . . of the motions & designes of the enemy," but his distance from the political establishment would allow the official to pursue an Indian policy without worrying about political fallout. Additionally, the plan confirmed colonists' charter rights, thus negating any fears of designs on their liberties, and during peacetime the commander-in-chief would surrender military control back to local militias.[11]

In fact, some English officials had already attempted modest reforms along the lines of Locke's report. Responding to repeated complaints that the smaller colonies in New England failed to provide aid for their neighbors—and particular charges that Rhode Island provided refuge to those fleeing taxes or military service—imperial authorities tried on several occasions to place the Connecticut and Rhode Island militias under the authority of their larger neighbors. First the king ordered Massachusetts governor Sir William Phips to take control of the two colonies' militias—drawing a storm of protest that made actual enforcement of the order nearly impossible. Several years later Whitehall tried again, granting New York's governor Benjamin Fletcher authority over Connecticut's militia. Fletcher's theoretical powers increased even more when the crown appointed him governor of Pennsylvania, extending his influence from Delaware to New England.[12]

Fletcher believed in the king's prerogative and did his best to further the cause of royal governance in the colonies. An ally to the Tory faction in England and a close associate of William Blathwayt, Fletcher naturally settled into the political circles previously occupied by Sir Edmund Andros and Francis

Nicholson. Fletcher believed that Albany was the strategic center of the continent, and he continued the efforts of previous New York governors and city leaders to convince neighboring colonies to provide military support to the region. For Fletcher, moreover, the campaign to protect Albany became the main plank in an effort to bring much of the region under his authority.

Fletcher found massive resistance to his program in Connecticut. In 1693 he received a royal decree allowing him to raise troops for Albany's defense from adjacent provinces, but he could not convince his neighbors to help out. To make matters worse, some New Yorkers fled to Connecticut, New Jersey, and Pennsylvania to avoid paying taxes to support the war effort. In October the governor visited Hartford to present his commission directly to the government there, but instead of a warm welcome he found "A perfect spirrit of Rebellion." Not only did Connecticut's leaders refuse to grant any assistance; they had "blown up the Mob and ordered the Millitia to Arms" to protest the governor's presence, "and I am told my Life is in some Danger." The New Englanders argued their case by pointing to English precedent, noting that Fletcher's commission allowed him to draw whatever numbers of men he thought necessary, in contradiction of English legal precedent on the subject of militia regulation. Nonetheless, to Fletcher this insubordination indicated that the people of Connecticut were "Enimyes to Monarchs" who desired to "sett up for Absolute Power and make warr upon Theire neighbours."[13]

Fletcher's failure to find support for his military plans showed the limits of royal authority in 1690s America. He was wrong to blame antimonarchical elements for his failure. Nearly everyone in the colonies supported the king in an abstract constitutional sense, but people gave first priority to the protection of their own communities, and proved reluctant to help a "Souldier of fortune" like Fletcher who appeared to place his own ambitions above disinterested service. Royal officials had no way to force colonial subjects to comply with the king's orders. Fletcher ranted and railed at his rivals, and even threw one unfortunate opponent down a stairwell of the capitol in Hartford. But however vicious or violent, Fletcher was only one man, and in the end he had to return to New York in disgrace.[14]

The only way for officials like Fletcher to prosecute the war—and compel obedience from neighbors—was with royal troops. As numerous English observers noted, the French sent frequent military reinforcements to North America. These soldiers not only guarded the frontiers but often stayed and became settlers. Despite the frequent admonitions against "standing armies" among late seventeenth-century English people, colonists would have probably welcomed the presence of redcoats—especially if they removed the need for colonial militias to patrol outside their home communities. Unfortunately for the governor, however, officials in Whitehall proved almost as stingy as their counterparts in Connecticut. The king did spare one company for New York, which had arrived in 1691 with governor Henry Sloughter and quickly became embroiled in the civil conflict that ended with Jacob Leisler's execution. The company ended up in Albany, and the town soon became the most militarized spot in English America—the closest thing to "garrison government" in all the mainland colonies. But as the king continued to focus on the European war, he provided little support for the few hundred troops who remained in North America.[15]

Service in Albany proved particularly onerous to the soldiers stationed there. As one of their commanders noted, "wee are in a Wilderness heareing nothing but Roarings of Boares howlings and such like noises of heathens Wolves & foxes." Moreover, the men were "soe hard dealt [wi]th" that many of them preferred the boars and heathens to the rigors of camp life. The soldiers received few provisions, and what they did have was rotten and infested with maggots so that even "the dogs in England would not eat it." The soldiers also lacked proper clothing. Another officer described them as "without either short stockins shirts or briches," and their near naked condition scandalized residents of Albany. To make matters worse, some soldiers charged that their commanders withheld some of the meager subsistence money they had due— probably because even those in charge received such little pay from England. In response to these conditions, nearly half of the three hundred soldiers at the fort had already left by 1695, and one officer predicted that the regiment would "unavoydably breake and disperse" without investment from England.[16]

The continuing desertions from the regiment posed a great challenge to the colony's leaders. The most dramatic incident occurred in April 1696, when a large group of soldiers stationed in Schenectady made off in the middle of the night with stolen powder and shot, apparently heading for New England. The officers immediately went out in pursuit of the deserters, and an ensuing gun battle resulted in the deaths of five runaways. During the court martial proceedings the surviving men revealed the reasons for their insubordination. One complained that he was "hardly dealt with by his officer" and mocked by the Dutch inhabitants, who called him "severall bad names." Aside from these tensions, the soldiers also could expect material awards for desertion. Governor Fletcher claimed the mutiny "was encouraged by the great wages given to labourers in the neighbouring Colonies where the people protected and concealed" the deserters. A later report claimed that wages for common laborers exceeded the soldiers' pay threefold.[17]

Governor Fletcher had no way to stop soldiers from abandoning the camp. Early in his tenure, he issued a dire proclamation calling for the inspection of all "Travellers or Passengers" in the province to make sure they were not deserting soldiers, runaway servants, or foreign spies. Two years later, though, he found cause to issue another proclamation, this one much less menacing, offering amnesty to any deserting soldier who returned to his post within thirty days. Finally, in 1697, Fletcher stopped threatening the deserting soldiers at all and focused instead on the people who harbored them, declaring that anyone who aided a deserter would be "detached to serve in their room." In fact, the shortage of men in service meant that Fletcher could not afford to execute people who abandoned their responsibilities to defend the colony during wartime. Even after the Schenectady mutiny, Fletcher executed only one ringleader but commuted the sentences of the others, "considering the scarcity of men in this Country."[18]

Administrators like Fletcher had little success in their centralizing efforts because colonists had no compelling reason to accept reforms that seemed to be against their interests. Many colonial subjects continued to see the king's men as enemies to their liberties, and Fletcher also contended with a central government that only occasionally considered the colonies, and proved reluctant to provide any material support for its programs there. The result, in Fletcher's case and many others, was that governors turned away from grand plans for imperial reform and focused on personal aggrandizement, trying to milk as much money out of their offices as circumstances would allow.[19]

In 1697, however, administrators in Whitehall seized another opportunity for reform. The governorship of Massachusetts had been vacant since Phips's death in 1695. The king had already chosen one of his longtime allies to fill the post, but some people suggested that the appointment could be extended beyond the Bay Colony. Edmund Harrison argued in a memorandum to the Board of Trade that the new "Governour of New England, may also be the Civill Governour of New York, & New Hampshire, and Generall of all the forces of New England[,] New York[,] New Hampshire[,] Connecticut[,] Road Island & the Jerseys." The "Union of their forces," he went on to argue, "may be able not only to oppose the enemies designes, but also (if assisted with some Regular troops) to remove the French from that part of America." Such an office required "a Person of honour & temper," and the king had just the man: one of his parliamentary allies, Richard Coote, earl of Bellomont.[20]

Bellomont was in some ways a typical Whig courtier but his various experiences since the Revolution had shaped his politics in distinctive ways. A nephew of Charles Coote, one of Ireland's most influential Protestants, Richard used his illustrious name to gain a position at court. During the reign of James II, however, he left for the Netherlands, where he joined William of Orange's retinue—not, as he told a member of James II's Privy Council, out of disloyalty, but "to apply my Selfe to the studdy of arms, the better to qualifie my selfe for the Service of my King and Country." Nonetheless, he soon became an enthusiastic revolutionary, accompanying William and Mary to Torbay, and eventually gaining a title as earl of Bellomont. He spent the 1690s focused on two things: foiling popish plots and seeing to his own professional advancement. For instance, in 1690 he took the lead in investigating the so-called "warming pan scandal," the widespread rumor that James II had faked the birth of his son the Prince of Wales, smuggling another child into the birthing room. After this effort led nowhere, Bellomont lobbied for a post as chief justice in Ireland, as he believed that the king suffered from "evill Counsel" in that troubled kingdom. Nonetheless, the earl confided that he was less than happy to return to his ancestral land; "I would not be oblig'd to live in Ireld. above 2 or 3 years for almost any reward," he wrote. Thus his happiness when a post in North America came available instead.[21]

•   •   •

The new union of colonies resulted from a combination of long-time strategy and short-term circumstance. While many people in Whitehall and the colonies believed that such a union was necessary to fight the French, it was Bellomont's desire for a higher salary, and perhaps a posting outside Ireland, that finally brought the plan to fruition. Like many landed nobles, Bellomont experienced an almost constant need for funds, and he knew that colonial administration could be an undependable livelihood. In most cases Whitehall assumed that colonial legislatures would provide salaries to their governors, but securing the money was not always easy. Knowing this uncertainty, Bellomont claimed that he "always desir'd to be sent governour of N. England" but asked that "N[ew] York were added, that I might be enabled to do the king and those countrys service & be certain of a salary suitable to the employment." From its inception, therefore, the new colonial union existed to benefit its commander as well as the king.[22]

Imperial leaders had trouble convincing nervous colonists to accept this new colonial union. As the earl of Bridgewater—the chair of the Board of Trade—recorded in his notes on the process, leaders of all the colonies feared being under the control of Massachusetts. Agents from New York noted that Boston was too far away to make an effective capital, and argued that the two places had always competed "in matters of trade" and politics, and that any governor would inevitably favor one over the other. Connecticut's agent Fitz John Winthrop protested Bellomont's control over his colony's militia, claiming that "Imposing a General" who could summon troops without the consent of local authorities "will be hard on the Inhabitants." In Massachusetts, meanwhile, more than a few colonists related the new union to the unpopular Dominion of New England. The minister John Higginson worried that the new governor could be "some Huffing Hectoring Blade" and a "Stranger who knows not N[ew] E[ngland]," while magistrate Richard Saltonstall viewed the new government as "a Consummation or Conclusion of E[dmund] A[ndros's] former designes." The new government, in short, had little support in the colonies, and revived fears of oppression by outsiders stoked during the struggles of the 1680s.[23]

Two factors helped to ease these fears. First, the fatigue of war had taken its toll on the colonies and made resistance to royal authority less likely. Lieutenant governor William Stoughton remarked to Bellomont that subjects in Massachusetts were "quiet and much rejoiced" about the governor's arrival, but even happier about the end of the war with France. The region still suffered from attacks by "the Indian Rebels," and a strong royal presence in Massachusetts could help bring the natives into "Obedience." New Englanders also began to learn more about their new governor—who unlike many of his predecessors was well connected in Whig political circles. Bellomont belonged to the Church of England, but had ties to the dissenting interest in England and Ireland—the same people who tried their best to defend New England in Parliament. One of the colony's best friends in England described Bellomont as "a Man of great bravery, and courage, and of a most condescending meek and affable temper, who minds Religion, and . . . does not go over with Designes for his own Advantage." Even Fitz John Winthrop—who had many qualms about the new colonial union—described its new chief as "a very good man." None were as effusive as the earl's New York supporter who, when the new governor made a speech, remarked "Is it possible that old Seneca is alive again?"[24]

In fact Bellomont's Williamite politics influenced the way he approached colonial governance. On the face of it, the new governor's aims did not differ much from those of his immediate predecessors: he wanted to make the colonies "flourish" and ensure they remained "usefull to England." In particular, he sought to enforce the newly strengthened Navigation Acts and secure the king's revenues. At the same time, however, the governor's politics rested on a more important desire: to preserve the Protestant succession against enemies both inside and outside the colonies who hoped to overthrow William and bring back James II and popery. Even though he ruled during a time of peace, Bellomont acted like a governor under siege, viewing anyone who crossed him as a possible Jacobite or papist. This intense anti-Catholicism shaped the policies of his administration and injected a religious purpose into the imperial project that had been far less visible in previous years.[25]

The contours of Bellomont's domestic policy appeared most clearly in New York. The governor arrived in a colony where "Faction and Sedition" had taken hold, as the followers of the executed Jacob Leisler continued to fight Leisler's former enemies for a share of government. Bellomont initially tried to remain neutral in the struggle, but soon gravitated toward the Leislerians, who smeared their opponents as a "Jacobite Party" who sought to steal the king's revenue and usurp his authority. Many of these supposed Jacobites were leading merchants who had benefited from Benjamin Fletcher's relaxed economic policies and showed great resistance to the new governor's attempts to limit piracy and enforce navigation laws. Bellomont understood these men not just as self-interested rivals, but as enemies to the king who hoped to throw off all authority. He responded by suspending several prominent anti-Leislerians from the council, thus endearing himself to the substantial numbers of New Yorkers who continued to revere Leisler and resent the leading merchants. At the same time, he made powerful enemies who used their influence in Whitehall to clamor for his recall.[26]

Bellomont placed his new colonial opponents into English political categories. He believed that all people "disaffected to the present Govern[men]t" could be identified as "Papists and Jacobites," and that all these people had been coddled by the previous governor Benjamin Fletcher—whose political persuasions had been different from Bellomont's. The main evidence of disloyalty came from the anti-Leislerians' actions at the time of the "late, happy revolution," when most of them opposed Leisler's regime. In fact, Bellomont merely recycled many of the charges of treason that Leisler himself had leveled against his opponents. When he removed William Pinhorne from the council, for instance, Bellomont mentioned a remark Pinhorne had made nearly a decade earlier when he speculated that the king of France would "devour" King William's forces in a manner that was "so like the cant that was among the Jacobites in England at that time" that Bellomont assumed he must be a Jacobite himself. Pinhorne also stood accused of "harbouring and entertaining one Smith a Jesuit in his house" when such papists could not live in safety in New York, another sure sign of disloyalty. The governor also targeted New York's Anglican minister William Vesey. When the minister emerged as a critic of some of Bellomont's policies, the governor impugned Vesey's loyalty, noting that his father had been convicted in Boston "for being the most impudent and avowed Jacobite that had been known in America."[27]

Foiling these Jacobite rivals became a central goal of Bellomont's governorship. His most concerted campaign targeted Albany's Dutch Reformed minister Godfrey Dellius, whose efforts to convert Mohawks had won acclaim throughout the colonies, even from such luminaries as Cotton Mather. Dellius had long been active in anti-Leislerian political circles, and Bellomont drew on his political views to accuse him of long-term disloyalty to King William and possible ties to popery. Leisler himself had forced Dellius into exile in 1690, considering him to be one of the "Popish Trumpets" who "preached up the damn'd Doctrins of Passive Obedience and Non Resistance" during the time of the Glorious Revolution. Since that time Dellius had become a particular friend of Benjamin Fletcher, and he also had close ties to Albany's merchant elite. Unlike his counterparts Henry Selyns and Rudolph Varick in New York, Dellius managed to maintain at least the nominal support of his congregation during these times of strife, but his political and economic meddling did cause some consternation among Albany's laity. Robert Livingston's wife claimed that Dellius was "so much in the hatred of the people" that many of them refused to attend church, charging that "he teaches that they shall not covet and covets for himself."[28]

The minister's covetousness eventually led to his downfall. In 1695 he joined a group of prominent merchants and city leaders—including Peter Schuyler and William Pinhorne—in purchasing a massive tract of land from the Mohawk Indians. The grant included much of the traditional Mohawk homeland, as well as some of the most valuable timber in the region. Such exorbitant land grants were not uncommon during Fletcher's tenure, as he sought to place as much land as possible in the hands of his political allies, but this particular conveyance raised several concerns among Albany residents. First, members of the city council feared the grant would "be the utter Ruine to the generall trade and commerce of this Citty," as it would displace the Mohawks and perhaps lead to the establishment of trading entrepots further in the backcountry. More important, however, Albany's leaders worried that the grant would alienate the

Mohawks from the English interest, inspiring them "to desert this Provence and fly to the French." To remedy the situation, Albany's council sent a memorial to the newly arrived Bellomont protesting the grant. The governor for his part seized an opportunity not only to redress Mohawk grievances, but also to bring down some of his most powerful political rivals.[29]

Dellius quickly emerged as a convenient target for the governor's aggression. The other patentees sold back their shares when they sensed the political fallout, leaving the embattled minister to face Bellomont alone. Moreover, Dellius appeared to be especially culpable in the matter because he had engineered the negotiations that led the Mohawks to part with their land—negotiations that some of the Indians claimed to be fraudulent. According to two Christian Mohawks who testified before the governor, Dellius "used artifice to circumvent them and their Companions into a bargain of Sale," claiming that the patentees would only act as "Guardians or Trustees" and preserve the land for the Indians. Dellius's interpreter Hilletie van Olinda abetted the fraud, misrepresenting the exchange so that the sellers had no idea that they had permanently alienated their land. According to Bellomont, pure greed motivated Dellius to perpetrate this design against the very Indians he claimed as friends and proselytes. The land contained many trees that could be used for masts, and the minister "proposes to himself a great profit by sending masts down the River and selling them" in New York. Not coincidentally, Bellomont himself had a plan for establishing New York as a center for the production of naval stores, and did not want one of his chief rivals to receive the profits.[30]

Bellomont claimed that the minister's fraudulent dealings with the Mohawks were part of a larger design to undermine the king's government in New York and strengthen both the Jacobite party and French papists. The governor used a variety of evidence to make his case against Dellius, including recycled charges from Leisler's tenure and more recent allegations. Bellomont also engaged in what modern commentators label "the politics of personal destruction," painting Dellius as a drunk and a libertine to sully his reputation in the English court.[31]

Bellomont traced Dellius's bad intentions back to the early 1690s. After the Glorious Revolution, the governor claimed, the minister refused to pray for King William—Bellomont alleged that the minister possessed "a personall hatred to the King." Even more ominously, Dellius maintained an active correspondence with French Jesuits, including one Pierre Millet, who lived as a captive among the Oneidas for much of the war, and former missionary Jacques de Lamberville. These contacts "gave people jealousie he was popishly affected." In fact, Dellius had written to Millet and even worked to ensure that the imprisoned priest received no cruel treatment during his captivity. Despite his protestations of innocence, the verifiable existence of such letters helped to suggest that the minister was actually a closet Catholic.[32]

The governor buttressed these old charges with new allegations against Dellius. Soon after Bellomont's arrival Dellius had accompanied Johannes Schuyler on an embassy to Montreal to settle the peace, and after the land grant controversy erupted some Albany townspeople became "jealous" that the minister had betrayed the country during his trip to Canada. Bellomont predictably shared these suspicions, and added the charge that Dellius had "tamper'd" with the Iroquois by telling them that he and his political allies possessed as much authority as the governor. During his first conference with the Iroquois Bellomont found them "so sullen and cold in their carriage that I thought we had quite lost their affections," and he blamed Dellius for their intransigence. Bellomont recognized that the Iroquois alliance provided security from New France, and he believed that Dellius's designs—both the fraudulent land purchase and his treacherous embassy—had the calculated aim of alienating the Iroquois from the English and forcing them to make peace with the French.[33]

The most damning charge against the minister concerned an alleged sexual dalliance with a French Canadian woman. After Dellius's return from Canada rumors began to circulate that he had seduced a woman there—a longtime acquaintance who had spent the last several years as a prisoner in Albany—and left her with a "big belly." The evidence consisted of a letter from the woman to Dellius demanding that he provide financial support for the child. Bellomont never actually saw the letter, but heard of its existence from several sources. To the governor, this report further highlighted Dellius's depravity—Bellomont compared the minister to the biblical sons of Eli, noting that "his familiarity with the French woman is parallel to the sin committed by those two at the door of the Tabernacle." Additionally, the allegation highlighted Dellius's similarity to Catholic ecclesiastics, who many Protestants believed were prone to sexual deviance.[34]

Bellomont's efforts resulted in Dellius fleeing the colony and returning to the Netherlands. The governor vacated the questionable grant and returned the land in question to the Mohawks. At the same time he removed Dellius from his ministerial position—a bold act for a secular ruler in a province dominated by Reformed Protestants. In the end, however, this victory proved hollow, as Bellomont's actions inspired significant resistance from Dellius's friends and supporters, who protested "a suspension of a minister by the civil power." Nearly every church in the colony wrote to European authorities lauding Dellius for his work converting the Indians and lamenting his departure. In the meantime, Bellomont became frustrated with his Leislerian allies, who neglected to put their accusations against the minister in writing, and failed to acquire the letter outlining Dellius's sexual transgressions.[35]

Dellius's personal response to the charges lambasted the governor as a self-interested tyrant and vigorously denied the allegations. Nonetheless, Bellomont's campaign forced the minister to debate the governor on his own terms, as he spent much of his protestation proving his anti-Catholic credentials. Far from being a papist, Dellius had preached against the Roman church from his pulpit during James II's reign—when a number of Jesuits roamed the province seeking proselytes—and his mission to the Mohawks helped prevent many Indian allies from defecting to the French and Catholicism. His correspondence with Pierre Millet had been an act of Christian charity, not an endorsement of his beliefs, and the Canadian woman in question was not a love interest, but a "woman of quality" who hosted Dellius during his embassy and wrote a friendly letter attempting to establish commercial ties with Albany. Even as he defended his conduct, Dellius realized that such charges of popery were hard to refute. "Although I am no Jesuit," the minister protested, "I must pass for one, for [Bellomont] forges the resemblance in his own brain." He might have added that such allegations resounded greatly among a nervous populace primed to believe that popish conspirators threatened them at every turn.[36]

Bellomont's extreme anti-Catholicism also influenced his foreign policy. While he arrived during peacetime, the governor did not trust the French—and he was particularly fearful that Jesuit missionaries still labored to seduce the Indians from their proper obedience to King William. To prevent this evil, Bellomont opened a two-front assault on the missionaries. He pledged to expel Jesuits from both the Iroquois country and the eastern borderlands beyond the Province of Maine. When the Jesuit Jacques Bruyas requested permission to return to his Iroquois mission site, Bellomont angrily refused, and he warned Canadian governor Louis Buade, comte de Frontenac, that any Catholic missionaries who ventured into Iroquois villages would be imprisoned and prosecuted under English law. The new governor's bluster provoked a similar response from French officials, who instructed their missionaries not to negotiate with him and requested that authorities in France send Irish priests who could covertly minister to New England's supposedly large Irish population.[37]

Bellomont's offensive against the Jesuits centered on the Iroquois country west of New York. The governor feared that the English would "intirely loose the Five Nations of Indians, unlesse an effectuall and speedy course be taken to retrieve their affection"—and a major part of this campaign was to send Protestant missionaries to counter Jesuit efforts. In April 1699 the interpreter Arnout Cornelisz Vielé represented Bellomont at the Iroquois capital of Onondaga, where he told the Indians "they should have protestant Instructors in their Countrey, at which they were extreamly rejoiced." In order to supply these missionaries Bellomont used his connections with the New England Company in London, who pledged to pay for several Harvard graduates to minister among the Iroquois. This arrangement ironically furthered a desire of Benjamin Fletcher, who had unsuccessfully tried to secure some of these funds for Dellius's mission, and proved unwelcome news to certain New Englanders who objected to the money leaving their region.[38]

The governor paid equal attention to New England's eastern frontier. Early in his tenure Bellomont received several reports that "French Priests" just beyond the Province of Maine labored to convert the Abenaki and maintain them in the French interest. The governor declared the Jesuits to be inveterate enemies; he noted to the New Hampshire legislature that while the Indians constituted "a cruel and perfidious enemy in their own nature," they had been "taught and encouraged to be more so by the Jesuits and other popish Missionaries from France," who taught their proselytes to "kill your people treacherously." Bellomont's first solution was not to send rival Protestant missionaries, but to remove the Jesuits by any means possible. The missionaries themselves learned of his intentions. One of them, Vincent Bigot, wrote an angry letter to an English correspondent remarking that Bellomont "earnestly desires to get us into his hands," and planned to "thrust us into a most loathsom prison." The missionary's brother and fellow Jesuit Jacques Bigot also knew of Bellomont's intentions; when he met an English ship on the coast of Maine he declined the captain's invitation to come aboard. "Had I done this," he wrote, "I think that I would not have seen my beloved Mission again for a long time."[39]

The policies and predilections of Bellomont's administration closely resembled those of his predecessor, Jacob Leisler—with an important difference. While Leisler's quest to rid North America of popery had placed him at odds with imperial power, Bellomont *was* the imperial power. For the first time, English officials tried to promote themselves as the guardians of Protestantism, and this change in rhetoric had great consequences for the future history of imperial governance, as it defined the empire in terms that most subjects could understand and support. In the short term, this new understanding of empire shaped Bellomont's response to the greatest crisis of his administration: the revelation of a new Indian design.

• • •

The events of the early months of 1700 provided Bellomont with an opportunity to pursue his imperial plans. The eighteenth century in New England began with an ominous portent. In several towns in the Connecticut Valley and elsewhere people observed "a Blazing Starr," accompanied by "the apperranc of a great Light and nois of guns." A booming voice accompanied this visual and aural phenomenon, "Saying Fight on fight on for the King of England." If these signs in the sky were correct—and history suggested that they often were—then the region was headed for another war.[40]

Other disturbing news accompanied this worrisome astronomical phenomenon. Early in the year rumors of a new Indian conspiracy surfaced in northeastern Connecticut. As in other similar panics, the rumors started with an Indian, the Mohegan sachem Owaneco. On January 16 the chief visited James Noyes in New Roxbury (now known as Woodstock), telling the Englishman about a visit by strange Indians a few weeks earlier. A Nipmuck chief named Toby—a particularly difficult character suspected of being an enemy agent during the last war—had come through the area carrying wampum belts from the north. Toby presented his belts to Ninequabbin—a Wabbaquasset sachem who lived near New Roxbury—and according to Owaneco, the belts signified an invitation to join a "general combination" of Indians that would "cutt off the English." These Indians invited Owaneco to join the plot, but he refused and instead brought the information to colonial authorities—first to Noyes and later to Connecticut governor Fitz John Winthrop.[41]

The plot had two major components. It began far to the west when a "duchman at Albany" informed local Mohawks "that king William had given order for the cuting off [of] all indians" and advised them to stock up on powder before the king stopped selling it to them. The king actually had proposed restricting arms sales to Indians, but not to allied Mohawks, and not in preparation for some kind of general slaughter. Some early reports suggested that the Dutch merchant acted out of self-interest in an attempt to boost his arms sales, but the rumors had drastic effects, supposedly inspiring the longtime allies of the English to consider war in the name of self-preservation. No one knew for sure whether friendly Mohawks would break the Covenant Chain and fight the English, but their Canadian brethren—the numerous Mohawks who lived in mission communities near Montreal—definitely did intend war. The longtime malcontent Toby was present at the war council that resolved to take on the colonists, and he helped to negotiate an alliance between the Mohawks and the "eastern Indians"—mostly Abenakis and Penacooks—who had menaced New England's northern and eastern frontiers during the previous war.[42]

The combination of Catholic Mohawks and Abenakis then endeavored to tempt the "friend Indians" who lived in New England to join the plot. As Toby told the Mohawks, they could "easily destroy the English" with the help of local natives, since they lived in the heart of English territory and could fall on their neighbors without warning. Toby himself traveled to the "praying town" of Natick and then on to Connecticut bearing wampum belts that invited local sachems to join the plan. As reported by Owaneco, these rumors seemed precisely calculated to arouse colonists' fears, drawing on their anxieties about a new Indian war and their distrust of the "pretend friends" who lived among them. This plan differed from previous ones by the sheer number of partners it included. One Indian illustrated the scope of the plot by drawing a bow over a map of the region, stretching from the eastern country, through New England and into Iroquoia: "the longest bow that ever was in New England" and one that united a vast majority of Indians against the colonists.[43]

Suspicious movements by local Indians accompanied these rumors. Early in February a militia captain from New London named Samuel Mason traveled to Oxford, just across the Massachusetts border, to inspect the native community there. When he reached his destination Mason found that many of the Indians had left, supposedly fearful of an attack by their Mohegan rivals. Their destination, it seemed, was north of New Hampshire in Penacook country—Toby's frequent place of lodging and a central meeting point for New England's enemies. If all these events were not enough, colonists in New Hampshire also noticed strange behavior on the part of neighboring Indians. Natives residing near the town of Dover suddenly withdrew in mid-February, "supposed to be occasioned by an Indian that came that afternoon out of the woods, and made all dispatch to gather the Indians together." Before they left the Indians seemed to be inspecting English houses in the vicinity, and this strange display convinced worried townspeople that the natives "designed mischiefe aga[in]st us."[44]

Over the following month colonists gathered more evidence about the coming assault. Owaneco's initial allegation provided an unstable foundation—the chief was a notorious drunkard described by one of his fellow sachems as "fals, untrue, and wicked"—but other reports seemed to confirm the details of his testimony, and as one Connecticut official noted, it was "better to be awakened by false reports to attend duty than secure to expose o[u]r selves to danger." One of the fullest accounts of the conspiracy came from a New Roxbury resident named John Sabin—a friend to local Indians who had done frequent service as a negotiator during the war. Sabin tramped to Boston in mid-winter to share his alarming news with Bellomont and his council, relating how his Indian correspondents had spoken of such a design for months, but Sabin had only credited their talk after hearing of Owaneco's revelations. An inhabitant of Oxford who signed his letters only as N. J. provided separate details of the plot, saying he heard from an Indian friend that a large army of natives "ware ready to fall upon the English Speedily."[45]

These various reports blamed the French and especially Jesuit missionaries for the impending war. Neither Owaneco nor the other Indian informers had mentioned the French, but their English auditors naturally amended the stories to add a Catholic dimension to the plot. James Noyes fit the design into the devil's perpetual war against New England, describing the Indians as Satan's "subjects that worship him" under the tutelage of "french jesuits." John Sabin actually implicated the French governor in the conspiracy. He asserted that the coming war would be fought "by the instigation of the Governour of Canada," who would use his "cunning men"—meaning Jesuit priests—to tell lies to the Indians and push them to war against the English. Sabin's speculation led to a number of wild rumors as colonists insinuated that Jesuits had planted the rumor that King William intended to disarm and conquer the Indians, apparently forgetting the initial reports blaming a Dutch merchant.[46]

The wave of fear caused New Englanders to look to authority to provide protection from the threat. Colonists in Connecticut sent off to Hartford and New London for aid, but they knew that real assistance had to come from a higher source: the imperial governor in Boston. While Bellomont had no authority over Connecticut's militia during peacetime, he did have access to the larger Massachusetts militia, and his authority stretched from New Hampshire to Iroquoia—most of the region affected by the supposed plot. By early February the governor was well informed of the details of the conspiracy; on 7 February the news had become common enough in Boston to warrant inclusion in Samuel Sewall's diary. But the nervous colonists who implored the governor for assistance had little reason to expect much from him. In the past imperial officials had rarely looked kindly on such popular panics, and concerned residents of Oxford and New Roxbury seemed to know that their appeals might not be favorably received. Oxford's minister and his neighbors insisted in letters to both Winthrop and Bellomont that "our Brains are not Addled nor is this writing the Effect of Lunacy or phrenzy but we speak of things Just as they are." As James Noyes recognized, Bellomont was a "stranger to these divelish Policies"—and strangers had too often ignored similar alarms in the past.[47]

Much to their surprise, the panicked people of Oxford and New Roxbury found an ally in the imperial governor. The revelation of an Indian plot fit Bellomont's conspiratorial worldview, and he never attempted to downplay or discount his subjects' fears. Instead, he used the revelations of a plot to further his political goals: in particular, his campaign against Jesuits and his efforts to increase the royal presence in North America. On the last day of February Bellomont first reported to the Board of Trade on the "ugly allarm . . . of a General Insurrection and Rebellion of all the Indians." John Sabin's report about the French governor and his "cunning men" proved that Jesuits were behind the plot, and blamed Jacques Bruyas in particular for spreading the rumors that turned the Indians against the English. Bellomont resolved to continue his plan to expel or capture any Jesuits among the Indians, hoping to send "those Vermin to England, there to be punished as they deserve." He also began a concerted campaign for more troops to defend the continent and more money to buy gifts for Indian allies, drawing an unfavorable contrast with the French on both counts. If the government did not begin investing in its colonies, Bellomont implied, they would soon be lost.[48]

On the local level, meanwhile, the governor rallied his subjects to foil the conspiracy. On 13 March Bellomont called in the Massachusetts General Court and informed them of the plot. His initial speech to the legislature elevated the "general Insurrection" from a rumor to a probability, and he called the province to arms, imploring the representatives "to Consider of a Way to make such levies of Souldiers as shall be sufficient to defend the Country, and being levied, to Discipline, and make them expert in the service and use of their arms." Over the next few days Bellomont also called on subjects to "undeceive" the Indians about the alleged English design against them, and he proclaimed a general fast. This last move adopted a convention of the old charter government, which had frequently placed coded political messages in fast day proclamations—often covertly critical of imperial designs. Bellomont's proclamation utilized the same language, calling on God to help New England in its time of trial, and also placing the region's problems in a global context by noting "the sore and bitter persecutions wherewith the People of God in France, and in some other parts of Europe, are grievously harrassed and oppressed." While fast proclamations in the 1680s had served to criticize imperial policy, this one implicitly promoted the empire as a force that would defend both New England and the international Protestant cause. Bellomont also saw that his speeches were published and sent home with the representatives after they dispersed, so that inhabitants of all New England's towns knew exactly what their governor was doing to defend the country from popish and Indian enemies.[49]

The colonial assembly responded warmly to Bellomont's entreaties. The governor wrote to Fitz John Winthrop that the council and representatives proved "vigorous" in their response to his call to arms—not an insignificant reaction from a legislature famous for nay-saying its chief executive. Bellomont's appeal succeeded because it managed to be firm without being condescending. The governor did not compel the assembly to take any course of action—thus respecting their autonomy—but he spoke firmly enough that they knew they had to do something. The effectiveness of this approach can be gauged from a letter that one representative sent home detailing the assembly's proceedings. William Bassett told his unnamed correspondent that the legislature had laid aside all other business to devote itself to "putting ourselves & neighbors in a capassety to secure ourselves" from the "Comon Enemie." He enclosed Bellomont's proclamation to share with his constituents, "by which you may see some thing is already done," but he also assured "our neighbors" that no one would be impressed to support the war effort. Bellomont's strategy was perfectly tailored to appeal to colonists' sensibilities: he pledged to meet the enemy, but did not demand that the region's young men be called to service outside their home towns.[50]

The governor's actions in the days after the assembly met further assured his subjects that he was serious about defending the region from the plot. In Oxford, for instance, Bellomont's actions helped demonstrate the efficacy of royal government. At the beginning of the month one Oxford resident implored Bellomont to send men to protect against the enemy, noting that no one with a commission had ever been stationed in the frontier town. On 18 March Benjamin Sabin wrote a desperate appeal to Fitz John Winthrop, complaining of the region's undefended state. Noting that Bellomont had promised only to send a messenger to gauge the town's defenses rather than a regiment, Sabin asked Winthrop to provide "at least 14 Souldiers." The very night that Sabin wrote, however, the people of Oxford were "Surprised by the Unexpected Coming in" of about 20 men "for our relief." The governor had come through after all, and the people of Oxford rested in safety.[51]

Bellomont also utilized his status as New York's governor to investigate the plot there. At the same time that he called New England to arms he sent a letter to the commissioners of Indian affairs in Albany who maintained close ties with the Iroquois, asking "whether there be any Indeavours us'd by the french to debauch them from us." His letter related the details of the plot, relating how the "french missionaries" had been "industrious to the last degree" in their efforts to destroy the alliance. Bellomont instructed the commissioners not only to counteract Jesuit deception, but also to give the Indians proper presents to maintain the alliance and to furnish the names and numbers of missionaries that worked among them. By the time the governor wrote these appeals to Albany, the Indians themselves had ceased to be primary players in a plan that the governor believed to be entirely controlled by Jesuits and the governor of New France.[52]

The commissioners' response would have chastened a less zealous governor. Robert Livingston immediately assured Fitz John Winthrop that "they know noething of any such designe, neyther can they believe it." Nonetheless, they did investigate the rumors, and their findings not only demolished the credibility of the original reports about the plot, but also provided a plausible explanation of how the rumors started in the first place. The key evidence came from three native informants; two Schaghticoke sachems who lived near Albany and the other a former resident of New Roxbury. The Indians confirmed that Toby had come to New Roxbury with wampum belts the previous spring, but he had not come to make war, but to celebrate peace. Excited that the end of King William's War allowed them to trade in places that had been off limits, the Penacooks had sent their ambassador to forge friendlier relations with New England's Indians. The New Roxbury natives had been afraid to share the news with their suspicious neighbors, however, because they believed "if the English should know that they had rec[eive]d a Belt or girdle of Wampum from the Pennecoke Indians" they would forbid the selling of powder to the Indians, thus robbing them of their livelihood and forcing them to leave their homes in search of a more hospitable dwelling place.[53]

The report underscored how dysfunctional Indian relations in New England had become. The Indians claimed the English were "so jealous of their Indians" that they did not allow them to hunt without an English escort, and any native hunting alone risked being killed. This climate of fear and mistrust also led the English to believe Owaneco's story—an outright lie calculated to discredit his rivals. As panic spread around the region, many of New Roxbury and Oxford's Indians fled, not to join a general conspiracy or convert to popery, but because they feared for their lives, and believed that the jealous English might cut them off at any time—not an unreasonable apprehension in light of recent events. In his own letter Livingston forcefully argued the Indians' innocence, claiming that even the widely suspected Schaghticokes were good subjects with no ill intentions. He also counseled Bellomont to make sure not to be too "Rigid and Jealous" in his treatment of the natives, noting that "keeping them in aw does rather Exasperate them than keep them under." As he wrote these words Livingston surely hoped that he had heard the last of the general insurrection.[54]

The governor ignored the substance of the report, however, focusing exclusively on the few marginal details that confirmed his previous beliefs. In one of their letters, for instance, the Albany commissioners doubted that Jesuits were active among the Iroquois, but confirmed that the French had a general desire to "debauch the Indians of the five nations from us," and that the Jesuits were major players in that design. Livingston elaborated on this suspicion, noting that large numbers of Mohawks had relocated to Canada, where priests instructed them in religion and maintained a "strange" authority over the proselytes, who even endured physical correction by the missionaries "upon the comission of any fault." Bellomont assiduously used this argument to buttress his own theory of Jesuit intrigue, not noting that the Jesuits had been ministering to Mohawks in Canada for decades, and Livingston had made identical arguments throughout the 1690s.[55]

Bellomont especially gravitated toward a relatively obscure section of Livingston's report. In his negotiations with the Iroquois Livingston decried "that diabolical practice which they have got of late in poysoning each other"— referring to the mysterious deaths of several Anglophile chiefs, perhaps by poison or witchcraft. This detail proved irresistible to Bellomont, and he included it in many of his letters home. Jesuits had long been associated with poison in the European imagination, and the very fact that Indians poisoned each other seemed to prove Jesuit involvement. The most calculated villain, Bellomont claimed, was the wife of an Onondaga sachem educated among the Jesuits, where she "was taught to poison, as well as to pray." The priests gave the woman a "subtill" poison that she placed under her long fingernails and let drop into the drinks of her victims. She "was so true a disciple of the Jesuits," the governor claimed, "that she has poison'd a multitude of our Five Nations that were best affected to us." In the end, however, the woman got her just reward, beaten to death in the streets of Albany by a relative of one of her victims. Aside from demonstrating how Jesuits schooled Indians in their deadly arts, Bellomont thus also adopted gender tropes common in anti-Catholic literature, showing how papists seduced spiritually weak but powerful women to accomplish their designs.[56]

The English also feared that Jesuits worked against them in the Eastern Country. In April Bellomont sent royal engineer Wolfgang William Romer to inspect Maine's fortifications, and he returned with news that the Abenakis had built two substantial forts and had "two Jesuits in each fort which do great hurt to the Kings interest . . . because they instil into those people an aversion & hatred for his Ma[jes]ty & his Subjects." More evidence corroborated Romer's report; Bellomont learned of a great meeting at the mission of Norridgewock, where there was "some mischief hatching between the Jesuits and those Indians." The missionaries allegedly chastised the Indians for negotiating with the English and demanded that the Abenakis consult them on all matters of policy. A leading Boston merchant in the region, meanwhile, learned from the powerful baron of Saint-Castin "that the Jesuits had Taken indefatigable pains to stir up the Indians every where to make war upon the english." In an added insult, the governor received a request from the Jesuit father in Norridgewock to sell him a bell for their church. Bellomont coldly refused, and pledged to "rout 'em out of that place, and all other places this side of the River Ste. Croix."[57]

The governor made good on his resolution to foil the Jesuits in another series of appeals to the legislature. Near the end of May 1700 he made a speech to the Massachusetts General Court, this time laying out his case against the Jesuits. He blamed the missionaries for the past decade's Indian troubles, claiming "it was at their instigation [the Indians] Murdered so many of Your People this Last War." He urged legislators to act against the menace, noting that allowing the missionaries to reside in the colonies was "Derogatory to English Laws, and Government." He urged lawmakers to "make a Law for punishing such Jesuits." This speech marked the most outward identification of English institutions with the fight against popery. To be a good Englishman, the governor implicitly argued, was to hate and oppose the papists, and colonists had better rally behind English institutions—including the empire—if they hoped to defeat the enemy. Once again, legislators heeded the call, quickly passing an act ordering all Jesuits and popish priests to leave the province. Anyone who broke the law risked perpetual imprisonment, and the legislature also threatened hefty fines for anyone who harbored a Jesuit. Within a month New York passed a nearly identical resolution, adding legal support to Bellomont's frequent threats against the missionaries.[58]

As if to prove the governor's point, new alarms began sounding in the days after his incendiary speech. Settlers in New Roxbury and Oxford once again reported that local Indians had abandoned their homes, and they heard reports that "an Unexpected number of Indians from all quarters" were massing near Penacook for a late summer assault on New England. This time the links to the Jesuits were clearer than ever. The Oxford Huguenot minister Jacques Laborie, who worked as a missionary among local natives, blamed Catholic missionaries for tempting his Indians away. When he asked his proselytes why they left, they "told me directly, that the religion of the Indians of Penicook was more beautiful than ours" and that "the french gave them silver crosses to put on their necks." The minister cautioned that the Indians would become slaves to the French if they deserted to the north, but they ignored his warnings. "The priests work vigorously," he concluded, and had used their charms and baubles to fool the hapless natives into serving the devil instead of God. Predictably, Bellomont pounced on this new report, citing it as "very plain evidence of the French Jesuits debauching those Indians."[59]

Beyond his legislative campaign in the colonies, Bellomont also attempted to change imperial policy in the center. The governor endeavored from the beginning of his tenure to convince his superiors in Whitehall to devote more attention to the colonies—especially in the form of troops and provisions—and the panic only underscored the need for new investment. Bellomont understood that no governor could use town-based militias to defend the country, since most colonists viewed them as local bodies whose task was to defend their own communities from outside attack. But even in the midst of a perceived serious crisis, Bellomont found a stingy royal administration unwilling to devote even meager resources to its overseas possessions. This reality pushed the governor to directly challenge his superiors in a manner uncommon among royal placemen; in a discussion of policy toward the Five Nations, for instance, Bellomont wondered that "the King seems to slight the Indians too much when in stead of taking measures to secure their affection and Obedience by protecting them from the french, the few Ragged souldiers are to be reduced and the Miserable woodden forts suffered to fall w[i]th meer rottenness." Throughout his correspondence the governor underscored the importance of the colonies to "the Nation," arguing that "the value of things . . . are not found out, but by the want of them."[60]

Bellomont's specific proposals resembled many of the others that had streamed into Whitehall over the previous decades. He drew an unfavorable comparison between the French and English colonies, noting that the French had attained a disproportionate influence in the region by sending adequate numbers of soldiers and cultivating Indian alliances. His two most important proposals, therefore, were to strengthen the garrison at Albany and build a "sod fort" near the Iroquois capital of Onondaga. The forts "are in so Ruinous a Condition that they will now scarse bear the firing of a Gun upon them," Bellomont reported to the Board of Trade. Officials in London proved sympathetic to the governor's suggestions. In October the Board of Trade heard a lengthy presentation on "the Defence of New York" that advocated building two new forts in the province and sending an Anglican missionary to combat Jesuit efforts. But despite these intentions, it proved difficult to find money to pay for such initiatives. The chair of the Board of Trade remarked with regret, "any thing that does Lay out money comes verry hard," and at first Whitehall proved reluctant to fund even the one sod fort at Onondaga, preferring that "the plantation"—meaning colonists—pay for it. In the end Bellomont did secure a small sum for the fort, but even the following year the crown resisted sending more troops to Albany or paying those already there a living wage.[61]

The end result of all Bellomont's efforts—both in the colonies and in London—was inconclusive. While the crisis undoubtedly raised the governor's stock in New England, he remained a polarizing figure in New York, and his enemies there continued to hound him and work for his recall. In London, meanwhile, the shifting of the political tides from the governor's Whig friends to his Tory enemies made him less influential. When he died in office in March 1701 many of his plans remained unfulfilled, and he was destined to be remembered more for his role in the rise and fall of the pirate William Kidd than for any policy endeavors.[62]

It would be a mistake to view the conspiracy of 1700, and the governor who cultivated it, as footnotes in colonial history. In fact, the episode had subtle but important effects, helping to push the region into an imperial age. The most obvious consequence of the panic was to make the colonies more English and more Protestant. The new laws against Catholic priests, while not unprecedented, placed the region's anti-Catholic ethos in statute, and tied it with other parts of the empire—Ireland in particular—that enacted new measures against Catholics at the same time. Moreover, the governor worked to connect this anti-Catholic sentiment with love for the king and loyalty to English laws and governance. His speeches and writings frequently invoked King William—already a storied hero among many colonists—praising the king as "the Glorious Instrument of Our Deliverance from the Pitious Fetters and Chains of Popery and Tyranny which had almost overwhelmed our Consciences, and Subverted all our Civil Rights." In an answer to one of Bellomont's speeches, the Massachusetts representatives expressed similar sentiments, calling William "our most Glorious Deliverer under GOD, from Popery and Slavery; Circumstances most intolerable and odious to true *English-men*, above any men in the World." This kind of rhetoric encouraged the new cult of monarchy in the colonies, but it was a peculiar kind of monarchism, built not on the king's God-given authority but on his status as the defender of Protestantism.[63]

More important, Bellomont tied this love of the king together with respect for the English legal and political system—another important bulwark against popery. He urged colonists to be more English, but his definition of Englishness was more juridical than ethnic or national. In New York, for instance, he attempted to downplay ethnic tensions by claiming that Dutch people could be just as "English" as the English—as long as they obeyed and reverenced English laws and government. Speaking with one Huguenot merchant, Bellomont lamented "the animosities between the English the french and dutch," and underscored that he did not discriminate between ethnicities but demanded that all true subjects give their allegiance to the king and state. In this way, Bellomont promoted the empire not as a totalizing institution that forced colonists to change the way they imagined politics, but as a means to retain the Protestant liberties they already possessed.[64]

The benefits of this benevolent imperialism did not extend to Americans who were not white or Protestant. The most lasting consequence of the panic of 1700, and perhaps of King William's War in general, was the further alienation of Indian people from colonial society—making future violence and misunderstanding almost inevitable. This transition can be seen in the shifting loyalties of the Penacook sachem Wattunomen—one of the most powerful native leaders in the region and a supposed ringleader of the conspiracy. Throughout the 1690s Wattunomen had attempted to remain aloof from the imperial battles that raged around him, and he continued his studied neutrality during the crisis of 1700. When Massachusetts officials suspected the sachem of ill intentions, for instance, he traveled to Boston to meet with the governor and allay his concerns, claiming to be "no wayes concerned in the Combination" and requesting freedom to travel and trade in English territories. This display did little to comfort the English; Lieutenant Governor Stoughton bluntly declared that he did not believe Wattunomen, and officials across the region moved to restrict native movements. When some of the Wabbaquasetts returned from Penacook to Connecticut, for instance, Fitz John Winthrop recommended that an English person be appointed to watch over the natives and prevent them from ranging about the country, as they had been "thornes in our sides that let out streames of blood and may yet be sharper if some meathods be not taken to settle them under better obediance." In New Hampshire, nervous legislators considered a bill that would ban Indians from even entering colonial towns.[65]

These policies eventually turned the conspiratorial fears of 1700 into a self-fulfilling prophecy. While the conspiracy never existed, English paranoia eventually convinced many natives that they could never live in peace with the English, and had to forge alliances with the French if they hoped to survive in the new imperial climate. Wattunomen was among those who abandoned neutrality and embraced the French cause in the eighteenth century. He became one of the leaders of an actual expedition against the English—the deadly 1704 raid on Deerfield that inaugurated the next round of imperial warfare. Even the Iroquois no longer proved to be as dependable allies. Tired of war and annoyed that the English did so little to maintain the alliance, the Iroquois signed a separate peace with the French in 1701, meaning that the English often had to fight future wars without the aid of their most powerful native allies.[66]

The conspiracy of 1700 culminated a period of transition in North America. Fears of Catholicism continued to motivate colonial Americans, but they had helped to engineer a wholesale change in political culture. Instead of being independent agents against popery, colonists became partners in an imperial, Protestant coalition. This transition had enormous consequences for the development of North America and the future of the British Empire. Over the first half the eighteenth century these imperial connections helped integrate the colonies more fully into a European world—making colonists more self-consciously English than they had ever been before. At the same time, the empire attained a level of power and sophistication unknown during the previous century—a dominance determined not just by authorities in Whitehall but by thousands of subjects around the globe who ventured their lives and fortunes to expand the king's dominions. This profound transformation of political culture would not have occurred without the efforts of administrators like the earl of Bellomont—astute statesmen who realized that the empire could only win the hearts and minds of its subjects if it became the defender of Protestantism against popish enemies. By making anti-Catholicism a state ideology, Bellomont helped usher in the age of empire in North America.[67]

Epilogue: Nicholson's Redemption

IN 1710 A set of verses circulated around Boston paying homage to the recent English conquest of Acadia. The work began by praising the hero of the moment, the man who had commanded the victorious expedition. "Queen Anne sends Nicholson from London," the poet began, "To save New-England from being undone; / Who being come does forward push, / Regards nor Coin nor Life a Rush." The man in question, Francis Nicholson, must have been pleased, and perhaps a bit surprised, to be lauded in verse by a New Englander—even one of such questionable talent. After all, Nicholson had not always been such a popular man in the region. His first trip to the region had been in 1687, when he served as an officer in the Dominion of New England; his tenure as Sir Edmund Andros's lieutenant ended in disgrace when he fled his post in New York to avoid arrest. Two decades later, however, he was back, hailed as a hero by people who had previously denounced him as a possible popish agent. The author of the verses, Samuel Sewall, had been one of the most steadfast opponents of the Dominion, and a defender of New England's autonomy. In 1710, these two men stood together, along with many other people in America and Britain, to celebrate a victory that had emerged from the cooperation of provincial New Englanders and imperial officials. Clearly, something had changed in the years since Nicholson's first American tour.[1]

Nicholson's redemption provides a fitting opportunity to reflect on how the empire had developed over the course of one man's career. Few people played such a prominent role in the English America's transformation. Nicholson served as an imperial agent for over four decades in seven colonies, from the Mediterranean outpost of Tangier to the Dominion of New England, the Chesapeake, Nova Scotia, and South Carolina. Nicholson himself was a pugnacious character who relished his role as a representative of royal authority; this fact remained constant from his early days in Charles II's army to his retirement during the reign of George I. But the old soldier succeeded in his task largely because, as the empire changed, he changed with it. He held on to his fundamental beliefs but shifted his tactics, so that the embarrassment of 1689, when subjects rose up against the king's agents, became unthinkable, or at least unlikely, for most of the eighteenth century. In short, Nicholson witnessed the transformation of British America from a place that resisted the empire to one that embraced it. His own actions, and the actions of people like him, at least partially fueled this change.[2]

Nicholson succeeded because he came to embrace the central tenets of the new imperial political culture that emerged during the era of the Glorious Revolution. One important aspect of that culture, a belief in centralizing authority under the king, came naturally out of Nicholson's Restoration experiences. On his arrival in the Dominion of New England, he presented himself as an agent of imperial state-building. Though New Englanders were naturally "very cuning," Nicholson hoped to "convince them what a happy Change they made, liveing under a Great and Gratious King now where formerly they were under a number of Tyarants." Nicholson never lost this zeal for the royal mission, but he learned that centralization could not be imposed by fiat; he needed to show colonial subjects why they should accept the inevitable loss of autonomy that came with the expansion of empire. He did this by stressing two things: the dangers of popery and the need to provide for defense. His tactics looked quite similar to those of his contemporary the earl of Bellomont, a man from the opposite side of the political spectrum.[3]

• • •

The first stage of Francis Nicholson's redemption occurred in the Chesapeake colonies of Virginia and Maryland. Like other disgraced officers of the Dominion of New England, Nicholson had no trouble explaining his conduct to ministers in Whitehall, many of whom were holdovers from James II's reign. His task was made easier by his connection to the Williamite duke of Bolton. In fact, while Sir Edmund Andros had to endure a trial before returning to America, Nicholson spent only a year in England before winning appointment as lieutenant governor of Virginia, where he arrived in May 1690. He found a colony fatigued by political unrest and worried about the prospect of war. The previous executive (who continued to hold his commission) was Francis Howard, lord Effingham, a high Tory who had governed in the same domineering style as the rulers of the Dominion of New England, feuding with popular leaders in the House of Burgesses. His departure for England in 1688, before the revolutionary ferment began, calmed the waters, but Virginians remained skeptical of imperial rule. More to the point, they were frightened, both of "strange Indians" that periodically lurked beyond the borders and of French Canadians.[4]

Over the course of his half-decade initial tenure in Virginia, Nicholson succeeded in calming people's fears. He "directed the People from Mallancholy Thoughts," as the council maintained, mainly by providing for security and respecting the House of Burgesses. He made enemies, but they were members of the governing council, the kind of local oligarchs who had been his best friends in New York. In Virginia, he took the opposite tack, befriending members of the more popular House of Burgesses and the people themselves. He did so by stressing defense, and specifically by capitalizing on fears of Indian attacks. For instance, he strengthened the network of backcountry forts that protected the colony from invasion, and he investigated new ways to organize the Indian trade to reduce tensions between natives and colonists. He traveled around the colony personally inspecting fortifications, and even organized a local version of the "Olympick Games" to train young men in martial pursuits.[5]

Nicholson did not adopt this policy out of sheer benevolence; he still aimed at centralizing imperial administration as a whole. While Nicholson understood, from his own experience, that combining all the colonies together in one political union had certain pitfalls, he continued to believe that only a coordinated effort could save English America from a French invasion. In the wake of Sir William Phips's failed Canada expedition, for instance, Nicholson conducted a thorough investigation, even interviewing several veterans of the mission who somehow ended up in Virginia. Not surprisingly, he blamed the failure on that fact that "all the Neighbouring Colonies of New England New Yorke and Maryland are in Confusion and have no Gov[erno]rs appointed by their Sacred Ma[jestie]s." In addition to the three colonies he singled out, Nicholson also targeted Pennsylvania, where he argued that the leaders' pacifist views threatened the empire. Widespread rumors implied that Pennsylvanians "have given out that if the French or Indians come against them they would goe out and Meet them without Armes, and acquaint them they had no quarrel with them." He urged not only the settlement of governments in all the colonies, but official coordination between them, in the creation of "a Post or Posts . . . to goe from one Government to another, that soe wee may have a Continuall and Speedy Correspondence of anything that may happen."[6]

All this sounds quite a bit like the Nicholson of 1687—though somewhat more sensitive to public opinion. But there was a new side to him as well. Throughout his two separate terms in Virginia and, between them, as royal governor of Maryland, Nicholson thoroughly embraced the Protestant side of imperial political culture. To be sure, his brand of anti-Catholicism differed in important respects from that of Reformed radicals like Jacob Leisler. He acted as one of the foremost champions of the Church of England, trying to build institutions so that colonists would no longer be, as he put it, "sheep without a Shepherd." He urged Lambeth Palace to send ministers and Books of Common Prayer, especially to places like Maryland and Pennsylvania where dissenting groups predominated, and in Virginia he was an early champion of the College of William and Mary, the colony's conformist answer to Harvard College in the north.[7]

Nicholson's antipopery also had an aggressive side. He fully embraced the conspiratorial mindset of English politics, and he set out to thwart the various forces of evil that threatened Virginia and Maryland from within. Like many Tories, he tended to lump dissenters and Catholics together, claiming that Protestant nonconformists were unwitting dupes of the papists—or perhaps worse. He reserved the worst of his ire for Quakers, whom he suspected of sharing information with the enemy. Their "inner light," he wrote, was really a "dark lanthern." He also believed that many New Englanders were natural foes of English monarchs and would aid the French. Nicholson clearly believed that Phips and his expedition were disloyal; he asked witnesses what flag Phips flew from his ship, implying that he served a master other than the king. In addition, he collected information from John and Robert Mason—relatives of the deceased New Hampshire proprietor—claiming that they knew of "Vessells sailing directly from New England to France," including one whose master was "an Irishman and a known Papist," who would probably pass on intelligence so that the French could invade the country.[8]

The starkest example of his Tory anti-Catholicism appeared in 1698 after Nicholson had moved from Virginia to Maryland. The old malcontent John Coode was causing trouble again, forming a faction of people who resisted imperial reforms and generally made trouble for Nicholson and his allies. The governor responded with a personal smear campaign, which he attempted to coordinate with Sir Edmund Andros, his former superior and sometime rival, then governing Virginia. Coode was, according to a proclamation from Virginia, "a dangerous & profligate person not only in his Rebellious & Seditious practises but also in his Morals." He naturally attracted "the unlearned

& younger Sort . . . which makes him not fit for human much less Christian society!" In a private letter, Nicholson went farther. Not only was Coode a Masaniello, a disturber of the peace, an atheist and deviant, he was also, naturally, a papist. Nicholson observed, "tis apparent tht the papists and Jacobites are concerned wth thm as also Mr. Pin," placing William Penn and John Coode in the same party, "who no doubt would be very glad to have me removed." Like Edwyn Stede, the earl of Bellomont, or, for that matter, John Coode himself at an earlier date, Nicholson presented himself as the Protestant hero, the one who could save the empire from popish enemies. This was the key to popular political success in the postrevolutionary empire.[9]

Like the rebel leaders of 1689 before him, Nicholson publicly targeted those he thought to be enemies of the state. Aside from the old Williamites, one of his main targets was the same group Coode had decried, Maryland's Catholic minority. While Maryland's revolution had excluded Catholics from political office and open expressions of faith, Nicholson found a wide degree of informal toleration. The papists, one memorandum stated, are "our professd Enemyes," and Nicholson hoped "They may not have so large a Liberty as now They enjoy The papists not being Excepted in the Matter of keeping their Chappells and fraternitys open To all they perswade to Joyn with Them." In 1698 he lamented that "zealous Papists" had been "visiting the sick during this time of common callamity" to "seduce, delude & perswade" Protestants to change faiths. He noted that Catholic masters often prevented their Protestant servants from praying. All these charges repeated anti-Catholic mantras that would have been familiar to Protestants in Maryland, or any other part of the empire, decades before. He set out to "countermine the wicked designs" of Catholics in a number of ways. First, he created a census of enemies, ordering sheriffs to list all the chapels, priests, and practicing Catholics (as well as Quakers) in the various counties. He also called for the strict enforcement of laws against Catholic worship.[10]

Nicholson related all these plans—marginalization of Catholics and dissenters, strengthening of the frontiers, promotion of piety and education—to his desire to advance the English empire in America. And the greatest threat, to be sure, came from France. Even from his perch in the Chesapeake, hundreds of miles from Canada, Nicholson studied French imperial strategy, and he came to see all the threats to English America as subsumed under the villainy of Louis XIV. In one report on American affairs submitted during his tenure in Maryland, Nicholson suggested that Louis was planning a new, diabolical assault on North America not only from the northeast, but from the west and southwest as well. Hearing of the exploration of the Mississippi Valley, Nicholson noted that the French king designed to "lay an ambush behind all the Kings colonys in the Continent of America." No colony would be safe from the French, and therefore it was imperative to defeat the Sun King's designs for America by whatever means possible.[11]

Nicholson himself took a leading role in this cause. After 1702 England and France went to war again after a dispute over the succession to the Spanish throne, a conflict that became known as Queen Anne's War in North America in recognition of the empire's new monarch. Violence quickly returned to the American borderlands, in much the same form as during the previous war. The worst depredations, once again, occurred in the northeast, in the Province of Maine and western Massachusetts, where French and Indian raiding parties attacked English communities. Descriptions of the violence resembled not just those from Schenectady or Maine the previous decade, but virtually all descriptions of popish violence against Protestants from the Irish Rebellion to the persecution of Huguenots. "At Porpudock they ript up one Goody Weber that was big with child and laid her child at her breast and so left her," noted one resident of Maine. "At Spurwink river they knockt one Jordans sucking Childs brains out agt a Tree." In other words, the Catholic-Indian plot was resurgent, determined once again to overtake Protestant America.[12]

New Englanders of all political persuasions agreed that only by invading the French colonies could the English stay safe in North America. Thus, they began to advocate renewed conquests of Acadia—which the French had reconquered soon after Phips's 1690 attack—and New France itself. Samuel Sewall noted that "bringing [the French colonies] under Her Maj[estie]s Obedience, would vastly enlarge the English Empire," and guarantee "the happy increase of the English Trade, and the Protestant Religion." These three fundamentals—empire, trade, and religion—once again combined to justify expansion. Joseph Dudley, a New Englander of almost opposite principles from Sewall who returned to the region as royal governor in 1702, remarked that "It is plain to every Considering man that while there is a French Nation in Europe so bigoted to the Romish Religion & so set upon perfidy and Destruction of all protestants, that have dependent Colony's in our Neighbourhood, we shall have no rest or Ease." He also repeated arguments of Robert Livingston and John Nelson from past years, claiming that "Indians must inevitably become Vassals & Servants to us" after the English defeated the French.[13]

All this resembled the rhetoric of the 1690s, but with a slight difference. Alongside the frequent invocation of the Protestant interest was an unmistakable sense that the various colonies faced a virtually identical threat. From London to Boston to Philadelphia, people interpreted the situation in very similar ways. The New Englander John Higginson, for example, looked at the French as a scourge not just to New England, but to the whole empire, as they were "endeavouring Might & Maine to gain over to their Religion & Intrest all the Indians," from Canada south to the backcountry of Virginia and Carolina to their new colony of Louisiana, founded near the mouth of the Mississippi River. The result would be to make the English "Slaves to the Heathen." At the same time, royal agent Robert Quarry, then in Philadelphia, said that the French "have inclos'd all the Queens Empire on North America." Both of these views mirrored Nicholson's earlier warnings about the French "ambush" of the English colonies, and were based in a great part on the writings of Louis Hennepin, a priest who had accompanied French explorers in the west. Hennepin's book even ended up on Increase Mather's reading list, demonstrating the extent to which New Englanders' geographical outlook had changed due to imperial war.[14]

The next assault on French Canada, therefore, came about as a partnership between local leaders such as the Mathers and Dudley and imperial officials. The leading imperial representative was none other than Nicholson, who had lost his posting in Virginia and had come back to America not as an executive, but as the chief military strategist for the war effort. He teamed up with an unlikely partner, Samuel Vetch, a Scottish covenanter who had assisted in the failed effort to establish the Scottish colony of Darien in Central America a few years earlier. Despite coming from opposite ends of the political spectrum, Nicholson and Vetch worked together, serving as the leaders of an expedition that would begin by taking Port Royal and Acadia, considered a nest of privateers, and end by finishing the work of Phips and Wheler by taking Quebec City. Vetch's commission demonstrated the role that colonial public opinion played in bringing the expedition to life. It reflected, as the queen said, "frequent applications, which have been made to us by our good subjects, the Inhabitants of those Parts, to deliver them from the Neighbourhood of the French at Canada, which of late years hath been so troublesome to them."[15]

Nonetheless, the granting of the commission was not the end of the story. The partnership worked better in theory than in practice, not because colonists resisted imperial exactions—though some officials did complain about their stinginess—but because officials in London proved reluctant to devote resources to the colonies that could be reserved for Europe or the

Mediterranean. For instance, Vetch and Nicholson had to call off the first expedition against Port Royal when expected reinforcements did not come through. The expedition's leaders chafed at the insult, as did local leaders and the women of Boston, who harangued returning soldiers with insults as they returned to port. One petition to the queen claimed that the French and their allies "doe looke on us, as a people forsaken of Your Majesty and as left to be a prey to their teeth." Once again, defense proved to be the pivotal issue in colonial politics, but this time everyone in New England, from people on the streets to royal representatives, agreed on the proper response. They only had to convince those in London to support them.[16]

In 1710 Nicholson and Vetch finally received the support they needed to conduct their expedition against Acadia. In order to gain the necessary support from the metropole, Nicholson traveled to London to make a personal appeal on behalf of New Englanders, finally receiving enough soldiers and ammunition to go ahead with his plans. The expedition resulted in the conquest of the French province, this time for good—it became the new British colony of Nova Scotia, regaining the name of a short-lived Scottish venture there nearly a century earlier. The taking of Port Royal temporarily buoyed the spirits of New Englanders, leading to the celebratory verses lauding Nicholson's service. At the same time, everyone perceived it, like Phips's earlier attack on the same port, as a preliminary venture to the taking of all New France and, eventually, the North American continent. One colonial theorist wrote that victory over the French would give the British "ground and scope to Setle 40 provinces with all the supernumeraries of Europe or refugees." They would gain the fisheries, accomplish mastery of the seas, and use the fruits of their American possessions to become "Soll arbiters of Europ." Nicholson himself laid out another rationale for the conquests. They were done, he wrote, "for Gods Glory," and for "the Extirpacon of the Roman Catholick Religion."[17]

The conquest of New France would have to wait. In 1711 a joint British–New England expedition under the command of Sir Hovenden Walker attempted to take Quebec, but abandoned their plans after several ships ran aground in the St. Lawrence River. The failure led to new rounds of recriminations, as colonial subjects and imperial planners blamed each other for the failure. This time, however, Nicholson stood on the colonists' side. According to Cotton Mather, he spoke on behalf of New England in Whitehall, arguing against those who blamed colonial subjects for Walker's failure. For this service, Mather noted in a private letter, Nicholson deserved to be "thanked for his activity and fidelity." He had made a stunning transition, which reflected a change of political tactics on Nicholson's part, but also a cultural change in the colonies themselves. By 1711, Protestant, anti-French imperialism held the empire together. It was an imperfect bond, to be sure, but one that worked remarkably well. Moreover, adaptations of the same political philosophy appeared in most British colonies. They retained their local quirks, but were all comfortably ensconced within an imperial system that valued monarchy, Protestantism, and the common defense.[18]

• • •

Nicholson's last imperial posting came in the colony of South Carolina. A proprietary colony perched, both culturally and geographically, between the mainland and the Caribbean, South Carolina became a royal colony in 1720, with Nicholson serving as the first royal governor. The transformation of South Carolina itself, like that of its first royal executive, illustrated the same processes that occurred in most of Britain's American colonies. But the circumstances in that colony, a remote outpost in the 1680s that gradually turned into a pivotal plantation society, revealed some other sides of the imperial transition. Whereas in the Northeast the French served as primary targets for Britain's expansionistic project, people in South Carolina increasingly viewed imperial relations through the prism of race. This particular manifestation of imperial politics, one that adapted the language of British politics to fit American circumstances, proved remarkably influential wherever Americans of different races and cultural backgrounds met.[19]

South Carolina's intensive introduction to the politics of empire began in 1701, nearly two decades before Nicholson arrived there. Though founded in the 1660s, the colony remained an insignificant outpost for the next few decades. The original proprietors included many power players in English politics, from both the Whig and Tory parties, but few settlers came in the early years. Whereas colonists fought among themselves, and repeatedly challenged the proprietors, the colony largely avoided the strife of 1689, and though South Carolina bordered the Spanish colony of Florida, the alliance between England and Spain kept inhabitants of the two colonies from intruding too much on each other's territory. In other words, the two forces that caused conflict in many colonies during the 1690s—rebellion and war—largely bypassed Carolina.[20]

Matters changed at the beginning of the new century. Even before the official return of war, Carolinians recognized the potential for a new conflict, as dynastic changes in Europe now placed Spain on the French side. This proved alarming because of the close proximity of St. Augustine to Charles Town, but to make matters worse the French had begun to envision a colony in Louisiana, only a few hundred miles to the west. In 1701 governor James Moore—a member of the Tory "Goose Creek" faction whose livelihood depended on the Indian slave trade—illustrated the dangers of the new century. "We are sure to be always in danger & under the trouble & Charge of keeping out Guards," the governor told the assembly, "even in time of Peace so long as those french live near us." In order to underscore the danger he compared South Carolina to its northern counterparts: "to put you in mind of the french of Canada's Neighbourhood to the Inhabitants of New England is to Say Enough on this Subject."[21]

Moore's strategy to meet the threat proved very similar to that of New England's leaders during the previous decade. He embraced the empire, but only to an extent, hoping to keep control of the mission in his own hands, rather than surrender power to imperial outsiders. After the coming of war Moore first planned an expedition against Florida's network of Franciscan missions to the Appalachee and Timucua Indians. The expedition had obvious religious implications; it fed on the common belief that Catholic missionaries trained their proselytes to serve as military bulwarks for the popish cause. At the same time, a strike against the missions appealed to Moore and his Goose Creek allies for other reasons, as it provided thousands of new bodies for the burgeoning Indian slave trade. These "Spanish Indians" ended up all around the empire, though some colonies, like Rhode Island, banned their importation when they became too "troublesome." Glossing over the economic rewards, Moore portrayed the assault as a necessity of imperial defense. "Before this expedition we were more afraid of the Spaniards of Appalatchee and their Indians in conjunction [with] the French of Mississippi, and their Indians doing us harm by land, than of any forces of the enemy by sea. Now they are totally undone."[22]

The next step was an attempted conquest of St. Augustine in 1702. Like Quebec City or Port Royal, the small Spanish garrison in Florida had long served as a tempting target for English raiders, especially the pirates who often spent their time in Charles Town or the nearby Bahama Islands. So once again, the expedition served the economic needs of prominent South Carolinians. Moore hoped that by eliminating Queen Anne's enemies in the region, colonial leaders would prove their worth to the empire—which would then give them liberty to manage their own affairs. As the governor put it, conquering

St. Augustine would "make us knowne & Recomend us to her Matie" and guarantee "her protection & Royall Aide."[23]

The last part of this statement demonstrated the ambiguity of South Carolina's situation. Like New England in the previous war, South Carolinians wanted the blessings of empire without its exactions. This proved to be a difficult balance that ordinary colonists in South Carolina could not maintain. As had happened with the earlier strikes in the north, Moore and his underlings could not conquer St. Augustine. They had enough forces to conquer and burn the small town, but could not capture its fortifications, eventually ending the siege when Spanish reinforcements arrived. In the meantime, circumstances in the colony made white Carolinians increasingly nervous. The Spanish enemy, like the French in the Caribbean, discovered South Carolina's greatest vulnerability: its slaves.[24]

South Carolina had been a slave society virtually since its foundation, but the rise of rice and indigo as cash crops furthered the region's dependence on enslaved African labor. By 1708 the colony became the first on the mainland to have a black majority, and this demographic imbalance created the same problems of defense as in the Caribbean colonies. Moreover, the Spanish learned early that they could manipulate these insecurities. From the early eighteenth century, the Spanish offered refuge to anyone, slave or free, who abandoned South Carolina and offered services to the Spanish. This offer proved tempting to many slaves, and throughout the early part of the century a steady stream of escaped slaves headed toward the colony, eventually founding the town of St. Teresa de Mose just north of St. Augustine. These former slaves, now free Catholics in the service of the Spanish king, proved formidable enemies during times of war.[25]

The defection of slaves quickly turned into a religious drama. The Spanish offered priestly instruction and baptism to escapees. Moreover, some of these Africans, it seemed, were already Catholic before arriving in the New World. A large number of slaves in Carolina came from either the Portuguese colony in Angola—where Jesuit priests routinely performed mass baptisms of captives before sending them into slavery—or the Kingdom of Kongo, an independent African state with its own Catholic Church. The numbers of Catholic slaves are difficult to measure, but their existence appears clearly in the letters of Francis Le Jau, an Anglican missionary of Huguenot descent who served the new Society for the Propagation of the Gospel in the colony during the first decade of the eighteenth century. In his missions to slaves, Le Jau encountered a number who had been baptized and received instruction in the Catholic faith. The missionary managed to convert several of these former Catholics to Protestantism, and set out on a program to promote Protestantism by sending New Testaments and Books of Common Prayer to St. Augustine. This last goal united Le Jau with people of very different theological persuasions, like Cotton Mather, who learned Spanish in order to write a catechism called *La fe del cristiano*, which he hoped would encourage a Reformation in the Spanish colonies. These efforts reflected the old notion that the struggle for North America was a contest of faiths as well as empires, but it held little purchase for native South Carolinians. Planters may have believed the papists targeted their slaves for conversion, but this did not turn them into advocates of missions. Instead, it made them more militant in their opposition to Spanish Florida.[26]

These fears of slaves, when combined with another crisis in intercultural relations, did succeed in transforming South Carolina's relations with Whitehall. In 1715 the Yamasee War broke out, a deadly conflict pitting white Carolinians against their former allies the Yamasee Indians, and which arose in part from the poisonous relations engendered by the Indian slave trade. In the wake of that conflict, the public clamored for greater protection from all enemies, black, Indian, or European. The result was the end of the proprietary government and the creation of a new royal colony—this one by popular acclaim. As perhaps the most accomplished veteran of the imperial service, Francis Nicholson arrived as governor in 1721, replacing James Moore and his faction. While the European peace during his governorship prevented him from leading any more conquests, his post in yet another North American colony demonstrated the extent to which the new imperial political culture extended across the colonies.[27]

In order to see how this political culture worked we must look a bit further into the future, to the next conflict between Spain and Britain. In 1739 the two kingdoms went to war over Spanish threats to British trade in the Caribbean, and fears of enemy attack returned to the region. During the summer, for instance, a suspicious stranger arrived in the new town of Savannah, Georgia, just south of South Carolina. The newcomer first claimed to be a Jew, then a German, but finally admitted he was "born in Old Spain." The man continued on his way, but events several months later in South Carolina led Georgians to rethink the encounter. A group of slaves near the Stono River had risen against their masters, killing several and heading south toward Florida before being apprehended by the militia. In the new reading, the stranger must have been "corrupting the Negroes of Carolina" to rebellion—an adaptation of antipopery that claimed that blacks, like Indians, were naturally susceptible to the advances of papists. Another source of concern was the fact that many of the slaves came from Angola, where "the Jesuits have a Mission and School . . . and many Thousands of the Negroes there profess the Roman Catholic Religion." The slaves may have come from the Kingdom of Kongo, or they may have not been Catholics at all. What was significant was that frightened planters definitely *thought* they were. They naturally fit their fears of slave conspiracies into the framework of Catholic plots and imperial military rivalry.[28]

These fears of a black fifth column spread to other colonies as well. In 1740 Georgia governor James Oglethorpe circulated reports, ostensibly originating from Indians in the vicinity of St. Augustine, that "the Spaniards had employed emissaries to burn all the magazines and considerable towns in the English North America," and that priests in disguise—like the Jewish-German-Spaniard in Savannah—were lurking and insinuating into the good graces of weak-minded people around British America. Thus the alarm when a number of suspicious fires appeared around New York City in 1741 and some slaves were implicated in setting them. As rumors of a conspiracy surfaced, officials could not accept that "these silly unthinking creatures could of themselves have contrived and carried on so deep, so direful and destructive a scheme." They naturally assumed that Spanish papists were behind the design.[29]

In the legal proceedings that followed, paranoid fears of popery served as a prominent backdrop in one of the most disturbing episodes in early American history. Prosecutors located the conspiracy in the long history of popish intrigue during the trial of John Ury, a schoolteacher identified as a "popish priest" who encouraged slaves to rebel and claimed that "he could forgive sins." The trial recycled a number of standard anti-Catholic arguments. Roman Catholics, according to the prosecutor, "hold it not only lawful but meritorious to kill and destroy all that differ in opinion from them," and held a particular goal to destroy "the Northern heresy." Their first method was to trick the laity into serving the church through "juggling tricks," before moving on to easier targets such as slaves. Moreover, this latest plot was just one in a string of outrages, from the "tragical instances of popish cruelty" in the Piedmont during the 1600s, the massacres in Paris, "the horrible slaughters of the duke d'Alba" in the Netherlands, and in general "that ocean of foreign blood with which the scarlet whore hath made herself perpetually drunk." Protestants in New York added more blood to the ocean, executing thirty slaves and four whites, some of whom were burned at the stake.[30]

Looking from the turmoil of 1741 back to the era of the Glorious

Revolution, one understands both the changes and continuities in imperial political culture. On one hand, the rhetoric of the New York conspiracy was nearly identical to that of the colonial rebellions of 1689; in both cases, ordinary people decried what they considered massive and diabolical plots against their lives and liberties. It was fear of these plots, more than any single factor, that pushed colonists to redefine their politics in the period after the Revolution. And yet at the same time, the political effects of this fear changed markedly. In 1689 ordinary people channeled their fear into dissent and rebellion, but by 1741 it was the powerless, not the powerful, who bore the brunt of popular rage. The British empire was a place in which people like Francis Nicholson and Cotton Mather could come together based on their mutual fear of Catholics, Indians, slaves, and other marginalized outsiders. This new kind of union emerged from the Glorious Revolution, and it proved remarkably durable. Only after the British finally defeated the French did North America face another age of imperial reckoning.

Abbreviations

Arch. Md.	W. H. Browne et al., eds., *Archives of Maryland* (Baltimore and Annapolis, 1883–).
AAS	American Antiquarian Society, Worcester, Mass.
BL	British Library, London.
CW	Rockefeller Library, Colonial Williamsburg.
DHNY	E. B. O'Callaghan, ed., *Documentary History of the State of New York*, 4 vols. (Albany, 1850).
DHSM	James Phinney Baxter, ed., *Documentary History of the State of Maine*, 19 vols. (Portland, Me., 1889–1916).
HL	Huntington Library, San Marino, Calif.
NYCD	E. B. O'Callaghan and John Romeyn Broadhead, eds., *Documents Relative to the Colonial History of the State of New York*, 15 vols. (Albany, 1853–87).
N.Y. Col. Mss.	New York Colonial Manuscripts, New York State Archives, Albany.
NYHS Coll.	Collections of the New-York Historical Society.
Mass. Arch.	Massachusetts Archives Collection, Massachusetts Archives, Boston.
MHS	Massachusetts Historical Society, Boston.
Randolph	Robert Noxon Toppan and Alfred T. Goodrick, eds., *Edward Randolph; Including his Letters and Official Papers . . . 1676–1700*, 7 vols. (Boston, 1898–1909).
TNA	The National Archives, Kew, England.
WMQ	*William and Mary Quarterly.*

Notes

INTRODUCTION: POPERY AND POLITICS IN THE BRITISH ATLANTIC WORLD

1. Benjamin Wadsworth, *King William Lamented in America: Or, A Sermon occasion'd by the very Sorrowful tidings, of the Death of William III* (Boston, 1702), 7, 9–10.

2. Edward Cranfield to the Committee on Trade and Plantations, 30 December 1682, CO 1/50/135, TNA. On New England political theory see T. H. Breen, *The Character of the Good Ruler: Puritan Political Theory in New England, 1630–1730* (New Haven, 1970). On the constitution of the empire see especially Bernard Bailyn, *The Origins of American Politics* (New York, 1969); Jack P. Greene, *Peripheries and Center: Constitutional Development in the Extended Polities of the British Empire and the United States, 1607–1788* (Athens, Ga., 1989); and Mary Sarah Bilder, *The Transatlantic Constitution: Colonial Legal Culture and the Empire* (Cambridge, Mass., 2004).

3. Memorial from the Agents from Albany to the Government of Mass., 20 March 1690, *NYCD*, 3: 695–98. Fear has been a subject of inquiry among historians and political theorists. See especially Corey Robin, *Fear: The History of a Political Idea* (New York, 2004); Peter N. Stearns, *American Fear: The Causes and Consequences of High Anxiety* (New York, 2006); and the classic essay by Richard Hofstadter, "The Paranoid Style in American Politics," in *The Paranoid Style, and Other Essays* (New York, 1965), 3–40. On the culture of conspiracy at this time see Barry Coward and Julian Swann, eds., *Conspiracies and Conspiracy Theory in Early Modern Europe: From the Waldensians to the French Revolution* (Aldershot, 2004). This book builds on the one comprehensive survey of the colonies during the era of the Glorious Revolution, David S. Lovejoy, *The Glorious Revolution in America* (New York, 1972).

4. The phrase "crisis of popery and arbitrary government" comes from Jonathan Scott, *England's Troubles: Seventeenth-Century English Political Instability in European Context* (Cambridge, 2000).

5. The fullest account of the plot remains John Kenyon, *The Popish Plot* (London, 1972); see also John Miller, *Popery and Politics in England, 1660–1688* (Cambridge, 1973); Jonathan Scott, "England's Troubles: Exhuming the Popish Plot," in Tim Harris, Paul Seaward, and Mark Goldie, eds., *The Politics of Religion in Restoration England* (Oxford, 1990), 107–31; and Tim Harris, *Restoration: Charles II and His Kingdoms, 1660–1685* (London, 2005), 136–202.

6. On antipopery in Elizabethan and early Stuart England see Peter Lake, "Anti-Popery: The Structure of a Prejudice," in Richard Cust and Ann Hughes, eds., *Conflict in Early Stuart England: Studies in Religion and Politics, 1603–1642* (London, 1989), 72–106; Michael C. Questier, "Practical Antipapistry During the Reign of Elizabeth I," *Journal of British Studies* 36 (1997): 371–96; Robin Clifton, "The Popular Fear of Catholics During the English Revolution," *Past and Present* 52 (1971), 23–55; Clifton, "Fears of Popery," in Conrad Russell, ed., *The Origins of the English Civil War* (London, 1973), 144–67; Carol Z. Wiener, "The Beleaguered Isle: A Study of Elizabethan and Early Jacobean Anti-Catholicism," *Past and Present* 51 (1971): 27–62; Caroline M. Hibbard, *Charles I and the Popish Plot* (Chapel Hill, 1983).

7. Henry More, *Apocalypsis Apocalypseos; or the Revelation of St. John the Divine* (London, 1680), 32. For details of this theology see Peter Lake, "The Significance of the Elizabethan Identification of the Pope as Antichrist," *Journal of Ecclesiastical History* 31 (1980): 161–78. On binary thinking in general see Stuart Clark, *Thinking with Demons: The Idea of Witchcraft in Early Modern Europe* (New York, 1999).

8. [Henry Care], *The Character of A Turbulent, Pragmatical Jesuit and Factious Romish Priest* (London, 1678), 3. On the political and economic effects of popery see Slingsby Bethel, *The Interest of the Princes and States of Europe*, 2nd ed. (London, 1681); and *The Political Mischiefs of Popery* (London, 1689).

9. *The True Spirit of Popery: or the Treachery and Cruelty of the Papists Exercis'd against the Protestants in All Ages and Countries where Popery has had the Upper-hand* (London, 1688), 3, 35. For the larger significance of the revolt see Aidan Clarke, "The 1641 Rebellion and Antipopery in Ireland," in Brian MacCuarta, ed., *Ulster 1641: Aspects of the Rising* (Belfast, 1993), 139–58; and Ethan Howard Shagan, "Constructing Discord: Ideology, Propaganda, and the English Response to the Irish Rebellion of 1641," *Journal of British Studies* 36 (1997): 4–34.

10. [Slingsby Bethel], *An Account of the French Usurpation upon the Trade of England, And what great damage the English do yearly sustain by their Commerce, and how the same may be retrenched, and England improved in Riches and Interest* (London, 1679), 2. On fears of "universal monarchy" during this period see Steven Pincus, "The English Debate over Universal Monarchy," in John Robertson, ed., *A Union for Empire: Political Thought and the British Union of 1707* (Cambridge, 1995), 37–62.

11. Philolaus, *A Character of Popery and Arbitrary Government* (London, 1681), 1. Later Stuart historians have debated whether or not Charles II and James II intended to set up an "absolute government" in England; for various perspectives, see John Miller, "The Potential for 'Absolutism' in Later Stuart England," *History* 69 (1984): 187–207; John Morrill, "The Sensible Revolution," in Jonathan Israel, ed., *The Anglo-Dutch Moment: Essays on the Glorious Revolution and its World Impact* (Cambridge, 1991), 76–81; Tim Harris, *Restoration: Charles II and his Kingdoms, 1660–1685* (London, 2004), 211–59; and Harris, *Revolution: The Great Crisis of the British Monarchy, 1685–1720* (London, 2006), 182–236. Steve Pincus has been the latest historian to contend that James II was a doctrinaire absolutist in the mold of Louis XIV; see *1688: The First Modern Revolution* (New Haven, 2009), 118–78.

12. [Charles Blount], *An Appeal From the Country To the City, For the Preservation of His Majesties Person, Liberty, Property, and the Protestant Religion* (London, 1679), 2.

13. Roger Morrice, *The Entring Book of Roger Morrice*, ed. Mark Goldie et al. (Woodbridge, 2007), 2: 158; [Pierre Jurieu], *The Last Efforts of Afflicted Innocence: Being an Account of the Persecution of the Protestants of France* (London, 1682), 2; [Robert Ferguson], *The Third Part of No Protestant Plot: with Observations on the Proceedings upon the Bill of Indictment against the E. of Shaftesbury: and A Brief Account of the Case of the Earl of Argyle* (London, 1682), 8. The fullest scholarly account of the exclusion crisis is Mark Knights, *Politics and Opinion in Crisis, 1678–81* (Cambridge, 1994).

14. [Alexander Shields], *A Short Memorial of the Sufferings and Grievances, Past and Present, of the Presbyterians in Scotland: Particularly of those of them called by Nick-name Cameronians* ([London], 1690), 3. The best account of party politics is Tim Harris, *Politics Under the Later Stuarts: Party Conflict in a Divided Society* (London, 1993). For a good account of the Whig political program see Mark Goldie, "Priestcraft and the Birth of Whiggism," in Nicholas T. Phillipson and Quentin Skinner, eds., *Political Discourse in Early Modern Britain* (Cambridge, 1992), 209–31.

15. Clare Jackson, *Restoration Scotland, 1660–1690: Royalist Politics, Religion, and Ideas* (Woodbridge, 2003); Harris, *Restoration*, 329–76. On anti-Calvinism see Nicholas Tyacke, *Anti-Calvinists: The Rise of English Arminianism, c. 1590–1640* (Oxford, 1990); Peter Lake, "Anti-Puritanism: The Structure of a Prejudice," in Kenneth Fincham and Peter Lake, eds., *Religious Politics in Post-Reformation England: Essays in Honour of Nicholas Tyacke* (Woodbridge, 2006); Patrick Collinson, "Antipuritanism," in John Coffey and Paul C. H. Lim, eds., *The Cambridge Companion to Puritanism* (Cambridge, 2008), 19–33.

16. [George Hickes], *The Spirit of Popery Speaking out of the Mouths of Phanatical-Protestants, or the Last Speeches of Mr. John Kid and Mr. John King, Two Presbyterian Ministers, Who were Executed for High-Treason and Rebellion at Edinburgh, August the 14th. 1679* (London, 1680), 2; *The Politicks of Malcontents, Shewing The Grand Influence the Jesuits Have in all their Desperate Undertakings* (London, 1684). On the program behind intolerance see Mark Goldie, "The Theory of Religious Intolerance in Restoration England," in Ole Peter Grell, Jonathan I. Israel, and Nicholas Tyacke, eds., *From Persecution to Toleration: The Glorious Revolution and Religion in England* (Oxford, 1991), 331–68.

17. "The Trial of Benjamin Harris, Bookseller, at Guildhall . . . ," in T. B. Howell, ed., *A Complete Collection of State Trials and Proceedings for High Treason and Other Crimes and Misdemeanors* (London, 1810), 7: 927; Mark Goldie, "The Hilton Gang and the Purge of London in the 1680s," in Howard Nenner, ed., *Politics and the Political Imagination in Later Stuart Britain* (Woodbridge, 1998), 43–73. On the radical Whig program during this period see Melinda Zook, *Radical Whigs and Conspiratorial Politics in Late Stuart England* (University Park, 1999).

18. *Journal of the Hon. John Erskine of Carnock, 1683–1687*, ed. Walter Macleod (Edinburgh, 1893), 113–14; Jurieu's *Accomplissement des propheties* first appeared in French in 1686, and in English translation the same year.

19. Cotton Mather, *Magnalia Christi Americana*, Books I and II, ed. Kenneth B. Murdock with Elizabeth W. Miller (Cambridge, Mass., 1977), 91; Karen Ordahl Kupperman, "Errand to the Indies: Puritan Colonization from Providence Island Through the Western Design," *WMQ* 3rd ser. 45 (1988): 70–99; L. H. Roper, *Conceiving Carolina: Proprietors,*

Planters, and Plots, 1662–1729 (New York, 2004); A. G. Roeber, " 'The Origin of Whatever Is Not English Among Us': The Dutch-Speaking and German-Speaking Peoples of Colonial British America," in Bernard Bailyn and Philip D. Morgan, eds., *Strangers Within the Realm: Cultural Margins of the First British Empire* (Chapel Hill, 1991), 220–83. There has been little in the way of sustained scholarship on early American antipopery, but see esp. Thomas More Brown, "The Image of the Beast: Anti-Papal Rhetoric in Colonial America," in Richard O. Curry and Thomas More Brown, eds., *Conspiracy: Fear of Subversion in American History* (New York, 1972), 1–20; Mary Augustina Ray, *American Opinion of Roman Catholicism in the Eighteenth Century* (New York, 1936); and Gayle Kathleen Pluta Brown, " 'A Controversy Not Merely Religious': The Anti-Catholic Tradition in Colonial New England" (Ph.D. dissertation, University of Iowa, 1990).

20. Frank Lestringant, "Une Saint-Barthélemy américaine: l'agonie de la Floride huguenote (septembre–octobre 1565), d'après les sources espagnoles et françaises," in *L'expérience huguenote au Nouveau Monde (XVIe siècle)* (Geneva, 1996), 229–42; A. M. Brookes and Annie Averette, eds., *The Unwritten History of Old St. Augustine* (St. Augustine, 1909), 14–19; Francisco Lopez de Mendoza Grajales, "The Founding of St. Augustine," *Old South Leaflets* 89 (New York, n.d.).

21. Quoted in Karen Ordahl Kupperman, *The Jamestown Project* (Cambridge, Mass., 2007), 51; Kupperman, *Roanoke: The Abandoned Colony*, 2nd ed. (Lanham, 2007), 87–88; J. Leitch Wright, Jr., *Anglo-Spanish Rivalry in North America* (Athens, Ga., 1971), 28–29.

22. Richard Hakluyt, "Discourse of Western Planting, 1584," in E. G. R. Taylor, ed., *The Original Writings & Correspondence of the Two Richard Hakluyts* (London, 1935), 2: 216, 239, 258. On Hakluyt's religious vision see David Harris Sacks, "Discourses of Western Planting: Richard Hakluyt and the Making of the Atlantic World," in Peter Mancall, ed., *The Atlantic World and Virginia, 1550–1624* (Chapel Hill, 2007), 410–53.

23. William Crashaw, *A Sermon Preached in London Before the right honourable the Lord Lawarre* (London, 1610); Douglas Bradburn, "The Eschatological Origins of the English Empire," in Douglas Bradburn and John Coombs, eds., *Early Modern Virginia: New Essays on the Old Dominion* (Charlottesville, forthcoming 2011).

24. The uses of antipopery during England's Civil War years are well covered in Lake, "Anti-Popery," as well as in Clifton, "The Popular Fear of Catholics During the English Revolution," 23–55. For the colonies during this time see Carla Gardina Pestana, *The English Atlantic in an Age of Revolution, 1640–1661* (Cambridge, Mass., 2004). As Pestana and Kupperman have underscored, much of the anti-Catholic colonizing push at this time focused on the West Indies rather than the mainland.

25. Benjamin Schmidt, *Innocence Abroad: The Dutch Imagination and the New World, 1570–1670* (Cambridge, 2001), 176–243.

26. M. Halsey Thomas, ed., *The Diary of Samuel Sewall, 1674–1729* (New York, 1973), 1: 359. The best account of the Western Design is in Pestana, *The English Atlantic in an Age of Revolution*. See also Steven C. A. Pincus, *Protestantism and Patriotism: Ideologies and the Making of English Foreign Policy, 1650–1668* (Cambridge, 1996).

27. Nathaniel Mather to Increase Mather, 19 December 1678, MHS, *Collections* 4th ser. 8 (1868): 16; Samuel Petto to Increase Mather, 21 [February] 1679, ibid., 345; Thomas

Waterhouse to Increase Mather, 27 February 1679, Mather Papers, vol. 3, fol. 4, Boston Public Library; Nicholas B. Shurtleff, ed., *Records of the Governor and Company of Massachusetts Bay in New England* (Boston, 1854), 5: 221; Order for a fast, 30 May 1681, Mass. Arch., 11:8.

28. Increase Mather Diaries, vol. 3, AAS [transcript at MHS], 79, 88, 131; Cotton Mather to Richard Chiswell, 27 November 1683, Rawlinson Letters 108, f. 87, Bodleian Library, Oxford; William Byrd to Perry and Lane, 8 August 1690, in Marion Tinling, ed., *The Correspondence of the Three William Byrds of Westover, Virginia, 1684–1776* (Charlottesville, 1977), 1: 135. For a sense of the dissenting networks that brought this news see Francis Bremer, "Increase Mather's Friends: The Trans-Atlantic Congregational Network of the Seventeenth Century," *Proceedings of the American Antiquarian Society* 94 (1984): 59–96.

29. The humble Peticon of Francis Branson, CO 1/48/45, TNA; Charles II to Governor and Council of Connecticut, 30 September 1682, Connecticut Colonial Records, 1664–1702, Connecticut State Library, Hartford. Kelso left only one other trace: a printed deposition of his role in the rebellion taken in Ireland: *News from Ireland. Being the Examination and Confession of William Kelso, A Scotch Rebel, Taken in Ireland* ([London], 1679).

30. Humble Proposition faite au Roy et à Son Parlement pour donner retraite aux Etrangers protestans et au proselites dans ses Colonies de L'amerique et sur tout en la Carolina, March 1679, in A. S. Salley, ed., *Records in the British Public Record Office Relating to South Carolina, 1663–1684* (Columbia, 1928), 62–68; Opinion of the Proprietors, 6 March 1679, ibid., 71; "Humble Proposalls for Carolina," March 1679, ibid., 75.

31. The humble Peticon of Francis Branson, CO 1/48/45, TNA; John Dunton, *The Life and Errors of John Dunton, Citizen of London* (London, 1818), 1: 96. For a personal narrative of one Monmouth rebel in Jamaica see John Coad, *A Memorandum of the Wonderful Providences of God to a poor unworthy Creature, during the time of the Duke of Monmouth's Rebellion and to the Revolution of 1688* (London, 1849).

32. Jenny Hale Pulsipher, *Subjects unto the Same King: Indians, English, and the Contest for Authority in Colonial New England* (Philadelphia, 2005); Wilcomb E. Washburn, *The Governor and the Rebel: A History of Bacon's Rebellion in Virginia* (Chapel Hill, 1957); Stephen Saunders Webb, *1676: The End of American Independence* (New York, 1984); Michael Craton, *Testing the Chains: Resistance to Slavery in the British West Indies* (Ithaca, 1982).

CHAPTER I. IMPERIAL DESIGNS

1. An overture for the better regulation of the forreigne Plantations, [c. 1675?], Egerton Mss. 3340, f. 148, BL. On the crisis in the empire at this time see Stephen Saunders Webb, *1676: The End of American Independence* (New York, 1986).

2. For this campaign in England itself see Paul Halliday, *Dismembering the Body Politic: Partisan Politics in England's Towns, 1650–1730* (Cambridge, 1998); Gary S. De Krey, *London and the Restoration, 1659–1683* (Cambridge, 2005), 341–86; Tim Harris, *Restoration: Charles II and His Kingdoms, 1664–1685* (London, 2006), 293–300; Scott Sowerby, "James II's Revolution: The Politics of Toleration in England, 1685–1689" (Ph.D. dissertation, Harvard University, 2006), 114–98.

3. The imperial transformations of New Hampshire and Bermuda have attracted little attention from historians, but see, on the former, Theodore B. Lewis, "Royal Government in New Hampshire and the Revocation of the Charter of the Massachusetts Bay Colony, 1679–1683," *Historical New Hampshire* 25 (1970): 3–45; Richard R. Johnson, "Robert Mason and the Coming of Royal Government to New England," *Historical New Hampshire* 35 (1980): 361–90; and on the latter, Henry C. Wilkinson, *The Adventurers of Bermuda: A History of the Island from its Discovery until the Dissolution of the Somers Island Company in 1684* (London, 1958), 374–84; Wilkinson, *Bermuda in the Old Empire: A History of the Island from the Dissolution of the Somers Island Company until the End of the American Revolutionary War: 1684–1784* (London, 1950), 1–27; and Richard S. Dunn, "The Downfall of the Bermuda Company: A Restoration Farce," *WMQ* 3rd ser. 20 (1963): 487–512.

4. These partisan divisions approximated, but did not reproduce, the rift between Whigs and Tories that struck England at the same time; for a summary of the vast dispute on that "age of party" see the roundtable "Order and Authority: Creating Party in Restoration England," *Albion* 25 (1993): 565–652.

5. The existence of these two forms of conspiratorial thought resembled both early Stuart and Restoration England; see Peter Lake, "Anti-Popery: The Structure of a Prejudice," in Richard Cust and Ann Hughes, eds., *Conflict in Early Stuart England: Studies in Religion and Politics, 1603–1642* (London, 1989), 72–97; Tim Harris, *London Crowds in the Reign of Charles II: Propaganda and Politics from the Restoration until the Exclusion Crisis* (Cambridge, 1987); Mark Knights, "Faults on Both Sides: The Conspiracies of Party Politics Under the Later Stuarts," in Barry Coward and Julian Swann, eds., *Conspiracies and Conspiracy Theory in Early Modern Europe: From the Waldensians to the French Revolution* (Aldershot, 2006), 153–72.

6. R. B., *The English Empire in America: Or a Prospect of His Majesties Dominions in the West-Indies* (London, 1685). For an analysis of Crouch's career as a printer who bridged the gap between elite and popular print culture, see Robert Mayer, "Nathaniel Crouch, Bookseller and Historian: Popular Historiography and Cultural Power in Late Seventeenth-Century England," *Eighteenth-Century Studies* 27 (1994): 391–419.

7. The best portraits of this empire remain Charles McLean Andrews, *The Colonial Period of American History* (New Haven, 1934); and G. L. Beer, *The Old Colonial System, 1660–1754* (New York, 1912); but see also Jack M. Sosin, *English America and the Restoration Monarchy of Charles II: Transatlantic Politics, Commerce, and Kinship* (Lincoln, Neb., 1980). For a great sense of the Restoration empire in the East see Philip Stern, " 'A Politie of Civill & Military Power': Political Thought and the Late Seventeenth-Century Foundations of the East India Company-State," *Journal of British Studies* 47 (2008): 253–83.

8. Analysts of the Restoration empire usually divide between those who emphasize its centralizing mission, as in Stephen Saunders Webb, *1676*; or those who stress its lack of actual power, as Sosin, *English America and the Restoration Monarchy*; or Richard R. Johnson, *Adjustment to Empire: The New England Colonies, 1675–1715* (New Brunswick, 1981). For eighteenth-century origins, see David Armitage, *The Ideological Origins of the British Empire* (Cambridge, 2000).

9. Steven C. A. Pincus, "From Butterboxes to Wooden Shoes: The Shift in English

Sentiment from Anti-Dutch to Anti-French in the 1670s," *Historical Journal* 38 (1995): 333–61.

10. Blathwayt to Edward Randolph, 10 March 1688, *Randolph*, 4: 216. On Blathwayt's early career see Stephen Saunders Webb, "William Blathwayt, Imperial Fixer: From Popish Plot to Glorious Revolution," *WMQ* 3rd ser. 25 (1968): 3–21.

11. Stapleton to the Lords of Trade and Plantations, 14 June 1678, CO 1/42/75, TNA; Stapleton to the Lords of Trade and Plantations, 29 June 1678, CO 1/42/98; Daniel K. Richter, *The Ordeal of the Longhouse: The Peoples of the Iroquois League in the Era of European Colonization* (Chapel Hill, 1992), 148–61; Francis Jennings, *The Ambiguous Iroquois Empire: The Covenant Chain Confederation of Indian Tribes with English Colonies* (New York, 1984), 172–94.

12. The best statement on the origins of this ideology is Nicholas Tyacke, *Anti-Calvinists: The Rise of English Arminianism, c. 1590–1640* (Oxford, 1987). For the Restoration see Harris, *London Crowds*, 130–55. For James II's views on toleration see Scott Sowerby, "Of Different Complexions: Religious Diversity and National Identity in James II's Toleration Campaign," *English Historical Review* 124 (2009): 29–52; and on toleration in the colonies, Evan Haefeli, "The Creation of American Religious Pluralism: Churches, Colonialism, and Conquest in the Mid-Atlantic, 1628–1688" (Ph.D. dissertation, Princeton University, 2000).

13. Randolph to Lords of Trade, 3 December 1684, *Randolph*, 3: 336. For a classic Tory anti-Jesuit tract, see *The Politicks of Malcontents, Shewing The Grand Influence the Jesuits Have in all their Desperate Undertakings* (London, 1684). On Randolph's life and career see Michael Garibaldi Hall, *Edward Randolph and the American Colonies, 1676–1703* (Chapel Hill, 1961).

14. Petition of Robert Mason and Ferdinando Gorges, recd. 9 January 1678, CO 1/42/15.vii, TNA.

15. The definitive account of Mason's long career in London and New England is Johnson, "Robert Mason and the Coming of Royal Government to New England." See also David E. Van Deventer, *The Emergence of Provincial New Hampshire, 1623–1741* (Ithaca, 1974), 40–51.

16. Wm Forbes Testificacon, 8 May 1681, CO 1/46/134, TNA; Jn Machins Testimony, 17 May 1681, CO 1/46/147; Warr[ant] for apprehending Mr Mason, 18 May 1681, CO 1/46/143. See also Humble Petition of Robert Mason Esq agst ye Councill of New Hampshire, 10 November 1681, CO 1/47/88; "A Narrative of the proceedings of the Councill of the Province of New Hampshire in New England," 6 September 1681, *Randolph*, 3: 104–7.

17. Most of the negative portrayals of Cranfield adopt the language and tone—and often much of the evidence—of Jeremy Belknap, *The History of New Hampshire* (Boston, 1791), 1: 188–227. For Cranfield as "rapacious," see Robert M. Bliss, *Revolution and Empire: English Politics and the American Colonies in the Seventeenth Century* (Manchester, 1990), 229; Mary Lou Lustig, *The Imperial Executive in America: Sir Edmund Andros, 1637–1714* (Madison, N.J., 2002), 142. The most even-handed account is in Jere R. Daniell, *Colonial New Hampshire: A History* (Millwood, N.Y., 1981), 81–95. For Cranfield's mission to Surinam see CO 278/3, TNA.

18. Cranfield to the Committee on Trade and Plantations, 1 December 1682, CO 1/50/116, TNA; Cranfield to the Committee, 29 January 1683, CO 1/50/124. Cranfield's letters to William Blathwayt, reprinted in *Randolph*, vol. 6, repeat much of the same information as those to the Committee.

19. Cranfield to the Committee on Trade and Plantations, 30 December 1682, CO 1/50/135, TNA.

20. Cranfield to Leoline Jenkins, 10 January 1683, CO 1/51/3, TNA; Cranfield to the Committee on Trade and Plantations, 23 January 1683, CO 1/51/14; Cranfield to Blathwayt, 10 January 1683, *Randolph*, 6: 130; Edward Randolph, "A Short Narrative of the late Transactions and Rebellion in the Province of New-Hampshier, in New England," ibid., 3: 261.

21. The most reliable account of what actually happened comes from the transcript of Gove's trial, Trial Proceedings of Edward Gove, CO 1/51/34.i, TNA. The leading narrative accounts are Randolph, "Short Narrative;" Robert Mason to William Blathwayt, 22 March 1683, Blathwayt Papers, vol. 12, folder 1, CW; see also Mass. Arch., 3: 463–65. Cranfield repeated the allegation that Gove intended to murder him, but not until a year later: Cranfield to the Lords of Trade, 16 January 1684, CO 1/54/8.

22. Gove to the Justices of the Court of Sessions, 29 January 1683, in Nathaniel Bouton, ed., *Documents and Records Relating to the Province of New Hampshire* (Concord, 1867–73), 1: 460–61; Randolph, "Short Narrative," 3: 261; Mason to Blathwayt, 22 March 1683, Blathwayt Papers, vol. 12, folder 1, CW. Trial Proceedings of Edward Gove, CO 1/51/34.i, TNA.

23. The quotation is from Cranfield to the Committee on Trade and Plantations, 30 December 1682, CO 1/50/135, TNA. Virtually every one of his letters from 1683 voices similar sentiments.

24. Cranfield to Jenkins, 20 February 1683, CO 1/51/34, TNA; Cranfield to Jenkins, 19 June 1683, CO 1/52/18; Cranfield to Jenkins, 19 October 1683, CO 1/53/12.

25. Cranfield to Jenkins, 20 February 1683, CO 1/51/34, TNA. On Gove's efforts to secure freedom, see "Proofe that Edw Gove is at times a distracted man," CO 1/51/24; Petition of Hannah Gove, [February] 1683, CO 1/51/40; Sunderland to James II, 14 September 1685, Misc. Mss., MHS; Petition of Gove to the King, 9 April 1686, ibid.

26. Bouton, ed., *Documents and Records*, 1: 482–84.

27. Warrant of Commitment of Rev. Joshua Moodey, MHS, *Collections* 4th ser. 5 (1861): 115–16; Moodey to Thomas Hinckley, 12 February 1684, ibid., 116–20; Bouton, ed., *Documents and Records*, 1: 482–83; Cotton Mather, Notes of Sermons, 1686, Cotton Mather Papers, HM15212, HL; William Vaughan to Nathaniel Weare, 4 February 1684, in Bouton, ed., *Documents and Records*, 1: 528.

28. For Cranfield's view of the financial crisis, see Cranfield to Jenkins, 14 May 1684, CO 1/54/99, TNA; Council of New Hampshire to the Committee on Trade and Plantations, 23 May 1684, CO 1/54/106.

29. Cranfield to the Committee on Trade and Plantations, 15 November 1683, CO 1/53/53, TNA; Thomas Thurton's deposition, 6 January 1685, CO 1/57/2.iv, TNA. Cranfield sent detailed records of colonists' refusal to pay. His collectors visited 422 households, of which only 44 (10%) agreed to pay the tax. All of those who agreed resided in Portsmouth,

and 40 of them were from Great Island, a stronghold of mostly Anglican merchants where Cranfield received most of his support. See CO 1/55/25.i–viii.

30. Cranfield to the Committee on Trade and Plantations, 6 January 1685, CO 1/57/2, TNA. He first requested a new assignment on 23 May 1684 (CO 1/54/105). Most historians contend that Cranfield was removed for misconduct. While the Committee on Trade and Plantations did chastise him for his lack of success, they did not punish Cranfield; indeed, his post in Barbados was in some ways a better assignment. On Cranfield in Barbados, see his letters to William Blathwayt, Blathwayt Papers, vol. 12, folders 5–6, CW.

31. Cranfield to the Committee on Trade and Plantations, 14 May 1684, CO 1/54/98, TNA; Bouton, ed., *Documents and Records*, 1: 499–500.

32. Population figures are from Wilkinson, *Bermuda in the Old Empire*, 14. On Bermuda's religious climate see A. C. Hollis Hallett, *Chronicle of a Colonial Church: 1612–1826, Bermuda* (Bermuda, 1993).

33. Francis Burghill Letterbook, Rawlinson Mss., D 764, Bodleian Library, Oxford; J. H. Lefroy, ed., *Memorials of the Discovery and Early Settlement of the Bermudas or Somers Islands* (Hamilton, 1932), 2: 460. See also Dunn, "The Downfall of the Bermuda Company."

34. Samuel Trott and William Righton to Francis Burghill, 15 August 1684, CO 1/55/19, TNA ; Coney to Nottingham, 21 October 1684, CO 38/1/115.

35. Burghill to Samuel Trott, 31 December 1681, Rawlinson Mss., D 764, f. 35, Bodleian Library; Artickels of Complaint & other High Misdemeanors, Humbly Offered against Richard Cony . . . , CO 1/55/60, TNA.

36. See Richard Lilburne, "A Relation of ye Spaniards Invading and taking this Island," CO 1/54/9, TNA; "Narrative of Passages at the Island of New Providence," CO 1/56/70; A. S. Salley, ed., *Records in the British National Archives Relating to South Carolina, 1685–1690* (Columbia, 1929), 184–86.

37. The best histories of Monmouth's Rebellion are Peter Earle, *Monmouth's Rebels: The Road to Sedgmoor, 1685* (London, 1977); and Robin Clifton, *The Last Popular Rebellion: The Western Rising of 1685* (London, 1984). For a good brief survey that covers both England and Scotland see Tim Harris, *Revolution: The Great Crisis of the British Monarchy* (London, 2006), 66–100.

38. William Dyer to William Blathwayt, 12 June 1685, Blathwayt Papers, vol. 4, folder 3, CW; Effingham to Blathwayt, 14 November 1685, in Warren M. Billings, ed., *The Papers of Francis Howard, Baron Howard of Effingham* (Richmond, 1989), 228; Effingham to Blathwayt, 6–24 February 1686, ibid., 240; H. R. McIlwaine, ed., *Executive Journals of the Council of Colonial Virginia* (Richmond, 1925), 1: 75.

39. Richard Coney to the Earl of Nottingham, 21 October 1684, CO 38/1/115, TNA. See also the depositions in CO 1/60/41. xvii, xix, liv, lvi–lvii. On Coney's Catholic connection see Michael J. Jarvis, "'In the Eye of all Trade': Maritime Revolution and the Transformation of Bermudian Society, 1612–1800" (Ph.D. dissertation, College of William and Mary, 1998), 306.

40. Abstracts of Depositions transmitted by Colo Coney the 4th of June [1685], CO 1/57/137, TNA; Declaration of Samuel Trott, CO 1/58/121.v. Coney describes his initial

problems with the people in great detail in a letter to William Blathwayt, 4 June 1685, Blathwayt Papers, vol. 36, folder 1, CW.

41. Attestacon touching ye Dept Sheriffs Seizure of ye Magazine, CO 1/59/3.i, TNA.

42. Coney to Sunderland, 4 June 1685, CO 1/57/135, TNA; Coney to the Committee on Trade and Plantations, 3 January 1686, in Lefroy, ed., *Memorials*, 2: 560–61.

43. Deposition of Capt Wm Phips, June 1685, CO 1/57/170, TNA; Declaration of George St. Lo, CO 1/63/74. The book in question was probably Henry Care, *English Liberties; or, the Free-born Subject's Inheritance* (London, 1679).

44. Articles against Capt. Bartholomew Sharpe . . . , CO 1/59/47.iv, TNA; Proceedings agt Capt Sharpe and Company at Nevis, 30 December 1686, CO 1/61/35. On Sharpe's earlier career as a pirate, see William Hacke, *Collection of Original Voyages* (London, 1699), part 2.

45. Petition to Coney, 3 January 1686, CO 1/59/12.i, TNA; William Peniston to Justices of the Peace, 22 March 1686, CO 1/59/47.iii.

46. Sharpe to Sunderland, 2 April 1686, CO 1/59/48, TNA; Proceedings agst Capt Bartho: Sharpe, 12 February 1687, CO 1/61/64.i; Deposition of Thomas Burton, 6 September 1686, CO 1/60/43.

47. George St. Lo to the earl of Sunderland, 10 September 1686, CO 1/60/47, TNA. For the case of the five prisoners, see Order on a Report for Discharging the Bermuda Prisoners, 10 December 1686, CO 38/2/95–6, TNA; on the Glorious Revolution in Bermuda, see Robert Robinson to the Committee on Trade and Plantations, 11 May 1689, CO 38/2/226–28.

48. Cranfield to Jenkins, 20 February 1683, CO 1/51/34, TNA; Francis Howard, Lord Effingham to William Blathwayt, 13 December 1685, in Billings, ed., *The Papers of Francis Howard, Baron Howard of Effingham*, 180; Randolph to the Archbishop of Canterbury, Tanner Mss. 30, fol. 97, Bodleian Library, Oxford.

49. Many historians have studied the charter controversy; see especially Viola Barnes, *The Dominion of New England: A Study in British Colonial Policy* (New Haven, 1923); T. H. Breen, *The Character of the Good Ruler: A Study of Puritan Political Ideas in New England, 1630–1730* (New Haven, 1970), 110–50; David Lovejoy, *The Glorious Revolution in America* (New York, 1972), 122–59; Richard R. Johnson, *Adjustment to Empire*, 3–70. The labeling of the political parties seems to have originated with John Gorham Palfrey, *History of New England* (Boston, 1858–90), 3: 359–63.

50. Certaine Notes and Informations concerning New England (c. 1675), Egerton Mss. 2395, f. 415, BL.

51. Edward Randolph to Sir Leoline Jenkins, 3 August 1683, *Randolph*, 3: 251–52.

52. Peter Thacher Diaries, 2: 99, 108–9, MHS.

53. *Popery and Tyranny: Or, the Present State of France: In relation to Its Government, Trade, Manners of the People, and Nature of the Countrey* (London, 1679), 7; Cranfield to Blathwayt, 5 October 1683, *Randolph*, 6: 149.

54. On the town meeting see M. G. Hall, ed., "The Autobiography of Increase Mather," *Proceedings of the American Antiquarian Society* 71 (1962), 308–9; Increase Mather Diaries, vol. 3, AAS [transcript at MHS], 23–25; *A Report of the Record Commissioners of*

Boston, Containing the Boston Records from 1660 to 1701 (Boston, 1881), 164; Abstract of a Letter from Randolph, 14 March 1684, *Randolph*, 3: 283–84.

55. William Dyer to William Blathwayt, 16 November 1685, Blathwayt Papers, vol. 4, folder 3, CW; Hall, ed., "Autobiography of Increase Mather," 313. On Kirke and Tangier see E. M. G. Routh, *Tangier: England's Last Atlantic Outpost, 1661–1684* (London, 1912); Stephen Saunders Webb, *The Governors General: The English Army and the Definition of the Empire, 1569–1681* (Chapel Hill, 1979), 504–8.

56. Randolph to Sir Robert Southwell, 29 January 1684, *Randolph*, 4: 3; Edward Gove to Edward Randolph, 11 June 1683, CO 1/52/10, TNA; Richard Stafford to John Tucker, 19 October 1686, CO 1/60/74; Edward Randolph to Sir James Hayes, 20 November 1686, in J. W. Fortescue, ed., *Calendar of State Papers, Colonial Series, America and West Indies, 1681–85* (London, 1897), #2157.

57. Joseph Dudley to William Blathwayt, 1685, Blathwayt Papers, vol. 4, folder 4, CW; "Dudley Records," MHS *Proceedings* 2nd ser. 13 (1899, 1900): 237–38.

58. "A Short Account of the English Plantations in America," [1688], George Chalmers Collection, Peter Force Collection ser. 8A, no. 34, Library of Congress. Direct evidence of Charles and James's intentions in fashioning the dominion is difficult to find, but see Barillon au Roi, 7 decembre 1684, in Charles James Fox, ed., *A History of the Early Part of the Reign of James the Second* (London, 1808), appendix, vii–viii; and van Citters to the States General of the Netherlands, 4 July 1687, Additional Mss. 34510, fol. 39, BL. Many thanks to Scott Sowerby for the references.

CHAPTER 2. CATHOLICS, INDIANS, AND THE POLITICS OF CONSPIRACY

1. Francis Nicholson to [Thomas Povey?], 31 August 1688, *NYCD*, 3: 552; Nicholson to [William Blathwayt], [October] 1688, Blathwayt Papers, vol. 15, folder 1, CW.

2. Receipt for New England seal, 29 September 1686, CO 1/60/57, TNA; for the illustration see William Cullen Bryant and Sydney Howard Gay, *A Popular History of the United States* (New York, 1879), 3: 9. For leading interpretations of the Dominion of New England see especially Viola Barnes, *The Dominion of New England: A Study in British Colonial Policy* (New Haven, 1923); Richard R. Johnson, *Adjustment to Empire: The New England Colonies, 1675–1715* (New Brunswick, 1981), 71–88.

3. On King Philip's War see especially Jenny Hale Pulsipher, *Subjects unto the Same King: Indians, English, and the Contest for Authority in Early New England* (Philadelphia, 2005); Jill Lepore, *The Name of War: King Philip's War and the Origins of American Identity* (New York, 1996); James D. Drake, *King Philip's War: Civil War in New England, 1675–1676* (Amherst, 1998). On Bacon's Rebellion, see Wilcomb Washburn, *The Governor and the Rebel: A History of Bacon's Rebellion in Virginia* (Chapel Hill, 1957). Stephen Saunders Webb, *1676: The End of American Independence* (New York, 1986), combines both events.

4. See esp. William S. Maltby, *The Black Legend in England: The Development of Anti-Spanish Sentiment, 1558–1680* (Durham, N.C., 1971).

5. Baltimore to Governor Calvert, 21–23 November 1642, *The Calvert Papers* (Baltimore,

1889–99), 1: 217; John D. Krugler, *English and Catholic: The Lords Baltimore in the Seventeenth Century* (Baltimore, 2004), 152–91; Antoinette Sutto, "Lord Baltimore, the Society of Jesus, and Caroline Absolutism in Maryland, 1630–1645," *Journal of British Studies* 48 (2009): 631–52.

6. *Domestick Intelligence*, no. 10, 8 August 1679.

7. *The Jesuite Unmasked, or, a Dialogue between the Most Holy Father La Chaise, Confessor of his Most Christian Majesty, the Most Chaste Father Peters, Confessor of the King of England, and the Most Pious Father Tachart, Ambassador from the French King to His Majesty of Siam* (London, 1689), 25–32.

8. John Cooper to John Hall, 9 May 1642, box 2, folder 12, Maryland Provincial Archives, Society of Jesus, Special Collections Division, Georgetown University Library; Catechism, 1675–77, Box 4, Folder 9.

9. "Extracts from the Annual Letters of the English Province of the Society of Jesus," in Clayton Colman Hall, ed., *Narratives of Early Maryland, 1633–1684* (New York, 1910), 120. See Babette M. Levy, "Early Puritanism in the Southern and Island Colonies," *Proceedings of the American Antiquarian Society* 70 (1960): 205–10. Baltimore estimated that three-fourths of Maryland's population were Protestant dissenters.

10. *Popish Cruelties: Wherein may be seen that Romish Traitors Have now the same Murthering and Treasonable Principles and Practices They had in Q. Elizabeth's Reign, Against the Established Governour and Government of these Kingdoms* (London, 1680), preface, 1.

11. Comparisons between colonization of Ireland and America abound, but few have seriously considered the role of religion; see especially the work of Nicholas Canny: "The Ideology of English Colonization: From Ireland to America," *WMQ* 3rd ser. 30 (1973): 575–98; *Kingdom and Colony: Ireland in the Atlantic World, 1560–1800* (Baltimore, 1988). See also James Muldoon, "The Irishman as Indian," *Essex Institute Historical Collections* 111 (1975): 267–89.

12. Aidan Clarke, "The 1641 Rebellion and Anti-Popery in Ireland," in Brian Mac-Cuarta, ed., *Ulster 1641: Aspects of the Rising* (Belfast, 1993), 139–58; Ethan Howard Shagan, "Constructing Discord: Ideology, Propaganda, and the English Response to the Irish Rebellion of 1641," *Journal of British Studies* 36 (1997): 4–34.

13. *The True Spirit of Popery: or the Treachery and Cruelty of the Papists Exercis'd against the Protestants in All Ages and Countries where Popery has had the Upper-hand* (London, 1688), 39, 41–42.

14. Andrew Marvell, *An Account of the Growth of Popery and Arbitrary Government in England* (Amsterdam, 1677), in *The Works of Andrew Marvell*, ed. Edward Thompson (London, 1776), 1: 449–50.

15. "An Act concerning Religion," 21 April 1649, *Arch. Md.* 1: 244–47.

16. The best narrative of these events is Krugler, *English and Catholic*, 152–91; see also Carla Gardina Pestana, *The English Atlantic in an Age of Revolution, 1640–1661* (Cambridge, Mass., 2004), 150–54.

17. *Virginia and Maryland, or the Lord Baltamore's printed Case, uncased and answered* (London, 1655), in *Narratives of Early Maryland*, 200; Leonard Strong, *Babylon's Fall in Maryland* (London, 1655), ibid., 236, 242.

18. "Complaint from Heaven with a Huy and crye and a petition out of Virginia and Maryland, 1676," *Arch. Md.,* 5: 134–35, 147–48.

19. Baltimore to Anglesea, 19 July 1681, *Arch. Md.*, 5: 280–81; Culpeper to the Lords of Trade and Plantations, 18 June 1681, CO 1/47/36, TNA.

20. David W. Jordan, "John Coode, Perennial Rebel," *Maryland Historical Magazine* 70 (1975): 1–28.

21. Deposition of Collen Mackenzie, *Arch. Md.*, 15: 391; Trial of John Coode, CO 1/48/16.ii, TNA.

22. Deposition of John Bright, *Arch. Md.*, 15: 388; Deposition of John Tyrling, ibid., 15: 387.

23. Deposition of John Bright, *Arch. Md.,* 15: 389; Deposition of William Boyden, ibid., 15: 403.

24. *Arch. Md.*, 8: 138. The complete trial transcripts are in *Arch. Md.,* 5: 311–34; CO 1/48/16, TNA. On the evolution of relations between the various branches of the colonial government see David Jordan, *The Foundations of Representative Government in Maryland, 1632–1715* (Cambridge, 1987).

25. Christopher Rousby to Robert Ridgely, extract, 6 December 1681, CO 1/47/101, TNA; Culpeper, "The Present State of Virginia," 12 December 1681, CO 1/47/105.

26. Jasper Danckaerts, *Journal of Jasper Danckaerts, 1679–1680*, ed. Bartlett Burleigh James and J. Franklin Jameson (New York, 1913), 44, 65, 79, and passim.

27. Claude Dablon to Rev. Fr. Pinette, Provincial of France, 24 October 1674, in Reuben Gold Thwaites, ed., *The Jesuit Relations, and Allied Documents* (Cleveland, 1912), 59: 73–75.

28. Randolph, "The Present State of New England," *Randolph*, 2: 243; Nathaniel B. Shurtleff, ed., *Records of the Governor and Company of Massachusetts Bay in New England* (Boston, 1854), 5: 141, 162, 166; Mary Rowlandson, *The Sovereignty and Goodness of God*, ed. Neal Salisbury (Boston, 1997), 89.

29. Indictment of Joshua Atwater, Suffolk Court Files, vol. 21, no. 1793, Mass. Arch.; John Noble, ed., *Records of the Court of Assistants of Massachusetts Bay* (Boston, 1901), 1: 145–46. For international news of the fire see *Domestick Intelligence*, no. 33, 28 December 1679, no. 43, 2 December 1679; Nathaniel Mather to Increase Mather, 31 December 1679, MHS, *Collections* 4th ser. 8 (1868): 22; Abraham Kick to Increase Mather, 15 December 1679, Mather Papers, 3: 46, Prince Collection, Boston Public Library. On London, see *London's Flames, Discovered by Informations Taken before the Committee Appointed to Enquire after the Burning of the City of London, And after the Insolency of the Papists, &c* (London, 1667).

30. Alden T. Vaughan and Edward W. Clark, eds., *Puritans Among the Indians: Accounts of Captivity and Redemption, 1676–1724* (Cambridge, Mass., 1981), 87.

31. Joseph Storer to Jonathan Corwin, 17 March 1682, Curwen Family Papers, box 1, folder 8, Peabody Essex Museum, Salem, Mass.; Edward Cranfield to William Blathwayt, 23 October 1682, *Randolph*, 6: 116; Deposition of James Dennes, 28 January 1684, in Franklin B. Hough, ed., *Papers Relating to Pemaquid and Parts Adjacent in the Present State of Maine* (Albany, 1861), 61, 63.

32. Rapport touchant les Sauvages Abenaquis de Sillery, [c. 1680], Francis Parkman

Papers, vol. 29, 407–8, MHS; "A Journal of what occurred in the Abnaquis Mission from the feast of Christmas, 1683, until October 6, 1684," *Jesuit Relations*, 63: 27–97. For background on Odanak see especially Gordon M. Day, *The Identity of the Saint Francis Indians* (Ottawa, 1981).

33. Saint-Castin to Simon Bradstreet, 1 July 1680, Thomas Prince Papers, #12, MHS; Richard Pateshall Informeth Against Mr John Kelson [Nelson] Mcht in Boston, *Papers Relating to Pemaquid*, 89–91; Letter from the Eastward, 27 March 1684, Mass. Arch., 70: 112. For more on Saint-Castin see Owen Stanwood, "Unlikely Imperialist: The Baron of Saint-Castin and the Transformation of the Northeastern Borderlands," *French Colonial History* 5 (2004): 43–61.

34. Cranfield to Thomas Hinckley, 14 February 1684, MHS, *Collections* 4th ser., 5 (1861), 121; Council of New Hampshire to Thomas Dongan, 21 March 1684, in Nathaniel Bouton, ed., *Documents and Records Relating to the Province of New-Hampshire* (Concord, 1867–73), 1: 500.

35. Information of John Pynchon, 17 June 1685, Mass. Arch., 3: 37b.

36. The fullest recent analysis of Andros's rule is in Mary Lou Lustig, *The Imperial Executive in America: Sir Edmund Andros, 1637–1714* (Madison, N.J., 2002).

37. Depositions of Ruth and Richard York, 7 February 1687, *DHSM*, 6: 325–28.

38. Edward Randolph to Thomas Povey, 21 June 1688, *Randolph*, 4: 224–25.

39. Andros to Jonathan George, 14 May 1688, *DHSM*, 6: 395; Edward Randolph to the Lords of Trade, 8 October 1688, *Randolph*, 4: 240–42; *Rose* log, ADM 51/3955/152, fol. 120, TNA.

40. Rapport de Monsieur de Meneval, Gouverneur de l'Acadie, 10 septembre 1688, in *Collection des manuscrits contenant letters, mémoires, et autres documents historiques relatifs à la Nouvelle France* (Québec, 1883–85), 1: 435.

41. Randolph to the Lords of Trade, 8 October 1688, *Randolph*, 4: 240–42.

42. Deposition of Edward Taylor, Caleb Ray, and Robert Scott, 28 January 1690, *DHSM*, 5: 38; Edward Tyng to Andros, 18 August 1688, *DHSM*, 6: 420; Deposition of Thomas Stevens, 4 September 1688, *DHSM*, 6: 422.

43. Edward Tyng to [Council of the Dominion of NE], 18 September 1688, *DHSM*, 6: 429–30; Examination of Henry Smith, 31 October 1688, *DHSM*, 6: 443–47. Joshua Pipon to [Andros?], 22 September 1688, *DHSM*, 6:432.

44. John Pynchon to Edmund Andros, 21 August 1688, in Carl Bridenbaugh, ed., *The Pynchon Papers*, vol. 1, *Letters of John Pynchon* (Boston, 1982), 185; Andros to Nathan Gold, 25 August 1688, in W. H. Whitmore, ed., *The Andros Tracts: Being a Collection of Pamphlets and Official Papers of the Andros Government and the Establishment of the Second Charter of Massachusetts* (New York, 1868–74), 3: 86–87; M. Halsey Thomas, ed., *The Diary of Samuel Sewall, 1674–1729* (New York, 1973), 1: 174–75; Examination of Magsigpen, 1688, Mass. Arch., 30: 310–11; Nicholson to [Blathwayt], [October] 1688, Blathwayt Papers, vol. 15, folder 1, CW.

45. Andros to Edward Tyng, 20 September 1688, *Andros Tracts*, 3: 87–88; Randolph to Lords of Trade, 8 October 1688, *Randolph*, 4: 243.

46. *Sewall Diary*, 1: 176; Account of forces raised against Indians in 1688, *Andros Tracts*, 3: 31–33. Opponents claimed the number of troops to be 1000; "Declaration of Grievances,"

in Michael G. Hall, Lawrence H. Leder, and Michael G. Kammen, eds., *The Glorious Revolution in America: Documents on the Colonial Crisis of 1689* (Chapel Hill, 1964), 45; Depositions of Kerley and How, 27 December 1689, Mass. Arch., 35: 147a.

47. Complaint of Joseph Emerson and Jacob Whiticker, 17 December 1689, *DHSM*, 5: 21; Richard Hodges's complaint against John Jourdan, *DHSM*, 5: 39; Complaint against John Jourdan, 28 January 1690, *DHSM*, 5: 40.

48. Isaac Miller's Testimony, 21 December 1689, *DHSM*, 5: 22–23; Deposition of Edward Taylor, 27 January 1690, *DHSM*, 5: 35.

49. On Calvinist resistance theory see especially Quentin Skinner, *The Foundations of Modern Political Thought* (Cambridge, 1978), 2: 302–48.

50. John Higginson, *Our Dying Saviour's Legacy of Peace to His Disciples in a troublesome World, from John 14.27. My Peace I give unto you, &c. Also a Discourse on the Two Witnesses: Shewing that it is a Duty of all Christians to be Witnesses unto Christ, from Rev. 11.3* (Boston, 1686), 149–51; Samuel Willard, *The Fiery Tryal no Strange Thing; Delivered in a Sermon preached at Charlestown, February 15. 1681. Being a day of Humiliation* (Boston, 1682).

51. Notes on Sermons by Joshua Moodey, f. 2, 302, MHS. On the importance of sermons in Restoration politics see Tim Harris, "Understanding Popular Politics in Restoration Britain," in Alan Houston and Steve Pincus, eds., *A Nation Transformed? England After the Restoration* (Cambridge, 2001), 135–36.

52. *Sewall Diary*, 1: 140; [Increase Mather], *A Brief Discourse Concerning the unlawfulness of the Common Prayer Worship* (Cambridge, 1686), 1, 4, 15. On the establishment of the Church of England see *Sewall Diary*, 1: 116, 135, 139, 163; Mark Peterson, *The Price of Redemption: The Spiritual Economy of Early New England* (Stanford, 1997), 177–78.

53. Proceedings against Wise and others of Ipswich for misdemeanors, *Randolph*, 4: 171–81; Declaration of John Wise, Mass. Arch., 35: 138–40.

54. On Mather's mission to England see especially. Johnson, *Adjustment to Empire*, 136–82; Michael G. Hall, *The Last American Puritan: The Life of Increase Mather* (Middletown, Conn., 1988), 212–54.

55. Petition of Peter Reverdy to the King, 12 September 1686, CO 1/60/49, TNA; Robert N. Toppan, ed., "Andros Records," *Proceedings of the American Antiquarian Society* 13 (1899–1900): 248; A Memorial concerning salt ponds, Fulham Papers, vol. 6, 174–75, Lambeth Palace Library, London (microfilm, Library of Congress).

56. Mass. Arch., 35: 191; Deposition of Samuel Eldred, 16 September 1688, Mass. Arch., 35: 129a.

57. Joshua Moodey to Increase Mather, 8 February 1689, Mather Papers, vol. 7, 67, Prince Collection, Boston Public Library; Abstract of a Letter dated Boston New England, 20 August 1688, CO 1/65/43, TNA.

58. Randolph to Sir Nicholas Butler, 29 March 1688, *Randolph*, 6: 242–43; Randolph to William Blathwayt, 2 April 1688, ibid., 6: 251; Randolph to Blathwayt, 8 November 1688, ibid., 6: 279–82; Randolph to Sir James Hayes, 6 January 1689, ibid., 6: 284–85.

59. This very brief summary of pre-revolutionary history draws from the latest new scholarship on the Revolution in England and Europe, especially Tim Harris, *Revolution: The Great Crisis of the British Monarchy, 1685–1715* (London, 2006); Steve Pincus, *1688: The*

First Modern Revolution (New Haven, 2009); and Scott Sowerby, "Of Different Complexions: Religious Diversity and National Identity in James II's Toleration Campaign," *English Historical Review* 124 (2009): 29–52; Sowerby, "Forgetting the Repealers: Religious Toleration and Historical Amnesia in Later Stuart England," *Past and Present*, forthcoming.

60. *Sewall Diary*, 1: 175; *Arch. Md.*, 8: 44.

CHAPTER 3. RUMORS AND REBELLIONS

1. There have been several influential surveys of these events; see David Lovejoy, *The Glorious Revolution in America* (New York, 1972); Richard R. Johnson, "The Revolution of 1688–9 in the American Colonies," in Jonathan I. Israel, ed., *The Anglo-Dutch Moment: Essays on the Glorious Revolution and Its World Impact* (Cambridge, 1991), 215–40; and Richard S. Dunn, "The Glorious Revolution and America," in Nicholas Canny, ed., *The Oxford History of the British Empire*, vol. 1, *The Origins of Empire: British Overseas Enterprise to the End of the Seventeenth Century* (Oxford, 1998), 445–66.

2. Randolph to the Bishop of London, 25 October 1689, *Randolph*, 4: 305–7.

3. For the role of rumors in early modern history, see, for example, Ethan H. Shagan, "Rumours and Popular Politics during the Reign of Henry VIII," in Tim Harris, ed., *The Politics of the Excluded, c. 1500–1850* (Basingstoke, 2000), 30–66; Arlette Farge and Jacques Revel, *The Vanishing Children of Paris: Rumor and Politics Before the French Revolution* (Cambridge, Mass., 1993); Gregory Evans Dowd, "The Panic of 1751: Rumors on the Cherokee-South Carolina Frontier," *WMQ* 3rd ser. 53 (1996): 527–60.

4. Accot of the Celebration of the Birth of the Prince of Wales, 19 August 1688, CO 1/65/50.iii, TNA.

5. On the Irish see Hilary McD. Beckles, "A 'Riotous and Unruly Lot': Irish Indentured Servants and Freemen in the English West Indies, 1644–1713," *WMQ* 3rd ser. 47 (1990): 503–22; Jenny Shaw, "Island Purgatory: Irish Catholics and the Reconfiguring of the English Caribbean, 1650–1700" (Ph.D. dissertation, New York University, 2008).

6. For Stede's challenge to the French see Stede to the Committee on Trade and Plantations, 17 November 1686, CO 1/61/3, TNA.

7. "The past and present state of the Leeward Charribbee Islands," 15 March 1678, CO 1/42/36, TNA; C. S. S. Higham, *The Development of the Leeward Islands Under the Restoration, 1660–1688* (Cambridge, 1921).

8. Montgomery to Lords of Trade and Plantations, August 1688, CO 29/4/6–7, TNA. The Montgomerys were a prominent Ulster Scot Protestant family with strong ties to the Stuart dynasty and the Church of Ireland, though I have not been able to trace Sir Thomas's particular genealogy. In general see William Montgomery, *The Montgomery Manuscripts (1603–1706)* (Belfast, 1869).

9. Stede to Sunderland, 1 September 1688, CO 1/65/54, TNA; Humble Petition of Thomas Montgomery, 7 March 1689, CO 28/37/7.xx.

10. Proceedings of the Governor and Council of Barbados, 7 March 1689, CO

31/4/121–22, TNA. On the numbers of attendees see A List of The Psons . . . att Mass att the house of Mr. Willoughby Chamberlaines . . . , CO 28/37/7.xxx; Deposition of Edward Bishop, 13 March 1689, CO 28/37/7.xlvi.

11. Proceedings of the Governor and Council of Barbados, 2 October 1688, CO 31/4/96–97, TNA; Proceedings of the Court against Mr Wilson, 2 October 1688, CO 1/65/65.xxi; Examination of Mr Wilson, CO 1/65/65.xxii; Deposition of Thomas Ebourne, 6 September 1688, CO 1/65/65.xxiv.

12. Stede to Blathwayt, 16 August 1688, Blathwayt Papers, vol. 31, folder 4, CW; Stede to Blathwayt, 23 October 1688, ibid., vol. 32, folder 5; Stede to Sunderland, 1 September 1688, CO 1/65/54, TNA.

13. Proceedings of the Assembly of Nevis, 20–28 November 1688, CO 153/1/107–8, TNA.

14. Stede to Blathwayt, 16 March 1689, Blathwayt Papers, vol. 32, folder 5, CW; Blenac to Montgomery, 7 January 1689, CO 28/1/1, TNA; Johnson to the Committee on Trade and Plantations, 15 July 1689, CO 153/4/119. On communication links to Barbados see Ian K. Steele, *The English Atlantic, 1675–1740: An Exploration of Communication and Community* (Cambridge, 1986), 97.

15. Order of Council agt Sr Tho Montgomery, 25 February 1689, CO 28/1/6, TNA. See also Stede to Blathwayt, 16 March 1689, Blathwayt Papers, vol. 32, folder 5, CW.

16. Order of Council agt Sr Thomas Montgomery, 25 February 1689, CO 28/1/6, TNA.

17. Stede to Blathwayt, 16 March 1689, Blathwayt Papers, vol. 32, folder 5, CW. The documents are in two different places in the Colonial Office Papers: CO 28/37/7 and CO 28/1. I am grateful to Jenny Shaw for bringing these sources to my attention.

18. Proceedings of the Governor and Council of Barbados, 7 March 1689, CO 31/4/121–2, TNA; Examination of Tho: Brown, 7 March 1689, CO 28/37/7.xix; Deposition of Benjamin Cryer, 18 March 1689, CO 28/37/7.liii.

19. The Humble Petition of Sir Thomas Montgomery, 7 March 1689, and Stede's comments, CO 28/37/7.xx, TNA. Stede offered no philosophical or legal justification for the applicability of the penal laws in Barbados. For his earlier pledge to protect the priest see Stede to Sunderland, 1 September 1688, CO 1/65/54, TNA.

20. Blenac to Montgomery (copy), 7 January 1689 (and Stede's comments), CO 28/1/1, TNA; De la Forest to Montgomery (copy), n.d., CO 28/1/3; De la Forest to Chamberlain (copy), n.d., CO 28/37/7.iv; Lady Superior of the Ursulines to Montgomery (copy), 10 February 1689, CO 28/37/7.ii. The Latin letters, like the French ones, consisted mostly of news from Europe, much of it inaccurate. I am grateful to Mary Zito for translating the letters.

21. Garrat Trant to Montgomery, 23 February 1689 (Stede's comments), CO 28/1/5, TNA; Proceedings of the Governor and Council of Barbados, 2 October 1688, CO 31/4/114–15; Deposition of James Bradshaw, 22 April 1689, CO 28/37/7.lxiv.

22. Deposition of John Thompson, 23 February 1689, CO 28/37/7.v, TNA; Depositions of John Kelly and John Bowen, 23 February 1689, CO 28/37/7.vi.

23. Deposition of Martha Custley, 4 March 1689, CO 28/37/7.xvii, TNA; Deposition of Cesar Crawford, 4 March 1689, CO 28/37/7.xvi. Temple published *The Irish Rebellion* in 1644, but editions appeared throughout the Restoration period. The same phenomenon

appeared in the 1641 rebellion itself, in which reports of Catholic violence multiplied and increased in intensity as they traveled through the countryside; see Nicholas Canny, *Making Ireland British, 1580–1660* (Oxford, 2001), 461–550.

24. Deposition of Philipp Price, CO 28/37/7.xl, TNA; Deposition of Charles Collins, 11 March 1689, CO 28/37/7.xli. Barbados had experienced several recent insurrection scares, though incredibly this was the first speculation that slaves could provide aid to Catholic enemies; in general see Michael Craton, *Testing the Chains: Resistance to Slavery in the British West Indies* (Ithaca, 1982), 105–14.

25. Humble Petition of Montgomery (Stede's commentary), CO 28/37/7.xx, TNA; Stede to Blathwayt, 28 May 1689, Blathwayt Papers, vol. 32, folder 5, CW. One of Montgomery's servants witnessed his master writing letters to Petre and other prominent allies of James II, which he allegedly sent to England with the Jesuit Michel in January 1689, but which may have been lost at sea; Examination of Thomas Brown, 7 March 1689, CO 28/37/7.xix.

26. On the invasion of St. Christopher see Chapter 5.

27. William Dyre to William Blathwayt, 5 March 1685, 12 June 1685, Blathwayt Papers, vol. 4, folder 3, CW. The definitive account of this period in New England's political development is Richard R. Johnson, *Adjustment to Empire: The New England Colonies, 1675–1715* (New Brunswick, 1982), but see also Viola Barnes, *The Dominion of New England: A Study in British Colonial Policy* (New Haven, 1923); and T. H. Breen, *The Character of the Good Ruler: Puritan Political Thought in New England, 1620–1720* (New Haven, 1970).

28. Francis Nicholson to Fitz John Winthrop, 16 February 1689, Winthrop Family Papers, MHS; John West to Fitz John Winthrop, 23 February 1689, ibid.; Mass. Arch., 35: 216; John Borland to Andrew Russell, 28 March 1689, RH 15/106/690, #39, National Archives of Scotland, Edinburgh; Borland to Russell, 8 April 1689, RH 15/106/801, #2.

29. Deposition of Thomas Jentt and William Willcott, 27 January 1689, *DHSM*, 5: 36; Testimony of Waterman and David, 4 May 1689, Mass. Arch., 107: 29; Testimony of Stephen Greenleafe, Jr., 9 April 1689, *DHSM*, 6: 472–73; Testimony of George Little, ibid., 6: 473.

30. John West to Fitz John Winthrop, 23 February 1689, Winthrop Family Papers, MHS; Deposition of Caleb Moody, 9 January 1690, *DHSM*, 5: 28–29; Deposition of Joseph Bayley, 9 January 1690, Mass. Arch., 35: 166.

31. Testimonies of Joseph Graves, Mary Graves, and John Rutter, 3 January 1689, *DHSM*, 4: 446–47; Depositions of Thomas Browne, John Grout, Sr., John Goodenow, Jonathan Stanhope, and John Parmenter, 22 March 1689, ibid., 4: 448–49; Deposition of William Bond, 23 January 1689, Mass. Arch., 35: 179a.

32. Affidavits concerning the agreement of Andros with the Indians, *NYCD*, 3: 659; CO 5/1081/41, TNA.

33. Affidavit of Greveraet and Brewerton, 13 December 1689, *NYCD*, 3: 660; Deposition of John Winslow, Mass. Arch., 35: 216.

34. Deposition of Caleb Moody, *DHSM*, 5: 29; Depositions of Browne, et al., ibid., 4: 449; Testimony of Graves et al., ibid., 4: 446. For inexplicable reasons, Caleb usually chose to spell his surname without the letter "e," unlike his brother Joshua.

35. "A Particular Account of the Late Revolution at Boston in the Colony and Province

of Massachusetts, 1689," in Charles McLean Andrews, ed., *Narratives of the Insurrections, 1675–1690* (New York 1915), 196–97; John Palmer, *An Impartial Account of the State of New England* (London, 1690), in W. H. Whitmore, ed., *The Andros Tracts: Being a Collection of Pamphlets and Official Papers of the Andros Government and the Establishment of the Second Charter of Massachusetts* (New York, 1868–74) 1: 30–31. Most narratives of the Boston revolution came from the various pamphlets supporting or opposing the action. The most reliable first-person account, while still from a biased party, is John Riggs, "A Narrative of the Proceedings at Boston in New England upon the Inhabts seizing the Governmt there," CO 5/905/85–87, TNA.

36. "A Particular Account of the Late Revolution," in Andrews, ed., *Narratives of the Insurrections,* 196; *New England's Faction Discovered, Or a Brief and True Account of their Persecution of the Church of England* (London, 1690), *Andros Tracts,* 2: 206; Edward Randolph to the Committee for Trade and Plantations, 5 September 1689, *Randolph,* 4: 297. Randolph to the Lords of Trade, 29 May 1689, ibid., 272–73; Edmund Andros to William Blathwayt, 4 June 1689, Blathwayt Papers, vol. 1, folder 4, CW; *The Politicks of Malcontents, Shewing The Grand Influence the Jesuits Have in all their Desperate Undertakings* (London, 1684), 8.

37. Works that have pushed this interpretation include Barnes, *Dominion of New England;* Stephen Saunders Webb, *Lord Churchill's Coup: The Anglo-American Empire and the Glorious Revolution Reconsidered* (New York, 1998), 187–95 (who coined the phrase "Protestant putsch"), and Ian K. Steele, "Origins of Boston's Revolutionary Declaration of 18 April 1689," *New England Quarterly* 62 (1989): 75–81.

38. Edward Randolph to the Lords of Trade and Plantations, 29 May 1689, *Randolph,* 4: 279; "Account of forces raised agt Indians in 1688," *Andros Tracts,* 3: 33; Warrant for Assistance to Capt Jno Floyd on his March to Saco, 12 April 1689, *DHSM,* 6: 474–75.

39. Report of Samuel Mather, in Michael G. Hall, Lawrence H. Leder, and Michael G. Kammen, eds., *The Glorious Revolution in America: Documents on the Colonial Crisis of 1689* (Chapel Hill, 1964), 39–40; Thomas Danforth to Thomas Hinckley, 20 April 1689, MHS, *Collections* 4th ser. 5 (1861): 191; Thomas Danforth to Increase Mather, 30 July 1689, in Thomas Hutchinson, ed., *Hutchinson Papers* (Albany, 1865), 2: 310–11.

40. Information of the crew of the Rose Frigate, 29 April 1689, Mass. Arch., 107: 4; Information of the Rose Frigott Company, 1 May 1689, ibid., 9–10; John George to Samuel Pepys, 12 June 1689, in Andrews, ed., *Narratives of the Insurrections,* 215–19; Thomas Danforth to Increase Mather, 30 July 1689, *Hutchinson Papers,* 2: 313.

41. Samuel Prince to Thomas Hinckley, 22 April 1689, in Hall, Leder, and Kammen, eds., *Glorious Revolution in America,* 41; Riggs, "Narrative of Proceedings," CO 5/905/85, TNA; Extract of a Letter from Bristoll in New England unto Mr Mather and Others, 29 April 1689, CO 5/855/2; Nathaniel Byfield, *An Account of the Late Revolution in New England . . .* (London, 1689), in Hall, Leder, and Kammen, eds., *Glorious Revolution in America,* 47; "Diary of Lawrence Hammond," MHS, *Proceedings* 2nd. ser. 7 (1891, 1892): 150.

42. "Sir Edmund Andros's Report of his Administration," *NYCD,* 3: 723; Riggs, "Narrative," CO 5/905/85–7, TNA; Committee of Safety to John Pipon, 19 April 1689, in Robert

Earle Moody and Richard Clive Simmons, eds., *The Glorious Revolution in Massachusetts: Selected Documents, 1689–1692* (Boston, 1988), 53.

43. Nicholson and the Council of New York to the Board of Trade, 15 May 1689, *NYCD*, 3: 575; Declaration of the Freeholders of Suffolk County, 3 May 1689, ibid., 577.

44. Nicholson and Council to the Board of Trade, 15 May 1689, *NYCD*, 3: 575; "Documents Relating to the Administration of Leisler," *NYHS Coll.* 1 (1868), 260.

45. "Documents Relating to Leisler," *NYHS Coll.* 1: 265–66.

46. Affidavits against Francis Nicholson, *DHNY*, 2: 27; Depositions of Andries and Jan Meyer, 26 September 1689, ibid., 28; *An Account of the Proceedings at New-York. 1689* (Boston, 1689), CO 5/1081/11, TNA; *A Modest and Impartial Narrative . . .* (London, 1690), in Andrews, ed., *Narratives*, 323; Stephanus van Cortlandt to Edmund Andros, 9 July 1689, *NYCD*, 3: 592; "Documents Relating to Leisler," *NYHS Coll.*, 1: 284–85.

47. Van Cortlandt to Andros, 9 July 1689, *NYCD*, 3: 593; Depositions of Hendrick Jacobse and Albert Bosch, 10 June 1689, *DHNY*, 2: 12–13. This incident marked the event known to historians as Leisler's Rebellion. Virtually every historian of colonial New York has attempted to interpret the event; the most influential to me have been David William Voorhees, "'In Behalf of the True Protestants Religion': The Glorious Revolution in New York" (Ph.D. dissertation, New York University, 1988); Voorhees, "The 'fervent Zeale' of Jacob Leisler," *WMQ* 3rd ser. 51 (1994): 447–72; and John M. Murrin, "The Menacing Shadow of Louis XIV and the Rage of Jacob Leisler: The Constitutional Ordeal of Seventeenth-Century New York," in Stephen L. Schechter and Richard B. Bernstein, eds., *New York and the Union: Contributions to the American Constitutional Experience* (Albany, 1990), 29–71.

48. Van Cortlandt to Andros, 9 July 1689, *NYCD*, 3: 594; "Documents Relating to Leisler," *NYHS Coll.* 1: 268, 288.

49. Affidavit against Col. Bayard and certain parties on Staten island, 25 September 1689, *DHNY*, 2: 29–30; Declaration of Barth. le Roux, CO 5/1081/65, TNA; Meeting of the Committee of Safety, 6 June 1689, CO 5/1081/46.

50. While there is relatively little scholarship on the rebellion in Maryland, it includes perhaps the best monograph on the period, Lois Green Carr and David W. Jordan, *Maryland's Revolution in Government, 1689–1692* (Ithaca, 1974).

51. "Mariland's Grievances Wiy The[y] Have Taken Op Arms," January 1690, in Hall, Leder, and Kammen, eds., *Glorious Revolution in America*, 182–83.

52. *Arch. Md.*, 8: 56, 67. Similar fears surfaced in Maryland in the 1650s and 1681; see Michael Graham, S.J., "Popish Plots: Protestant Fears in Early Colonial Maryland, 1676–1689," *Catholic Historical Review* 79 (1993): 197–216.

53. John Addison to John West, 25 March 1689, *Arch. Md.*, 8: 93; John Courts to Lawrence Washington, 26 March 1689, ibid.; Testimony of Matthew Tennison, 22 December 1690, ibid., 224; see also Deposition of John Atkey, ibid., 71.

54. Examination of Burr Harrison, *Arch. Md.*, 8: 77–78, 84–86; Nicholas Spencer, Richard Lee, and Isaac Allerton to William Joseph, 22 March 1689, ibid., 82; Nicholas Spencer to William Blathwayt, 27 April 1689, Blathwayt Papers, vol. 16, folder 5, CW; H. R. McIlwaine, ed., *Executive Journals of the Council of Colonial Virginia* (Richmond, 1925), 1: 104–5.

55. Henry Jowles to William Digges, 24 March 1689, *Arch. Md.*, 8: 70–71; Jowles to

William Joseph and Deputy Governors, 24 March 1689, ibid., 72; Henry Darnall to William Joseph et al., 26 March 1689, ibid., 81. For a biographical sketch of Jowles, see Carr and Jordan, *Maryland's Revolution of Government*, 266–68.

56. William Digges to Hanslap et al., *Arch. Md.*, 8: 79–80; William Joseph et al. to Darnall, 26 March 1689, ibid., 82; *Executive Journals of Virginia*, 1: 105; Spencer to William Blathwayt, 10 June 1689, Blathwayt Papers, vol. 18, folder 3, CW.

57. William Joseph et al. to Robert Doyne, 25 March 1689, *Arch. Md.*, 8: 77; Edward Pye to [William Joseph?], 28 March 1689, ibid., 88–89; Declaration by William Barton, et al., ibid., 91; William Digges to "Gentlemen" of Charles County, 26 March 1689, ibid., 78–79; Proclamation against the plot, 27 March 1689, ibid., 86; Joseph et al. to Henry Jowles, 24 March 1689, ibid., 73.

58. Spencer to Blathwayt, 10 June 1689, Blathwayt Papers, vol. 18, folder 3, CW; "The Randolph Manuscript: Memoranda from Virginia Records, 1688–90," *Virginia Magazine of History and Biography* 20 (1912): 3–4, 10; Spencer to William Digges, [March 1689], *Arch. Md.*, 8: 92; Gilbert Clarke to Digges, 29 March 1689, ibid., 93–94; William Fitzhugh to Nicholas Hayward, 1 April 1689, in Richard Beale Davis, ed., *William Fitzhugh and His Chesapeake World, 1676–1701: The Fitzhugh Letters and Other Documents* (Chapel Hill, 1963), 250.

59. "The Randolph Manuscript," 5; Nicholas Spencer to the Lords of Trade and Plantation, 29 April 1689, CO 5/1305/30–31, TNA; Spencer to Blathwayt, 10 June 1689, Blathwayt Papers, vol. 18, folder 3, CW.

60. Pierre Bertrand to the Bishop of London, 12 September 1689, *Arch. Md.*, 8: 116; Nicholas Spencer to William Blathwayt, 10 June 1689, ibid, 112; The Narrative of Barbarah wife of Richd Smith, 30 December 1689, ibid., 8: 153. Baltimore did not send orders to proclaim William and Mary in the colony until August 31, by which time his government had already been overturned (ibid., 112).

61. Peter Sayer to Lord Baltimore, 31 December 1689, *Arch. Md.*, 8: 158. The best sketch of Coode's career is David W. Jordan, "John Coode, Perennial Rebel," *Maryland Historical Magazine* 70 (1975): 1–28. On the reference to Masaniello, used against Leisler as well as Coode, see Lovejoy, *Glorious Revolution in America*, 296–311.

62. Narrative of Henry Darnall, 31 December 1689, *Arch. Md.*, 8: 156; Memorandum of Smith's Case, 16 December 1689, ibid., 148.

63. Narrative of Darnall, *Arch. Md.*, 8:157; Articles of Surrender, 1 August 1689, ibid., 107–8; Nicholas Taney to Barbara Smith, ibid., 119.

64. Alexander Plunkett to Thomas Montgomery, 24 February 1689, CO 28/37/7.vii, TNA.

CHAPTER 4. THE EMPIRE TURNED UPSIDE DOWN

1. Peter R. Christoph, ed., *The Leisler Papers, 1689–1691: Files of the Provincial Secretary of New York Relating to the Administration of Lieutenant-Governor Jacob Leisler* (Syracuse, 2002), 44; John Palmer, *An Impartial Account of the State of New England* (London, 1690), in W. H. Whitmore, ed., *The Andros Tracts: Being a Collection of Pamphlets and Official*

Papers issued during the Period between the Overthrow of the Andros Government and the Establishment of the Second Charter of Massachusetts (Boston, 1868), 1: 25.

2. My understanding of Whig ideology draws heavily from Mark Goldie, especially "Priestcraft and the Birth of Whiggism," in Nicholas T. Phillipson and Quentin Skinner, eds., *Political Discourse in Early Modern Britain* (Cambridge, 1992), 209–31; and *Roger Morrice and the Puritan Whigs* (Woodbridge, 2007). On Calvinist resistance theory see Quentin Skinner, *The Foundations of Modern Political Thought* (Cambridge, 1978), 189–358; Robert N. Kingdon, "Calvinism and Resistance Theory, 1550–1580," in J. H. Burns and Mark Goldie, eds., *The Cambridge History of Political Thought, 1450–1700* (Cambridge, 1991), 193–218. A few scholars have examined the political thought of the colonial rebellions of 1688–89. For New England, see T. H. Breen, *The Character of the Good Ruler: Puritan Political Ideas in New England, 1630–1730* (New Haven, 1970), 134–79; and Craig Yirush, "From the Perspective of Empire: The Common Law, Natural Rights, and the Formation of American Political Theory, 1688–1775" (Ph.D. dissertation, Johns Hopkins University, 2004), 121–56; for New York, John M. Murrin, "The Menacing Shadow of Louis XIV and the Rage of Jacob Leisler: The Constitutional Ordeal of Seventeenth-Century New York," in Stephen L. Schechter and Richard B. Bernstein, eds., *New York and the Union: Contributions to the American Constitutional Experience* (Albany, 1990), 29–71; and David William Voorhees, "'The World Turned Upside Down': The Foundations of Leislerian Political Thought," in Hermann Wellenreuther, ed., *Jacob Leisler's Atlantic World in the Later Seventeenth Century* (Berlin, 2009), 89–118; and in general, Jack P. Greene, *Peripheries and Center: Constitutional Development in the Extended Polities of the British Empire and the United States, 1607–1788* (Athens, Ga., 1986), 19–42.

3. For a sense of these connections see Mark A. Peterson, "Boston Pays Tribute: Autonomy and Empire in the Atlantic World, 1630–1714," in Allan I. Macinnes and Arthur H. Williamson, eds., *Shaping the Stuart World, 1603–1714: The Atlantic Connection* (Leiden, 2005), 311–36; Peterson, "*Theopolis Americana*: The City-State of Boston, the Republic of Letters, and the Protestant International, 1689–1739," in Bernard Bailyn and Patricia L. Denault, eds., *Soundings in Atlantic History: Latent Structures and Intellectual Currents, 1500–1830* (Cambridge, Mass., 2009), 329–70; David William Voorhees, "The 'fervent Zeale' of Jacob Leisler," *WMQ* 3rd ser. 51 (1994): 447–72. For two very different readings of "liberty" in early modern England, see Tim Harris, "'Lives, Liberties, and Estates': Rhetorics of Liberty in the Reign of Charles II," in Tim Harris, Paul Seaward, and Mark Goldie, eds., *The Politics of Religion in Restoration England* (Oxford, 1990), 217–41; J. C. D. Clark, *The Language of Liberty, 1660–1832: Political Discourse and Social Dynamics in the Anglo-American World* (Cambridge, 1992). On the "empire of liberty" see David Armitage, *The Ideological Origins of the British Empire* (Cambridge, 2000), 195 and passim.

4. Peter Onuf, *Jefferson's Empire: The Language of American Nationhood* (Charlottesville, 2000).

5. See for example, *Popery and Tyranny: Or, the present State of France, in Relation to Its Government, Trade, Manners of the People, and Nature of the Countrey* (London, 1679).

6. *The Declaration of the Gentlemen, Merchants, and Inhabitants of Boston, and the*

Country Adjacent (Boston, 1689), in Robert E. Moody and Richard C. Simmons, eds., *The Glorious Revolution in Massachusetts: Selected Documents, 1689–1692* (Boston, 1988), 45.

7. Andrew Marvell, *An Account of the Growth of Popery and Arbitrary Government in England* (Amsterdam, 1677), in Edward Thompson, ed., *The Works of Andrew Marvell, Esq.* (London, 1776), 1: 441, 448; Philolaus, *A Character of Popery and Arbitrary Government, With a Timely Caveat and Advice to all the Free-holders, Citizens and Burgesses, how they may prevent the same, By choosing Good Members To Serve in this New Parliament* (London, 1681), 7; [Henry Care], *English Liberties; or, the Free-born Subject's Inheritance* (London, 1679), 106.

8. *Declaration of the Inhabitants*, 45–46; [Edward Rawson and Samuel Sewall], *The Revolution in New England Justified* (Boston, 1690), *Andros Tracts*, 1: 79–80; [Benjamin Harris], *The Triumph of Justice over Unjust Judges* (London, 1681), 14.

9. Care, *English Liberties*, 4–5; [Harris], *The Triumph of Justice over Unjust Judges*, 1 and passim; Roger Morrice, *The Entring Book of Roger Morrice*, ed. Mark Goldie et al. (Woodbridge, 2007), 3: 163, 4:235; John Gorham Palfrey, *History of New England* (Boston, 1858–90), 3: 547; [Increase Mather], *A Narrative of the Miseries of New England* (London, 1688), *Andros Tracts*, 2: 6. For a sense of how this campaign fit into the larger "Tory reaction" see Tim Harris, *Restoration: Charles II and his Kingdoms, 1660–1685* (London, 2005), 260–328.

10. *A Letter From a Person of Quality, To His Friend in the Country* ([London], 1675), 2; "A Vindication of New England (Prepared Chiefly by Increase Mather,) and Containing the Petition of the Episcopalians of Boston to the King," *Andros Tracts*, 2: 27, 50. The best study of the debate on the standing army in England during this period is Lois G. Schwoerer, *"No Standing Armies!": The Antiarmy Ideology in Seventeenth-Century England* (Baltimore, 1974).

11. Morrice, *Entring Book*, 3: 182, 4: 235, 419, 5: 182, and passim; [Care], *English Liberties*, 104; "A Vindication of New England," *Andros Tracts*, 2: 45.

12. *A Letter From a Person of Quality, To His Friend in the Country*, 32. [Pierre Jurieu], *The Last Efforts of Afflicted Innocence: Being an Account of the Persecution of the Protestants of France* (London, 1682), 3. On the anticlericalism inherent in Whig thought see Goldie, "Priestcraft and the Birth of Whiggism;" and J. A. I. Champion, *The Pillars of Priestcraft Shaken: The Church of England and its Enemies, 1660–1730* (Cambridge, 1992).

13. On the connections between Puritanism and Whiggism see Goldie, *Roger Morrice and the Puritan Whigs*, esp. 149–51; on composite monarchy see J. H. Elliott, "A Europe of Composite Monarchies," *Past and Present* 137 (1992): 48–71; on William as a Protestant hero see Tony Claydon, *William III and the Godly Revolution* (Cambridge, 1996).

14. Diarmiad MacCulloch, *The Reformation: A History* (New York, 2003), 170–72, 175; [Alexander Shields], *A Short Memorial of the Sufferings and Grievances, Past and Present, of the Presbyterians in Scotland* ([London], 1690), 23. In general see Martin van Gelderen, *The Political Thought of the Dutch Revolt* (Cambridge, 1992); Allan I. Macinnes, "Covenanting Ideology in Seventeenth-Century Scotland," in Jane H. Ohlmeyer, ed., *Political Thought in Seventeenth-Century Ireland: Kingdom or Colony?* (Cambridge, 2000), 191–220.

15. Pierre Jurieu, *Seasonable Advice to all Protestants in Europe, Of what Persuasion soever, for Uniting and Defending themselves against Popish Tyranny* (London, 1689), 8; Mather, *The Wonderful Works of God Commemorated* (Boston, 1689), 50.

16. [Rawson and Sewall], *Revolution in New England Justified*, in *Andros Tracts*, 1: 85; Declaration of John Wise, Mass. Arch., 35: 168; Complaints of John Wise and others, ibid., 138. There is some dispute over which official uttered the "sold for slaves" comment; Cotton Mather later blamed Joseph Dudley, but contemporary evidence points to Robert Mason.

17. [Rawson and Sewall], *Revolution in New England Justified*, in *Andros Tracts*, 1: 111–12; Depositions of Kerley and How, 27 December 1689, Mass. Arch., 35: 147a.

18. [Rawson and Sewall], *Revolution in New England Justified*, in *Andros Tracts*, 1: 87–90, 125–26; Mass. Arch., 35: 145.

19. Palmer, *Impartial Account*, in *Andros Tracts*, 1: 35–38; [Rawson and Sewall], *Revolution in New England Justified*, ibid., 124–28; *The Present State of the New-English Affairs* (Boston, 1689), ibid., 2: 17; M. G. Hall, ed., "The Autobiography of Increase Mather," *Proceedings of the American Antiquarian Society*, 71 (1962), 333. On "imperium" and "dominium" see Armitage, *Ideological Origins*, 30–31, 63.

20. W. Trail to John Cotton, 15 August 1690, Curwen Family Papers, box 1, folder 4, AAS; Dutch Church of New York to the Classis of Amsterdam, 21 October 1698, in "Documents relating to the Administration of Leisler," *NYHS Coll.*, 1 (1868), 399.

21. On the prehistory of country thought see especially Johann Sommerville, "Ideology, Property, and the Constitution," in Richard Cust and Ann Hughes, eds., *Conflict in Early Stuart England: Studies in Religion and Politics, 1603–1642* (London, 1989), 47–79. On apocalypticism see Warren Johnston, "Revelation and the Revolution of 1688–89," *Historical Journal* 48 (2005): 351–89; Ernestine van der Wall, " 'Antichrist Stormed': The Glorious Revolution and the Dutch Prophetic Tradition," in Dale Hoak and Mordechai Feingold, eds., *The World of William and Mary: Anglo-Dutch Perspectives on the Revolution of 1688–89* (Stanford, 1996), 152–64; Peterson, "Boston Pays Tribute," 331.

22. [Samuel Lee], *Ecclesia Gemens; or, Two Discourses on the mournful State of the Church, with a Prospect of her Dawning Glory* (London, 1677), 57–58.

23. Eliot to Baxter, 6 July 1663, in N. H. Keeble and Geoffrey F. Nuttall, eds., *Calendar of the Correspondence of Richard Baxter* (Oxford, 1991), 2: 39–40; Mather, *Wonderful Works of God*, 37–38.

24. Sewall to John Wise, 12 April 1698, MHS, *Collections*, 6th ser., 1 (1886), 197; Sewall to Nehemiah Walter, 4 December 1703, ibid., 287; Sewall to Stephen Sewall, 27 January 1704, ibid., 289; Sewall, *Phenomena quaedam Apocalyptica Ad Aspectum Novi Orbis configurata* (Boston, 1697), 5, 10.

25. Moody and Simmons, eds., *Glorious Revolution in Massachusetts*, 53–54; Austin Woolrych, *Britain in Revolution, 1625–1660* (Oxford, 2002), 228, 274–75; Richard Coney to William Blathwayt, 2 January 1685/6, Blathwayt Papers, vol. 36, folder 1, CW.

26. "A Memoriall to explain and Justify the principall articles in the Declaration, published by the Gentlemen & Merchants and Inhabitants of Boston on Aprill 18th 1689," Misc. Bound Mss., MHS.

27. "An Account of the Late Revolution in New England by A. B.," in Michael G. Hall,

Lawrence H. Leder, and Michael G. Kammen, eds., *The Glorious Revolution in America: Documents on the Colonial Crisis of 1689* (Chapel Hill, 1964), 51; Samuel Prince to Thomas Hinckley, 22 April 1689, ibid., 41. On Andros's imprisonment see Edward Randolph to Mr. Chaplain, 28 October 1689, *Randolph*, 5: 21.

28. Benjamin Davis to Edward Hull, 31 July 1689, in Moody and Simmons, eds., *Glorious Revolution in Massachusetts*, 398; Thomas Danforth to Increase Mather, 30 July 1689, in Thomas Hutchinson, ed., *Hutchinson Papers* (Boston, 1865), 2: 311–12; Letter from New England, 13 July 1689, CO 5/855/25, TNA; Petition of Joseph Dudley, 4 October 1689, *Andros Tracts*, 3: 104; Simon Bradstreet to Joseph Dudley, 16 July 1689, CO 5/855/21.ix, TNA; Petition of John Winslow, 18 July 1689, Mass. Arch., 107: 210a; Edward Randolph to William Blathwayt, 20 July 1689, in Hall, Leder, and Kammen, eds., *Glorious Revolution in America*, 63.

29. The Committee's investigations are reported in vol. 35 of the Mass. Arch., and summarized in *Andros Tracts*, 1: 149–73. For the *Rose* see Moody and Simmons, eds., *Glorious Revolution in Massachusetts*, 57.

30. Fitz John Winthrop, "An Order to the Field Officers," 1689, Winthrop Family Papers, MHS; John Allyn to Fitz-John Winthrop, 2 May 1689 and 6 May 1689, Winthrop Family Papers; William Pitkin to Fitz-John Winthrop, 6 May 1689, Winthrop Family Papers; J. Hammond Trumbull, ed., *The Public Records of the Colony of Connecticut* (Hartford, 1850–90), 3: 250. See Richard L. Bushman, *From Puritan to Yankee: Character and the Social Order in Connecticut, 1690–1765* (Cambridge, Mass., 1967), 90–91.

31. Moody and Simmons, eds., *Glorious Revolution in Massachusetts*, 64–65, 71–73, 82–83, 90; Thomas Danforth to Increase Mather, 30 July 1689, *Hutchinson Papers*, 2: 313.

32. In addition to the many works of David William Voorhees, especially "'The World Turned Upside Down,'" and Murrin, "The Menacing Shadow of Louis XIV and the Rage of Jacob Leisler," see also Simon Middleton, *From Privileges to Rights: Work and Politics in Colonial New York City* (Philadelphia, 2006).

33. For background on Leisler see Voorhees, "The 'fervant Zeale' of Jacob Leisler," and "'Hearing . . . What Great Success the Dragonnades in France Had': Jacob Leisler's Huguenot Connections," *de Halve Maen* 67 (1994): 15–20. On his confrontation with Plowman see *A Modest and Impartial Narrative . . .* (London, 1690), in Charles McLean Andrews, ed., *Narratives of the Insurrections, 1675–1690* (New York, 1915), 322.

34. Jacob Leisler et al. to Major Wildman, 20 October 1690, Blathwayt Papers, vol. 8, folder 1, CW; Frederick Philips and Stephanus Van Cortlandt to William Blathwayt, 5 August 1689, *NYCD*, 3: 609; Mr. Tuder to Francis Nicholson, August 1689, ibid., 618; Thomas Dongan to Wait Winthrop, 24 April 1690, Winthrop Family Papers, MHS; Leisler to William and Mary, 20 August 1689, *NYCD*, 3: 615.

35. *A Modest and Impartial Narrative*, in Andrews, ed., *Narratives of the Insurrections*, 326; Fragment of a letter from Leisler to Governor and Council of Connecticut, June 1690, *DHNY*, 2: 262; George Mackenzie to Francis Nicholson, 15 August 1689, *NYCD*, 3: 613–14; Depositions of Peter Godfrye and Henry Carmer, 22 July 1689, CO 5/1081/33, TNA; *Loyalty Vindicated from the Reflections of a Virulent Pamphlet . . .* (London, 1698), in Andrews, ed., *Narratives of the Insurrections*, 387; van Cortlandt to Andros, 9 July 1689, *NYCD*, 3: 595.

36. Voorhees, "'The World Turned Upside Down'"; Donna Merwick, "Being Dutch: An Interpretation of Why Jacob Leisler Died," *New York History* 70 (1989): 373–404.

37. Declaration of Jonathan Bull, 1 June 1689, Connecticut Archives, War, 2: 6a, Connecticut State Library, Hartford.

38. Albany Council Records, *DHNY*, 2:104, 150. On Milborne see David William Voorhees, "'Fanatiks' and 'Fifth Monarchists': The Milborne Family in the Seventeenth-Century Atlantic World," *New York Genealogical and Biographical Record* 129 (1998): 67–75, 174–82.

39. Albany Council Records, *DHNY*, 2: 119, 130–31.

40. Lois Green Carr and David W. Jordan, *Maryland's Revolution of Government, 1689–1692* (Ithaca, 1974), 232–88. On the Association see Gilbert Burnet, *History of My Own Time*, pt. 1, *The Reign of Charles the Second* (Oxford, 1897), 2: 264–65; *The History of the Association, Containing all the Debates in the Last House of Commons At Westminster: Concerning an Association, for the Preservation of the King's Person, and the Security of the Protestant Religion* (London, 1682).

41. *The Declaration of the Reasons and Motives For the Present Appearance in Arms of Their Majesties Protestant Subjects In the Province of Maryland* (St. Mary's City, 1689), in Andrews, ed., *Narratives of the Insurrections*, 183–84, 305–13; "Mariland's Grievances Wiy The[y] Have Taken Op Arms," January 1690, in Hall, Leder, and Kammen, eds., *Glorious Revolution in America*, 179–83; Articles against the Lord Baltemore, recd 22 November 1691, *Arch. Md.*, 8: 215–18.

42. *Arch. Md.*, 8: 110; Narrative of Darnall, ibid., 157; Narrative of Barbarah Smith, ibid., 154; Bertrand to the Bishop of London, ibid., 117; Peter Sayer to Baltimore, 31 December 1689, ibid., 158.

43. Reports from the Committee of Secresy, 4 September 1689, *Arch. Md.*, 13: 240; Sayer to Baltimore, ibid., 8: 159–61; Richard Hill to Lord Baltimore, 20 September 1689, ibid., 8: 122; Act prohibiting Catholic lawyers, ibid., 448; "Annual Letters from Maryland," in Henry Foley, ed., *Records of the English Province of the Society of Jesus* (London, 1877–83), 3: 394–95.

44. Coode to Leisler, 26 November 1689, *DHNY*, 2: 42–3; Leisler to the Assembly of Maryland, 26 September 1689, ibid., 33; Leisler to the Assembly of Maryland, n.d., ibid., 34.

45. Leisler to Stede, 23 November 1689, *DHNY*, 2: 40–41; Coode to Leisler, 4 April 1690, ibid., 225–26; H. R. McIlwaine, ed., *Executive Journals of the Council of Colonial Virginia* (Richmond, 1925), 1: 127. For Leisler's knowledge of West Indian events see his letter to William and Mary, 20 August 1689, CO 5/1081/50, TNA.

46. James Lloyd to Thomas Brinley, 10 July 1689 (abstract), CO 5/855/29, TNA; Benjamin Davis to Edward Stule, 31 July 1689 (abstract), ibid.; Francis Brinley to Thomas Brinley, 14 July 1689 (abstract), ibid.; Palmer, *Impartial Account*, in *Andros Tracts*, 1: 35–38.

47. Bulkeley expressed his views in two tracts: *The People's Right to Election Or Alteration of Government in Connecticott* (Philadelphia, 1689), in *Andros Tracts*, 2: 85–109; and "Will and Doom, Or the Miseries of Connecticut by and under a Usurped and Arbitrary Power," Connecticut Historical Society, *Collections*, 3 (1895), 69–269. For the specific quotations see *People's Right to Election*, 94, and "Will and Doom," 83, 90, 192. See also Bulkeley to Fitz John Winthrop, 11 October 1689 and 28 October 1689, Winthrop Family Papers, MHS.

48. Bulkeley, "Will and Doom," 82; *The People's Right to Election*, 98–99; William Fitzhugh to the County Court, 10 November 1691, in Richard Beale Davis, ed., *William Fitzhugh and his Chesapeake World, 1676–1701: The Fitzhugh Letters and Other Documents* (Chapel Hill, 1963), 297; Extract of a letter from Samuel Miles, 29 November 1690, CO 5/855/124, TNA; Humble address of your Majties most Loyal and Dutifull Subjects of the Church of Engld in your Majties Territory and Dominion of New England, CO 5/855/58, TNA; *New England's Faction Discovered, Or a Brief and True Account of their Persecution of the Church of England* (London, 1690), in *Andros Tracts*, 2: 212; Randolph to Dr. William Sancroft, Archbishop of Canterbury, 28 May 1689, *Randolph*, 4: 270.

49. Randolph to Francis Nicholson, 26 July 1689, *Randolph*, 4: 287; Randolph to the Committee on Trade and Plantations, 5 September 1689, ibid., 4: 294; Van Cortlandt to Francis Nicholson, 5 August 1689, *NYCD*, 3:610.

50. Albany Council Records, *DHNY*, 2: 104, 108.

51. Moody and Simmons, eds., *Glorious Revolution in Massachusetts*, 60–61, 66–67, 96–100; Albany Council Records, *DHNY*, 2: 84.

52. For the "Mohawk Plot" see Bulkeley, *The People's Right to Election*, 103; on the "Christian compact," Moody and Simmons, eds., *Glorious Revolution in Massachusetts*, 144–46.

53. Propositions made by the Agents for Massachusetts, Plymouth, and Connecticut to the Five Nations or Cantons of Indians, 23 September 1689, in Carl Bridenbaugh, ed., *The Pynchon Papers*, vol. 1, *Letters of John Pynchon, 1654–1700* (Boston, 1982), 213–14; Propositions made by Pynchon et al. to the River Indians, 12 September 1689, Mass. Arch., 107: 316–17; Lawrence H. Leder, ed., *The Livingston Indian Records, 1666–1723* (Gettysburg, Pa., 1956), 149–53.

CHAPTER 5. THE PROTESTANT ASSAULT ON FRENCH AMERICA

1. Sir Francis Wheler to [?], 4 June 1693, CO 166/1/22, TNA. For complaints about the crew see Isaac Addington to William Blathwayt, 23 October 1693, Blathwayt Papers, vol. 5, folder 3, CW.

2. King William's War has not attracted as much scholarship as it deserves, but see Douglas Edward Leach, *Arms for Empire: A Military History of the British Colonies in North America, 1607–1763* (New York, 1973), 80–115; Ian K. Steele, *Warpaths: Invasions of North America* (New York, 1994), 137–50; Ann M. Little, *Abraham in Arms: War and Gender in Colonial New England* (Philadelphia, 2005); Jenny Hale Pulsipher, " 'Dark Cloud Rising from the East': Indian Sovereignty and the Coming of King William's War in New England," *New England Quarterly* 80 (2007): 588–613. On the West Indies see William Thomas Morgan, "The British West Indies During King William's War (1688–97)," *Journal of Modern History* 2 (1930): 378–409.

3. Some of the best histories of the 1690s have taken the form of biographies of its leading participants. See especially Emerson W. Baker and John G. Reid, *The New England Knight: Sir William Phips, 1651–1695* (Toronto, 1998); and Richard R. Johnson, *John Nelson, Merchant Adventurer: A Life Between Empires* (New York, 1991).

4. Richard Upton to William Blathwayt, 18 April 1689, Blathwayt Papers, vol. 39, folder 3, CW; Stede to Shrewsbury, 16 July 1689, CO 29/4/121–2, TNA.

5. On the French and Irish sack of St. Christopher, see Edwyn Stede to Shrewsbury, 16 July 1689, CO 29/4/121–2, TNA; on French-Indian connections, see John Pike to William Stoughton, 4 July 1695, *DHSM*, 5:420; Charles Frost to Stoughton, 7 September 1695, ibid., 429; "A Short account of the losse of Pemaquid ffort in New England August the 3rd 1689," CO 5/855/27, TNA. The declaration of war appears in Thomas Southey, *Chronological History of the West Indies* (London, 1827), 147.

6. Albany Council Records, *DHNY*, 1: 302. On Schenectady during this period see Thomas E. Burke, Jr., *Mohawk Frontier: The Dutch Community of Schenectady, New York, 1661–1710* (Ithaca, N.Y., 1991).

7. List of ye people kild and destroyed by ye French of Canida and there Indians at Skinnechtady, 9 February 1690, *DNHY*, 1: 304–5; Leisler to Maryland, 4 March 1690, ibid., 307. He repeated the same reports to Governor Stede of Barbados in May; ibid., 301. For earlier examples of violence against pregnant women, see Ethan Howard Shagan, "Constructing Discord: Ideology, Propaganda, and the English Response to the Irish Rebellion of 1641," *Journal of British Studies* 36 (1997): 12–13; Pierre Jurieu, *Pastoral Letters, Directed to the Protestants in France, Who Groan under the Babylonish Captivity* (London, 1688), among many others. David William Voorhees noted the similarities between Leisler's rhetoric and Blount's seminal tract; " 'The World Turned Upside Down': The Foundations of Leislerian Political Thought," in Hermann Wellenreuther, ed., *Jacob Leisler's Atlantic World in the Later Seventeenth Century* (Berlin, 2009), 89–118.

8. Henrico County, Record Book #5 (Deeds, Wills, Etc.), 1688–97 [transcript], 532–35, Library of Virginia, Richmond.

9. Declaration of Silvanus Davis, [1690], *DHSM*, 5: 146–47.

10. Declaration of Davis, 147. For the conception of America as "beyond the line," see Eliga H. Gould, "Zones of Law, Zones of Violence: The Legal Geography of the British Atlantic, circa 1772," *WMQ* 3rd ser. 60 (2003): 471–510.

11. Stede to Shrewsbury, 16 July 1689, CO 29/4/121–2, TNA; Joseph Crisps to Col. Buyer, 10 June 1689, CO 152/37/10. For the surrender see Narrative of proceedings of the French att the siege of the fort of St. Christopher from the 17th of July to the 5th of August 1689, CO 152/37/33.ii.

12. On Stede's efforts against the French during the reign of James II see Stede to the Committee on Trade and Plantations, 19 September 1687, CO 1/63/38, TNA. On the Caribs see Philip Boucher, *Cannibal Encounters: Europeans and Island Caribs, 1492–1763* (Baltimore, 1992).

13. Stede to the Committee on Trade and Plantations, 17 March 1687, CO 1/62/11, TNA; Deposition of Richard Harwood, 15 November 1686, CO 1/61/14.i; Order in council concerning Sr Timo Thornhill, 23 November 1686, CO 1/61/14.iii.

14. Stede to William Blathwayt, 3 September 1689, Blathwayt Papers, vol. 32, folder 5, CW; Christopher Codrington to the Committee on Trade and Plantations, 15 August 1689, CO 153/4/153, TNA.

15. Thomas Spencer, *A True and Faithfull Relation of the Proceedings of the Forces of*

Their Majesties K. William and Q. Mary in their Expedition against the French, in the Caribby Islands, in the West-Indies (London, 1691). For Kidd's involvement see Christopher Codrington to the Committee on Trade and Plantations, 15 August 1689, CO 153/4/150, TNA.

16. *A True and Faithful Account of an Intire and Absolute Victory over the French Fleet in the West-Indies, by Two East-India Ships, and Other Vessels, at Barbadoes, Made into Men of War* (London, 1690); Thomas Hill to Committee on Trade and Plantations, 11 January 1691, CO 153/5/1, TNA.

17. Jacob Leisler to Simon Bradstreet, 7 April 1690, *DHNY*, 2: 228; Depositions against Robert Livingston, ibid., 206–10.

18. Memorial of the Agents from Albany, &c., to the Government of Connecticut, 12 March 1690, *NYCD*, 3: 692–94.

19. Memorial from the Agents from Albany to the Government of Mass., 20 March 1690, *NYCD*, 3: 695–98. The original is in Mass. Arch., 35: 333–41.

20. Mather, *Souldiers Counselled and Comforted* (Boston, 1689), 36–37; he presented similar themes in *Present State of New-England* (Boston, 1690). The same themes appeared in a tract by a French Protestant minister in Boston that used Jesuit materials from Livingston along with commentary from Mather; see Ezechiel Carré, *Echantillon, de la Doctrine que les Jésuites enségnent aus sauvages du nouveau monde* (Boston, 1690); and, for a translation and interpretation, Evan Haefeli and Owen Stanwood, "Jesuits, Huguenots, and the Apocalypse: The Origins of America's First French Book," *Proceedings of the American Antiquarian Society* 116 (2006): 59–120.

21. M. Halsey Thomas, ed., *The Diary of Samuel Sewall, 1674–1729* (New York, 1973), 1: 252; Sewall to the Governor and Council of Connecticut, 29 March 1690, Connecticut Archives, War, 2: 48a, Connecticut State Library, Hartford.

22. Governor and Council of Massachusetts to Thomas Hinckley, 11 April 1690, MHS, *Collections*, 4th ser., 5 (1861), 239. Sewall mentioned the meeting but left few details, *Sewall Diary*, 1: 257.

23. Meeting of the Commissioners at New York, 1 May 1690, *DHSM*, 5:94; Instructions to William Stoughton and Samuel Sewall, 17 April 1690, Mass. Arch., 36: 8–9.

24. For Nelson's early efforts see Proposals of John Nelson, 4 January 1690, *DHSM*, 5: 26–27; Richard Earle Moody and Richard Clive Simmons, eds., *The Glorious Revolution in Massachusetts: Selected Documents, 1689–1692* (Boston, 1988), 135–6; "Journal of Dr. Benjamin Bullivant," MHS, *Proceedings* 16 (1878): 106. On the power struggle between Phips and Nelson see Baker and Reid, *New England Knight*, 84–85; Johnson, *John Nelson*, 57–69.

25. See Deposition of Capt Wm Phips, June 1685, CO 1/57/170, TNA; John Knepp, "Journal of Our Intended voyage by Gods Assistance in his Maties shipp ye Rose William Phips Commander from the Downes to Boston in New England on the maine Continent of America," Egerton Mss. 2526, BL; Hender Molesworth to William Blathwayt, 18 November 1684, CO 1/56/82, TNA. Many of the details of Phips's life come from the interesting but somewhat unreliable contemporary biography by Cotton Mather, *The Life of William Phips*, ed. Mark Van Doren (New York, 1929).

26. Moody and Simmons, eds., *Glorious Revolution in Massachusetts*, 238; Jefferies to John Usher, 29 March 1690, Frederick Lewis Gay Transcripts, Phips Papers, 1: 23, MHS;

"Journal of Dr. Benjamin Bullivant," MHS, *Proceedings* 16 (1878); Memorial of the Agents from Albany to the Government of Massachusetts, 20 March 1690, *NYCD*, 3: 696; *A Journal of the Proceedings in the late Expedition to Port-Royal* (Boston, 1690), 9.

27. *Journal of the Proceedings in the late Expedition to Port-Royal*, 5–6; "Relation de ce qui s'est passé de plus remarquable en Canada, depuis le depart des vaisseaux, au mois de novembre, 1689, jusqu'au mois de novembre, 1690," in *Collection de manuscrits contenant lettres, mémoires, et autres documents historiques relatifs à la Nouvelle-France* (Québec, 1883–85), 1: 502–3; "Prise du Port Royal par les Anglois de Baston, 19–27 may 1690," in "Historical Documents relating to Acadia, the Commonwealth of Massachusetts, the French Colonial Government, and the Abenaquis," Parkman Papers, vol. 30, MHS.

28. *Journal of the Proceedings in the late Expedition to Port-Royal*, 6; "Relation de ce qui s'est passé . . . " in *Collection de manuscrits*, 1: 502.

29. Moody and Simmons, eds., *Glorious Revolution in Massachusetts*, 245; List of Plunder from Port Royal, 14 June 1690, Mass. Arch., 35: 122a, 123–24a; *Sewall Diary*, 1: 260.

30. Cotton Mather to James Brown, 30 June 1690, in Kenneth Silverman, ed., *Selected Letters of Cotton Mather* (Baton Rouge, 1971), 26–67; Bradstreet to Jacob Leisler, 30 May 1690, *DHNY*, 2: 260; Extract of a Letter to John Usher from Boston, 27 May 1690, CO 5/855/100, TNA.

31. Robert Livingston to Francis Nicholson, 7 June 1690, *NYCD*, 3: 725; Governor and Council of Connecticut to Governor and Council of Massachusetts, 15 May 1690, *DHSM*, 5: 96–97; Fitz John Winthrop to the Governor and Council of Connecticut, 20 May 1690, MHS, *Collections*, 5th ser., 8 (1882), 303; Fitz John Winthrop to Wait Winthrop, 7 June 1690, ibid., 304; Bradstreet to Leisler, 27 May 1690, *DHSM*, 5: 111; Richard S. Dunn, *Puritans and Yankees: The Winthrop Dynasty of New England, 1630–1717* (Princeton, 1962), 289–94. On Milborne's background see David William Voorhees, "'Fanatiks' and 'Fifth Monarchists': The Milborne Family in the Seventeenth-Century Atlantic World," *New York Genealogical and Biographical Record* 129 (1998): 67–75, 174–82.

32. Livingston to Nicholson, 7 June 1690, *NYCD*, 3: 728; Jacob Leisler to the Earl of Shrewsbury, 23 June 1690, ibid., 731–73; Leisler to John Coode, 27 June 1690, *DHNY*, 2: 268; Governor and Council of Massachusetts to Shrewsbury, 19 July 1690, in William H. Whitmore, ed., *The Andros Tracts: Being a Collection of Pamphlets and Official Papers of the Andros Government and the Establishment of the Second Charter of Massachusetts* (New York, 1868–74), 3: 49.

33. Bullivant to John Usher, 10 July 1690 (extract), Blathwayt Papers, BL242, HL; Thomas Newton to Francis Nicholson, 26 May 1690, *NYCD*, 3: 720; Mather, *Present State of New England*; John Emerson to Wait Winthrop, 26 July 1690, MHS, *Collections* 5th ser., 1 (1871), 437–38; *Sewall Diary*, 1: 262.

34. Fitz John Winthrop to Peter Schuyler, 23 July 1690, MHS, *Collections*, 5th ser., 8 (1882), 307; Winthrop to the Governor and Council of Connecticut, 29 July 1690, ibid., 308–9; Fitz John Winthrop to Wait Winthrop, [1690], Winthrop Family Papers, MHS; Stephanus van Cortlandt to William Blathwayt, 1 August 1690, Blathwayt Papers, vol. 9, folder 1, CW; Milborne to Fitz John Winthrop, 9 August 1690, Winthrop Family Papers, MHS.

35. Propositions made by the Majr Genll John Winthrop . . . to some of the heads

of Maquas, Onydes, Schagtcookes and River Indians, 8 August 1690, Winthrop Family Papers, MHS; "Journal of the Expedition to Canada," MHS, *Collections*, 5th ser., 8 (1882), 313–19; Fitz John Winthrop to the Governor and Council of Connecticut, 15 August 1690, ibid., 310–12; Journal of Capt. John Schuyler, *DHNY*, 2: 286–87; Certificate of Sander Glen, 21 August 1690, Winthrop Family Papers, MHS.

36. John Allyn to Jacob Leisler, 23 August 1690, *DHNY*, 2: 284; *Sewall Diary*, 1: 265.

37. Leisler to [Governor and Council of Connecticut], 30 September 1690, *DHNY*, 2: 301; Winthrop to the Governor and Council of Connecticut, 6 October 1690, MHS, *Collections*, 5th ser., 8 (1882), 323.

38. Leisler to [Governor and Council of Connecticut], 30 September 1690, *DHNY*, 2: 300–302; Copy of letter by Leisler, 15 October 1690, Jacob Melyen Letterbook, 30–31, AAS; Leisler and the Council to the Earl of Shrewsbury, 20 October 1690, *NYCD*, 3: 752. The charges of adultery were technically true, as Winthrop kept a common law wife for much of his life; see Dunn, *Puritans and Yankees*, 204.

39. Leisler to [Connecticut], 30 September 1689, *DHNY*, 2: 303; Leisler to Robert Treat, 1 January 1691, ibid., 317–19. The language of Leisler's letter closely resembles that in Isaiah 46–47.

40. John Allyn to Leisler, 1 September 1690, *DHNY*, 2: 288–89; J. Hammond Trumbull, *The Public Records of the Colony of Connecticut* (Hartford, 1850–90), 4: 38; William Jones to Wait Winthrop, 16 September 1690, Winthrop Family Papers, MHS.

41. Simon Bradstreet to Thomas Hinckley, 6 June 1690, MHS, *Collections*, 4th ser., 5 (1861), 259; Fitz John Winthrop to Robert Livingston, 16 June 1690, Winthrop Family Papers, MHS; John Cotton [Jr.] to John Cotton [Sr.], 5 August 1690, Curwen Family Papers, box 1, folder 4, AAS; Anonymous account of the Phips Expedition, MHS, *Proceedings* 2nd ser. 15 (1901, 1902): 305.

42. *Sewall Diary*, 1: 263; *The Diaries of Benjamin Lynde and of Benjamin Lynde, Jr.* (Boston, 1880), 1; Report concerning New-England, 12 June 1690, CO 5/905/222, 223–24, TNA; Moody and Simmons, eds., *Glorious Revolution in Massachusetts*, 264, 272; Baker and Reid, *New England Knight*, 96–97.

43. Anonymous Account of Phips Expedition, MHS, *Proceedings* 2nd ser. 15 (1901, 1902): 306–12; Relation de Monseignat (Extrait), in Ernest Myrand, ed., *Sir William Phips devant Québec: histoire d'un siège* (Québec, 1893), 20, 22; Frontenac à M. de Seignelay, 12 novembre 1690, ibid., 7; Relation de l'officier Janclot, ibid., 74.

44. Mather, *Life of Sir William Phips*, 73–75; Relation de l'intendant Bochard de Champigny, in Myrand, ed., *Phips devant Québec*, 81.

45. Louis Amand de Lom d'Arce, baron de Lahontan, *New Voyages to North America* (London, 1703), 162–64; Relation de Monseignat, in Myrand, ed., *Phips devant Québec*, 26; Frontenac à Seignelay, ibid., 13. English versions of Frontenac's famous speech contained an additional passage, charging that the colonists had "made a Revolution, which if it had not been made, New-England and the French had been all One" (Mather, *Life of Phips*, 75). This addition meant to demonstrate that Edmund Andros had really been plotting to deliver the colonies to France. No French accounts corroborate this passage, which seemed to originate with Silvanus Davis's testimony.

46. Lettre pastorale de Mgr de St-Vallier Pour disposer les peuples de ce diocèse à se bien défendre contre les Anglais, in Myrand, ed., *Phips devant Québec*, 153; Relation de Jeanne-Françoise Juchereau de la Ferté, ibid., 85, 89; "Account of the defeat of the English at Quebec," in Rueben Gold Thwaites, ed., *The Jesuit Relations and Allied Documents* (Cleveland, 1896–1901), 64: 45–47; Relation de Mgr de Laval, 20 novembre 1690, in Myrand, ed., *Phips devant Québec*, 121. No English documents contained any plans for the colony's religious in case of a successful invasion, but it is easy to imagine that many ordinary New Englanders would have threatened to treat the Jesuits as the captives claimed.

47. "The Narrative of Mr. John Wise, Minister of Gods Word at Chebacco," MHS, *Proceedings* 2nd ser. 15 (1901, 1902): 287–90, 296; "Major Walley's Journal," in Myrand, ed., *Phips devant Québec*, 43–47; Frontenac à Seignelay, 12 novembre 1690, ibid., 9; Relation de Jeanne-Françoise Juchereau de la Ferté, ibid., 91; Lahontan, *New Voyages*, 163. Another interesting second-hand account appears in Johannes Kerfbyll to Abraham de Peyster, 20 November 1690, De Peyster Papers, Dutch Translations by Dingman Ver Steeg, 4–7, New-York Historical Society.

48. "Narrative of John Wise," 296; Stephanus van Cortlandt to William Blathwayt, 7 May 1691, Blathwayt Papers, vol. 9, folder 1, CW.

49. Information of Henry Graveraett regarding New York, 16 December 1690, CO 5/855/128, TNA; Jacob Melyen to Jacob Leisler, 11 December 1690, *DHNY*, 2: 316.

50. Ingoldesby to Leisler, 30 January 1691, in "Documents Relating to the Administration of Leisler," *NYHS Coll.*, 1 (1868), 300; Leisler to Ingoldesby, 14 February 1691, ibid., 303.

51. Affidavit of Thomas Jeffers, 19 February 1692, "Documents Relating to the Administration of Leisler," *NYHS Coll.*, 1: 320; Affidavit of Kiliaan van Rensselaer, 1 March 1692, ibid., 330; Declaration of the Freeholders and Inhabitants of Long Island and Parts Adjacent, March 1691, ibid., 305; William Jones to Wait Winthrop, 16 September 1690, Winthrop Family Papers, MHS.

52. Warrant for Jacob Leisler's Commitment to Prison, 26 March 1691, *DHNY*, 2: 363; Lawrence H. Leder, ed., "Records of the Trials of Jacob Leisler and his Associates," *New-York Historical Society Quarterly* 36 (1952): 431–58; Dying Speeches of Leisler and Milborne, 16 May 1691, *DHNY*, 2: 378; Jacob Melyen to Abraham Governeur, 3 September 1691, Jacob Melyen Letterbook, 36–37, AAS.

53. Cotton Mather, *Decennium Luctuosum* (Boston, 1699), in Charles H. Lincoln, ed., *Narratives of the Indian Wars, 1675–1699* (New York, 1913), 242–47; James F. Cooper and Kenneth P. Minkema, eds., *The Sermon Notebook of Samuel Parris, 1689–1694* (Boston, 1993), 199–205.

54. The connections to the Indian war are explored most fully in Mary Beth Norton, *In the Devil's Snare: The Salem Witchcraft Crisis of 1692* (New York, 2002), although she expanded an argument that first appeared in James E. Kences, "Some Unexplored Relationships of Essex County Witchcraft to the Indian Wars of 1675 and 1689," *Essex Institute Historical Collections* 120 (1984): 179–212. The literature on Salem witchcraft is far too vast to cover here, but my interpretation is particularly indebted to David Thomas Konig, *Law and Society in Puritan Massachusetts: Essex County, 1629–1692* (Chapel Hill, 1979), 158–85;

and John Murrin, "Coming to Terms with the Salem Witch Trials," *Proceedings of the American Antiquarian Society* 110 (2000): 309–47.

55. Essex County Quarterly Court Records, WPA Transcripts, vol. 49, fol. 57–1, 57–2, Peabody Essex Museum, Salem; Narrative of the Conspiracy of the Negros, CO 28/1/101.ii, TNA. Thanks to Jason Sharples for the latter reference.

56. [Hammond], *To the King's Most Excellent Majesty, the Humble Address of divers of the Gentry, Merchants, and others . . .* (London, 1691), CO 5/856/145, TNA; Bulkeley, "Will and Doom, Or the Miseries of Connecticut by and under a Usurped and Arbitrary Power," Connecticut Historical Society, *Collections* 3 (1895): 203.

57. "Reflections upon the Affairs of New England," [June 1691] Connecticut Historical Society, *Collections*, 21 (1924), 325–38.

58. Benjamin Davis to Nicholson, 17 April 1691, Blathwayt Papers, vol. 4, folder 4, CW; Abstract of the Address of divers Gentlemen Mercht & others of Their Mats Subjects in New England, CO 5/855/122, TNA; Francis Foxcroft to Charles Lidget, 2 April 1690, CO 5/855/79; Samuel Sewall to Increase Mather, 19 December 1690, MHS, *Collections*, 6th ser., 1 (1886), 115.

59. For the new charter, see Michael G. Hall, Lawrence H. Leder, and Michael G. Kammen, eds., *The Glorious Revolution in America: Documents on the Colonial Crisis of 1689* (Chapel Hill, 1964), 76–79; Richard R. Johnson, *Adjustment to Empire: The New England Colonies, 1675–1715* (New Brunswick, 1981), 226–41; and David S. Lovejoy, *The Glorious Revolution in America* (New York, 1972), 376–77.

60. Stede to the Committee, 30 May 1689, CO 29/4/116–17, TNA.

61. Christopher Codrington to the Committee on Trade and Plantations, 8 November 1689, CO 153/4/194, 197, 199–200, TNA.

62. Morgan, "King William's War in the British West Indies." On the elder Wheler see Richard S. Dunn, *Sugar and Slaves: The Rise of the Planter Class in the English West Indies, 1624–1715* (Chapel Hill, 1972), 124.

63. Council of War, 20 April 1693, CO 166/1/1, TNA.

64. Phips to Blathwayt, 12 October 1692, Blathwayt Papers, vol. 5, folder 1, CW; [Blathwayt] to [Phips], 20 February 1693, Blathwayt Papers, vol 5, folder 1, CW; Blathwayt to Increase Mather, 20 February 1693, Blathwayt Papers, vol. 5, folder 6, CW.

65. Wheler to Phips, 8 July 1693, CO 5/857/68; Phips to Wheler, 12 July 1693, CO 5/857/69; Mass. Arch., Court Records, 6: 295; Phips to Blathwayt, 26 September 1693, Blathwayt Papers, vol. 5, folder 2, CW.

66. Phips to William III, 30 September 1693, Blathwayt Papers, vol. 5, folder 2, CW.

CHAPTER 6. AMBIVALENT BONDS

1. Petition of the Inhabitants of the Isles of Shoals, 17 February 1692, *DHSM*, 5: 350; Instructions to Capt. Willey, 17 February 1692, ibid., 351; Edward Willey to the Governor and Council of Massachusetts, 11 March 1692, ibid., 358; Samuel Sewall to John Cotton,

22 February 1692, Curwen Family Papers, box 1, folder 4, AAS; Address of some of the Inhabitants of the Isles of Shoals to the Governor and Council of Massachusetts, 12 March 1692, *DHSM*, 5: 363.

2. Bellomont has attracted little attention from historians, and the rumors of 1700 even less. See Frederic de Peyster, *The Life and Administration of Richard, Earl of Bellomont, Governor of the Provinces of New York, Massachusetts, and New Hampshire, from 1697 to 1701* (New York, 1879); John D. Runcie, "The Problem of Anglo-American Politics in Bellomont's New York," *WMQ* 3rd ser. 26 (1969): 191–217; John C. Rainbolt, "A 'great and usefull designe': Bellomont's Proposal for New York, 1698–1701," *New-York Historical Society Quarterly* 53 (1969): 333–51; Rainbolt, "The Creation of a Governor and Captain General for the Northern Colonies: The Process of Colonial Policy Formation at the End of the Seventeenth Century," *New-York Historical Society Quarterly* 57 (1973): 100–120; Kenneth M. Morrison, *The Embattled Northeast: The Elusive Ideal of Alliance in Abenaki-Euramerican Relations* (Berkeley, 1984), 146–53; Jack M. Sosin, *English America and Imperial Inconstancy: The Rise of Provincial Autonomy, 1696–1715* (Lincoln, Neb., 1985), 153–74; Evan Haefeli and Kevin Sweeney, *Captors and Captives: The 1704 French and Indian Raid on Deerfield* (Amherst, 2003), 85–86.

3. John Oldmixon, *The British Empire in America, Containing the History of the Discovery, Settlement, Progress and present State of all the British Colonies, on the Continent and Islands of America* (London, 1708), 1: iv.

4. Chidley Brooke to William Blathwayt, 23 November 1694, Blathwayt Papers, vol. 11, folder 4, CW. Aside from the well-known introduction of royal government in Massachusetts, Whitehall also took steps to vacate the charters of Pennsylvania and Maryland—both of which were ruled by allies of the deposed James II. In both cases the crown eventually restored the rights of the proprietors; William Penn regained his colony in 1694, and the Calvert family won back Maryland in 1715 after the family converted from Catholicism to Anglicanism.

5. The humble Representation and Address of the Lieutenant Governor, Council and Assembly of . . . Massachusetts Bay in New England, 24 September 1696, CO 5/859/44.i, TNA; reprinted in *DHSM*, 5: 448–51; Plan submitted by Mssrs. Brooke and Nicoll for securing New-York, *NYCD*, 4: 183–84.

6. Benjamin Davis to Edward Hull (abstract), 2 January 1697, CO 5/859/55, TNA; Petition of the Inhabitants, Traders, and Proprietors in the North Parts of America, CO 5/859/62; The Humble Representation of the Merchants, & others concerned in the trade to New England, CO 5/859/81; Stephen Sewall to Edward Hill (extract), Frederick Lewis Gay Transcripts, State Papers, 8: 2–3, MHS.

7. For a detailed sketch of Nelson's negotiations in London during this time see Richard R. Johnson, *John Nelson, Merchant Adventurer: A Life Between Empires* (New York, 1991), 87–106.

8. Nelson's Analysis of the position of the French in America, and his plea for British action [1696], Temple-Nelson Papers, Houghton Library, Harvard University.

9. Draft of "A Brief and Plaine Scheam," ca. 8 February 1697, in Richard S. Dunn and Mary Maples Dunn, eds., *The Papers of William Penn* (Philadelphia, 1986), 3: 482–83; John

Miller, *New York Considered and Improved, 1695*, ed. Victor Hugo Paltsits (Cleveland, 1903), 75–85. Penn's proposals appeared in an influential work of political economy, Charles Davenant, *Discourses on the Publick Revenues and the Trade of England* (London, 1698), 259–61.

10. [Richard] Daniel, "Note About New England," 23 December 1695, BL 249, Blathwayt Papers, HL; Daniel, "The Present State of New England," 23 December 1695, Blathwayt Papers, vol. 6, folder 5, CW.

11. Report of the Lords of Trade on the Northern Colonies in America, 30 September 1696, *NYCD*, 4: 227–30. For Locke's authorship see Johnson, *John Nelson*, 94.

12. For complaints about Rhode Island, see for example Isaac Addington to William Blathwayt, 21 February 1693, Blathwayt Papers, vol. 5, folder 3, CW; Francis Brinley to Blathwayt, 29 December 1692, ibid., vol. 11, folder 4. On Fletcher's tenure in Pennsylvania see Gary B. Nash, *Quakers and Politics: Pennsylvania, 1681–1726* (Princeton, 1968), 181–87.

13. Fletcher to Blathwayt, 15 August 1693, *NYCD*, 4: 37; Fletcher to the Committee of Trade, 10 November 1693, ibid., 73–74; Fletcher to Blathwayt, 28 October 1693, Blathwayt Papers, vol. 8, folder 4, CW; "The Case of Connecticut and Reasons for Explaining the Commission of the Governour of New Yorke," Connecticut Colonial Records, 1664–1702, Connecticut State Library, Hartford; Fletcher to Blathwayt, 28 March 1694, Blathwayt Papers, vol. 8, folder 4, CW; Fletcher to [Blathwayt], 19 November 1694, BL191, Blathwayt Papers, HL.

14. "The Case of Connecticut and Reasons for Explaining the Commission of the Governour of New Yorke," Ct. Colonial Recs., 1664–1702, Connecticut State Library; James S. Leamon, "Governor Fletcher's Recall," *WMQ* 3rd. ser. 20 (1963): 528.

15. For "garrison government" see Stephen Saunders Webb, "Army and Empire: English Garrison Government in Britain and America, 1569 to 1763," *WMQ* 3rd. ser. 34 (1977): 1–31; *The Governors-General: The English Army and the Definition of the Empire, 1569–1681* (Chapel Hill, 1979).

16. George Sydenham to [William Blathwayt], 7 October 1695, Blathwayt Papers, vol. 10, folder 3, CW; The Memorial of Capt James Weems, 3 September 1696, N.Y. Col. Mss., 40: 193; Board of Trade to the King, Report on the Complaints of three lieutenants serving in the province of New York, 18 February 1697, BL169, Blathwayt Papers, HL.

17. Petition of Abraham Bickford, N.Y. Col. Mss., 41: 128; Abraham Bickford to Benjamin Fletcher, March 1696, *NYCD*, 4: 161–62; Minutes on the Court Martial on the Schenectady Deserters, 21 April 1696, ibid., 163–64; Fletcher to the Lords of Trade, 10 June 1696, ibid., 160; Representation of the Lords of Trade concerning New-York, ibid., 707.

18. *By His Excellency Benjamin Fletcher . . . A Proclamation* (New York, 1693), N.Y. Col. Mss., 39: 106; *By His Excellency Benjamin Fletcher . . . A Proclamation* (New York, 169[6]), ibid., 40: 134; *By His Excellency Benjamin Fletcher . . . A Proclamation* (New York, 1697), ibid., 41: 131; Fletcher to Lords of Trade, 10 June 1696, *NYCD*, 4: 160.

19. See Leamon, "Governor Fletcher's Recall." For a good summary of colonial governance during this period, see Ian K. Steele, "The Anointed, the Appointed, and the Elected: Governance of the British Empire, 1689–1784," in P. J. Marshall, ed., *The Oxford History of the British Empire*, vol. 2, *The Eighteenth Century* (Oxford, 1998), 105–27.

20. Edmund Harrison's memorandum on uniting the northern colonies in America, 1

February 1697, CO 5/859/60, TNA. The final version gave Bellomont the administration of New Hampshire, Massachusetts, and New York and control of the Connecticut and Rhode Island militias, but only during time of war. The union was approved on 25 February 1697, and Bellomont's appointment finalized on 16 March (CO 5/859/72, 75.)

21. Richard Coote to Lord Middleton, 12 August 1687, Add. Mss. 41820, fol. 273, BL; Coote to Middleton, 5 April 1688, Add. Mss. 48121, fol. 74; Mem of pceedings in ye matter of Pr. W., Add. Mss., 29587, f.73; Bellomont to Edward Clarke, 23 August 1690, Misc. Mss. Bellomont, New-York Historical Society; Bellomont to Edward Clark, 9 September 1690, ibid.

22. Bellomont to the Earl of Bridgewater, 23 February 1697, EL9671, Bridgewater Papers, Ellesmere Collection, HL. The most complete reconstruction of the salary negotiations is in Rainbolt, "The Creation of a Governor and Captain General for the Northern Colonies."

23. EL9658, EL9664, Bridgewater Papers, Ellesmere Collection, HL; Chidley Brooke and Richard Nicolls to the Committee on Trade and Plantations, 8 February 1697, CO 5/859/68, TNA; Fitz John Winthrop to the Committee on Trade and Plantations, recd. 8 February 1697, CO 5/859/67; John Higginson to John How, 1 August 1694, MHS, *Collections*, 80 (1972), 214–15; Richard Saltonstall to Rowland Cotton, 20 April 1698, ibid., 256.

24. Stoughton to Bellomont, 13 December 1697, Mass. Arch., 3: 61; William Ashurst to William Stoughton and the Commissioners, 16 July 1697, Company for the Propagation of the Gospel in New England, Letter Book, 1688–1761, 19, Alderman Library, University of Virginia (microfilm, MHS); Fitz John Winthrop to Wait Winthrop, 13 July 1695, MHS, *Collections*, 5th ser., 8 (1882), 324; Staats to de Peyster, 12 June 1699, De Peyster Papers, Dutch Translations by Dingman Ver Steeg, 21, New-York Historical Society.

25. Bellomont to Bridgewater, 12 May 1699, EL9764, Bridgewater Papers, Ellesmere Collection, HL.

26. *His Excellency, The Earl of Bellomont his Speech To the Representatives of his Majesties Province of New-York, the 21th of March, 1699* (New York, 1699), EL9776, Bridgewater Papers, Ellesmere Mss., HL; *To his Excellency Richard Earl of Bellomont . . . The Humble Petition and Remonstrance of the Representatives of this His Majesties Province of New-York in America* (New York, 1699), ibid., EL9777; Herbert L. Osgood, ed., *Minutes of the Common Council of the City of New York, 1675–1776* (New York, 1905), 2: 27

27. Bellomont to the Lords of Trade, 22 June 1698, *NYCD*, 4: 322; Bellomont to the Lords of Trade, 21 October 1698, ibid., 398–400; Bellomont to the Lord Bishop of London, 11 September 1699, *NYCD*, 4: 581. "Father Smith" was actually one of the more fascinating characters in late-seventeenth-century America, an English Jesuit probably named Thomas Harvey who resided in New York during the Catholic Thomas Dongan's governorship, and spent many of the next years traveling the colonies and hiding out under a number of assumed names, including John Smith. He resided with Pinhorne sometime in 1690, during Leisler's administration. See Thomas Hughes, ed., *History of the Society of Jesus in North America, Colonial and Federal* (Cleveland, 1908), 2: 148–51; Henry Foley, *Records of the English Province of the Society of Jesus* (London, 1877–83), 7: 342–43. Vesey's father, also named William Vesey, was convicted of refusing to observe a fast day for King William's

deliverance from a Jacobite plot in 1696; see Case of William Vezy, April 1697, Suffolk Court Files, vol. 38, no. 3443, Mass. Arch.

28. "Loyalty Vindicated, 1698," in Charles McLean Andrews, ed., *Narratives of the Insurrections, 1675–1690* (New York, 1915); Alida Livingston to Robert Livingston, 12, 25, 27 January 1698, Livingston Papers, Gilder Lehrman Collection, quoted in Lawrence H. Leder, *Robert Livingston, 1654–1728, and the Politics of Colonial New York* (Chapel Hill, 1961), 128.

29. N. Y. Col. Mss., 40: 72b; "City Records," in Joel Munsell, ed., *The Annals of Albany* (Albany, 1850–59), 3: 32, 35; Memorial of Messrs. Bleecker and Schermerhorn, 6 June 1698, *NYCD*, 4: 330; Daniel K. Richter, *The Ordeal of the Longhouse: The Peoples of the Iroquois League in the Era of European Colonization* (Chapel Hill, 1991), 191–92.

30. Depositions of Henry and Joseph, Christian Mohawks, 31 May 1698, *NYCD*, 4: 345–46; Examination of Hendrick the Mohawk, 10 June 1699, ibid., 539–41; Peter Wraxall, *An Abridgement of the Indian Affairs, Contained in Four Folio Volumes, Transacted in the Colony of New York, from the year 1678 to the year 1751*, ed. Charles Howard Martin (Cambridge, Mass., 1915), 30; Bellomont to the Lords of Trade, 17 April 1699, *NYCD*, 4: 503–4; Bellomont to Abraham de Peyster, 3 and 21 August 1699, in de Peyster, *Life and Administration of Bellomont*, "Appendix: Letters of the Earl of Bellomont to Colonel Abraham de Peyster," v–vii (originals in De Peyster Papers, New-York Historical Society).

31. On this particular brand of politics see Patricia U. Bonomi's interesting study of Bellomont's successor in New York, *The Lord Cornbury Scandal: The Politics of Reputation in British America* (Chapel Hill, 1998).

32. Bellomont to Lords of Trade, 13 April 1699, *NYCD*, 4: 488–89; Bellomont to Lords of Trade, ibid., 533–34. These charges originated with Leisler; see *DHNY*, 2: 268.

33. Bellomont to the Lords of Trade, 13 April 1699, *NYCD*, 4: 488; Bellomont to the Board of Trade, 14 September 1698, ibid., 362–63. For the records of Dellius's embassy to Montreal see ibid., 340–41, 348–51.

34. Bellomont to the Lord Bishop of London, 11 September 1699, *NYCD*, 4: 581–82; Bellomont to Abraham de Peyster, 3 August 1699, de Peyster, *Life and Administration of Bellomont*, "Appendix," v. The biblical reference is to 1 Samuel 2: 22, in which the sons of the priest Eli "lay with the women that assembled at the door of the congregation."

35. Instructions to Messrs. Hanse and Schermerhorn, 19 May 1699, *NYCD*, 4: 566; Bellomont to the Lords of Trade, ibid., 528–29; Church of Albany to the Classis of Amsterdam, 5 June 1699, in Edward T. Corwin, ed., *Ecclesiastical Records of the State of New York* (Albany, 1901), 3: 1317; Bellomont to de Peyster, 21 August 1699, 9 September 1699, de Peyster, *Life and Administration of Bellomont*, "Appendix," vii, x. For the many petitions on the minister's behalf see Corwin, ed., *Ecclesiastical Records*, 2: 1305–11, 1321–25.

36. "The Defence of Rev. Godfridus Dellius, against the Charges of Lord Bellomont made Oct. 13, 1699," *Ecclesiastical Records*, 2: 1410–18, quotation on 1415–16.

37. Bellomont to Frontenac, 13 August 1698, *NYCD*, 4: 367–68; Jacques Bruyas to Bellomont, 13 octobre 1699, CO 5/861/4.xxix, TNA; Joseph Robineau de Villebon à ministre, 27 octobre 1699, in *Collection de manuscrits contenant lettres, mémoires, et autres documents historiques relatifs à la Nouvelle-France* (Québec, 1883–85), 2: 330.

38. Bellomont to the Lords of Trade, 1 July 1698, *NYCD*, 4: 333–34; Journal of Arnout Cornelisse Viele's Negotiations at Onondaga, April-May 1699, ibid., 560 (but see the Iroquois response to Bellomont's message on 565, which belies Vielé's optimism and suggests that the Indians were not eager to receive Protestant missionaries); Wraxall, *Abridgment of the Indian Affairs*, 28–29; Bellomont to the Secretary of the Board, 19 October 1700, *NYCD*, 4: 766–67; William Ashurst to William Stoughton, 8 March 1699, Company for the Propagation of the Gospel in New England, Letter Book, 24–25, Alderman Library, University of Virginia.

39. Nathaniel Bouton, ed., *Documents and Records Relating to the Province of New-Hampshire* (Concord, 1867–73), 2: 318–19; John Nelson and Silvanus Davis to Bellomont, 24 November 1699, CO 5/861/4.xxii, TNA; Bellomont's Speech to the Council and Representatives of New Hampshire, 7 September 1699, in Bouton, ed., *Documents and Records*, 3: 66; Vincent Bigot to George Turfrey, 5 October [?], *DHSM*, 5: 456; Jacques Bigot to a Jesuit, 26 October 1699, in Rueben Gold Thwaites, ed., *The Jesuit Relations and Allied Documents* (Cleveland, 1896–1901), 65: 95.

40. Josiah Cotton to [John Cotton?], 22 February 1700, Misc. Bound Mss., MHS; John Dexter to Fitz John Winthrop, 26 March 1700, Winthrop Family Papers, MHS; James Noyes to Fitz John Winthrop, 18 January 1700, ibid.

41. James Noyes to Fitz John Winthrop, 16 January 1700, Winthrop Family Papers, MHS; Information respecting a rumored Rising of the Indians, 22 January 1700, *NYCD*, 4: 613–16.

42. Noyes to Winthrop, 16 January 1700, Winthrop Family Papers, MHS; Josiah Cotton to [John Cotton?], 22 February 1700, Misc. Bound Mss., MHS; Information respecting a rumored Rising of the Indians, 22 January 1700, *NYCD*, 4: 614.

43. Information respecting a rumored Rising of the Indians, 22 January 1700, *NYCD*, 4: 614; Fitz John Winthrop to Bellomont, 29 January 1700, ibid., 612; Information of Mr. John Sabin, 20 February 1700, ibid., 619.

44. A Journall of the Expedition from N london to Woodstock p[er] order of the Govr & Councill, under the Comand of Samll Mason . . . , Winthrop Family Papers, MHS; Bouton, ed., *Documents and Records*, 2: 324; William Partridge to Bellomont, 20 February 1700, *NYCD*, 4: 617.

45. The declaration of Ben Uncas, Winthrop Family Papers, MHS; Robert Treat to Fitz John Winthrop, MHS, *Collections* 6th ser., 3 (1889), 45; Information of Mr. John Sabin, *NYCD*, 4: 619–20; Letter from Oxford re Penacook Indians, 4 March 1700, Mass. Arch., 70: 430. For Owaneco's dealings with Connecticut officials during this period see Richard L. Bushman, *From Puritan to Yankee: Character and the Social Order in Connecticut, 1690–1765* (Cambridge, Mass., 1967), 82–87.

46. James Noyes to Fitz John Winthrop, 18 January 1700, Winthrop Family Papers, MHS; Information of Mr. John Sabin, *NYCD*, 4: 619; Caleb Stanley to Fitz John Winthrop, 1 March 1700, MHS, *Collections* 6th ser., 3 (1889), 48–49.

47. Fitz John Winthrop to Bellomont, 29 January 1700, *NYCD*, 4: 612–13; John Pynchon to Bellomont, 5 February 1700, Carl Bridenbaugh, ed., *The Pynchon Papers*, vol. 1, *Letters of John Pynchon, 1654–1700* (Boston, 1982), 310; M. Halsey Thomas, ed., *The Diary of*

Samuel Sewall, 1674–1729 (New York, 1973), 1: 424; Inhabitants of Woodstock to Fitz John Winthrop, 11 March 1700, Winthrop Family Papers, MHS; Josiah Dwight to Bellomont, 11 March 1700, CO 5/861/31.viii, TNA; Noyes to Winthrop, 18 January 1700, Winthrop Family Papers, MHS.

48. Bellomont to the Lords of Trade, 28 February 1700, *NYCD*, 4: 606–10. For a similar sentiment from someone of very different political persuasions, see John Usher to William Blathwayt, 25 February 1700, Blathwayt Papers, vol. 6, folder 2, CW.

49. Mass. Arch., Court Records, 7: 51–54; Mass. Arch., 11: 143; *His Excellency the Earl of Bellomont's Speech to the Honourable the Council, and House of Representatives, Assembled in General Court . . .* (Boston, 1699 [1700]), CO 5/861/31.ii, TNA; *By His Excellency, Richard, Earl of Bellomont, Captain General and Governour in Chief . . . A Proclamation* (Boston, 1699 [1700]), CO 5/861/31.iv; *By His Excellency, Richard, Earl of Bellomont, Captain General and Governour in Chief . . . A Proclamation for a general fast* (Boston, 1699 [1700]), CO 5/861/31.v.

50. Bellomont to Winthrop, 17 March 1700, Winthrop Family Papers, MHS; William Bassett to "Rev'd Sr," 15 March 1700, Misc. Bound Mss., MHS.

51. Letter from Oxford re Penacook Indians, 4 March 1700, Mass. Arch., 70: 430; Benjamin Sabin to Fitz John Winthrop, 18 March 1700, Winthrop Family Papers, MHS; Josiah Dwight to Winthrop, 19 March 1700, Winthrop Family Papers.

52. Bellomont to Winthrop, 17 March 1700, Winthrop Family Papers, MHS; Winthrop to Bellomont, 20 March 1700, Winthrop Family Papers; Bellomont to the Commissioners of Indian Affairs in Albany, 21 March 1700, CO 5/861/31.ix, PRO; Instructions to Schuyler, Livingston, and Hanson, 21 March 1700, CO 5/861/31.xii.

53. Fitz John Winthrop to the Council of Connecticut, 23 March [1700], MHS, *Collections*, 5th ser., 8 (1882), 380; Examination of Suckquans & Sasquehaan, two Sachems of Skachkook and of Nichnemeno a new Roxbury Indian . . . 7 April 1700, CO 5/861/31.xv, TNA.

54. Examination of Suckquans, et al, CO 5/861/31.xv, TNA; Livingston to Bellomont, 8 April 1700, CO 5/861/31.xiv.

55. Commissioners of Indian Affairs at Albany to Bellomont, 9 April 1700, CO 5/861/31.xiii, TNA; Mr. Robert Livingston's Report of his Journey to Onondaga, April 1700, *NYCD*, 4: 648–49.

56. Livingston's Report, *NYCD*, 4: 649; Bellomont to the Lords of Trade, 25 May 1700, ibid., 644; Bellomont to the Lords of Trade, 26 July 1700, ibid., 689. On the gendered nature of English antipopery see Frances E. Dolan, *Whores of Babylon: Catholicism, Gender, and Seventeenth-Century Print Culture* (Ithaca, 1999).

57. Memorial of Col. Wolfgang William Romer, 11 April 1700, *DHSM*, 10: 49; Bellomont to [?], 16 July 1700, ibid., 72; Memorial to his Excellency Earle of Bellomont of my . . . voyage to the Kennebeck River in the Months of June & July 1700 . . . , Cyprian Southack Letters, MHS; Bellomont to the Lords of Trade and Plantations, 22 June 1700, CO 5/861/46.i, TNA; Bellomont to the Lords of Trade and Plantations, 15 July 1700, CO 5/861/53.

58. Mass. Arch., Court Records, 7: 74–75; *His Excellency the Earl of Bellomont's Speech to*

the Honorable the Council and House of Representatives . . . (Boston, 1700), CO 5/861/41.xvi, TNA; Mass. Arch., 30: 456a; *The Acts and Resolves, Public and Private, of the Province of the Massachusetts Bay* (Boston, 1869), 1: 423–24; Corwin, ed., *Ecclesiastical Records*, 2: 1368–70.

59. Josiah Dwight to Fitz John Winthrop, 10 June 1700, Winthrop Family Papers, MHS; Colossians Discovery, 21 June 1700, *DHSM*, 10: 63–65; Jacques Laborie to Bellomont, 17 juin 1700, ibid., 59–60; Mary de Witt Freeland, *The Records of Oxford, Mass. including Chapters of Nipmuck, Huguenot and English History from the Earliest Date, 1630* (Albany, 1894), 168–69; Bellomont to the Lords of Trade, 9 July 1700, *DHSM*, 10: 68–70.

60. Bellomont to the Lords of Trade, 20 April 1700, *NYCD*, 4: 638; Bellomont to the Earl of Bridgewater, 22 June 1700, EL9782, Bridgewater Papers, Ellesmere Collection, HL.

61. Report of the Council of Trade upon My Lord Bellomonts proposals for the Security of the plantations, 4 October 1700, Lansdowne Mss. 849, fol. 29–44, BL; Extract of a Representation to the Board of Trade to the Lords Justices Octor 4th 1700 relating to the Defence of New York, Plantation Reports, Ayer Mss. #339, Newberry Library, Chicago; Lords of Trade to the King, 24 April 1700, *NYCD*, 4: 639–40; Bridgewater to Bellomont, n.d., EL9783, Bridgewater Papers, Ellesmere Collection, HL; Board of Ordnance to the Earl of Romney, 4 May 1700, *NYCD*, 4: 641; Lords of Trade to Bellomont, 21 June 1700, ibid., 666; Bellomont to [William Blathwayt], 1 January 1701, BL148, Blathwayt Papers, HL.

62. See Runcie, "The Problem of Anglo-American Politics in Bellomont's New York;" and, on the Kidd affair, Robert Ritchie, *Captain Kidd and the War Against the Pirates* (Cambridge, Mass., 1986). Bellomont was one of the original investors in Kidd's filibustering mission, but turned on him after it became apparent that Kidd had engaged in illegal piracy, presiding over the pirate's arrest.

63. Mass. Arch., Court Records, 7: 6–7; *The Answer Of the House of Representatives, to His Excellency the Earl of Bellomont's Speech* (Boston, 1699), CO 5/860/65.iii, TNA. On the Irish comparison, see D. W. Hayton, "The Williamite Revolution in Ireland, 1689–1691," in Jonathan Israel, ed., *The Anglo-Dutch Moment: Essays on the Glorious Revolution and its World Impact* (Cambridge, 1991), 185–213.

64. Bellomont to the Lords of Trade, 27 April 1699, *NYCD*, 4: 508; Gabriel Bernon to the Consistory of the French Church in New York, 27 mars 1699, in *Collections of the Huguenot Society of America* (New York, 1886), 1: 338.

65. Capt. Jerathmeel Bowers his Acct of his Observation of the Indians at Pennicook, Winthrop Family Papers, MHS; Caleb Stanley to Fitz John Winthrop, 18 August 1700, MHS, *Collections*, 6th ser., 3 (1889), 57–59; Memorial of Watanomen and Cadanonokas, sagamores of Penacook, Mass. Arch., 30: 459; William Stoughton to Fitz John Winthrop, 19 August 1700, Winthrop Family Papers, MHS; Winthrop to Stoughton, 22 August 1700, ibid.; Bouton, ed., *Documents and Records*, 3: 108.

66. On Wattunomen's role in the Deerfield attack see Haefeli and Sweeney, *Captors and Captives*, 78–92. On the Iroquois see Gilles Havard, *The Great Peace of Montreal of 1701: French-Native Diplomacy in the Seventeenth Century* (Montreal, 2001).

67. Bellomont's efforts represented an early stage of the "Anglicization" of the colonies, on which see John M. Murrin, "Anglicizing an American Colony: The Transformation of

Provincial Massachusetts" (Ph.D. dissertation, Yale University, 1966); Brendan McConville, *The King's Three Faces: The Rise and Fall of Royal America, 1688–1776* (Chapel Hill, 2006).

EPILOGUE: NICHOLSON'S REDEMPTION

1. Verses on the Capture of Port Royal, MHS, *Collections* 6th ser., 1 (1886), 406. For analysis of the verses and background see John G. Reid, "The 'Conquest' of Acadia: Narratives," in Reid et al., *The "Conquest" of Acadia, 1710: Imperial, Colonial, and Aboriginal Constructions* (Toronto, 2004), 3–5.

2. Nicholson's career has attracted a number of historians. The best account, though my interpretation differs from his in many respects, is Stephen Saunders Webb, "The Strange Career of Francis Nicholson," *WMQ* 3rd ser. 23 (1966): 513–48. See also Bruce T. McCully, "From the North Riding to Morocco: The Early Years of Governor Francis Nicholson, 1655–1686," *WMQ* 3rd ser. 19 (1962): 534–56; McCully, "Governor Francis Nicholson, Patron *Par Excellence* of Religion and Learning in Colonial America," *WMQ* 3rd ser. 39 (1982): 310–33; Kevin Hardwick, "Narratives of Villainy and Virtue: Governor Francis Nicholson and the Character of the Good Ruler in Early Virginia," *Journal of Southern History* 72 (2006): 39–74.

3. Nicholson to William Blathwayt, 7 February 1687, Blathwayt Papers, 15, folder 1, CW.

4. Nicholson to the Committee on Trade and Plantations, 20 August 1690, CO 5/1358/20–22, TNA. On Effingham's rule see Warren M. Billings, *Virginia's Viceroy: Their Majesties' Governor General, Francis Howard, Lord Howard of Effingham* (Fairfax, Va., 1991).

5. H. R. McIlwaine, ed., *Executive Journals of the Council of Colonial Virginia* (Richmond, 1925), 1: 244; Nicholson to the Committee on Trade and Plantations, 4 November 1690, CO 5/1358/29–33, TNA; Nicholson to the Committee, 26 January 1691, CO 5/1358/37–39; Webb, "Strange Career of Francis Nicholson."

6. McIlwaine, ed., *Executive Journals*, 1: 141.

7. Nicholson to the Archbishop of Canterbury, 8 March 1696, Fulham Papers, vol. 2, fol. 50, Lambeth Palace Library [microfilm, Library of Congress]; Henry Hartwell, James Blair, and Edward Chilton, *The Present State of Virginia, and the College*, ed. Hunter Dickinson Farish (Williamsburg, 1940). On these efforts in general see McCully, "Governor Francis Nicholson."

8. Nicholson to the earl of Bridgewater, 30 June 1697, Nicholson Letters, Blathwayt Papers (uncataloged), HL; McIlwaine, ed., *Executive Journals*, 1: 161, 212.

9. McIlwaine, ed., *Executive Journals*, 1: 419; Nicholson to [William Blathwayt], 19 August 1698, Francis Nicholson Letters, Blathwayt Papers (uncataloged), HL [microfilm, CW].

10. Memorandums of severall Letters relating To Maryland and Pensilvania dictated to me by ye Governor of Maryland at Patuxent Maryland, 26 May 1698, Bridgewater Papers, Ellesmere Mss., EL 9599, HL; Nicholson to the Archbishop, 29 March 1698, Fulham Papers, vol. 2, fol. 98, Lambeth Palace [microfilm, Library of Congress]; Fulham Papers, vol. 2., fol. 108–10.

11. Memorandums of severall Letters . . . , Bridgewater Papers, Ellesmere Collection, HL.

12. John Hornabrook, Account of Indian attacks, *DHSM*, 9: 178–79.

13. Samuel Sewall to Nathaniel Higginson, 21 October 1706, MHS, *Collections* 6th ser., 1 (1886), 340; Governor's Speech, 25 May 1709, *DHSM*, 9: 296–97.

14. A Memorial from New-Engld, relating to the French Settlements in Canada, *DHSM*, 9: 211; Robert Quary, A memoriall humbly presented . . . to Lord Godolphin, [May? 1702], BL28, Blathwayt Papers, HL; Increase Mather Diaries, vol. 9, AAS [microfilm at MHS], 20. The book in question was Louis Hennepin, *A New Discovery of a Vast Country in America* (London, 1698).

15. Instructions to Samuel Vetch, 1 March 1709, CO 5/9/59, TNA. On the conquest see especially Elizabeth Mancke and John G. Reid, "Elites, States, and the Imperial Contest for Acadia," and Geoffrey Plank, "New England and the Conquest," both in Reid et al., *The "Conquest" of Acadia*, 25–47, 67–86. On the region more generally see Geoffrey Plank, *An Unsettled Conquest: The British Campaign Against the Peoples of Acadia* (Philadelphia, 2001).

16. Address of the Inhabitants, Merchants of Boston, 24 October 1709, CO 5/9/82, TNA; John Winthrop to Fitz John Winthrop, July 1707, MHS, *Collections* 6th ser., 3 (1889), 387–89.

17. John Stewart to Lord Secretary, 8 June 1712, CO 5/9/53, TNA; Nicholson to [?], 20 February 1711, CO 5/9/135.

18. Cotton Mather to Samuel Penhallow, 17 April 1712, in Kenneth Silverman, ed., *Selected Letters of Cotton Mather* (Baton Rouge, 1971), 101. On this synthesis see Brendan McConville, *The King's Three Faces: The Rise and Fall of Royal America, 1688–1776* (Chapel Hill, 2006); T. H. Breen, *The Marketplace of Revolution: How Consumer Politics Shaped American Independence* (New York, 2004), 33–192; John M. Murrin, "Political Development," in Jack P. Greene and J. R. Pole, eds., *Colonial British America: Essays on the New History of the Early Modern Era* (Baltimore, 1984), 408–56; and in a slightly different vein, Jack P. Greene, *Pursuits of Happiness: The Social Development of Early Modern British Colonies and the Formation of American Culture* (Chapel Hill, 1988).

19. My understanding of early South Carolina politics depends primarily on L. H. Roper, *Conceiving Carolina: Proprietors, Planters, and Plots, 1662–1729* (New York, 2004); and M. Eugene Sirmans, *Colonial South Carolina: A Political History, 1663–1763* (Chapel Hill, 1966). In addition, see the interesting overview of imperial politics in Alan Gallay, *The Indian Slave Trade: The Rise of the English Empire in the American South* (New Haven, 2003).

20. The one main exception was the Spanish destruction of the Scottish Covenanter colony of Stuart Town in 1686. The Scots intended to avenge the assault, with English help, but colonial officials succeeded in preventing the design; see Sirmans, *Colonial South Carolina*, 44.

21. A. S. Salley, ed., *Journal of the Commons House of Assembly of South Carolina, For the Session Beginning August 13, 1701 and Ending August 28, 1701* (Columbia, 1926), 4.

22. James Moore to the Lords Proprietors, 16 April 1704, in Mark F. Boyd, Hale G. Smith, and John W. Griffin, eds., *Here They Once Stood: The Tragic End of the Apalachee*

Mission (Gainesville, Fla., 1951), 94–95; Margaret Newell, "The Changing Nature of Indian Slavery in Colonial New England," in Neal Salisbury and Colin Calloway, eds., *Reinterpreting New England Indians and the Colonial Experience* (Boston, 2004), 116–17.

23. A. S. Salley, ed., *Journals of the Commons House of Assembly of South Carolina for 1702* (Columbia, 1932), 64.

24. On the St. Augustine raid see Charles W. Arnade, *The Siege of St. Augustine in 1702* (Gainesville, 1959).

25. On slave society in South Carolina see especially Peter H. Wood, *Black Majority: Negroes in Colonial South Carolina from 1670 Through the Stono Rebellion* (New York, 1972); Robert Olwell, *Masters, Slaves, and Subjects: The Culture of Power in the South Carolina Low Country, 1740–1790* (Ithaca, 1998); and S. Max Edelson, *Plantation Enterprise in Colonial South Carolina* (Cambridge, Mass., 2006). On St. Teresa de Mose see Jane Landers, *Black Society in Spanish Florida* (Urbana, 1999), 29–60.

26. Frank J. Klingberg, ed., *The Carolina Chronicle of Dr. Francis Le Jau, 1706–1717* (Berkeley, 1956), 58 and passim; Mather, *La fe del christiano* (Boston, 1699). Like Samuel Sewall, Mather had come to believe that the conversion of Spanish American Catholics might be a sign of the coming apocalypse. This does not seem to have been a belief shared by South Carolinians.

27. See Sirmans, *Colonial South Carolina*, 103–28.

28. Landers, *Black Society in Spanish Florida*, 37; "The Journal of William Stephens," in Mark M. Smith, ed., *Stono: Documenting and Interpreting a Southern Slave Revolt* (Columbia, S.C., 2005), 3–4, 14; John K. Thornton, "The African Dimensions of the Stono Rebellion," *American Historical Review* 96 (1991): 1101–13. As Thornton has demonstrated, it is plausible, but far from certain, that the slaves were Kongolese Catholics.

29. Thomas J. Davis, *A Rumor of Revolt: The "Great Negro Plot" in Colonial New York* (New York, 1985), 160; Daniel Horsmanden, *The New York Conspiracy*, ed. Thomas J. Davis (Boston, 1971), 341. For New York's ties to the empire at this time see Serena Zabin, *Dangerous Economies: Status and Commerce in Imperial New York* (Philadelphia, 2009). This and the following paragraph draw from Owen Stanwood, "Catholics, Protestants, and the Clash of Civilizations in Colonial America," in Chris Beneke and Christopher S. Grenda, eds., *The First Prejudice: Religious Tolerance and Intolerance in Early America* (Philadelphia, 2010), 218–40.

30. Horsmanden, *New York Conspiracy*, 342–43, 369.

Index

Acknowledgments

I could not have written this book without the aid of friends, patrons, and a number of "remarkable providences." At Grinnell College, Alison Games and Don Smith unwittingly turned me into an English Atlanticist. Alison in particular convinced me that academic history was a glamorous life filled with Caribbean vacations. While I have spent very little time on the beach, I remain grateful for her inspiration and friendship. Ethan Shagan performed a similar service at Northwestern University, introducing me to early modern religious history and popular politics, and sending me in unexpected new directions. Tim Breen was a model mentor, in that he left me to follow my interests, but was not shy to let me know when I went astray. He also taught me how to write—thus saving the reading public a great deal of pain and suffering.

A number of institutions offered valuable financial assistance. Northwestern's Graduate School and History Department helped out, as did the Catholic University of America and Boston College. (Thus proving that neither the Catholic Church nor the Society of Jesus is quite as bad as this book's protagonists believed.) The Massachusetts Historical Society and the Folger Shakespeare Library gave me fellowships and opened up their collections and facilities. In addition, I benefited from the librarians and archivists at these and many other institutions, including the British Library, the National Archives at Kew, the National Archives of Scotland, the Massachusetts Archives, the American Antiquarian Society, the Connecticut State Library, the New-York Historical Society, and the Huntington Library. The Newberry Library—and especially the D'Arcy McNickle Center for American Indian History—served as an intellectual home during my years in Chicago, and the Library of Congress—and its phenomenal John W. Kluge Center—served the same purpose in Washington. I am particularly grateful to all of the librarians, staff, and fellows of those fine institutions. Special thanks are due to my colleagues at Catholic University and Boston College—and especially my students, for years of encouragement, astute questions, and reminding me why I became a historian in the first place.

In my travels I have encountered hundreds of fellow scholars who have not only helped to shape this book, but have become valued friends as well. While I cannot possibly name everyone, I am particularly grateful to those who have helped me to clarify my ideas over the years by reading and commenting on sections of the book, including Bernard Bailyn, Josef Barton, Justin Behrend, Chris Beneke, Doug Bradburn, Mike Guenther, Karl Gunther, David Hall, April Hatfield, Chris Hodson, Ron Hoffman, Richard Johnson, Kevin Kenny, Karen Kupperman, Brendan McConville, Brett Rushforth, David Silverman, David Voorhees, and Craig Yirush. Steve Pincus, Justin Pope, Jason Sharples, Jenny Shaw, and Stephen Taylor shared knowledge and sources from their own research. Mary Zito translated several letters from Latin. Max Edelson provided advice, companionship, and some inspired, if ultimately discarded, title suggestions. Tim Harris and John Murrin inspired me with their scholarship, and later became tireless supporters of this work; I am grateful for their friendship and scholarly generosity. Michael Kimmage never read a word of the manuscript, but shaped it nonetheless through years of conversations about the historian's craft and less lofty subjects. Two fellow historians influenced this book and its author in extraordinary ways. Evan Haefeli was one of the first people to show interest in this project, and he has continued to be a model reader, supporter, collaborator, Dutch translator, and friend. Scott Sowerby has taught me most of what I know about later Stuart history, offered astute (and sometimes spirited) readings of the manuscript, and also helped to keep me sane. For all of this I am most grateful.

I have also been blessed with fine editors. Bob Lockhart has provided the perfect combination of prodding and support (and many drinks along the way), while Dan Richter has been the most astute reader and critic a young historian could hope for. Three readers for the press—Ned Landsman, Mark Peterson, and Geoff Plank—offered cogent critiques of the manuscript at several different stages.

My family and friends may not all be historians, but they have been most supportive of this book and its author. My parents Leslie and Patricia Stanwood provided financial and moral support for many years. Don Elmore, Julie Prentice, and Karen O'Brien offered their homes to me on research trips. Many other friends, too many to name, listened to my treatises on antipopery and empire, and often made helpful comments (or listened politely). No one contributed more in the final year of writing than Jennifer Zartarian, who provided writing retreats from Brooklyn to Black Mountain, listened to stories about Quakers and sea monsters, and told me what the empire was really doing. Finally, this book is for my favorite writer, Simon, whose youthful enthusiasm for academic prose certainly places him outside the mainstream, but even closer to my heart. I hope he enjoys the book.